BRAVOS FO

(more . . .)

SHELLEY WINTERS

Shelley II

The Middle of My Century

POCKET BOOKS

New York London Toronto Sydney Tokyo Singapore

Photos in picture sections researched, edited and arranged by
Vincent Virga

POCKET BOOKS, a division of Simon & Schuster Inc.
1230 Avenue of the Americas, New York, NY 10020

ISBN: 0-671-70142-8

First Pocket Books printing September 1990

10 9 8 7 6 5 4 3 2 1

POCKET and colophon are registered trademarks of
Simon & Schuster Inc.

Cover photo by PHOTOFEST

Printed in the U.S.A.

AUTHOR'S NOTE

The first part of my autobiography, *Shelley: Also Known as Shirley*, was at the top of best-seller lists for fourteen weeks. And when *The New York Times Book Review* year-end roundup cited one hundred outstanding books chosen from the forty thousand published that year in the United States, my book was there.

When critics reviewed it, they said I had written an insightful book about my life before, during, and a few years after the Second World War. But whenever Donahue or Carson interviewed me, all they wanted to talk about was my love affairs.

So in this second part of my autobiography I have been a little less specific about who, what, where, and when. But I am certain, reader, that I have left enough clues to stimulate your erotic imagination.

ACKNOWLEDGMENTS

To my friend Jimmy Haspiel, who remembers when I did what film or play—and if not, he knows where to find out.

To Ellis Ambrun, my amanuensis, who knows how to develop *sitzfleisch* in a writer and, more importantly, knows how to dissipate the angst.

To Vincent Virga, who knows how to find those pictures that verify my memories—even some I didn't want verified.

To my editors, Nancy Nicholas and Michael Korda, whose heads may be a little bloodied but, I hope, unbowed.

To the many young women all over the country who typed, drove, ran interference and laughed in the right places.

For my mother, Rosie, who convinced me before an audition that if they hired me <u>they</u> were lucky.

Maiden, the world's supremest spirit
  Beneath the shadow of her wings
Folds all thy memory doth inherit
  From ruin of divinest things,
    Feelings that lure thee to betray,
    And light of thoughts that pass away.

—Percy Bysshe Shelley

Introduction

How could I possibly have done all the work I did in the
fifties and sixties? I have researched the films, the television shows, the plays—those are the facts. I mean I won
Oscars and Emmys; the pictures were released; the television shows were seen and reviewed. It's in the film and
theater books, so I can't argue with it, but I must have
worked day shift, night shift, and swing shift.

Looking at the list reminds me of the stories I have
read about silent films in which actors like Charlie Chaplin, Buster Keaton, and Harold Lloyd made a new two-
reel comedy every other day (sometimes one hundred
silent films a year). But most of the films I made took
from four to ten weeks to shoot, and I was in three
Broadway plays during that time, too—which ran for almost a year each.

Logically I can't account for it. My friends, my relatives, my lovers, husbands, directors, may all remember
these incidents differently, but this is how I remember
them.

I seem to be in some kind of emotional time warp because, as I write, everything that I'm writing about seems
to have happened yesterday. Recently, in an acting class,
two young people did a scene from *For Whom the Bell
Tolls*. When I was critiquing them, I told them about a
young veteran of the Abraham Lincoln Brigade who had

come home to Brooklyn without his right arm. The students seemed to understand what I was talking about, but after class the boy who had been playing the scene came up to me and whispered, "Miss Winters, did you really know someone who knew Abraham Lincoln?"

I realized then that my acting students had no idea what the hell I was talking about. They thought it had been a story about the American Civil War or perhaps the Spanish-American War. They had no idea of the importance of the Spanish Civil War or of the way it affected political thought and the arts and the theater they would work in for the rest of this century.

I know I often confuse these students when I refer to incidents from the thirties, the forties, the fifties, and even the sixties in the way they seem to me—like recent events, barely under my skin. I tell them my stories about the Depression, the Second World War, Roosevelt, Truman, Eisenhower, Kennedy, Johnson, Korea, Vietnam, Martin Luther King, civil rights, the assassinations. The world I worked in and what happened in the theater they will be working in seems like history to them. But to me it all seems like yesterday. I guess I am still stuck in the middle of my century.

What I am sure about is that those years were extraordinary. It was the best of times for me, and although sometimes I hide from knowledge, I know it was also the worst of times.

It was during those times that I finally escaped the cunning dumb blonde-bombshell image Universal and I had created and broke through the crippling sexual double standard that had been imposed on women throughout history. I hope I stopped playing The Star, much of whose energy was devoted to self-aggrandizement, and became a woman who took responsibility for her actions and who helped fight for equality and dignity for herself and her sisters.

I retreat into the dumb blonde-bombshell image less and less. Nowadays I only present that persona late at night on the Johnny Carson show and we both have fun with her.

PART
1

*International Star of
Stage, Screen, &
Schwab's Drugstore*

1

*E*arly in 1954, I was returning from Europe—more exactly Rome—and as I flew westward on the TWA clipper I looked out the window and examined my life and the aurora borealis. In those days of prop planes you often stopped at Shannon, Ireland, or Gander, Newfoundland, en route to New York. I was sleepless and in despair. Here I was an international movie star and an internationally rejected sex goddess. My divorce from Italian matinee idol Vittorio Gassman was on the front pages of the world's press.

I had done a film called *Mambo* with my about-to-be-ex-husband, Vittorio. For God's sake, it's bad enough to live through a divorce without having to act with the man during the rough separation discussions. Why couldn't he at least have left me for an older girl? Anna Maria Ferrero —sixteen, gorgeous, and a fine actress . . . it would ruin my career, destroy my self-esteem . . . and I couldn't get into any of my clothes because of all the pasta I had cried into for the last three months.

As I tried to sleep on that long-ago plane ride, I had already forgotten and changed everything so that it was all "his fault." Never mind that he didn't want to become an American movie star and live in Hollywood for the rest of his life. Never mind that I didn't want to become an Italian actress and live in Italy for the rest of my life.

The whole goddamn plane was fast asleep—only I, barefoot and girdleless, roamed the aisle. I was afraid to have another drink. My feet, my soul, my teeth and hair felt rejected and sleepless.

Before I had left Rome, I had gone to a pharmacy and bought a hundred Seconal suppositories. It seems to me that most medicine in Europe is prescribed in suppository form; I guess that's because they don't always have bottled water handy. In 1954 you didn't need prescriptions for those things. After I had paid my lire and had the medicine safely in my purse, I asked the Italian pharmacist, "How come you don't need a prescription for these dangerous sleeping things?" The man fixed me with a fishy eye and said in English, "Signora Gassman, in the whole history of Italian medicine, no one—but no one—has ever committed suicide in that fashion."

So I had used two of these Seconal suppositories and had had two martinis. But I still felt as though I would never sleep again. I date my chronic insomnia from that flight. Only later did I realize that my feeling of unattractiveness was a product of my life conditioning, *not that divorce*. I felt I could not be desirable unless I was attached to a desirable man. As I sat on that plane that night so long ago, I remember wondering whether all other American women had the same conviction and made the same mistakes I had.

Even now I wonder if women's lib arrived too late for women of my generation. When I think of the victim roles that I fought for (and for which I often got nominations and twice Oscars), I hope I was helping raise the public's consciousness so that the process of rectifying the age-old plight of women could begin. Gloria Steinem and Betty Friedan say that's what I was doing, and I hope they're right.

Arriving in New York in the early morning hours, I felt I had been away from the U.S.A. for a hundred years. Once you have been subjected to the legal systems of other countries, especially if you are a woman (the Napoleonic Code was still in force in Italy then), my God, how you respect the laws and the judicial system of the United States.

I rushed to my little apartment at the Meurice Hotel on West Fifty-eighth Street. I had paid rent for this little haven since 1948 when I had played Ado Annie in *Oklahoma!* I had used it very seldom since then and had often lent it to my California friends who were spending time in New York. As I sent up my twelve suitcases, I thanked God that I still had this apartment. I tipped the bellhop and phoned my mother and father and ten-month-old baby in California and told them some white lies. I had to convince my mother, as per instructions from Jerry Giesler, the famous lawyer who was representing me, that she had to testify that Vittorio was guilty of mental cruelty. It seemed that if we got the divorce in California, it would make our Mexican marriage more legal in the United States and Italy.

He had given our daughter a glorious property settlement, which we had signed in Venice, Italy. In the coming years he was more than generous. He paid all my daughter's school bills and gave me a large down payment on an apartment in New York.

But that was later. When the day of the divorce trial arrived, the judge had great difficulty getting my mother, Rose, to say anything negative about Vittorio. She said, "Well, I heard fights downstairs," but the judge couldn't get her to say whether it was a male or female voice screaming.

Finally, when the judge reached the point of exasperation, she did quietly say, "Well, he studied *Hamlet* all the time, which is a very big role, and that was mentally cruel to Shelley." In utter disgust, the judge pounded his gavel and said, "Some witness." But he granted me an interlocutory degree, which would become final in a year.

Back in New York and legally separated, I was desperately trying to think of a way to get my life together. The newly formed Actors Studio was holding sessions on Tuesdays and Fridays. Sometime in 1948, Elia Kazan had asked me to be an observer. That year, 1954, I began to attend regularly and tried to work on something called a "private moment," which is very difficult for me to do. Other actors I know have greater freedom doing this. It is something you do in front of the class that you would only do in the privacy of your home, alone, such as acting out a fantasy, conducting an orchestra, dancing or singing to recorded music, pretending that you're greatly accomplished at all of the above things, since no one is watching or listening to you—except the entire class.

Everything changed for me at a Friday session at the Actors Studio in 1954, when I saw Gerry O'Loughlin do a remarkable private moment. A young man comes into a dark empty room. He has on a hat, overcoat, and scarf. It is cold in the apartment. It is snowing outside. He is carrying a box of fried chicken. He thinks about turning on the light but doesn't bother. He takes off his gloves and scarf and puts the chicken on a high stool. He just stands there with his hat, coat and galoshes on and eats the chicken. It was the quintessence of loneliness. I found myself weeping quietly, knowing how sad it is to eat only because one must, without enjoyment, without sitting down, and then to try to think of somewhere else to go.

I had always thought that only women suffered from this kind of loneliness, but watching that exercise and the way that the actor used the cold and the dark and the unappetizing greasy chicken was a revelation. He got a glass of water and started to cry. He manfully stopped himself, wiped his tears, blew his nose, put his gloves back on, put the empty box back in a bag, looked at a newspaper—searching for a movie, I think—and then went out. It was one of the most powerful things I had ever seen. Every human being has experienced this sense of pointlessness and desolation.

Lee Strasberg quietly asked Gerry how he had arrived at this "moment" and why he was doing it. O'Loughlin explained that he was searching for the essence of a character he was going to play in the film *Lovers and Lollipops*. His character was too discouraged and tired to make an effort anymore. That day I learned something about sense memory that I was able to use in acting and writing for the rest of my life: the cold, the dark, the smell of the greasy chicken, how his wet clothes felt on his body, the silence of the uninhabited room, how power-fully it affected the actor and consequently the audience.

Lee told us that inadvertently the actor, in recalling the sensory memory of this experience, had done an exercise called "affective memory." I thought Lee was saying "effective." So for the next twenty-five years that's what I called it because it was *so* effective. Not until New Year's Eve 1982 did I realize my mistake.

Lee was discussing a role I was working on, an alco-holic woman in *Gingerbread Lady*. He suddenly asked me how I spelled "affective memory." I told him "e-f-f-e-c-t-i-v-e" and said that I had spelled it that way ever since I had seen that exercise in 1954. He laughed one of his rare, beautiful laughs and said, "Shelley, you still think onomatopoeically. The exercise is called 'affective memory.' It is called that because acting is the process of going through your own human experience and memo-ries. You can read the playwright's words but an actor can't possibly know the sources he used to write them. Even if the writer reads the lines to the actor, it becomes an empty imitation. That's why we see so many Hamlets or other great roles. When the words are profound, and they go through the actor's life experience, they will then speak to the audience with universal truths."

I left the Actors Studio that day with my depression gone and remembering again that I was an artist who, in 1951, had been nominated for the Best Actress Oscar for *A Place in the Sun*. I was capable of giving people plea-sure and even perhaps knowledge that would help them change their lives. No more was I just a rejected wife and an abandoned mother. I was a person in my own right with a responsibility and a life to fulfill. I suddenly real-ized, too, that I would never be able to do it in California, where I succumbed so easily to the blonde bombshell image. I began to think about the ways I could emotion-ally and literally move my little family to New York.

When I got back to my hotel, there was a message from my agent about a film in Mexico called *The Treasure of Pancho Villa* and, after that, the first color NBC televi-sion broadcast of *The Women*, in which I was to play

Crystal. The film was to be done for RKO and they would pay me $50,000.

I knew Howard Hughes, who owned RKO, and I called him at Sam Goldwyn Studios, where, for some mysterious reason, he had his office. By a miracle I got through and quickly asked him if he could pay me $1,000 a month for four years to do *The Treasure of Pancho Villa*. There was a long pause.

"Shelley," he said, "why do you want forty-eight thousand dollars for doing a picture instead of fifty thousand? Have you discussed this interesting idea with your agent?"

I stuttered, "Hugh"—which is what I called him when I was nervous—"I am getting a divorce from Vittorio Gassman, and I've decided to move to New York with my baby and her nurse . . . and I think the security of knowing that I have a thousand dollars a month will make the transition much easier for me."

This was 1954, when $1,000 was comparable to $4,500 now. Lovely Howard Hughes then said, "Shelley, in the past year with all the worldwide publicity, you have become an international star, and I think even though you will be studying and working on the New York stage, you will soon be making films all over the world. So as this picture will not be released for at least a year, I suggest I pay you sixty-six thousand dollars, which will give you one thousand a month for five years and six thousand dollars' commission for your agent."

As I tried to thank him, he said sternly, "Shelley, just be careful in Mexico. Remember they are Latins, too."

When I got the script, I found out that the plot is about six mules carrying a great deal of gold to Pancho Villa from the Pacific to the Atlantic side of Mexico or maybe vice versa.

My mind was filled with so many artistic and financial concerns then that it wasn't until recently, when I saw the film on late-night television, that I realized it is one of the funniest films I have ever done, although at the time I didn't mean it to be. Rory Calhoun, Gilbert Roland, and some other fine character actors in the cast were doing a cowboy picture. I was doing a revolutionary film about the exploitation of Mexican peasants. I think I modeled my character on Emma Goldman. They acted; I made speeches. Howard Hughes, who was very anticommunist, must have had a fit when he saw it.

From the neck up I was Universal's blonde bombshell: platinum hair with every curl in place and long black eyelashes. From the neck down I was a revolutionary. I wore a man's shirt with the sleeves rolled up, a wide leather belt, Mexican worker pants, old boots, and a gun. So maybe I rewrote a few of the lines. The producer, Edmund Granger, let me.

The Indians and Mexican soldiers were being played by students from the University of Mexico, and every time I opened my mouth somebody would translate my speech into Spanish and they would all cheer. All the American actors were pretending I was reciting love lyrics in the direction of Rory Calhoun.

I acted as fast as I could because I was on my way to New York and stopping in Cuernavaca just long enough to make my money. In those days Cuernavaca wasn't yet a tourist trap and at dawn the Mexican peasants on their way to the fields would sing to greet the sun.

At the wrap party the Mexican minister of film made a speech in English thanking the American actors, producers, and crew for doing this film in Mexico. Approximately ten words out of his mouth, the students began booing and hitting the tables with their spoons and yelling that this was Mexico and he should speak Spanish. To quiet this budding riot I jumped onto the table and started dancing and singing "La Cucaracha" or something dipsy like that and since the students liked me they began to laugh and throw flowers. No riot.

Back in New York, I wandered around the cold streets, seeing eight shows a week and having lunch and dinner with old friends. But now they treated me differently. I have never had a sense of being different from other working actors; realistically, I know that if you get good roles and do them well, you get money and fame. But some section of my mind denies fame's "apartness." Even now, I need to sometimes think that Shelley Winters is invisible, and Shirley Schrift, the name I was born with, is walking around among regular folk. If I'm done up and am at an opening or a party, I'm Shelley Winters —and people have the right to ask me for autographs and all the other stuff of the celebrity life. When I have on blue jeans and no makeup and I'm shopping in the supermarket, however, I'm surprised and look around to see whom he or she is addressing when some stranger approaches me with a huge smile and starts talking to me.

That winter of '54, I was so bruised from the continual notoriety in the world press about Vittorio Gassman and Shelley Winters's fights and separation during the filming of *Mambo* that I was desperately trying to wrap the cloak of anonymity around me. We had been in the headlines of the New York and London *Times, France-Soir,* and *Il Tempo.*

I had two films playing on Broadway, and the *Daily News* and the *Mirror* were still carrying details of my impending divorce, "with pictures." My New York friends tried to help me hide, but I found that many of them had gone to California or had gotten married or given up show business. Some of them suddenly had relatives who wanted to meet Shelley Winters at Sardi's. I was in no shape to meet anybody anywhere.

Finally, my dear friend Connie Dowling showed up in New York. If you ever see *Up in Arms* with Danny Kaye, the striking blonde girl playing opposite him is Connie Dowling, who was as lovely inside as she was outside. Connie was married to Ivan Tors, a successful Hungarian producer. She managed to get me out of the doldrums. I had been sitting immobile in New York for three weeks and, believe it or not, had often forgotten to eat. I had gotten quite thin and looked like hell. Connie took me to "A Day at Elizabeth Arden's," and we went shopping at Bergdorf's, and Ivan and Connie then took me to "21" for dinner. I wore a black velvet hat with feathers (I still have it), sexy high-heeled F.M. shoes, and thick false eyelashes. With my mink coat casually draped over the chair, I suddenly pivoted back to life.

Here I was, a world-famous actress who still had a lucrative year left on her Universal contract, a studio to take care of me, a family to love me, thousands of fans, and I found out from Ivan that Warners was trying to borrow me for a film with Jack Palance and Lee Marvin.

As I sipped a champagne cocktail in the elegant "21" restaurant, a handsome blond giant said, "Hello, Shelley." I looked up and saw Sterling Hayden. He sat down, and Ivan and he began to discuss a film they were planning. He also managed to hold my hand under the table.

I had met Sterling various times since the end of the Second World War—sometimes under rather bizarre circumstances. I believe the first time was at the Actors' Lab, which was the California home of the Group Theatre, the forerunner of the Actors Studio. It was in a large old reconverted house in back of Schwab's drugstore on Sunset Boulevard. The ground floor had been converted to a theater with about a hundred seats, and I saw some of the greatest acting that I have ever seen in that little theater. Lee Cobb performed *The Evils of Tobacco,* Ruth Nelson and the then-redheaded actor Norman Lloyd (later a regular in "St. Elsewhere") did *The Boor,* and Morris Carnovsky, John Garfield, and Stella Adler did a revival of *Awake and Sing!*

It was in one of the classes at the Actors' Lab that I saw the most beautiful man I had ever seen in my life. He seemed about six feet six, and he looked like a blond Scandinavian god. He had been a wonderful athlete, and had achieved instant stardom in the late thirties.

Vittorio and I had met him and his wife, Betty, at various parties and performances, and I recalled that they had about five children. So that night at "21" I was very sorry to hear that they were divorcing. As Ivan Tors ordered us all more champagne, I suddenly remembered the strange circumstances under which I had last seen Sterling.

A couple of years earlier, in December of '52, during my lonely pregnancy, there was a knock at the door at about seven o'clock one morning. My house had an upstairs apartment, which was for rent, and there was a sign out on my lawn in Beverly Hills stating that fact. I looked through the peephole to see who it was, as I was rather frightened that anyone would be knocking at my door at such an early hour.

"Shelley," a famliiar voice said, "I see you have an apartment for rent upstairs."

I recognized the voice, opened the door, and got a terrible shock. It was Sterling Hayden, but it wasn't. His face seemed destroyed and old. I stared at him and he finally asked, "Could I please come in for a cup of coffee, Shelley?" I was alone in the house and had an old heavy robe over my flannel pajamas. I couldn't think of any reason to turn away a friend who obviously was in distress. It was barely dawn, but I invited him in and went to heat up yesterday's coffee.

He explained to me that his wife and he were separating, and he was going to get the children part of the time, and his psychiatrist's office was two blocks south on Burton Way. He now saw his psychiatrist every day, sometimes twice a day.

I got us both coffee and soda crackers and asked him to stop pacing around my living room and sit down, because he was making me dizzy. The only evasive answer I could give him about the upstairs apartment was that my business manager was handling the rental and Sterling would have to talk to him. I could not understand how he could have custody of all his very young children. I believe the youngest was about eighteen months, and, in any event, I didn't want them running around on the floor above me—all five. As he drank his coffee, I watched his hands shake and his left foot twitch. I was determined to remain calm.

After a long pause, this huge, blond, destroyed giant said to me, "Shelley, why do you think I'm being offered scripts and Larry Parks isn't? We both said practically the same thing."

I truly did not know what he was talking about. In great confusion, all I could blurt out was, "Where?"

He laughed and said, "You obviously haven't been looking at the television or listening to the radio. In Washington, of course, in front of the House Un-American Activities Committee."

I did not want to discuss it. I did not want to know.

Larry Parks did not give the same testimony as Sterling. Larry refused to name names. Sterling had been coerced into naming friends and could not now live with that. As always when I felt I was in a dangerous situation, I retreated into my dumb blonde-bombshell role and started babbling incoherently. I murmured something inane like, "I think you should do war films, since your experience in the Second World War was so interesting." He just stared at me. I had been told that he had parachuted behind the Nazi lines and been a liaison with Tito's Yugoslav guerrillas.

He yelled, "Shelley, shut up," and he repeated, "Why do you think Larry Parks was blacklisted, and I am not?"

I had known Larry Parks at Columbia when I'd been under contract at that studio, but all I would answer was, "Maybe you're a more commercial type than he is."

Apparently he didn't believe me, because he again asked, "Shelley, you really didn't hear my testimony on the radio or read it in the newspapers?"

I told him truthfully that I hadn't. He then seemed to look through me as he mumbled, "I'm a foundling. My adoptive father was an organizer with the longshoremen's union. He was Harry Bridges's right-hand man. When he heard my testimony, he had a heart attack and died."

I had nothing to say. I was busy protecting my pregnancy. I don't remember how the conversation ended, but when he finally left, I cried and cried, and then I called Vittorio, who was performing *Hamlet* in Milan.

Now it was two years later, and as I sat in my elegant outfit at the "21" club, Sterling Hayden seemed completely recovered. He made sardonic jokes, and he drank three double shots of aquavit with champagne chasers in half an hour. When our dinner finally arrived, he got up and said, "Since we're both getting divorces, I hope if I come by to see you in Beverly Hills again, you won't throw me out." I think he was asking me something else, but I didn't want to pursue it there and then, so all I said was, "I'd like very much to see you, Sterling, and I hope our kids can play together on my front lawn."

He smiled his sardonic smile and said, "That's a

date." As he left the restaurant, towering above everyone else, my friend Connie took my hand and whispered in my ear, "Shelley, don't believe in those old Italian proverbs."

"Which ones, Connie?" I whispered back.

"Well, like 'The best way to drive out a nail is with another nail.' "

Twenty-five years later, I did a film called *King of the Gypsies* with Sterling, who played the king, and I was the queen of the Gypsies. It was Eric Roberts's first picture, and he looked like both of us. In the first scene we shot (the end of the film, naturally), I sit by Sterling's bed in a hospital where he is dying. He had a beard which Dino de Laurentiis offered him $100,000 to cut off. Gypsies do not wear beards. Sterling refused, and I asked him why he was so obstinate, since he had not worn a beard in *The Godfather* or *Dr. Strangelove*.

"In one I played a bigoted cop," he replied, "and in the other, an insane general. My naked face is exactly right for those roles."

I sat and watched him and thought how old we were now and how young we had been in 1954. The director yelled, "Roll 'em." And Sterling held my hand and said, "You know, he's dead now. Larry Parks is dead. Why do you suppose I worked and Larry never did again? We both gave the same testimony to that committee." And the director of *King of the Gypsies* yelled, "Action."

After that therapeutic day at Arden, Bergdorf's, and "21," my courage surfaced, and I returned to California with Connie and Ivan. I was now very grateful that I owned that un-movie-starrish duplex apartment house. My parents lived upstairs now, and the nurse, Kathy, and my little daughter and I lived downstairs. The first thing I did was to buy swings and seesaws and a huge tire, which was tied to the pine tree on a high branch in the front of the house. I established a sort of Shelley Winters Park for the young children of the neighborhood.

In those days, there were many middle-class families in my section of Beverly Hills, which was on the wrong side of the trolley tracks. There was a little red streetcar that went all the way from Union Station downtown to the beach. For some reason, Southern Pacific had to run an engine over that route every night. I remember vividly rocking my child and listening to that lonesome whistle, but, alas, all of it is gone. No trolley, no tracks, no trains, no Shelley Winters Park. Now the neighborhood is very chic high-rise apartments, and they are very expensive; I believe there's no one on my block under fifty, including me. I refuse to tear down my little duplex apartment and build a high rise. My house is still a home and not an investment.

Anyway, back in California I decided that the best way for my daughter not to feel deprived was to have her play only with children whose mothers were divorced or widowed (one of my less-than-great decisions). If I had a problem, I would first try to solve it by denying its existence. I reasoned that my daughter wouldn't notice that she didn't have a father until she was eight if none of her friends had one. I did this for a number of years and, even though Vittorio came to visit quite often, she never noticed the difference in her living arrangements until one day when she was three, after we had moved to New York and her nursery school had a "father's day." My well-behaved child suddenly lay down on the floor and cried and screamed till we took her home. I recently learned that that nursery school no longer has father's day. It is now "parent's day," which I think is a much better idea, given the percentage of one-parent households with young children these days.

At that time studios still had the suspension system (although since then Olivia de Havilland has gone to court and gotten it changed. She fought it through and won). You would sign a contract for seven years and then any time you took off from making the studio's movies, for the stage or to do a movie for another studio, even though you had to get their permission your studio suspended you and added the time you had taken off onto the end of your contract and you owed it to them. My agent and lawyer were having a fight to the death with

Universal, which claimed that I owed them another two years because of the suspensions I had taken over the past six years. I had been suspended for artistic and romantic reasons—like staying in Rome with Vittorio for six months when they needed me back in the San Fernando Valley to do a gangster film they had written for me called *Playgirl*. I eventually did that film for them to settle the contract. Nobody remembers it, and I have never even seen it.

Much of an actor's life is spent staring at the telephone. Stars are no exception. Despite the fact that I have done over a hundred films and fifty plays, I'm always sure, at the final curtain or after the last shot of a film, that I will never work again. The sweetest words an actor can ever hear are *"They want you."* So I guess, during the middle fifties when I was coming to the end of my seven-year contract and the end of my marriage to Vittorio Gassman, despite my resolve to do only films I could be proud of, I began accepting any film that would stifle this dreadful "occupational disease."

One morning after returning from a walk, having pushed my daughter's baby carriage all over the hills of Beverly, I found a novel on my doorstep. It was a book called *Night of the Hunter* by Davis Grubb. In it was a letter from my lovely and brilliant teacher, Charles Laughton. Mr. Laughton told me this would be the first film he would direct, and that United Artists had hired the distinguished writer James Agee to do the screenplay. He wanted Robert Mitchum and me to star in it with Lillian Gish.

I parked the carriage under a tree in my garden and made sure the baby was fast asleep and sat down and read that whole powerful novel. I had done nothing important for more than two years, and I was trembling with joy at the thought of being directed by Charles Laughton and working with Robert Mitchum. To this day I think it was Bob's best film. I know it was one of mine.

After reading the book, I ordered my agent to make the best deal he could with United Artists, but, in any case, *I would do this film.*

During the month that I waited for the screenplay to be

completed, I had many meetings with James Agee and Charles Laughton. I finally began to understand, maybe for the first time, that films are what happens on the screen and how the audience reacts. That's why it is my opinion that the experience of sitting in a dark theater with other people is a whole different and deeper experience than watching anything ever on television, including tapes and cassettes. In a theater, you are part of an audience, and that is what brings the whole artistic process to fruition. Film art is not realized till it jumps from the page into the director's hands, through the actor's imagination, and the audience opens up to realize and experience it. When you are in a theater there is a proscenium, stage, or screen, but you forget those things and laugh or weep. There is a literary term for it: "willing suspension of disbelief." This cannot be done unless you are connected with other human beings as part of a living, breathing audience.

Working with Charles Laughton was like being given a gift. He had worked on my speech with Margaret Pendergass McLaine, a famous speech therapist. So now Brooklyn Shirley could with great confidence play a Southern farm woman. I believe I simply reverted to my Missouri accent, having been born in St. Louis and moved to Brooklyn when I was nine.

Sometime during that period, I was sent the television script of *Sorry, Wrong Number* and offered a small fortune to do it. It entailed three weeks of rehearsal and then a live broadcast and the whole show was practically a monologue. It's about a rich young woman, an invalid, who overhears a crosswire telephone call in which her husband is discussing his plans to murder her. The piece is practically a forty-eight-minute monologue (twelve minutes of commercials in an hour show). The husband's shadow is seen once in a while as he walks around the house. The only way the director could get any pace during this one-character show was to have six cameras swinging around, about, above, and beneath me.

These live shows were very scary but exciting. You had the sense of rehearsing fully and almost doing a play as on the stage. But the technical problems of suffering and weeping and still looking beautiful and sexy in my white satin nightgown almost undid me. In *Sorry, Wrong Number*, my husband must strangle me very realistically in the last scene. Then I'm supposed to lie still and dead in my sexy nightgown. When we finally did this live, at the end of the show I thought the cameras were finished with me and were photographing his shadow, so I casually got up out of bed, drank a glass of water for my aching throat, and walked off the set. Those cameras were not through with me. I hadn't understood that they wanted to intercut shots of him trying to escape and me dead on the bed. Ah, live television!

Sometimes I get angry that they never show my *Sorry, Wrong Number* on television, just the Burt Lancaster–Barbara Stanwyck movie. When I call my agent to inquire why, he reminds me that in those days they had not as yet invented tape. Strange—it still feels as if I did that performance yesterday.

About a year later I did another TV play, called *The Dark Wall*. I played a split personality—split three ways. I was an inhibited, restrained young woman of about thirty; a hooker type, brash and loud, of about twenty; and an eleven-year-old retarded child. You have to remember this was live, live, live television. If you made a mistake, you just had to continue and hope the millions of people watching their black-and-white sets wouldn't notice your mistake, or you prayed that the cameraman was pointing his camera at something else.

In *The Dark Wall,* the silly art director had put two closets on the set—for no reason. Toward the end of the play, the psychiatrist, played by Shepperd Strudwick, attempts to reason with me, playing the eleven-year-old. I'm supposed to tumble into a closet that is open to the camera and is properly lit. What the director didn't understand was that I now was a very Method actress. When I became the hysterical eleven-year-old I tumbled into the closet, then I cried and hit out at the doctor and struggled with my schizophrenia. But I had tumbled into the wrong closet. I was acting deeply but, with some section of my brain, I heard walls being torn apart and lights going on. The crew was literally tearing the set apart so that the camera could get at me. I thought I was acting just great, but nobody in America could see me. Camera, lights, and microphones were sneaking into the scene. I was unaware of this until after the show was over.

Then, as I waited for the director to come out of the booth and congratulate me, I noticed that all the crew were staring at me. Silent admiration, I thought, because of my fine acting. When the director, feeble and white-faced, came onto the set, he whispered, "When you change the blocking, let the director know in advance."

Joanne Woodward later did the same sort of role and won an Oscar for *Three Faces of Eve*. I have to admit that Joanne was very good too. Deep in my heart, I know I helped kill live television. Or if you want to be more positive about it, I hurried the scientists into developing videotape.

I did *Sorry, Wrong Number* while I was waiting for the screenplay of *Night of the Hunter* to be completed. During the rehearsals of this show, Sterling Hayden called me and asked if I would have dinner at his beach house, as he still had trouble going out anywhere in Hollywood. I thought it was agoraphobia. Maybe it was.

My self-esteem reasserted itself because this very attractive and famous actor wanted to see me. One night I decided that he was exactly the right person to cue my lines in *Sorry, Wrong Number* since I talked for forty-eight minutes nonstop. I mean, I couldn't possibly think of anybody else in the world to help me learn those lines —well, not anybody as attractive anyway. I don't remember *exactly when it was*, but I remember *exactly what I wore*: black velvet capri pants (two sizes smaller than the ones I'd worn when I'd left Rome), a white satin V-neck blouse, thick false eyelashes, black satin F.M. sandals, and bright pink lipstick outlined in dark red.

His house was perched on the edge of a cliff overlooking Santa Monica Bay. There were some long steps from the road down to it. I arrived just as the stars were twinkling on the water, and I brought Sterling some delicious Chinese food, a large bottle of cold aquavit, and me.

This relationship lasted until I started shooting *Night of the Hunter,* when I had to get up at five every morning. Whether it was two weeks or two months, I have no idea. All I know is that at the end of it I was able to go through with my divorce from Vittorio Gassman, and I hoped that Sterling had gotten his life together too, and no more agoraphobia. I subsequently read that he had done something definitive, like sailing around the world on his three-masted schooner, *The Wanderer,* "borrowing" his children for the two-year voyage. He wrote a best-seller about this trip called *Wanderer.*

I reported for work on the set of *Night of the Hunter.* The first night's shooting was scheduled in front of an eerie house in Malibu Canyon. In the daytime I was still rehearsing one of those TV shows, and Robert Mitchum was just finishing a film of his own. So we were both rather tired when the first day of shooting started at 8:00 P.M.

I was late, but Mitchum was even later. The producer, Paul Gregory, got into a terrible snit. He was running around the set screaming about how much it would cost if the stars delayed like this all through the film. Laughton just sat quietly with the distinguished cameraman James Wong Howe, carefully lighting the first scene. Gregory's screaming unnerved me, and since the first day of shooting is always stressful, I was hoping somebody would shut him up. Good acting cannot be performed in an ambiance of chaos and pressure. That's what's wrong with television today: they insist on quantity and not quality, and the actors sometimes seem like talking machines.

Finally Mitch arrived, made up and ready, and all they had to do was get him in his costume and write "L-O-V-E" on one hand and "H-A-T-E" on the other. Gregory continued to scream, and Mitch just looked at him—he'd already seen me shaking—so he walked over to Gregory's new white Cadillac and peed on it. Gregory could not very well fire either Mitchum or the now-hysterically-laughing me. He had financed this picture with our names. So when the set quieted down and the prop man got a hose and washed down the Cadillac, the filming of *Night of the Hunter* began.

It is a classic film that has played all over the world for the past thirty years. And every day of shooting was a joy. I played a character unlike any I'd ever played before or since, a countrified young widow whose husband has gone to prison for stealing a great deal of money during the Depression. His cellmate is a crazy preacher played by Mitch, who finds out that the money is hidden somewhere on our little farm. Mitchum finds out the money is hidden in my little girl's doll. To get at the child he kills me and follows the children during a long, terrifying chase down the Mississippi River. Lillian Gish played the heroic caretaker of the children who foils Mitchum and saves the children.

Mitchum, who was and is famous for playing jokes and kidding around on the set, was contained and serious throughout the filming. Charles Laughton directed the film slowly and carefully. And we knew when we saw the first rushes that we were part of something classic and timeless. *Night of the Hunter* is probably the most thoughtful and reserved performance I ever gave.

The studio released the film very quietly, and the public seemed to ignore it. I believe Charles Laughton had been "named" by someone and was therefore blacklisted. A decade later, both in Europe and in the U.S., the film was finally recognized as a unique poetic achievement.

Some years later, I had a little shack right on the beach, where my eight-year-old daughter and I were spending weekends. It was August 18, and I was having a birthday party. Kids from up and down the beach made a huge fire in front of the balcony of my green shack. We were going to have roast potatoes, corn on the cob, hot dogs, hamburgers, and punch.

We were all gathered around the fire when out of the darkness came Charles Laughton, carried by his chauffeur. I had heard he was very ill in the hospital, and I

21

couldn't believe he was able to show up for my birthday. But there he was.

He sat in a deck chair and recited all the sonnets of Shakespeare, performing for all the kids on the beach, who in a few minutes numbered several hundred. At about midnight, he did most of *King Lear* for us. All my life, I will never forget that night. None of those young people made a sound; we just heard his magical voice giving us the great poetry and the truths and words of Shakespeare. When he finished *King Lear*, I kissed his hand, and the chauffeur carried him up to his car.

That was the last time I saw Charles Laughton. The only person who was allowed to see him in the hospital was Albert Finney. It's forever in my memory—the music of Charles Laughton's voice on that long-ago night. Nowadays when I see and hear the antiestablishment anger in the "music" and "lyrics" of the kids of this generation, I know how deprived and poor they are. I know it by their dissonant music and my rich memory of Laughton's voice.

2

*T*he late forties. I'm regressing, but that's how my memories work. Hollywood. The in place was a gourmet restaurant on Sunset Boulevard called the Players. It was on a second-floor veranda, overlooking a trafficless Sunset Boulevard. The famous director Preston Sturges owned it, and I'm sure it wasn't a money-making proposition, but he was there every night. The food was superb, especially the rare roast beef and Caesar salad, and all of Preston's Oscar-winning writer and director buddies hung out there.

When I was making all those blonde-bombshell Westerns and gangster films, I would stop there almost every night. I would relax with *one* martini and the above menu, and Christopher Isherwood, Ivan Moffat or Harry Brown, who had written the screenplay for *A Place in the Sun*, would cue me in my pedestrian dialogue that I had to memorize for the next day's filming. I remember Mel Frank (an Oscar winner for *A Touch of Class* and many other nominations) sitting with me as I ate and drilling the stupid dialogue into my head. The Universal producers never understood how my dialogue improved so remarkably from page to performance. They just thought I was an inventive actress, classing up their B pictures. There was a writer at Universal who bragged that he wrote five of my scripts a year. He never knew that Oscar-winning writers and directors were rewriting his scenes as they were helping me to learn them over martinis.

One night, when I showed up exhausted from filming *Frenchie*, complete with platinum hair and padded bra, Christopher Isherwood and Ivan Moffat were seated with an ugly, funny-handsome young Welshman. He had very black, curly, almost kinky hair, rather a stocky build (just a little taller than I), and very rumpled clothes. He was altogether charming, and I gathered it was his first night in Hollywood.

His name was something Thomas—I didn't catch the first part—but since we were retaking a scene the next day, and I didn't have to learn any new lines, I could enjoy the conversation with this cute Welshman. When I asked Mr. Thomas what he did, Ivan told me, "He draws accurate and biting images of people and events." So I assumed he was a cartoonist, and they all let me assume this for a long time. The young man, of course, was Dylan Thomas, but he didn't look like any writer I had ever met in Hollywood. In those days writers wore suits and ties. My friends told me he was working for some London newspaper.

In the course of dinner, I asked Mr. Thomas why he had come to Hollywood. He looked deep into my blue eyes and whispered sexily, "To touch the titties of a beautiful blonde starlet and to meet Charlie Chaplin." I gazed at the two literary figures beside us. They said nothing.

"Okay," I said, "I can grant both your wishes."

When we had finished the dessert and brandy, I announced, "You may touch each of my breasts with one finger, and the day after tomorrow will be Sunday, and Charlie Chaplin has open house, as Christopher and Ivan well know. I will take you up there."

Ivan bought us a bottle of champagne and poured it. Then, with great ceremony, Mr. Thomas sterilized his index finger in the champagne and delicately brushed each breast with the finger, leaving a streak in my pancake body makeup. A look of supreme ecstasy came over this Welsh elf's face. "Oh, God, Nirvana," he uttered. "I do not believe it's necessary for me to meet Charlie Chaplin now."

Against the studio's rules, I had worn one of my Western blouses home. It was a very low-cut off-white blouse with a ruffle around the neck that barely covered my nipples and a push-up bra. In the early fifties, the studio would paste your costume to your cleavage with liquid adhesive. The Legion of Decency decreed, "No cleavage," but the mounds on each side were okay to photograph, as long as the rosebuds did not show on film. But ripping the blouse off at the end of the day was a painful and slow process, and, for many years, I was afraid I was going to develop hair on my chest. I'm happy to report it never happened.

Christopher and Ivan were laughing uproariously. I knew I was being joshed, and I informed my dinner companions that the brakes on my car were not too good, and, since Charlie lived on top of Summit Ridge Drive, we could pass on that trip.

"No, no," said Ivan. "I've loaned Dylan my green Hornet while he's in California, and if you keep him on the right side of the road, he can drive you up to the Chaplin house Sunday night. He really is longing to meet Charlie, and I'm sure Charlie is anxious to meet him."

Why Chaplin would want to meet this obscure Welsh cartoonist was a mystery to me. Also he just sat there when the check came, so it was obvious he had very little money. So I invited him to an early Sunday dinner the next night with me and my then-roommate, Marilyn Monroe. Then we would all drive up to Charlie's house after dinner.

By the time I left the Players that night, I realized that Mr. Thomas had a serious drinking problem, and, if Ivan or Christopher couldn't drive us up to Charlie Chaplin's house, I decided *I* would drive the green Hornet myself.

Sunday, Marilyn and I spent the entire day cleaning the apartment, and we prepared dinner. The arrangement was that I did the real cooking and she did the dishes and cleaning up. Not only could Marilyn not cook, if you handed her a leg of lamb, she just stared at it. Once I asked her to wash the salad while I went to the store. When I came back an hour later, she was still scrubbing each leaf. Her idea of making a salad was to scrub each lettuce leaf with a Brillo pad.

I didn't know at the time why she was making such a big deal of this occasion. She went to the empty lot next door (which is still there on Holloway Drive west of La Cienega; I think Hollywood has forgotten who owns it) and collected lots of white wildflowers, which she put in glasses on our little TV tables out on our little balcony. Maybe she knew Dylan Thomas was a famous poet, but she certainly didn't tell me if she did. She had set up this nest of tables on the balcony so we could overlook the lights of Hollywood (on those smogless nights you could see all the lights, all the way to the airport; there were no tall buildings or Century City to obstruct the view, and on a clear day you could see Catalina). She put Japanese lanterns along the awning and set out a hurricane lamp with candles. Marilyn loved lamps that had plants growing out of their bases, and she got an extension cord and put one out on the balcony. Our other guest was Sidney Skolsky, the famed columnist, and if he knew what an illustrious guest we had, he kept it a secret too.

I had roasted a loin of pork, very crispy, with wedges of garlic, and with it was serving mashed potatoes with green onions and sour cream, and well-washed salad with Roquefort dressing. Marilyn was to make the applesauce. All she had to do was open a jar and heat the contents and add a little Cointreau and orange peel. She obviously didn't understand my instructions, because we *drank* the applesauce, which had a whole bottle of Cointreau in it and the diced pulp of the orange. Thank goodness she threw the peel away. Anyway, the dinner was delicious, and the company was charming and hilarious.

Mr. Thomas drank practically all his dinner. Marilyn had made a pitcher of gin martinis, and since we didn't have a pitcher, she made it in a milk bottle. She and I had two juice glasses of martini each, Sidney had none, and Mr. Thomas drank the rest. To slow him down, Sidney suggested a straw. A bottle of red and a bottle of white wine at his elbow disappeared next, followed by six bot-

tles of beer he had bought in a supermarket. He told us
with great amazement that in California you could buy
tobacco and alcohol in the supermarket. He was so enchanted with this idea that I was sure he was going to
move immediately from London to Los Angeles.

Memories always evoke music to me. Or music evokes
memories. That night, on our little candlelit balcony,
Dylan Thomas sang a Welsh song for Marilyn and me. It
had a haunting melody in a minor key, and the words
were as follows:

Come all ye fair and tender maids, who flourish in
   your prime, prime
Beware, beware, keep your garden fair, let no man
   steal your time, time, let no man steal your time
'Cause when your time is past and gone, he'll care
   no more for you, you
And many a day that your garden is waste, 'twill
   spread all over with rue, rue, 'twill spread all
   over with rue
A woman is a branch, a tree—a man a clinging
   vine, vine
And from her branches carelessly he takes what he
   can find, find, he takes what he can find

I was deeply touched by the song. Over the years, the
only other person I ever heard sing it was Richard Burton. Marilyn and I were so touched we were almost
weeping, but Mr. Thomas was still drinking everything in
sight. Sidney Skolsky was taking notes for his column in
the *Citizen-News*.

Although Mr. Thomas teased and kidded me with his
risqué Welsh wit, he was quiet and respectful to Marilyn.
Marilyn was so sure things were bound to go awry that I
think she unconsciously made things happen to get the
waiting over with. I saw her do this time and time again.
Dylan Thomas seemed aware that behind the eyelashes
and platinum hair and terrific body, there was a fragile
and sensitive girl. I guess he sensed that I was tougher,
having survived the Brooklyn ghetto. He was obviously
a horny Welshman, but he never once made any kind of

pass at Marilyn. Not even a verbal one. I don't think it was because her looks didn't turn him on; he was obviously mad about platinum-blonde starlets. I think this poet sensed that she very badly needed not to be thought of as just a tits-and-ass cutie. By the end of the meal she was quite smitten with him, and, although I promised we could wait till she drove Sidney Skolsky to his next assignment, she did not want to go to Charlie Chaplin's house that night. It was a long time before Marilyn ever felt intelligent enough to mix socially with important intelligent people, if she ever did. Maybe that feeling is what was behind her marriage to Arthur Miller. (If you don't graduate high school—marry an intellectual.)

When I examine the years of the early fifties, I suddenly realize how much of a role model I was for my friend Marilyn. Even in the late forties, when I studied at the Actors' Lab in Hollywood and with Charles Laughton in Santa Monica, she did the same. She became intimidated by The New York Group Theatre teachers who were now teaching at The Actors' Lab behind Schwab's, so while I was studying with Lee Cobb or Morris Carnovsky, Marilyn worked and did a couple of plays in little amateur theaters somewhere on La Brea Avenue (in the "unchicest" and most unartistic section of Hollywood). I believe she started doing this as soon as she finished her "Rosie the Riveter" phase right after the war. I went to see one of these plays and, although I was in the third row, I could hardly hear her. I believe it was an amateur production of Aben Kandel's *You Only Twinkle Once,* a play I had done earlier, during the Second World War, with the paraplegics from Birmingham Veterans Hospital.

Something was wrong with Marilyn's used black Cadillac, which Jack Benny had given her as a bonus when she'd done his radio show at my suggestion. So I loaned her my secondhand beige Cadillac with the bad brakes to drive Sidney around the Sunset Strip, and Mr. Thomas and I got in Ivan's green Hornet. This little car was a convertible down to the axle. There was no top, no doors. It was tied together with heavy string, and a fender was missing. But it had very good brakes and a great engine. I think Ivan kept it in this condition because, no matter where he parked, the police would *never* tow it away. One look at the car and they would be sure that the owner could not come up with the $10 to take it out of the police pound. My escort got in on the right side of the car since he was British, and I of course climbed into the left. He was quite drunk.

"Where's the bloody steering wheel?" he yelled.

"Mr. Thomas, it's over here on the left, where I'm sitting."

He looked a little confused and muttered, "Every fucking thing's backwards in this country. But since you're over there, you drive."

I never had any intention of letting him drive. We started out for Charlie Chaplin's house. After stopping at a supermarket along the way for six bottles of beer we wound our way up Benedict Canyon to Summit Ridge Drive. Artie Shaw had written and performed with his clarinet a superb and scary melody called "Summit Ridge Drive," and it had recently been released, and I had often played it on my Capehart record player. The ride that night with Dylan Thomas up that mountain road in the green Hornet seemed to act out the record. I never was very good at coordinating my left foot on the clutch and my right hand switching gears. I would shift from first to third, forgetting about second gear, and the car would stall, then start to roll backwards down the hill. Dylan, trying to help me, would step on the gas when I got it into the right gear. He had pulled a pint bottle of cheap gin out of some hidden pocket, and after he had drunk half of two bottles of beer, he poured the gin into the beer bottles. Somehow he managed to stay seated in the lurching car and mix this formula and help me with the clutch and steer with his elbow and drink this warm, loathsome mixture.

Chaplin's house was perched on a cliff, and his tennis court was about fifteen feet below. There was one driveway to the house and another one to the tennis court and swimming pool above the house. As we got up to Summit Ridge Drive, the car got a little out of control. Dylan grabbed the wheel, pulling it to the right side, but somehow we drove down to Charlie Chaplin's tennis court instead of up the driveway to his house. We knocked down the net, but luckily we had taken the wrong driveway so at least we didn't skid into the pool. I sat huddled in the green Hornet. Dylan didn't seem to notice anything amiss.

"Come on, girl," he yelled. "I want to meet the greatest comic genius of our century."

Leaving the green Hornet on the tennis court, tangled in the net, I slunk after him, and we climbed up the driveway steps to Charlie Chaplin's front door, as astonished faces peered at us from the solarium overlooking the tennis court.

Oona O'Neill Chaplin stood at the front door, very pregnant and very amused. She could see how upset I was, but she still greeted Dylan warmly and kissed me, saying, "Don't worry. No damage. Jerry will fix the net and back the car out into the street."

She was referring to Jerry Epstein, who was a friend of mine and Sydney Chaplin's. Jerry, a producer at the little Circle Theatre, later became Charlie Chaplin's producer when Charlie directed *A Countess from Hong Kong,* which starred Marlon Brando and Sophia Loren and was a very expensive British film.

Jerry had been a friend of mine since my Brownsville, Brooklyn, days, and we had recently been having strange tennis matches on Charlie's court. For many years, Charlie had been holding open house on Sunday afternoons. Oona always served a wonderful, elaborate brunch on the lawn, and very formal tennis was played on the court below. It was requested that players wear all white and they were graded carefully according to their ability. Jack Cushingham gave lessons on this court, as did Pancho Gonzales and William Haines, who became a noted interior decorator. Many other famous players took part in the matches. Charlie was often the referee, and Jerry and I were often linesmen and ballboys. The *pièce de résistance* of the afternoon was often a match between Jerry Epstein and myself. Since neither one of us had the proper white outfits customarily worn during that period, we would wear whatever gym clothes we had used in high school—for me, often it was my plaid romper suit and polka-dot bobby socks and old brown-and-white saddle shoes. Jerry had something left over from the Army. But we played ferociously, arguing each point and playing according to "Brownsville stickball rules." In the middle forties and early fifties, tennis was very much an English gentleman's game. So everyone loved to watch our savage Brooklyn to-the-death tennis matches.

To this day, I have the most expensive tennis game ever not learned. I have had $10,000 worth of lessons, and I've yet to develop a proper backhand. I still run around the ball. But, back then, I hadn't had one lesson. I remember one early-morning game with Marilyn and Sydney Chaplin when we had not yet learned the scoring system. Sydney called the points. He had just come back from the Army and was inclined to play jokes and found everything hilarious (no doubt because he was still alive). Every time he yelled "Love–fifteen" or "Love–forty," Jerry, Marilyn, and I would go off into gales of laughter. We really thought it was a description and not a score.

Sydney had been drafted into the American Army in the early forties and, because his father was Charlie Chaplin, who was suspected of leftist sympathies, he was sent to North Africa after only ten days of basic training. In the late forties he introduced me to an Army buddy of his who told me that they had marched through North Africa and Sicily, landed at Anzio, fought and marched up the entire boot of Italy, and finally been sent home after they'd liberated Paris. They were the sole survivors of their unit.

Sydney got me to join the Beverly Hills Tennis Club, and I took lessons faithfully twice a week for six years. When I got married, I brought my young husband, Vittorio Gassman, to the Beverly Hills Tennis Club and, although he had been on the Italian Olympic basketball team, he had never held a tennis racket in his hand. The first time we played, he beat me 6–0. I broke my racket and threw it away, and that was the last time I ever played tennis.

* * *

But that was still very much in the future. That night in the home of Charlie Chaplin, I was among the best tennis players and intellectuals of the film industry, dragging along my drunken cartoonist. I had made him leave his bottles of gin and beer outside in the bushes. But he was such a mess he looked like a stoned leprechaun. He wore strange brogues with flapping tongues that seemed to flap in unison with his belt and tie and his real tongue. I was ashamed to introduce him to anyone except Oona, and she quickly got him into an armchair with a cup of black coffee.

I looked around the room, and everyone was there—but I mean everyone. Garbo, George Stevens, Salka Viertel, George Cukor, Mr. and Mrs. Lion Feuchtwanger, Thomas Mann, Lotte Lenya, Elsa Lanchester, Marlene Dietrich, and Katharine Hepburn, who was almost a professional tennis player. Every morning of her life when she was in Hollywood, at 6:00 A.M., Katharine Hepburn took a lesson at the Beverly Hills Hotel. I would often go watch her practice before reporting to Universal for makeup. In those days Katharine Hepburn had such a lithe body and she was so beautiful it was like watching a prima ballerina.

Christopher Isherwood and Ivan Moffat were pretending they didn't know Dylan and me, but suddenly everyone was looking at Dylan and wanted to talk to him. Since he was very drunk, I couldn't think why. He, on the other hand, obviously didn't want to talk to anybody but Charlie Chaplin.

Charlie was sitting at the piano, playing a strange, beautiful tune. I quickly went over to Ivan and Christopher and asked them why they had asked me to take care of their difficult, drunken cartoonist friend. With a very straight face, as was his wont, Ivan asked me if I didn't like Mr. Thomas.

"When he's relatively sober, he's adorable," I replied. "But he has a terrible drinking problem, doesn't he? Perhaps I should make an appointment for him with a good Beverly Hills psychiatrist."

Ivan agreed and said, with a straight face, "You're a

modern, educated woman. You can take care of his problem."

Christopher hushed him and said, "You've been very sweet to Dylan. Please take care of him till we can get him back on the Super Chief at the end of the week."

"Okay, Christopher," I said. "But you owe me one."

Christopher Isherwood must have taken my remark seriously, because the next morning, on my doorstep, was a gift-wrapped copy of his book, *Berlin Stories,* which was soon made into a play by John van Druten called *I Am a Camera.*

At Chaplin's, I looked over to see if "my ward" was still upright. I couldn't hear what he was saying, but he had a large brandy glass in his hand, and any half-empty glass within reach he was pouring into his snifter. I wandered back to Mr. Thomas, picking up a cup of strong black coffee on the way. I took the snifter away from him, handed him the coffee, and sat on his lap, immobilizing him. He looked deep into my bosom with his big brown eyes and muttered something like, "Isn't that bloody genius ever going to talk to me? That's why I came to California. He's ignoring me like he's the governor and I'm the colonial."

I told him the coffee was laced with brandy, which it wasn't, and got him to drink it and calmed him down. I was sure that all the luminaries were staring and wondering what the hell I thought I was doing, sitting on this drunkard's lap, but I couldn't think of any other way to control him.

Charlie was staring with disapproval, and then he again played and hummed that beautiful, haunting melody. Sydney, who was tall and handsome and had a lovely voice, began to hum it along with his father.

The tune was the theme of *Limelight.* It was so lovely that, after one chorus, we were all humming softly with Sydney. Charlie Chaplin, Jr., suddenly got up. He was small and looked very much like his father and had grown a mustache exactly like the false one his father wore as his film character "The Tramp." He was a very introverted and friendless boy. He began to sing the melody with a strange, shrieking, toneless la-la-la-la, and all the guests froze. It was like watching a young, distorted version of Charlie Chaplin dancing around, singing, and mocking himself. Dylan Thomas abruptly got up, and I slid to the floor. He suddenly seemed cold sober and took Charlie junior's hands and danced around the room with him, humming the tune in his melodious voice. Charlie junior kept right on la-la-la-la-ing off-key and sort of sarcastically.

Charlie senior crashed his hands on the keyboard, got up, and knocked Charlie junior's hands away from Dylan. Unable to distinguish who was doing what, Charlie senior hissed at Dylan, "Even great poetry cannot excuse such rude, drunken behavior."

Sydney grabbed his father's upraised arm and gently led him away. Dylan turned on his heel and, in a very dignified manner, walked out into the solarium. Charlie junior sat on a hassock and began to weep bitterly.

"Sydney is playing the lead in the film," he screamed. "I won't be an extra. I won't, I won't."

As the guests left hurriedly, we heard a sound like running water. Dylan was peeing on a large plant on Charlie's porch. In this decade, I seem to have known a lot of gentlemen who peed as an act of revenge.

Sydney Chaplin had been a great friend of mine ever since mustering out of the Army at the end of World War II. Although there is much I admire about Charlie Chaplin's genius, I believe he was a very remiss father with his first family. Charlie junior and Sydney had been put in the Buckley Military Academy on Melrose Avenue in Hollywood and for most of their childhoods rarely came home to either their father or their mother. Whenever Sydney drove past that school, he would spit and shudder. He told me that when he and his brother were quite little, they had been brutalized by the ex–Army major who had run the school.

"I was pretty strong," Sydney remembered, "and handled it, but I can't be sure of the harm it did my brother."

I think Chaplin senior could not admit to himself that Charlie junior was emotionally backward and therefore had not sought special remedial education for him. The years have confirmed my opinion because, although he wrote a lengthy autobiography before he died, Chaplin senior never mentioned Charlie junior. In fact, he hardly mentioned Sydney, or anything else about his first family. In the late sixties, when his father had been living in Switzerland for more than a decade, Charlie junior committed suicide.

Sydney was a great friend of mine. We were something better than lovers: buddies. And, although he was certainly sexy and handsome and we met at the Beverly Hills Tennis Club almost every day, I had very strict rules. I could only be faithful to one man at a time. I was, at the time, involved with Burt Lancaster, who was involved with his wife.

He and I and Jack Cushingham (who was then the tennis pro and is now a producer) bummed around Los Angeles and its environs and had all the fun we could each and every day. Hollywood Park, Santa Anita, and Del Mar were our hangouts when I wasn't working or sitting by the phone waiting. We went to the burlesque shows downtown, free screenings at any of the studios, Ciro's, the Mocambo or Trocadero, the Coconut Grove, Romanoff's, Perino's, Chasen's—anyplace or anywhere, as long as some rich agent or producer was paying.

Sydney was given an allowance of $300 a month by his father and, although $300 was worth what $1,500 is now, it was just enough then to live pretty well and discourage initiative. Sydney was going through his F. Scott Fitzgerald period of "finding himself" a little late. But I guess after the long war, he wanted to enjoy life and the Hollywood he had been isolated from during his childhood.

Since his younger brother's name, Charlie Chaplin, Jr., was exploited constantly, Sydney would tell people that he was related to Saul Chaplin, the famous MGM composer, who, although a friend, was no relation. Thus he managed to avoid being known as Charlie Chaplin's son. He took the $300 every month, and he also took out most of the beautiful young starlets. I'm pretty sure he knew them in the biblical sense. But since he was a gallant gentleman, he never discussed those dates with me or anyone else. But he was clearly the Warren Beatty of his time.

During the filming of *Winchester '73* in 1949, in which Tony Curtis and Rock Hudson had very small roles—in fact, one line each—Harrison Carroll, a then-famous film columnist, kept calling me on the set, which annoyed James Stewart no end, since it was interrupting our one and only love scene. I finally took the call.

"Shelley, I must have an answer," Harrison demanded. "Is the romance between you and Sydney Chaplin serious?"

I told him the wildest fabrication I could think of:

"Well, Harrison, we are thinking of getting engaged—so Sydney has sent to the Cartier jewelry designer in Paris to design an emerald-and-diamond necklace for me, instead of an engagement ring. When the necklace arrives, we will be officially engaged."

I felt that Harrison, when he put the phone down, would realize that I had been "sending him up"—because he knew how broke Sydney usually was. Nevertheless, he printed that whole story in his column the next day. Charlie Chaplin immediately took Sydney's allowance away. I hurriedly phoned Charlie senior and told him that it was all a gag that had somehow misfired. He eventually restored his son's allowance, but not immediately.

In retrospect, I think Sydney would have been a more fulfilled actor and a bigger stage and film star if his father had not restored that allowance. Because of that allowance he never studied or worked very hard to find jobs. In fact, he would turn down films if they interrupted a tennis tournament.

My brother-in-law, George Boroff, owned a little theater called the Circle Theatre. My sister, Blanche, helped run it. Somehow or other, we talked Sydney, who had never acted on a stage, into doing *What Every Woman Knows* by J. M. Barrie. Ruth Conte, who was a talented actress from New York and married to Richard Conte, with whom I'd filmed *Cry of the City,* was to play the feminine lead. Then Sydney wanted Jerry Epstein (my Brownsville tennis partner) to be the producer. Well, it was only a little theater so, what the hell, they all agreed. But then all of a sudden, Charlie Chaplin, Sr., decided to direct this play in this little hundred-seat theater. Hollywood was stunned. It was as if Greta Garbo suddenly announced she was going to make a B picture at Universal.

We all managed to stay away from these fascinating rehearsals for weeks. Then one morning when I arrived at the Beverly Hills Tennis Club for my lesson, Sydney and Jack Cushingham were playing a ferocious game. Jack was a tournament player, and Sydney was making a nice income on the side playing tennis. But that morning Sydney was playing tennis like he wanted to kill Jack, the net, his racket, and the entire Beverly Hills Tennis Club.

After the game, we had breakfast. Jack was talking a blue streak, but Sydney, who was always a bit of a stoic, just sat there, eating despondently. He would not talk about the rehearsals, but finally I shut Jack up and told Sydney that everyone knew how difficult acting in live theater was, and here he was, doing his first part, the lead in a difficult English play.

He responded to that comment with something intellectual like, "Hey, Shell, you're sure the movies are easier? I would rather do something besides act, but I'm not trained to do anything else, so I guess I have to be an actor or reenlist in the Army."

I assured him films were easier because you do it until you get it right, then you are done with the scene forever. He asked me to come to the rehearsal that night with my friend Marilyn. "And bring her coach along," he stressed, saying perhaps we could all give him some suggestions, as he was having a very difficult time and thinking about quitting.

When we got to the theater that night, the three of us sneaked in very quietly in the dark after the rehearsal had started and sat in the back row. (I was to do *A Streetcar Named Desire* in that little theater with Dennis Weaver in a decade or so. It was the first theater-in-the-round in the United States.) As I watched Chaplin direct Sydney and Ruth, I realized that because the theater was so small and the audience so close, Charlie was giving them the basis of a wonderful, deep *film* technique that enables you to allow the camera to photograph your thoughts. Later, while I was filming *A Place in the Sun*, George Stevens told me, "*Movie acting is talking soft and thinking loud.*" And Charlie Chaplin, although he had played huge theaters in vaudeville and slapstick in many silent two-reel comedies, was giving his actors the basis of poignant, quiet, realistic, comic film acting, well suited to this small theater, where the actors were practically in the audience's laps.

The only problem was that his idea of directing seemed to be to act out all the roles, the women as well as the men, the young roles as well as the old. I don't know whether he directed his actors this way on film, but Marilyn and I and Natasha Lytess, her coach, sat there, stunned. Marilyn whispered to me, "No one on earth can do these parts as good as him." She was right.

At that moment, Charlie was enacting Ruth Conte's role. He captured the essence of *the little woman*, serene and slightly shy, slim but strong, and knowledgeable. He then acted out Sydney's role with words and gestures and thoughts. He became a tall, bumbling, strong, silent, slightly dumb, sexy man. I swear to God, as we watched him, he got taller and then shorter, huskier or slimmer, depending on which role he was acting. To watch him was like watching a miraculous chameleon changing colors.

Suddenly, Marilyn's coach, Natasha, got up and yelled, "Mr. Chaplin, you mustn't do that to your actors!"

Of course, she was right. But Marilyn and I got under the seats. Chaplin stopped the rehearsal and, with a voice like doom, thundered, "Who invited you people to this rehearsal?"

Sydney turned a violent red but managed to stutter, "Dad, I invited them. Ruth and I have the blocking now, and I would like Shelley and her friends to watch a run-through of the first scene."

He wasn't about to admit to his father that he had invited a drama coach to the rehearsal.

Charlie looked as if he was going to knock all our heads together, but he sat down in the front row and called, "Stage manager, run the first scene. CURTAIN." Jerry Epstein was also the stage manager.

I was frantically plotting how I could sneak out of the theater when the lights were lowered. The scene started, and I was amazed to see that Sydney and Ruth had somehow managed to interpret what Charlie had wanted and not be paralyzed by his genius or even try to imitate him.

Marilyn, her coach, and I crept out just before the lights came up at the end of that scene. As we looked at each other in astonishment, Marilyn whispered, "I've had directors get impatient with me, and act out the lines and expect me to recite and imitate them. It always makes me come apart at the seams."

I whispered back, "When you get some good Stanislavsky training and have worked with good directors, you can figure out what it is they want and then do it your own way."

Marilyn's coach muttered in disgust, "Shelley, don't give her any of that Stanislavsky nonsense. Charlie Chaplin is a genius, but he's just not a stage director." Maybe she was right, but I hated her telling Marilyn not to study.

As we came out of the little Circle Theatre that night, Marilyn seemed to be shaking, and I thought it was because of Charlie Chaplin. But she was staring at a building across the street from the entrance to the Circle Theatre.

"Don't be afraid of Charlie, Marilyn," I said. "He's never going to give us a job, anyway. He doesn't use blonde bombshells in his kind of pictures."

She shook her head, still staring at the building across the way, and finally she whispered, "That's the orphan asylum I lived in most of my life. That's where my foster parents would ship me back to when they decided they didn't want me anymore."

Even though my sister and brother-in-law owned the Circle Theatre, and I knew an orphan asylum was across the street, I had never known until this moment that Marilyn had grown up there.

We all got back in my car, and we went to Dolores's Drive-In on Sunset and La Brea and ordered hamburgers and chocolate milk shakes. As we waited for our burgers, Marilyn told us how she had recently gotten a man's name from that orphan asylum. Her mother had listed a Mortensen as her biological father. The night she had finished *The Asphalt Jungle*, after the wrap party, when her fellow actors and John Huston, the director, were assuring her that she was a wonderful actress and had the potential of a star, she called information in some place like Whittier, got the man's phone number, and called it. It was quite late at night, but she was feeling very happy because at long last she had a role in a distinguished film. She was convinced that this man was her biological father and she explained to the man who answered who she was (by then she was beginning to get a lot of publicity). A drunken male voice responded, saying, "Listen, you tramp, I have my own family, and I don't want anything to do with Hollywood bums. Don't you ever call me again." And he hung up.

I never liked Dolores's Drive-In much after that night.

Sometime in the early fifties, Columbia Studios' publicity department informed me that they were having a private screening of *On the Waterfront* and had been given a list—I guessed by Elia Kazan—of people who he thought might be interested in seeing it. They were putting aside two tickets for me for that evening. I asked Marilyn if she would like to go with me and see this much-discussed film. We were in the parking lot at Schwab's. She seemed to hesitate and then said, "Okay, but if Marlon Brando is there, we don't have to talk to him, do we?"

I looked at her, amazed, and said, "Marilyn, there isn't a chance in hell that Marlon will be at his own screening. I'm sure it'll be most of the people from the Actors Studio, and it isn't a press showing."

She hesitated and then said, "Okay, but you drive."

I assured her I would. So we agreed to go to the Hamburger Hamlet on Sunset Boulevard first and then see the film and make an early night of it. We both had early makeup calls. No drinks, no discussion with coffee and Danish afterwards.

We met Jerry Paris (later a famous comedy director), a longtime pal and a better driver than either one of us, in the Hamburger Hamlet parking lot, so I invited him along to see *On the Waterfront*—and drive. Marilyn was reluctant to take another person, as we only had two tickets. I assured her that since both of us had been under contract to Columbia at one time or another, they would let Jerry in. To this day, women's lib or no women's lib, I'm reluctant to go to any Hollywood event without a male escort. In New York, I'll go with another woman to any function, formal or not, and feel perfectly comfortable. But not in Hollywood. Marilyn felt the same way.

That night, the Columbia parking lot was full, and we had to park near the Hollywood Cemetery next to RKO. As we walked the two blocks up Gower Street to Columbia's entrance, our steps got slower and slower. Columbia had been the scene of the deepest humiliation for both of us. We had both been treated like pieces of meat, given sex-bomb bit parts, and when we'd asked or tried to do something worthwhile, we were told to stay in the tits-and-ass category and not bother Max Arnow, the head of casting. As we approached the front office, our steps faltered, and Marilyn whispered, "Why are they showing his picture in Harry Cohn's screening room?"

Jerry Paris whispered back, "Probably because Columbia financed the film for him."

When we got into the theater, the lights were just about to go down. Jimmy Dean and Nick Ray were sitting in the first—almost empty—row, and we sat on either side of them.

The film was riveting. Its theme, photography, script, and direction were the highest achievement in the art of film. I felt transported to that impoverished neighborhood. I remembered that the pigeons on the roof were the only pets one could keep in my Brooklyn tenement. Eva Marie Saint was so good in *On the Waterfront*, I almost couldn't hate her when, years later, she got my Broadway role in the film version of *A Hatful of Rain*. Marlon Brando, if possible, surpassed himself. The moment when he tells Rod Steiger, "I coulda' been a contender," broke our hearts. What a writer Budd Schulberg was; he doesn't write, "I could have been a champion." He writes, "I could have been a contender." And what an actor. Marlon usually has a powerful moment like that in every film. It's as if he opens a door to all human experience and longing, and he makes you understand the common denominator of humanity. These moments of genius are what has kept audiences going to Marlon Brando pictures for thirty-five years, even the undistinguished ones. He is worth all the millions the studios and public have given him.

Marilyn, Jerry, Jimmy Dean, Nick Ray, and I left the theater in silence—exhilarated yet strangely depressed. The end of the film had been brutal and strange. I didn't understand it, but I somehow knew it was wrong. Jimmy, as was his wont, attached himself to us. In fact, we were all rather huddling together. Nick Ray, who was a handsome, famous director, whispered to me, "Why don't you and Marilyn stop off at my bungalow at the Chateau Marmont, and we'll talk about Gadge's picture?" (Gadge was Elia Kazan's nickname—lately he wants to be called Elia, which I can never remember or pronounce.)

In the late forties Nick, the prestigious director of *They Live by Night* and *Knock on Any Door*, had been my steady beau. He had been my beau once for five or two months. He was somewhat older than the men I usually got attracted to, but he had lovely salt-and-pepper gray hair. He was probably too educated and successful for me to allow myself to get too serious about him. A few months after we stopped seeing each other, Marilyn, on my recommendation, started to go out with Nick. The very things that turned me off turned her on. But he had one talent we could both appreciate. He was older, had gray hair, and was articulate and intelligent. Now as I write, I remember that never to my knowledge did Marilyn ever have a relationship with a young, handsome actor, though she worked with many. Nick must have gotten discouraged with both of us because he married Gloria Grahame, another blonde bombshell but also a fine actress who was to get an Oscar for *The Bad and the Beautiful*.

But these events were in the past and the future. As we drove up Sunset Boulevard to drop Jerry off at his car at the Hamburger Hamlet, Jimmy Dean circled us on his motorcycle. He knew we were trying to get rid of him. He was playing chicken with us, and it was quite dangerous, both for him on the motorcycle, with no helmet, and for me and my passengers. At times it seemed as if I had a choice of hitting either Jimmy's motorcycle or another car. Thank goodness, in those days, there wasn't any traffic on Sunset that late at night.

When we got to the parking lot of Hamburger Hamlet, where Jerry got his car, Jimmy sped away up the hill on Doheny Drive. Jerry, Marilyn, and I were shaking. Jerry made sure that Jimmy was gone and then turned my car around for me. As Marilyn and I set off east on Sunset toward the Chateau Marmont, we hadn't gone more than three blocks when, somewhere around La Cienega, Jimmy came roaring down the mountain. He started the same deadly game of circling us. I was so angry, I was ready to run him over. I kept honking at him, and he kept putting his brakes on right in front of me. He was laughing and enjoying the game. I had once seen a cyclist's head crushed like a melon in an accident on Highland near Universal Studios, and we were scared out of our wits.

When we got to the Chateau Marmont, I quickly drove into the underground garage. Jimmy followed. Marilyn was rigid with fear, and I was ready to punch him out. He stood there grinning like a little boy who had been playing a practical joke. His face was so childlike. He knew we were going up to Nick Ray's bungalow, and he couldn't imagine that we wouldn't take him along with us. I don't recall whether this was before Nick directed him in *Rebel Without a Cause* or not, but they were friends. So I relented and took Jimmy along—much to Marilyn's disgust.

Now that I think about it, I realize that Jimmy and Marilyn treated each other like resentful siblings. As we walked to Nick's bungalow (the same one where John Belushi a few decades later died of an overdose), they ignored each other, and this attitude continued throughout a long night of conversation. Jimmy was sardonic and made fun of everything, especially things about Hollywood that pained or embarrassed him.

Nick's bungalow was surrounded by night-blooming jasmine. It was sparsely furnished, and he had a big Mad Man Muntz black-and-white TV set. There was a peculiar box on top of it which I didn't pay much attention to. I guess he had taken this bungalow unfurnished (nowadays, when actors or rock musicians die there, it's very elegantly furnished). What I didn't know was that the long, thick wire leading from the TV to the dial changer was rigged with a microphone leading to this mysterious box, which was one of those newfangled tape recorders. In those days, they were reel-to-reel and as large as a complicated computer is now.

Nick mixed rather strong piña coladas, and we were so shaken by both *Waterfront* and Jimmy Dean's motorcycle games that Marilyn and I abandoned our earlier resolution of a nonalcoholic early night. After a couple of piña coladas, I was able to calm down enough to complain to Nick how enraged we were by Jimmy's dangerous game and to tell Jimmy that if he wanted to play Russian roulette, he should do it by himself and not involve his so-called friends.

Jimmy just said, "It's midnight. We have to turn on Vampira."

Vampira was a girl posing as a dragon lady with as much bosom exposed as the traffic would bear and a long black wig, long black nails, and three sets of eyelashes and horror makeup. She MC'd the late-night horror movies on a local L.A. station. Jimmy was currently having a mad affair with Vampira—they probably made love in her coffin, from which she introduced the TV broadcast of old horror movies.

That night, Jimmy turned off the sound on the set and pretended to watch the movie as I harangued him about his self-destructive propensities. Around 4:00 A.M., he agreed to see Dr. Judd Marmor, a psychiatrist Marilyn and I were both seeing. It was sort of a bet. He eventually did spend an hour with Dr. Marmor and didn't say a word to the doctor. After an hour of silence, the doctor asked him why he was there.

"I lost a bet to Shelley Winters," Jimmy said.

The reason I remember is that I paid the $25 for his hour of "therapy."

3

*E*ven though, or perhaps because, my name is Winters, I'm allergic to cold weather. When other people are comfortable, I experience what they call mild weather as freezing agony.

The winter of 1954 was the coldest in many a year, but I was having such an exciting time that I hardly noticed the cold. There were great plays and musicals on Broadway. I was surrounded by loving friends and fellow actors at the Actors Studio, and I was solidifying my dream of returning to Broadway and/or London's West End.

The Actors Studio was meeting in a rehearsal hall above the Broadway Theatre at Forty-ninth and Broadway. Elia Kazan, Lee Strasberg, Danny Mann, and Marty Ritt were moderating. I attended an extraordinary session. Kazan was trying to make us understand that characterization comes from how you plan an "action." For instance, a man who is drunk does not try to be drunk. He is trying to be sober. That is his "action."

When Kazan moderated, he would lock the door at exactly 11:00 A.M.—the classes were from 11:00 A.M. to 1:00 P.M. exactly. There was a blizzard that morning, and I barely managed to get to the class from the Meurice Hotel at Fifty-eighth and Sixth. I dressed in snow boots, my long mink coat, sweater, slacks, long johns, a wool hat, and a wool muffler over my face. There were no cabs, but I fought the snow and the wind and got to the rehearsal hall at five minutes of eleven, having left my hotel a few blocks away at ten.

When the class started, Kazan locked the door, as usual. As Kazan was preparing an exercise to demonstrate how to plan an action, there was a banging on the door. We could hear the blizzard howling outside, and someone got up and opened the door. It was Arthur Kennedy and his wife and another couple. They came in, and Kazan stopped talking. We all froze in our seats with cold and fear.

"When the curtain goes up at eight-thirty, you have to be on the stage, ready to act," Kazan stated, glaring at the latecomers. "When this class starts at eleven, you must be ready to learn, and the door is locked. That is the discipline of this art. Without that discipline, there is no art."

He waited, and Arthur Kennedy and his wife and two other famous theatrical latecomers got up and left. He relocked the door and continued.

Kazan gave us the example of a man who is dog-sitting eight or nine imaginary dogs for a weekend. The owners are coming back to their home early, and he must get the dogs outside, the house straightened up and clean. For Tony Quinn, Kazan assigned the improvisation as follows: that the man had been writing a script, and he had not walked the dogs properly, and he had to clean up the place before the owners got back. For Tommy Ewell, Kazan gave the same assignment, but with the modification that although he had to get them outside, he was allergic to the dogs. Touching them made all his allergies flare up. Besides, the dogs didn't want to go outside. For Marlon Brando, Kazan qualified the assignment thus: Marlon had a beautiful girl showing up in five minutes, and he was determined to get the animals out of the place, glamorize it up a bit, and seduce the young lady before the owners of the dogs returned.

The results of this improvisation were hilarious, and the entire class understood clearly that although all three actors had the same assignment—TO GET THE DOGS OUTDOORS—how they did it and the reasons for doing it gave them three distinct and different characterizations. So although I saw this exercise in New York in the early fifties, forever afterward when I have searched for a character in a film or play, I have first asked myself, What is she doing? Second, Why and how is she doing it? And that has given me the characterization.

I left the Studio that afternoon knowing the Actors Studio would be a cornerstone of my life. And, like a pianist or a painter, I would be able to practice my craft all of my life and not have to wait for an audience or a camera. While I was waiting for the elevator, Kazan came up to me, put his arm around my shoulders, and asked me if I had understood the session. I said I thought I had and added that it was very valuable. And I thanked him. Then he asked me when I was going to audition for the Actors Studio, since I had been attending sessions since about 1948. I hemmed and hawed and said, "You know, Gadge, I live in California and, although I'm trying to get permission to do a play on Broadway, Universal suspends me every time I go to Malibu for brunch, let alone fly to New York."

Gadge smiled and said, "Shelley, we know this. But you are attending sessions, and you must be brave and have confidence in yourself and audition like everybody else. I'm sure you'll become a member of the Studio, and it would be another incentive for you to move to New York."

I never did have enough confidence. After I opened in *A Hatful of Rain*, with an entire Actors Studio company, and got rave reviews and standing ovations, Lee Strasberg, who understood my terror and my inability to face the possibility of rejection, let me do my audition in a classroom session, and I did a scene from Bill Marchant's *Faster, Faster* with Henry Silva. I became a member, but I was possibly their longest observer, the same length as my Universal contract—seven years, from 1948 to 1955.

When I got back to the hotel that day, there was a film script of *I Am a Camera*, based on Christopher Isherwood's *Berlin Stories*, the book he had given me for baby-sitting Dylan Thomas. I sat down on the floor in my mink and galoshes, and no matter that the snow was melting all over me, I immediately read the entire screenplay. The accompanying letter told me that Julie Harris would re-create the role she had done in John van Druten's Broadway adaptation. Laurence Harvey would play the Isherwood role, and I would play the German Jewish girl. The letter was signed by Henry Cornelius, who was a new, extraordinary director; he had just directed Kay Kendall and John Gregson in the very funny and successful *Genevieve*. I trembled with joy. I called my agent in Hollywood and told him I had to do this film. If Universal didn't let me, I would get a gun and shoot Mr. Goetz, the studio head, in his head.

"I don't think that'll be necessary," said Herb Brenner, my agent. "You're so busy turning down all Universal's pictures, or dragging back to New York, they'll be glad to send you to England and get you off suspension and make money loaning you out."

Herb also told me that I had to leave immediately for London, because I had to learn the very difficult accent. I had to speak English as a German girl who had been taught by a British teacher. I rushed to Bloomingdale's, got woolen underwear, rushed to the furrier and got a woolen lining for my mink coat, collected all the antibiotics and Vitamin C's I could, and rushed to the airport, where there was a round-trip ticket on the TWA clipper waiting for me.

I had been to England in 1950, during the Festival of Britain, with Farley Granger. It had been summertime, but it had been cold and damp. I couldn't imagine what it would be like in March. It was worse than I imagined.

I studied the script the whole fifteen hours it took my luxurious clipper to get to Gatwick Airport. As I reread the script, I realized that much of the filming would take place in Berlin. I hadn't thought about that the first time I'd read it. After all, the film was based on the play, and a play, of course, is done on a set inside a theater. I had seen the play, and Julie Harris had been dazzling. In the script, they kept indicating "Exterior, Berlin street." To this day, although I've made a hundred films, and I know a movie is pictures of what the characters do, not what they say, when I first get a script, I always first read what the characters say. Then on a second read-through, I read the directions. Probably because I still think like a theater actress.

It was a very, very foggy day in London town when we landed, and suddenly I had this dread feeling that I was in Berlin. I was already in my role to that extent. The terrible Second World War had ended a few years before, but the films and pictures of the devastation and concentration camps were still very much around in newspapers and on TV. I had only been able to look at them in the last year. Berlin had been razed, so how could we shoot a film there? I knew there were practically no prewar buildings left standing. So how?

The steward began to notice that I couldn't get off the plane. He kept telling me that we had landed, and I just stared at him. He had a tough time convincing me we were not in Berlin, but London. When I finally got off the plane and out of the reassuring English-speaking customs, I was met by the producers, the Fox brothers, Laurence Harvey, and Henry Cornelius. I barely let them greet me before I quietly and firmly stated:

"The money you have put in escrow with my agent in Hollywood will be returned to you, and I will pay for my own round-trip ticket. But I cannot go to Berlin. There is nothing to discuss. I love the film and my role, but you must recast me."

They looked at my face and knew there was no reasoning with me. I apologized, saying, "I'm sorry. I didn't realize that the exteriors were in Berlin."

The Foxes somehow persuaded me to get in their elegant Rolls-Royce. Henry Cornelius took off his glove and my glove and held my hand. In the weeks to come, I was to find that he was the kindest and most sympathetic of directors. He told me that, although he spoke English very well, he was a German refugee, and his family had barely escaped Germany with their lives. He understood my feelings, and he himself had no desire to work there. He had spent a month in Berlin looking at locations, and they were rebuilding the city, but he doubted that they would shoot in Berlin. *If* they went to Germany, they would have to use some other city, and make it look like Berlin.

I held his hand and said, "Mr. Cornelius, can't you make the Shepperton back lot look like Berlin? It will save you a lot of money, and, as Sam Goldwyn says, 'A rock is a rock; a tree is a tree. What's important is what's in the actor's eyes, so let's shoot it in Griffith Park.'"

Henry Cornelius laughed at this famous Goldwynism and said, "Shelley, Mr. Goldwyn has made some great pictures. Let me think this over. You get snug at the Dorchester Hotel and study your German-British accent. I'm sending you a wonderful teacher tomorrow morning. She works with the Royal Shakespeare Company. And you let me worry about the production."

I got some sleep at the hotel, and at tea time Laurence Harvey called me, and I joined him in the lobby for a fantastic British high tea—six different kinds of tea and cucumber and watercress sandwiches. When I complimented Larry on the wonderful pastry, he smilingly informed me that the Dorchester had imported the pastry chef from Munich.

I knew Laurence Harvey from parties I'd attended when I'd first visited London with Farley Granger a couple of years earlier. I had first met him at an engagement party that John Gielgud had given at his exquisite home for Farley and myself. We were just very engaged; we never married.

The next morning, I had to go to the studio for wardrobe fittings. Larry phoned and said that since he lived nearby at the Grosvenor House, he would take me.

"A terrible fog has settled over London," he explained. "Literally, people are expiring of it."

When he picked me up in his Rolls-Royce at 6:00 A.M. he had already collected Hannah, my German-British teacher. He had a thermos of coffee and a picnic basket with egg sandwiches and scones in it. I asked him if we were going to eat this well on the way to the studio every morning. Since he was playing the Christopher Isherwood character in the film, he had developed a clipped Mayfair British speech and he answered, "Darling, I have whiskey and beer in the boot. The fog is so bad this morning that it may take us till lunch to get to Shepperton. If it gets any worse, we're going to have to live down there. And there is no central heating in the Shepperton Pub."

My enthusiasm for *I Am a Camera* was rapidly diminishing.

We drove about twenty-five miles an hour and stopped every few blocks while the chauffeur examined the road ahead. There were bomb craters still all over and around London, and with the heavy fog, it made the going rather difficult. Larry began to drink warm whiskey and soda. After all, it was already 7:00 A.M. I drank coffee while Hannah, who was sitting up front, read my role aloud with a German-British accent. Larry kept making fun of my efforts until Hannah shut him up with, "Mr. Harvey, I can still hear your Lithuanian sibilants and the South African twang in your speech. If you're going to work at the Old Vic, as I have read you plan to do, perhaps you should have some speech therapy yourself."

Harvey glowered at her, but he shut up and let us work. Thank God it started to rain, and even though I hate the cold, relentless London rain, it was dispersing the fog. Hannah was a linguist and an Oxford don. She had studied with the professor who had invented phonetics, and although I am not very good at—and am fearful of using—dialects, by the time we reached the studio, I was comfortable and felt surer about being able to do this difficult role. Henry Cornelius kept her with me day and night, and Hannah became quite a friend. During the early days of shooting, when I was so cold and lonely, I would often go to Hannah's little flat for supper, and we would pull the table in front of her huge fireplace. Once a week, on Sundays, she would let me treat her to a roast beef dinner at a famous London restaurant. The English were still on ration stamps.

The costumes were lovely, but all during the fittings I kept telling the producers, the Fox brothers, that I could not go to Berlin. They kept reassuring me that I could handle the trip to Germany just fine. I couldn't. Thirty years later, I finally did a film in Berlin, called *Looping,* and the crew and the actors could not have been nicer.

They were mostly young people who only knew the Nazi horror from reading about it. But still, I hardly ever left the Bristol-Kimpinski Hotel.

One afternoon before shooting started on *I Am a Camera,* I was in makeup, and I started to sob. Julie Harris came over to me and put her arm around me. I explained to her that my Uncle Yaekel was endlessly searching for his family around the world, the U.S.A., Canada, everywhere. The Jewish Agency had told him that my aunt and cousins had been put in a boxcar and left on a siding, where they froze and starved to death. Yaekel did not believe it and was still searching for them. By the early fifties, while I was doing *I Am a Camera* in London, he was somewhere in Canada, still looking for them. He had already searched through all the refugee agencies in England, Germany, and Russia. Yaekel Schrift eventually died in Israel in his eighties. He was hit by a car while he was still searching.

Julie Harris kissed me and said, "I'll talk to the producers, Shelley. I'm sure there's a way they could fake it and send a second unit to Germany and do the close-ups here."

The next day I was informed that that was exactly what they were going to do. My first day of shooting, I attempted to thank Henry Cornelius. He kissed me and said, "I'm glad you made an issue about it. I'm not ready to go back to Germany yet, either.

"Just remember, Shelley, that the film we are making is about a people long famous for their music, poetry, and mathematical and mechanical genius. It's also about how they let their souls be twisted by an ugly philosophy and dictator, and in the process, they almost destroyed themselves, as well as the world."

For the rest of the shooting, I remembered that that was what I was involved in. But to this day, I cannot understand how the German people so lost their souls during the Nazi period. In retrospect, I realize that my investigation of the doomed intelligentsia of pre-Hitler Berlin for *I Am a Camera* was my artistic preparation for *The Diary of Anne Frank,* for which I won an Oscar a few years later.

I remember *I Am a Camera* as being extremely difficult but creatively most fulfilling. But driving back and forth to Shepperton was exhausting; neither Julie nor I wanted to move nearer the studio, but it would often take two hours at night while we crawled along in the fog. We would rehearse our lines in the car, and we trained ourselves to sleep sitting upright.

My part was not extensive, and, as Cornelius was shooting in exact sequence, I had many days off. The weather was not conducive to sight-seeing, and I was very cold and lonely.

One Sunday morning, I phoned my friends Peter and Mary Noble, who had said I must take a cab and come over to their flat for breakfast. They had two beautiful daughters, one a brand-new baby and one a four-year-old. Mary was an actress but not very ambitious. I thought Mary could have had a remarkable career, but she was modest, smart, and retiring, and her life was centered on her husband, home, and family. She would not do any film that took her away on location or tour with a play that took her out of London. Who knows? Maybe her life decisions were a lot better than mine.

Handsome, blond Peter was a writer, journalist, sometime actor, and host of a talk show on British television, which was then in its infancy.

Anyway, that lovely, sunny morning, I took myself to my chums' flat, which was on the first floor of a municipal housing development, and on the floor in the corner of the kitchen sat one of the tallest, most charming, most masculine young Scotsmen I was ever to meet. In the weeks that followed, I learned that he was *very* Scottish, and to this day I love all things from Scotland.

Peter and Mary Noble, although very broke, had invited me to an elegant breakfast. Their three-month-old daughter, Kara, was in a basinette on a wooden door which was resting on top of the bathtub, because the hot-water pipes were in the bathroom, and that was the warmest room in the house. Tina, their four-year-old, was sitting on the lap of Sean Connery (that was the name of the handsome but impoverished Scotsman). He was telling her a very serious story about real leprechauns. I

54

pulled up a kitchen chair, and Mary gave me my tea, and I listened, along with Tina, to the story.

It was a magical hour, and Sean was an enchanting storyteller. After tea, Sean and Tina and I went marketing for Mary, and it was an altogether different experience from the supermarkets in America. Sean carried a string shopping bag, in which he put all of his purchases. I tried to pay for some of them, but Sean would have none of it. He bought a joint of lamb, parsnips, brussels sprouts, and other strange British vegetables. He carried Tina on one shoulder and, since I was wearing three-inch spike heels, which were making me turn my ankles on the cobblestones, he was soon carrying me on his other shoulder. I weighed 116 pounds in those days.

In Edinburgh, Sean had driven a beer lorry drawn by a team of six horses, and had thrown around two-hundred-pound barrels of beer, so his muscles were the opposite of cosmetic. He had recently closed in the West End in *South Pacific*, in which he had had a small role and sung in the chorus.

I subsequently found out that, although he was flat broke at the time, he would never allow anyone, especially a female, to buy him a meal. So I could only eat with him if we dined at Peter and Mary's house or, best of all, when his brother, Neil, who was still in the army, brought in fish and chips and beer at their house.

They had the strangest sort of Dickensian flat I'd ever seen or could have imagined. It was right out of *David Copperfield*. It was only twelve feet square but had three floors piled on top of one another above a shop. And all the stories were joined by a rickety, crisscross iron staircase that they had painted red. I'd never before seen a fire escape on the *inside* of a tenement. Neil's room was on the second floor above the shop, the kitchen–living room was the third story, and Sean's room was the top floor (rather like *Seventh Heaven*). Their three stories were furnished in a modest but imaginative way, and Sean's room consisted of walls lined with secondhand books and a huge, very thin mattress on the floor, with an embroidered Indian throw on it. All through the house were mementos from all over the world that Sean had collected during his travels in the British merchant marine during World War II.

In the third-floor kitchen–living room stood an ancient, narrow coal stove, on which one could cook. It was the only source of heat in the building, but Sean was too thrifty to waste coal when there were sources of heat that he could generate without spending money. That little house was the coldest building I've ever been in. But somehow I spent some of my warmest nights there.

On Sundays, we would have elevenses at the Nobles', and at noon we would all walk up to Portobello Road, and we would buy the babies and each other little presents. Portobello Road on Sundays is a huge street fair, but I would get a threatening look from Sean if I tried to spend more than five shillings on any one gift. In the afternoon, when the pubs opened, we would go to his local, which was in a working-class district, and have mugs of warm beer. After one sip, I would give him mine, and we would chat up all his neighbors, who were, for the most part, laborers and active members of the Labour Party. So, because of the film *I Am a Camera,* I have a very firm grasp of the British labor movement in the fifties.

When I left London in the early spring, Peter Noble drove me to the airport in his dilapidated 1931 Rolls-Royce. As we clanked along, he mentioned that he feared Sean and Neil were going to lose their house, as they didn't have their yearly "ground rent," which was then the equivalent of about $300. Since I had paid my bill at the Dorchester and still had about a hundred big, white £5 notes (worth about $400) left from my per diem, I said, "Peter, give this to Sean."

With an exasperated expression, Peter said, "You know he wouldn't take it from you."

I knew that was so, but then I remembered that Peter had written several books, including *The Negro in Films.* So I plotted:

"Tell Sean that you've gotten a huge advance for another book, and you want to lend him the money so he won't lose his house."

Peter smiled, said, "What a bloody good idea, Shell," and took the money.

I forgot all about that money, but about ten years later, when Sean was in New York and already a millionaire playing James Bond, we went to see Sammy Davis, Jr., in the musical version of *Golden Boy*. Afterward, we went backstage to compliment Sammy. His then-wife, May Britt, modeled her new blond mink coat for me, while the men talked in the adjoining dressing room. I tried it on and adored it.

A few days later, Sean spent the night on my sofa, because he was still so thrifty he would often check out of his hotel room before that evening's date, in order to save paying another night at the Plaza. When I returned from driving him to the airport, there was a delivery man at my door with a huge Christian Dior box. I looked at him, aghast, and sputtered, "It's a mistake. I haven't ordered anything from Christian Dior."

"Nevertheless," the gentleman said, "this is for you, Miss Winters."

So I signed for it. When I opened the box in my living room, there was a new mink coat, the exact blond shade of May Britt's, and in my exact size. There was a note which said:

Dear Shell,
Interest on your money and a belated thank you.

Love,
Sean

4

When I returned from London, I had a *déjà vu* experience. I had done a film with John Garfield in 1950, and a few years later, after his death, I did one about him. What I lived through with him in the first film came to pass in the plot of the second film.

The film I did with John Garfield was called *He Ran All the Way*. Just before we worked together, Warners ended their contract with him. The film I did with him was his first independent picture, and it was released by United Artists, which had borrowed me from Universal. At first, Universal refused to let me do it. They wanted me to do some cockamamie film called *Little Egypt*. I did not want to do another forgettable film, and I was most anxious to work with John Garfield and the director, John Berry, but I did not want to risk suspension by flatly refusing *Little Egypt*. I needed the money, so I hit upon what I thought was an ingenious plan of action.

I went ahead and did the costumes for *Little Egypt*. I was about a size 9, so I began eating as if it was going out of style. In those days they did many costume tests for films, especially for Technicolor Baghdad nonsenses. So after I finished fitting the costumes, which consisted of fourteen spangled bras with veiled sleeves and sequined bottoms with veiled pantaloons (à la "I Dream of Jeannie"), I gained twelve pounds over one week and one weekend and then was very ready to test the wardrobe for this Universal epic.

When Messrs. Spitz and Goetz, who were the bosses at Universal, saw my wardrobe tests with my twelve pounds of fat, mostly around my bare midriff, and my belly button exposed and falling over the top of the sheer, sexy pantaloons, they screamed, "For God's sake, let John Garfield have her!" They made this sacrifice for $150,000, which in those preinflation days was equivalent to $700,000 now.

I then quickly fasted, drank only water, lived in the Beverly Hills Health Club steam room, and then took off fifteen pounds in a week, and happily ran all the way to Sam Goldwyn's studio to start rehearsals and wardrobe tests for *He Ran All the Way*. During this time I also took diet and water pills given to me by the studio doctor, and started my lifelong process of "ruining my metabolism." I determinedly put my romantic life on hold so that when I finally started rehearsing with John Garfield, whom I had seen in many movies, I was indeed smitten.

The film was about a fugitive hiding from the law in unlikely, clever places. I played the young daughter of a simple middle-class family who, to escape the dullness of her workaday existence, develops a very strong imaginary life. When John Garfield, swimming under water, bumps into her in a swimming pool in Long Beach, his romantic good looks dazzle her. When he casually admits he has no place to stay, she takes him home to her family's for dinner. Her Prince Charming has arrived.

Wally Ford, who played my father, is the only one able to resist this character's charm and starts questioning him. After the dinner scene, Garfield's character takes the family hostage and decides to hide out in our apartment. In one of the most horrendous scenes of this terrifying night, Garfield's character orders my mother to sew his shirt at gunpoint—and she's so terrified and rattled she puts the sewing machine needle through her hand. The next morning, using me as a shield, he takes me down through the tenement house and almost escapes from the police. By pretending to help him, I somehow manage to get his gun away from him and shoot him fatally.

He Ran All the Way was released in an almost clandestine manner. I never understood why until years later, when I found out that both John Garfield and John Berry had been named by someone as suspected fellow travelers, and they had refused to clear themselves by naming other people.

He Ran All the Way was one of the most remarkable and important films I was ever to do, and every frame was thought out carefully, with the intention of illuminating the behavior of a criminal who is created by society.

In the mid-fifties, a play called *The Desperate Hours* was done on Broadway starring Paul Newman. He had also been released from Warners after doing a lousy film called *The Silver Chalice*. He came home to the Actors Studio and then did this play. It was exactly the story of *He Ran All the Way*. This play turned Paul Newman's career around—and when he went back to Hollywood, he did *Somebody Up There Likes Me* and on its release became a superstar.

When I was doing *He Ran All the Way*, at each day's shooting I saw the writers and the director carefully emphasize the fact that the criminal that Garfield played could have been a productive citizen, but, owing to the environment he had been born into—the gangs, the slums, and the crowded schools—his fate was sealed very early, and he was almost programmed to become an enemy of society. Poverty Is Violence.

The time frame of *He Ran All the Way* covered twelve hours. It starts in the early afternoon in a swimming pool (the Long Beach Plunge). James Wong Howe's camera was at the side of the pool above the water. The director had arranged for a stuntman double to do Garfield's swimming. Garfield had had a severe heart attack at the Beverly Hills Tennis Club a few months earlier. I knew that underwater swimming was especially taxing to the heart. I rehearsed with the double, but when we came to the actual shooting of the scene, Garfield refused to let the double do it. We had to do the scene about ten times to get the lighting in the water right. It was scary and unnecessary. When John came up out of the water, the camera was on the back of his head and on my face, and all you saw on film was a figure moving through twenty feet of water, then surfacing.

Back then, I could not understand why John insisted on doing this dangerous shot himself. In retrospect, it seems almost as if he unconsciously wanted another heart attack. I didn't understand the political trouble he was in. I just knew that Warner Brothers, by breaking his contract and casting him adrift, were destroying one of their most valuable properties and breaking his heart. In New York, John Garfield had been called Julie Garfine, and he had been one of the shining lights of the Group Theatre.

He was so handsome, and he had a wonderful voice and acting intelligence and a sexy sweetness that made women all over the world adore him. Including me. He was so sensitive and intelligent, but on some days it was like acting with Dr. Jekyll *and* Mr. Hyde. He would go into rages about nothing at all, and, even though he was one of the producers, he would cause hours of delay in production. He was generous to me in every way a big star can be to a newcomer. He gave me the best camera angles in two-shots, made sure the camera favored me and the audience saw both of my eyes. He spent hours on my close-ups, and if he didn't like the rushes and felt I could look prettier, he insisted that the director relight the scene and reshoot it. I developed a big crush on him and I think he had one on me. Perhaps it was just wishful thinking on my part, but I know we necked a lot in preparing for the love scenes, which often started at the height of sexual passion when the director yelled, "Action!"

Quite recently, I was directing a play at the Actors Studio, and John Garfield's daughter, Julie Garfield, was playing a starring role. She looks a great deal like her father and is a consummate comedienne and actress. Julie has only one fault. She tends to fragment rehearsals —which means to break the concentration and start talking about something irrelevant, which is distracting to everyone (as I used to do if the reality got too real and painful). After this had happened many times, at a wonderful rehearsal Julie suddenly broke the scene and turned to me and said, "Shelley, did my father ever sleep with you?"

I was so angry with her for stopping this fine rehearsal that I shot back without thinking, "Oh, Julie, your father was a movie star. He slept with everybody."

Julie disappeared from the show, the Actors Studio, and, I believe, the borough of Manhattan. She moved to Brooklyn Heights. She has since returned to the Studio and, for all I know, to Manhattan.

That night, after the rehearsal ended, I put all the actresses in the show into a taxi station wagon and I took another taxi and had the driver take me around cold, snowy Central Park while I thought about *He Ran All the Way*.

I remembered how it had felt shooting in downtown Los Angeles in the dead of night in one of the coldest winters in California history. John Garfield would be sweet and loving to me one minute and then snarl questions at me as his daughter had just done. As I had watched the picture progressing, I had had this terrible conviction that the criminal he was playing in this film was in some ways really him. The twisting and turning and trying to escape his fate were analogous to his private, artistic, and political life. At that time, 1950, I was so young and too naive and unpolitical to understand what was happening to him and to Hollywood. I just knew that that night when we rehearsed, it was sleeting as if it would never stop, and the special-effects people were blowing choking smoke at us; John held me in his arms and, although there were hundreds of tourists around us, I was filled with a lonely, nameless dread, and I tried to comfort him in some unnosy, silent way.

I remembered clearly being in his trailer and the sound of the sleet on the tin roof; the greasy food they brought us for midnight supper; drinking rum and Coke, waiting the long hours they took to light the rain scenes; and watching a man in agony, not an actor preparing for a scene.

When we got to the last scene, in which I was supposed to shoot him because of what he had done to my family, John suddenly looked at me like an enemy. He flatly refused to let me do the scene. He wanted "the police" to kill him, which made no sense as far as the writer and director of the film were concerned. Now, in retrospect, I understand he didn't want *a friend* to kill him. (I think a friend had named him before the HUAC.) He wanted a nameless force, a blur. "Let the police do it."

We had a terrible fight that night, and at one point he hit me, hard. I stared at him in astonishment, and a girl-friend of mine, who was visiting the set, hit him back, hard. And then we all began to weep.

James Wong Howe thought it was getting too light to shoot the scene and we would have to come back another night, which meant the budget of the film would be wrecked, which it already was. And so, in a long shot, I decided it was now or never: I grabbed the make-believe gun and shot John Garfield with a make-believe bullet. He looked at me in disbelief and despair, a look that has haunted me ever since, and then he tumbled down the stairs and "died." I began to scream hysterically. A stuntman was supposed to fall down the stairs. I thought John was really dead. Maybe, in a sense, he already was.

He didn't actually die for a year or so, but he knew he was leaving Hollywood forever. When we finished filming at the Goldwyn Studios, John drove me and all my bundles and makeup home. As we drove west on Sunset Boulevard, I (the eternal backseat driver) said, "John, wouldn't Wilshire Boulevard be better?" He smiled his sweet smile at me.

"Quiet, my murderer," he whispered. "I'm saying goodbye to the palm trees."

As I had gotten to know him, I had realized that, like so many American kids, his life in the ghetto had been filled with longing to be "a movie star." Even though he'd been a fine actor on Broadway, the fame and money of Hollywood had given him things he had never believed possible—principally artistic and financial freedom. When I read of his actual death a year or so later, it seemed to be an anticlimactic suicide.

He had done *Peer Gynt* on Broadway, directed by Lee Strasberg. It was an enormous role, and he had been funny, poignant, tragic, and mostly inspiring in the part. When I went backstage to congratulate him, I realized he was neglecting his health, drinking a great deal, and not getting enough sleep. I later read in the press that he had died in bed with a strange woman he had picked up in a bar. Well, that's what the papers said.

I still don't know if I answered his daughter's question truthfully. I imagine I did. I was very democratic in those days, and if I had an affair with Sterling Hayden, who'd named names, I must have had an affair with John Garfield, who hadn't.

Now comes the *déjà vu*.

A year or so after I did *He Ran All the Way*, a messenger knocked on my door and handed me a copy of the film script of *The Big Knife* by Clifford Odets. It had been a hit play on Broadway and was soon to be made into a film, with Robert Aldrich directing. He wanted me to play the powerful but small role of Dixie.

I had known Odets from my teenage days as an usher at the Belasco Theatre, home of the Group Theatre. As I sat in the California sunshine, I read this one long scene that Dixie appears in; although it was a very warm day, I became quite cold, and I could feel the gooseflesh on my thighs and arms. This role embodied much of what I felt about Hollywood in those days.

Dixie was a pretty, sad Hollywood call girl. She was uneducated but not stupid, and she was very courageous and cunning. Although in the scene she is threatened, she will not shut up. She tells everybody off. I had seen Diane Cilento play the part on the London stage, and she had been extraordinary. My agent didn't want me to do this role for financial and artistic and maybe political reasons, even though the gifted Robert Aldrich was producing and directing the film. But I did it anyway.

The Big Knife is about a fine actor from New York, a

movie star. He commits suicide at the end of the film when the powerful studio, which has developed and protected him and built him into a superstar, suddenly decides to throw him to the wolves—to accommodate the terrible witch-hunt going on in Hollywood at that time.

In the days of the studio system, actors were conditioned to feel that the heads of the studios were father figures and their happiness and welfare depended on the approval, admiration, love, and protection of these studio heads. Judy Garland, Rita Hayworth, John Garfield, and certainly Marilyn felt that way. And for a long time, I did, too. Then I somehow got the courage and the financial security which enabled me to break away from the Hollywood star system and move back to New York, thus saving my sanity and perhaps my life.

In *The Big Knife*, Jack Palance played the star intent on destroying himself after his studio broke his contract and abandoned him. Ida Lupino played his patient wife, and Rod Steiger played the powerful, ruthless studio head. As I started to prepare for the role of Dixie, I was haunted by the sense of having lived through the actual events with John Garfield.

I would get up early in the morning and go have breakfast at Schwab's, where some of the real beautiful Hollywood call girls were having breakfast after having worked all night. They were careful and closed and very reluctant to talk to me about anything. But when I described the role I was researching and Dixie's courage and cunning and the way she was victimized by being told she was a starlet and then used as if she was a prostitute, they understood what I was trying to put on the screen. Then they began to tell me their sad, funny, and terrifying stories. In the script of *The Big Knife* Dixie is finally killed because she blabs too much about what the studio is doing to the doomed movie star. I thought it was a special case, an invention of Clifford Odets's. But after a few mornings at Schwab's with those tired, beautiful call girls, I realized that every time they turn a trick, they are aware that any kinky customer might be a psycho killer, and the fear of death is ever present behind their sexy smiles.

They were not exactly under contract with the studios. One of them was about eighteen years old and married to a very handsome stuntman. She was a Latin American and had come into America illegally via Mexico. Her husband had rented and furnished a yacht like an elegant bordello and cruised among the boats off San Diego, and she and another teenager were compelled to service all the rich yachtsmen. This was of course arranged by their husbands. One morning when I joined her for breakfast, she opened her purse to fix her lipstick and it was full of hundred-dollar bills. It was a very big and heavy purse.

She hated her husband, and some years later I read that she killed him on a causeway in Florida. She was never indicted. It was his gun, with a hair trigger, and even though she had shot him six times, the judge ruled it was an accident. I guess if you want to shoot someone, it's best to do it in Florida. This Latin American girl, who I believe could have been an actress, was my role model for Dixie.

The filming of *The Big Knife* was very strange and difficult. Robert Aldrich insisted that I be smart-ass, terrified, and courageous, all at the same time. I decided to seek Lee Strasberg's help, and when we finished rehearsing, on a Friday, I flew to New York. In the early fifties, one did not do this while shooting. It was outlawed by the film's insurance policy, but nevertheless I took the red-eye, eager to discuss my role with Lee Strasberg, who was a very close friend of Clifford Odets and had been the late John Garfield's director and friend.

I told Lee how I was having difficulty communicating the nameless fear of this courageous little actress within the limitations of the scene in the film script. Rod Steiger is trying to keep me from blabbing about what I have overheard, especially that Steiger has threatened the film star with blacklisting and physical violence. Blacklisting then as now was supposedly illegal. Dixie won't shut up because she knows how unjust this persecution is. She doesn't know it consciously, but squealing on one's friend is against every moral code that good men live by.

I couldn't seem to communicate Dixie's courage while enacting her fear. I was trying to do two opposite things with the same thoughts and words. When I arrived in New York midday Saturday, I went right to Paula and Lee Strasberg's apartment. Lee watched me do the scene. He of course knew that the script was based on John Garfield's life and death. When I finished, he thought about it quietly for a long while and then said, "Act her courage. Shelley, just be afraid of the furniture, as if it could come to life and hurt you." It was inspired direction. I knew exactly what he meant.

When I got back to Hollywood early Monday morning, exhausted—the plane trip took fourteen hours in those days—I arrived on the set a little late, but I had my makeup on, and I quickly got into my costume, took my place, and began examining the furniture as if the different pieces were inanimate enemies and would come alive at any moment and destroy me.

The assistant director, whoever he was, began to bawl me out for being late. Robert Aldrich was standing in the darkness, away from the lighted set, and he had been watching me rehearse. He yelled, "I don't know what Shelley did on Saturday or Sunday, but leave her alone now. This scene will be the pivot of the film." And so it was. Lee had helped me be funny and brave and at the same time communicate "nameless dread," that feeling of trying to function without knowing where or how your doom is going to strike.

The Big Knife had a very limited distribution, and I have never seen it on television. As I write this, I am hoping to get a cassette of it so I can reexamine my work and show it to my students. It's not in the video stores, though there are many famous actors in it. Mine wasn't a big role, and I was at the top of my career then, with every studio wanting me for leading roles in important films. I didn't care. *The Big Knife* was my personal salute to the angry and gifted, great, sad and sweet John Garfield. It was also my personal tribute to my many friends who had been so brave, facing that truly un-American HUAC committee.

5

When I was a kid, I began to think that if anyone was for the poor people or the relief recipients or the minorities, he or she must be a socialist or a communist. Those were the people in Brooklyn who put their money where their mouth was. They went down South and organized the black cotton workers who lived and worked in terrible poverty. They organized demonstrations against Hitler's Nazism and Mussolini's Fascism. That seemed to be true, too, during my late teens in Hollywood during the Second World War. I remember attending a meeting with Marilyn one night in the forties, listening to Henry Wallace and being sure that since he was for the underprivileged he must be a socialist. I remember I was afraid some committee would indict him.

At the height of the blacklisting in the fifties, Farley Granger and I were invited to a party at Gene Kelly's where Norman Mailer made a speech on behalf of the Hollywood Ten. These were ten distinguished producers, directors, and writers who had been blacklisted and eventually went to jail for standing on their constitutional and ethical rights not to name other people who might have been involved in left, or left-of-center, movements. Farley and I did not understand much of what was being said during the lecture and party that followed. All we knew was that Norman Mailer was attempting to have all the important people in Hollywood sign an *amicus curiae* brief, Latin for "friend of the court." Norman was hoping to present this case of the Hollywood Ten to the Supreme Court. He was trying to do this before these men were sent to jail by HUAC. Everyone who was anyone was at this party, AND I MEAN EVERYONE, in Hollywood. The Ten had stood on our Constitution's Fifth Amendment, which guarantees American citizens the right not to have to incriminate themselves.

Norman, who was then famous only for *The Naked and the Dead,* was a most eloquent speaker. He explained that, if only for humane reasons, these men should not be sent to a jail with criminals but deserved another, more effective legal defense, and an appeal to the Supreme Court. Everyone in the room was very excited and gave money. But I noticed no checks seemed to be given, only cash.

Farley and I had another party at Janet Leigh and Arthur Loew's house, so we hurriedly signed the *amicus curiae* brief and donated $50 each. Then Farley pulled me out the front door. The parking attendant seemed to have disappeared, so I leaned against a tree while Farley went to find his car.

I noticed in a dark convertible two people necking in a rather sexual manner. When I peeked again, I realized it was Montgomery Clift and Salka Viertel, Garbo's writer and a very important person in the Hollywood firmament. She was also about sixty years old. As I write this, I wonder wistfully if Aidan Quinn perhaps likes to neck with sixty-year-old ladies.

Farley came back with his car and made me stop peeking, and we drove to the next party.

Quite recently, thirty years later, I was in the Polo Lounge having lunch with my ex-husband Vittorio Gassman. Norman Mailer, who now had white hair, came and joined Vittorio and me for coffee. When Vittorio left for his rehearsal—he was doing a one-man show at UCLA —Norman said, "You know, Shelley, you've never thanked me properly."

"Norman, I've thanked you all my life for being such a great writer. What *are* you referring to in particular?"

His blue eyes twinkling, Norman said, "Remember about thirty years ago, the famous party at Gene Kelly's house, when everyone was yelling about the inhumanity of putting the Hollywood Ten in jail? And they were giving all that cash for a legal defense fund?"

"Yes, Norman. I remember."

He smiled his devilish smile and said, "Well, they did a lot of yelling, but the only people who signed the *amicus curiae* brief were you and Farley Granger."

"Norman, I don't believe it," I gasped. "What did you do with the brief?"

Norman Mailer smiled wickedly and said, "I just tore it up, Shelley. I needed a powerhouse of names to prepare a proper brief for the Supreme Court. I realized that you two kids didn't understand the danger you were putting yourselves in. Given the temper of the times, you two could have been blacklisted in the name of humanity."

There are people who reproach me for never having shunned those who had named names, but I cannot be sure how I would have behaved if my life and career and my child's welfare had been threatened the way those victims of the witch-hunt were. Two years after he had testified before HUAC I saw Elia Kazan at an Actors Studio party, sitting with Lee Strasberg, whose wife Paula he had named. I hesitated but then I said, "Hello, Gadge." Kazan looked at me with haunted eyes and said, "Thank you, Shelley."

After the film *The Big Knife*, I didn't like Hollywood anymore. Universal was getting about $100,000 a film lending me to other studios, which they did as often as they could. My response to the scripts they sent me was not very flattering. The final straw came when the studio publicity department called me in to have a discussion about the proper conduct of a star.

1. I wasn't to go to Schwab's drugstore for breakfast any longer.

2. I was now an important property, and I must only associate with people of equal importance in the industry.
3. It was bad for my career to be seen with people who weren't famous and/or important.

I explained that most of the actors I knew from New York were my friends and had respectable acting careers and made a very good living—even if they were not stars. Many of them had refused to sign a crippling seven-year contract. They preferred to do the best pictures they could and not just any crap that the studio might assign them to. The publicity department just told me I was wrong, but I knew they were wrong.

I went to the cocktail party that preceded the Golden Globe Awards. I was a nominee, and I won one that night. I believe Marilyn won an award that night, too, as most promising newcomer. I can't remember for which picture I won, and the little golden plaque has since fallen off my little Golden Globe and gotten lost. How it happened is another story. Later. I will probably never find out the name of the picture because the Hollywood foreign-press correspondents are very sketchy with their records, and in those days many of them couldn't speak or read English yet.

Anyway, several decades ago, I was at this cocktail party, looking gorgeous and chatting with gorgeous Gregory Peck. We were discussing something banal, and a character actor I knew stopped by, said hello, and joined in and improved the conversation.

Just then, one of the foreign photographers wanted to take a picture. Gregory Peck edged me away from the unimportant character actor so that we two stars could pose by ourselves—it would be safer for our careers. No doubt Peck had been given the same pep talk by the Selznick publicity office and was trying to obey his orders. I was shocked and offended. If being a star meant I couldn't associate with character actors, who weren't stars, I wanted no part of this kind of studio system.

When I got home that night, I started to pack. I did not

71

know how the baby and nurse and I would live in New York, but we were going.

I noticed a script on my pillow—which was where my mother usually put them, knowing I would be sure to read them before I went to sleep. It was from a British producer I'd never heard of by the name of Sydney Box. The script was based on a hit London play called *To Dorothy, a Son*, and Mr. Box was asking me to star and coproduce the film with him in London that summer.

I didn't even read the script. I talked to my agent first thing in the morning and told him I would do it for half my American salary and the American distribution rights. And I must have four round-trip tickets—for myself, my mother, my child, and her nurse. Of course, I must have first-class accommodations in London for all of us as well.

Lovely Sydney Box cabled that very evening his acceptance of my terms and put the seventy-five grand in the agent's escrow the next day. Although I wasn't finished with my seven-year contract, Universal knew I was so unhappy with their program B pictures, they would let me do this independently of my contract. They would just add three months onto the end of my seven years. Dealing with studio bosses had taught me how to negotiate "in bad faith." I had been under contract for four or five years. They had suspended me when I had a baby without their permission. Maybe I had wrecked their production schedule.

Universal had called me the day after I had gone into Cedars of Lebanon Hospital to have my baby. She was born prematurely, which is a terrifying experience. Nevertheless they were sending me a script called *From Here to Eternity*, based on James Jones's bestseller. Although I'd read the book, I never read the script. When Fred Zinnemann called me, I was barely polite to him. I just said, "Sorry, Mr. Zinnemann, I cannot do your picture. I have more important things to do." So Donna Reed got that Oscar.

But now my baby was a very healthy toddler, and I wanted my freedom to do only good independent films wherever in the world they were offered. Most importantly I wanted to live in New York and train myself with summer and winter stock and the Actors Studio and to be able finally to work on the Broadway stage.

I planned our trip very carefully and decided that all of us would go to New York first and stay there a couple of weeks and see a lot of shows and then fly on to England. With our thirty suitcases full of cans of special American baby food—I guess we didn't think that American babies could digest English baby food—we left for the L.A. airport. My father, protesting loudly, drove us. He could not understand why we were leaving sunny California and thriving America to go back to the Old Country, even if it was on a Pan Am clipper. My mother, who had never been out of the United States or on a plane, was eagerly looking forward to this great adventure.

When we landed in New York, it took us forty-five minutes to load everything into two taxicabs. My mother had not let me hire a limousine, because Rosie Schrift was having an attack of thrift. Universal had been supplying me with limousines for the past five years, and I must say I was rather put out at having to get in a taxi with the baby, her nurse, her stroller, her baby food, her diapers, and as much luggage as the cabdriver could pile around us. My mother took the other cab, sitting in front with the driver and the rest of the luggage filling the rest of the cab—the back, the trunk, and the roof rack. This was probably not an appropriate entrance for a Hollywood movie star. After this uncomfortable journey, I resolved that from here on in, my image demanded limousines, no matter what my mother said.

The Meurice Hotel had opened a door to another bedroom with twin beds off my little apartment, and they had put a crib in it for the kid. I had my own bedroom in glorious solitary splendor. Rose was overjoyed, because there was a little kitchen adjoining the living room. My mother was nervous about the baby even eating New York food; the baby had been premature and very delicate for several months but now she was sturdy and strong and even a little plump. There was a baby carriage in the hallway, and we moved into our makeshift apartment, while I settled down to attend to the business of becoming a New York stage actress again.

I was firm in my resolve that after finishing the English film I would return to the New York theater. My New York agents were arranging for me to meet Broadway producers and directors.

Universal's publicity department was aghast when they read in *The New York Times* that their hot blonde property was going to leave Hollywood, live in New York, and do a hit play on the New York stage. At that time, I didn't realize there was any other kind.

Suddenly, I was eighteen again, or so it seemed. The future was full of wonderful possibilities. I spent as much time as I could at the Actors Studio. The work the actors who lived in New York were doing stunned me. They were all doing classics and literate new plays. One Friday morning I saw a scene from a new play called *End as a Man*. Ben Gazzara played the lead, but there was a young actor in it by the name of Tony Franciosa, who had just gotten into the Actors Studio. He was marvelous—sexy and handsome—and he had a special, exciting talent. I met him briefly when I was leaving the Studio that day. Someone introduced us, and he said, "Hello, Miss Shelley Winters." I said, "Hello, Mr. Anthony Franciosa. What are you doing now?" He grinned and said, "I'm a mail boy at CBS, but rehearsing at night for *End as a Man*." I advised, "Good! Keep studying, and don't go to Hollywood too soon." I left then for a matinee.

I saw sixteen Broadway and off-Broadway plays. I took my mother to practically every theater in New York, even seeing plays that I had already seen. I took her to restaurants uptown, downtown, and on Broadway —Sardi's, "21," the Colony, El Morocco, Lindy's, the Stage Deli, and Lupowitz and Moscowitz on Second Avenue. Watching my mother enjoy New York *with money* was one of the happiest experiences of my life. We had moved from St. Louis when I was nine years old, and my mother had lived in Brooklyn till she and my father moved to California when I was seventeen. While I was growing up she had saved her pennies, and once a year she would go to a matinee at the Metropolitan Opera.

Rose would have certainly been a great actress, and she had a beautiful voice and could possibly have been an opera singer. She worked at Lerner's on Flatbush Avenue in downtown Brooklyn and stood on her feet for years and years, selling dresses. When I finally got a job on the New York stage, she had practically never been to Manhattan.

We saw matinees of *South Pacific; Kiss Me, Kate;* and *La Bohème*—and anything else that we could see at a matinee. Even though we had a nurse, and the baby slept soundly, my mother would not leave her alone at night. I remembered that she had never left my sister and me alone at night, and I realized that that was possibly the source of my feeling of security and ability to deal positively with the world. As a teenager, I was afraid of nothing and nobody.

While we were in New York, Mother had her birthday April 11, and I bought her a little blond mink cape, having heard how damp it was in England, even in summer. When I got back to our little apartment, Mother was in our minikitchen, cooking a complete dinner on a two-burner hot plate—cabbage borscht, salmon croquettes, and black-cherry Jello with bananas. She managed to cook gourmet healthy meals for all of us on a two-burner hot plate. I had gotten her a bunch of early mauve lilacs, which used to grow in front of our house in St. Louis, and a little chocolate birthday cake, which I had ordered the day before, and I was also carrying the big box with the mink cape.

The dinner table was set, and Kathy was feeding the baby fresh-cooked squash, which was being liberally sprayed all over the living room. Mother looked at the box and the flowers, and even the baby stopped eating. Mother sat down and just looked at the big box. She seemed afraid to open it. I took out the cake, we all sang "Happy Birthday," and she blew out the candles.

"Go ahead, Mom," I whispered in her ear. "Open the box."

She opened it slowly and then rushed back into the kitchen and washed her hands and then dried them carefully on her apron. The way she picked up that little mink cape was something I'll never forget. Mom had worked all her adult life. In St. Louis and Brooklyn, she had made all of our clothes. She had scrimped and saved and broken her heart when she could not get enough money together to send her highly intelligent daughter Blanche to medical school. To this day, my sister Blanche still insists she only wanted to go to nurses' training school (that was all my parents could afford). In my mother's hands that mink cape became something else. I think it became a symbol that she had done ''pretty good.'' It was her Oscar.

That night after dinner, as Kathy and I washed the dishes, Mom was singing to the baby and trying to get her to calm down and go to sleep. I got a call from downstairs that a Mr. Jay Julien was in the lobby with two other gentlemen. I remembered my agent had made an appointment with them, but, even though I racked my brain, I could not remember exactly who they were. All I could remember was that he was a lawyer and would-be producer, and they wanted to bring me a play that Mr. Julien was planning to do in the fall. I told the desk to send them up.

Mr. Jay Julien, Mr. William Marchant, and Mr. Alex Fondas walked into my apartment and my life, and they are still very much in my life now, more than thirty years later. Jay Julien is my lawyer and business manager, and William Marchant is a wonderful writer who has written plays, movies, and TV shows in England and America. Alex Fondas was then a CBS mailroom executive who is now an agent and has indeed become a good friend, and over the years we've had many fun times and adventures together. Alex and Bill once went to Greece to visit Alex's relatives for two weeks and stayed three years. They did the same thing in England, too.

Jay gave me a play called *Faster, Faster* that Bill had written. They wanted to discuss the play and my doing it on Broadway, but Mom insisted that they all sit down first and have some dinner. She served them the hot borscht, quickly made some more salmon croquettes and salad, and found some wine somewhere, and treated them all as if they were ''Mr. Jonas Schrift.'' After all,

76

they were offering her daughter a starring role on Broadway. Through all this, Mom never took off her new mink cape or her apron. I must say, this big Broadway producer, the famous Broadway writer, and the CBS executive seemed awfully hungry for people with steady jobs. But, at the time, I thought it was just Mom's terrific cooking that made them have second helpings of everything, including the birthday cake.

The baby flatly refused to go to sleep. She was still on California time and, as far as she was concerned, it was the cocktail hour, not time to go to sleep. After dinner, Alex lifted her out of her high chair, put her in her crib, sat next to her on the floor, and started to tell her funny stories. She was only a toddler, but she seemed to understand everything he discussed with her. They even found out they had the same birthday, Valentine's Day, February 14—and, during much of her childhood in New York, Alex would show up to share her birthday parties, dressed in funny costumes, such as a rabbit, a duck, or Mickey Mouse. But that night, dressed as himself, he got her to laugh herself to sleep by about 11:00 P.M. Mom, Kathy, and I sat down in exhaustion and relief and wondered how we would ever get her to adjust to London time. The nurse suggested Alex come along.

Bill told us facts about England, enchanting Mom with stories about British royalty. He gave us a long list of places we must see and emphasized the value of the bargains at the silver vaults. So, of course, I now have a beautiful and very valuable collection of Queen Anne silver worth a hundred times what Mom paid for it then.

When the theaters let out, the young men and I walked over to the Plaza Hotel to meet Frank Corsaro, a young off-Broadway director from the Actors Studio, who was to direct *Faster, Faster*. He is now a Broadway director, a director at the Metropolitan Opera, and the artistic director of the Actors Studio.

My fondest memories of Frank Corsaro are of him sitting in the orchestra at the Lyceum Theatre, playing scales on the piano. Then he didn't even know how to read music, but today he is one of the most famous opera directors in the world. He was very shy with girls then, although a girl he rather liked later married Oscar Hammerstein. He used to lose his temper quite easily, sometimes with cause, and, of course, he always had to be extremely thrifty. A few years ago, when he was in rehearsal with *Jesus Christ Superstar,* he had a terrible automobile accident, which put him in the hospital for several months. He just smiled and said, "Well, I was meant to do something else." In my book, Frank Corsaro is a mensch. I wonder who his analyst was.

Frank was fascinating and a warm Italian. He was one of the most literate young men I had ever met and had gotten his master's degree at the Yale Drama School at the age of twenty. Now, still in his early twenties, he was living at home in the Bronx due to financial duress. We discussed *Faster, Faster* and while Frank agreed it was funny and very well written, it unfortunately seemed to parallel the life of Frank and Nancy Sinatra and their turbulent marriage and couldn't be produced as it was. They all agreed that the play needed a major rewrite. On impulse, I told Corsaro I would trust his artistic judgment, and if he thought the play was ready, I would do it in the fall.

That long-ago evening in the Oak Room at the Plaza was a revelation. All these young men were completely theater-oriented. Certainly they wanted to make money, but they loved the theater and what it then stood for, and they spoke of how live theater could influence the lives and values of the audience. These men were artists, and they treated me like an intelligent peer. As I sat in the Oak Room surrounded by late-night theater people, I knew at long last I had come home. The next morning I left for England.

6

*I*t was a beautiful spring day, as we flew eastward. But I began to experience the trepidation I'd had when I'd left Italy. This was my third trip to England. Though England and America share a common language, perhaps I'm such a typical American that, as soon as my feet leave my native soil, I get scared. The reality, of course, was that it had taken three pictures, two television shows, and a couple of healthy romances for me to get back my feelings of worth. Maybe a divorce does that to some women. I had exercised and dieted and once again was a perfect size 10. They were going to design a glamorous wardrobe for me, which I could keep, and the producers of the English film had paid three months' rent in advance on a fashionable town house for me and my little entourage.

I sat on the plane and reviewed Bill Marchant's list of tourist attractions. I looked up from the list and saw my baby daughter, who had not taken step one yet, carefully propelling herself down the aisle of the Pan Am clipper. My first reaction was terror. She had been talking a blue streak for months, even if we couldn't understand her half of the time, but she had refused to walk. She crawled, she sat on a swing, and she rode a pony, but walking did not seem to interest her. She preferred being carried, or being pushed in her stroller. And here she was, calmly walking down the aisle without a seat belt on. My mother and I looked at each other in amazement.

"Don't be frightened," said the wise nurse Kathy. "The gravity makes them feel light, and walking is easier." The Pam Am clipper was a prop plane and of course did not fly as high as the jets do now.

In the mid-fifties, flying first-class to Europe was a big adventure. Today, when I fly the boring, three-hour transatlantic trip on the Concorde, I find it difficult to remember how it took half a day to make the same trip in the fifties. But what I remember is the food—as soon as we took off, they served us Russian vodka and fresh gray Russian caviar with onion and chopped eggs and/or sour cream on squares of pumpernickel bread. My mouth is salivating as I write about it. Then, after the plane had refueled in Newfoundland, you got around to the serious eating. Hot hors d'oeuvres with champagne. The roast beef or filet mignon was sliced in front of you, and none, but none, of the food was frozen. Chasen's catered the flights from Los Angeles to New York, and Le Pavillon from New York to London. And there were no microwave ovens in those days. You could have steaks charcoal broiled to order, or roast guinea hen under glass, and they would pass around enormous silver platters of fresh vegetables and baby roast potatoes, and three kinds of dessert, including chocolate éclairs. Of course, there was a different wine with every course. No movies, but by the time you'd eaten and drunk all the booze, you fell into a stuffed stupor. Somewhere over Shannon, they would wake you up for fresh-squeezed orange juice, eggs, and the most delicious Irish bacon I'd ever eaten.

There is a restaurant in the London airport that serves this special Irish bacon, and I always have breakfast there when I arrive in or leave London. I used to buy a pound or two of this bacon, and I smuggled a pound of it into Moscow on my way to a film festival there. Of course, when I put it in the Moscow Hotel refrigerator, it disappeared. On the return trip to New York, I bought another pound, put it in my purse, and tried to smuggle it into the U.S. It is against customs regulations to bring food or plants into the U.S. I was caught. Wouldn't you know, the New York customs officer asked me to open my purse. It was the last and only time, before or since, that I tried to smuggle anything into the States. He confiscated my Irish bacon with a brogue you could cut with a knife, and he said, "Have to send this back to London. The queen has to examine this hog."

"I'm sorry I don't have any eggs for you to confiscate, too," I replied, but I wasn't too snooty—I was glad he hadn't arrested me.

Back on the clipper, my mother, Kathy, and I, and especially the baby, could hardly get back into our coats. We had eaten our way across the Atlantic. Kathy was rather sleepy-eyed because the baby was still on Pacific time. As a matter of fact, she stayed on Pacific time the whole time we were in London, which meant she turned night into day. She would sleep all day long and wake up at 9:00 P.M. when I had to go to sleep, and demand her breakfast when I had just finished my dinner.

When we arrived in London, after we'd gone through customs and immigration, a battery of reporters and flashbulbs descended on us. I hadn't thought this was such an important film, but it was one of the first British-American coproductions after the war, and the British press treated me royally and with kindness. Whether it was the presence of my mother and daughter, they didn't ask me one personal question about my daughter's father or my recent much-publicized divorce. They handled me with such kid gloves that I began to feel like visiting royalty from the Kingdom of Brooklyn. Of course, this was long before the reign of Rupert Murdoch and the scandal press.

My mother was dressed in her mink cape and I in my new full-length mink coat with the enormous turnback cuffs; this mink was the second in a long line of minks. Kathy was in the old one that I had shared with Marilyn. That one was made of so many minks that the nurse, the baby, my mother, and I could all have fit into it. In London, we were glad we had all those minks, because it was so cold and damp that we Californians shivered as we piled into the vintage Rolls-Royce with some of our thirty suitcases. We were followed by a lorry carrying the rest of our luggage, and the British press followed the lorry in a red double-decker bus. The producer, Mr. Box, was obviously having a press conference about the picture on the way to the city.

We had been met by the film's director—surprise, surprise, *a woman,* Mrs. Muriel Box. In the eight weeks I worked with Mrs. Box, she never once took her hat or gloves off, and whenever I asked her a method question to clarify the script, she burst into tears. Her husband, Sydney Box, looked like all the wartime cartoons of Colonel Blimp, and he was the proud owner of a huge herd of black-and-white cattle.

Also in the welcoming committee was Betty Box, Mr. Box's sister, who was a prestigious director and producer in her own right. In a flash I knew it was a pity she wasn't directing *To Dorothy, a Son* because, when we'd been delayed at the airport for an hour, while I had been speaking to the press, and the airport officials had been scurrying around trying to find my work permit, she with great dispatch had straightened out the official snafu.

When the customs official of the Labour Party had informed me that I had to swiftly go to the nearest police station to be fingerprinted, I almost got back on the plane. But Betty Box convinced this officious man that I was not a Hollywood criminal who was going to steal the Crown Jewels that very night, and we would take care of this problem tomorrow. She probably slipped him ten pounds.

What I remember about that fingerprinting when it took place was that I was very angry at having to do it in order to work in Britain. This is one of the ways the British Labour Party was protecting its artists. But a very jolly bobby with a huge mustache started to tell me funny stories that weren't in Agatha Christie's mysteries: Like the initials F-U-C-K come from eighteenth-century police blotters and stand for "*For Unlawful Carnal Knowledge.*" I got to laughing, and I didn't mind being fingerprinted to protect the British cinema's leading ladies from Hollywood actresses whose pictures were shown all over the world, especially in the U.K. At that time not many British films got to the U.S.A.

In the Rolls, the passenger compartment was heated up to about eighty-five degrees—but the chauffeur's compartment was open to the elements, which distressed my mother very much. All through our stay in England, when we rode in these cabs, she worried about the driver "sitting outside." Betty and Muriel were sitting on the jump seats, and they told my mother not to worry about the chauffeur—he was already commenting that, if it got any hotter in the back compartment, his floorboards would get so hot he would demand heat pay. British film crews get that when they work in the jungle.

As we motored through the outskirts of London, I was struck by the enormous contrast between the ancient, Dickensian municipal tenements with the outdoor lavatories and the grandeur of the palaces on the mall, the houses of grace and favor, the great historic buildings, and royal apartments. In a flash, I realized what a dangerous political writer Dickens had been in his time.

The beauty and quiet splendor of London took my breath away. My mother and Kathy were silent. Kathy, like Sean Connery, was Scottish and not impressed by the royal trappings. But the baby seemed impressed, and quiet.

Although I had visited London twice before, I hadn't had time for real tourism. So I resolved that this time I would allow myself the joy of absorbing British history, tradition, and the England of great literature. Especially since Sean was away, working somewhere in Africa.

Quite recently, I did a wonderful play called *84, Charing Cross Road,* and I believe I was quite good in it. If I was, it was partly because of what I absorbed on that trip.

Muriel and Betty Box kept telling me about the beautiful house they had rented for us, which had belonged to an Earl of Something-or-other and which had recently been vacated by Gregory Peck so we could move in. We could hardly wait. We arrived at this impressive town house with the rain and sleet coming down as if it would never stop. The outside of the house looked like a castle. We went through the marble entrance hall, and there was my English chum, Peter Noble, with three bouquets of beautiful roses (why are the colors of English flowers more brilliant than any others?). Peter was to be the English coproducer for Gina Productions, which was my American company. The walls in the house were covered with a dark, dark red silk and dark mahogany paneling. There was a lovely curved marble staircase, but I noticed under it was creeping something called "rising damp." The house was cold, *cold*, damp, and dark, despite its beauty. Of course, there was no central heating. Noticing my mother's distressed face, Sydney Box said, "Madam, look at this beautiful Adam mantel."

Mother, clutching the baby, said, "You mean Charles Addams?"

Mr. Box said, "Please notice how perfectly restored the antiques are. The house and its furnishings are three hundred years old."

Rosie stared at him and said, "Three hundred years? And you expect us to live in it with a baby?"

Whereupon she headed back to the warmth of the Rolls-Royce, knocking down three pieces of luggage that were coming in the door in a handcart.

I gave the upstairs rooms a quick look. They indeed looked like a royal brothel. The bathroom looked like an ancient torture chamber. But Peter Noble was already on the phone frantically trying to get the Savoy to give us a suite immediately with central heating.

We left Muriel and Sydney and Betty Box standing in the cold mist and piled back in the Rolls-Royce. The thirty pieces of luggage were piled back in the lorry. Sydney was holding the bag of California baby food, and Muriel was holding the diapers, some of them wet. But I instructed the chauffeur to drive quickly to the Savoy before my mother got in a taxi and drove back to the airport to get my baby safely back home to sunny California.

When we got to the luxurious Savoy, they couldn't have been more gracious to me and my sodden entourage. We were exhausted from the time change and the traipsing all over London in the damp. They hurried us up to a beautiful, warm three-bedroom suite, taking our brand-new passports, but not even asking us to register in the lobby. A motherly housekeeper made us sit down in the living room and brought very hot tea. The staff went swirling around us. We watched in awe as they brought in the thirty pieces of luggage, got a crib and a high chair for the baby, a small Scotch for Scottish Kathy, an overseas telephone line for me, and an aspirin and an ice bag for Rose's headache, and ran hot baths for all of us.

I had no idea what time it was anywhere, but I was busy trying to call my agent in Los Angeles to find out if the English producers were going to pay for this elaborate suite and tender loving care or if I would have to, since I had refused to stay in the brothel mansion they had paid three months' rent on.

All the Boxes arrived, took the phone away from me, and assured me it was their responsibility, and Sydney spread around big white £5 notes to the army that was making us comfortable. Mrs. Box—Muriel—reassured Mother that after the film started they would find us a lovely service flat near the Serpentine. Since Mother did not know what a Serpentine service flat was, she took a couple more aspirins and said nothing. At this point, anything British sounded dangerous to her.

In what seemed like ten minutes, the electric fireplace was lit, the suite was full of glorious flowers and baskets of fruit, and hot tea and watercress and cucumber sandwiches were served. Sydney then handed me a new script of *Cash on Delivery,* which was the new title of *To Dorothy, a Son.* He also handed me a huge roll of £5 notes. It was about the equivalent of my weekly per diem, $2,000. It seemed so much money, which it was, that I promptly hid it in a boot. I later came to regret having done this, because I forgot where it was.

I luxuriated for two days, taking hot bubble baths in the immense tub, exercising, getting massages, dieting, sleeping, talking on the phone to my English chums, and, at night, staring out over the Thames.

A small problem developed. The baby had somehow

realized that the little panel with three buttons on the table contained a magic trick. When we weren't watching her closely, she would push these buttons. Then we would see her crawling over to the hall door and waiting. Lo and behold, in a few minutes, the chambermaid, the waiter, and the valet would appear. She would clap her hands with delight, and we would not know why they had shown up, since nothing was required. Finally, since we all more or less spoke English, except the baby, they explained to us that the lights in their service room were on, notifying them that we had pressed the buttons. Since American hotels have only a chambermaid, who shows up only when she feels like it, and you have to call downstairs for room service, we adults finally figured out what that little panel was for and put it out of the baby's reach, much to her disgust, and the staff's, too; they liked to play with her. Which was lucky because she was still on California time. She would crawl up and down the halls of the Savoy all night with an exhausted Rose or Kathy or me trailing after her. We took three-hour shifts. Finally, the night porter and night chambermaid took pity on us and took her on their rounds, and she helped them with their chores, such as shining shoes. They played with her as they did their work, and she laughed and gurgled, and we three guardians of the child fell into exhausted sleep. Any other hotel in the world would have asked us to leave, but the lovely Savoy simply changed the schedule, and perhaps the clientele, of our entire floor.

We had arrived on a Friday. So Monday morning I was notified to report to Berman's, a very old, very famous maker of costumes for both films and theater. I met a lovely young woman who was to do my clothes. She did one of the most intelligent things a designer ever did with me: she talked to me. We discussed the new script, and she tried to get my ideas about the character. I told her I understood the first script, but I was confused about the final script.

To this day, I'm not sure what it was about. I think it had something to do with an American girl going to London to claim an inheritance, but having to cross the international date line, which is somewhere in the Pacific, in order to arrive in London on the proper day to claim the fortune. The designer and I both laughed, and she told me to rely on the director, Muriel Box, who never took off her hat or gloves, to clarify the story for me. I must rent *Cash on Delivery* from a video store someday soon and find out what it was about.

There was a first-rate British cast, mostly stage actors from the West End. In those days British actors still considered films a silly art form. They would do any part in any film for the large sums of money involved, but their real careers were on the West End. Among the cast were Wilfrid Hyde-White, who seemed quite old even then, but I just recently did another film with him and he still seemed the same age. Also in the cast was a handsome young leading man by the name of John Gregson, who had just played the lead opposite Kay Kendall in *Genevieve;* and Peggy Cummins, who had been in Hollywood under contract to Twentieth and had played the lead in *Forever Amber* before it was reshot with Linda Darnell. I was surprised that our little British black-and-white picture was to have such an illustrious cast and resolved there and then that despite the delicious British high teas, I would continue dieting strenuously and study my script carefully.

The sketches of the costumes were wonderful. In a couple of weeks the Boxes found me a lovely, completely furnished flat on Park Lane, overlooking Hyde Park, and my little family settled in. The baby was beginning to speak with a slight English accent, Kathy was making friends in the park with all the British nannies, Rose explored the sales, especially the silver vaults, and I went to work on the glorious shooting schedule of the British working man in the film industry. In those days, that meant ready to shoot at 9:00 A.M. and an hour and a half before that for makeup. Before that they would serve me a full British breakfast at 7:00 A.M. (Irish bacon, eggs, orange juice, bubble-and-squeak, coffee, clotted cream, and crumpets). At 11:00 A.M. the tea trolley comes around, and you have tea with cream and ham-and-cheese rolls. You break for lunch at 1:00 P.M., when you have a full four-course meal: starters, then roast beef, Yorkshire pudding, two veggies, wines, and trifle with cream. At 4:00 P.M., everyone sits down to high tea, which for me usually was lemon tea and scones. The union shop foreman usually called the quarter at 5:15 P.M., which meant everyone had to stop working in fifteen minutes.

It must have been spring or summer by then, because I seem to remember going to the rushes in bright daylight. While we watched the rushes of the previous day's filming, we were served pink gin and chips. Then we would rush to the lovely pub across the way to discuss the rushes and have warm beer and chips. Then I would rush home at 8:00 P.M. and consume Rose's fantastic suppers. My valiant efforts to Anglicize my eating habits ended the first Friday, when the designer notified me that I had to fast over the weekend; I had gained a size and couldn't fit into any of my beautiful costumes. And as though we weren't getting enough food, one morning Rose opened the door, and there in the hallway, in my daughter's name, were orange juice, cod-liver oil, and milk, courtesy of the British Labour government. It seemed, during the fifties, all babies in Britain received these things free whether they wanted them or not. The British Labour government just said all children need them.

The summer I made *Cash on Delivery* was one of the happiest of my life. My British co-workers were enchanting. None of them took themselves too seriously. Since we were doing a comedy, Muriel and Betty Box, and especially John Gregson, managed to keep the atmosphere on the set very light and whimsical.

It took me about three days to figure out that Muriel was very intimidated by my sex-goddess publicity. She relaxed as soon as she realized that I was a serious actress and a pretty good comedienne and that I respected her and her script. And I soon realized that she was a very good film director who happened to be a woman. I had never had a woman film director before and I faced the fact that I had been prejudiced against her because of my stupid Hollywood sexist conditioning. Soon she began to give me skillful comic direction. It was altogether a new experience for this Method-oriented dramatic actress.

At the same time, I developed quite a crush on John Gregson. He was Peter Pan incarnate. We began to play practical jokes on each other and, during our love scenes, Muriel got a little confused as to when we were necking and when we were rehearsing. So did we.

Around the third week of shooting, the British polio drive had a big fund-raiser garden party in Brighton, and many celebrities, English stars, starlets, and royalty were attending this important event. John Gregson offered to furnish me transportation to Brighton. He had just bought an MG sports car, his first new car since the war, and it needed to be driven five hundred miles at thirty-five miles an hour to be broken in properly. Back then, one did that with new cars, even in the U.S. The evening before we left, John rang me up and told me to be sure and bring enough clothes, as it was a very long drive, and it would probably be best to spend the night in Brighton.

We were supposed to leave at 8:00 A.M., but by the time we cleared Hyde Park corner, where I insisted on stopping to hear the political speeches from all shades of soapboxes, it was more like 10:00 A.M. We finally got on the A1 after stopping at several pubs for fish and chips and beer, beer, beer. Driving on the left side of the road was not quite as terrifying as it might have been, because whenever we stopped, John would calm my nerves by kissing me a bit. It was a long trip, but altogether lovely.

I began to really look at him—not the character he was playing in the film. He had black, curly hair, very serious blue eyes, a puckish, sad, handsome face, and an English football player's body. He had played rugby semiprofessionally for some Northern city. His wit reminded me of Dylan Thomas.

At the beginning of this motor trip I had tried to keep up with him, beer for beer, although often pouring most of mine into his already empty glass. But by the fourth stop I was tipsy, and he was still sober as the proverbial judge. In the weeks to come, I was to find out that he could drink all day and most of the night and never get drunk. I believe British actors acquire this skill in adolescence.

By the time John and I arrived in Brighton, it was teatime, and the very proper British press was quite annoyed with us. I found out that a press conference had been scheduled, and the dignified journalists, including the correspondents from *The Manchester Guardian* and *The Times* of London, had been waiting for us and had finally given up. I caught a lot of flak.

There was no time for John and me to go to our rooms at the Brighton Inn, so I excused myself and dashed into what I thought was the unisex English rest room (they had those there at that time). I took off my slacks, sponged off quickly with cold water and cologne, fixed my makeup, sprayed on perfume, and put on my lime-green tulle hat with a pale pink rose in the back. I was standing in my hat, half-slip, and bra, putting on my false eyelashes, when I noticed in the mirror two distinguished gentlemen in morning suits. I grabbed my lime-green chiffon dress to cover myself, and as I turned, stunned and paralyzed, I realized one of the gentlemen was Prince Philip.

The prince nodded and smiled and said, "That's a lovely costume, Miss Winters. A Hartnell creation, isn't it?"

I think I mumbled, "Your Majesty," and curtsied. The prince smiled and looked at my size-10 figure in the mirror.

"Miss Winters," he inquired, "are you enjoying filming in London?"

I nodded dumbly. The other gentleman, very elderly and dignified, asked, "Shall I zip you up, Miss Winters?"

I continued nodding like one of those old Chevrolet kewpie dolls, but I stepped into my dress quickly, turned around, and Lord Whoever expertly zipped me up. I barely whispered, "Thank you," and dashed out of whatever room I was in.

John was waiting in the huge foyer of the Pavilion with a large beer in his hand. I grabbed his arm, splashing the beer over both of us, and shouted in a whisper, "Prince Philip just saw me in my bra and half-slip."

I think John thought I was drunk or hallucinating and replied, "Jolly good."

I babbled on, insisting that I had left my matching green purse, white gloves, hatbox, and makeup kit in the room with Prince Philip. He gave me a startled look and said, "My God, he was my superior officer in the Navy, and I'm still in the reserves."

I didn't know what that had to do with the prince's seeing me in my slip and bra, but nevertheless John whispered something to a man in uniform. He looked very startled but went into that strange rest room and returned with my belongings. He stowed the hatbox and makeup kit in John's car, first giving me the gloves and purse and a dirty look.

John and I then straightened ourselves and walked out onto a sort of dais, a step below a huge veranda. There were a few thousand people standing in front of us. Everyone was dressed in beautiful summery clothes, and, as I looked out, I saw a sea of white and pastel colors. The Union Jack was flying from every building, and the sea was a sparkling blue in back of us. Strung across and over the heads of the people was a huge banner in blue and white, which said HELP DEFEAT INFANTILE PARALYSIS. The scene would have been glorious except for the children, several in wheelchairs, some with braces trying to stand, and a couple of children in iron lungs. I didn't look too closely; I couldn't without crying. I'm not a stoic the way my fellow actors were—they'd lived through the Battle of Britain.

For me the day seemed suddenly to go gray, as if the sun had disappeared, and I remember saying a little selfish prayer to myself, for my child's sake. Dr. Jonas Salk had not yet even been heard of, and we didn't know anything about a polio vaccine. Now we hardly even hear about infantile paralysis or think about how dangerous and scary and hopeless that disease was.

Prince Philip came out on the veranda, followed by a very young Prince Charles carrying roses, which he gave to a beautiful, dignified lady who was obviously the head of the Brighton Infantile Paralysis Drive. Philip began to speak, and the sun came out again. With gentle humor, he joshed the crowd back into a more positive, happy, and proud mood. He reminded them that even though they were still recovering from the deprivation of the war, the English people had somehow raised millions of pounds to help research and defeat and cure this terrible disease. He made us feel positive and hopeful that that would happen soon. He reminded us that the English had already raised the money for the scientific research that had led to the discovery of penicillin in England during the Second World War.

That afternoon in Brighton was one of the few times in my life that I felt so connected with my environment. I truly belonged with my peers. In my long white gloves and green tulle hat (with the pink rose), I was a lady among ladies. After the long ceremony, all the stars went to an official dinner. It was given in a very elegant ballroom that had a stage at one end. I was so dazzled by the famous British actors seated at the huge U-shaped table that I can't even recall what we ate—Laurence Olivier, Vivien Leigh, Mr. and Mrs. Ralph Richardson, Michael Redgrave and his wife Rachel Kempson, Anthony Quayle, and Sam Wanamaker, the only other American present. All their wives looked like Lady Somebody. All I remember about that dinner is that the wines and champagnes and brandy were terrific.

After dinner and the VIPs' speeches, they had a floor show. The cockney MC must have been hilarious because everyone was laughing his head off. Sitting next to me, I saw John Gregson weeping with laughter. The comic, I guess, was very funny and dirty, but I didn't understand word one. John meanwhile kept filling my glass. Then as now, one drink and I feel great; two drinks and the room starts to roll; three drinks and I have to be carried to bed. My booze tolerance is very low, and I have developed the art of nursing one drink all evening long.

The last thing I remember about that floor show was Living Statues. It was a strange vaudeville act with muscular, beautiful young men and extraordinarily lovely young girls who seemed to be naked and were painted gold or silver. The French call such acts *tableaux vivants*.

When the curtain went up, they stood absolutely immobile. You couldn't see them breathe. Everyone applauded wildly. The curtain came down. A couple of seconds later, it went up again, and the statues were in different positions. These positions went on and on until the music and applause faded away. But by then I believe I had faded away too.

The next thing I remember is having breakfast with John on a terrace overlooking a sparkling blue sea, except the horizon seemed directly over my head. After John forced me to drink a very spicy Bloody Mary and take four aspirins, the horizon settled into its usual familiar position. It must have been a wonderful night, because both John and I were relaxed and glowing. I realized that we'd had that extraordinary kind of lovemaking you can only have with someone you don't love but whom you like and admire. No agony, no postcoital remorse, no "you have abandoned yourself or you are going to be abandoned." No lies, no pretense. Just lovely love.

We drove happily back to London after lunch, stopping at enchanting pubs all the way. To this day, the smell of fish and chips affects me like some sort of aphrodisiac.

About five miles from London, John suddenly asked me, "Shelley, tell the truth. Do you have sexual fantasies when you're making love?"

No one had ever asked me that question before. I must have looked startled, because he said immediately, "I'll tell you mine if you tell me yours."

I can't remember what he told me, but I quickly improvised something about a gorgeous hulking truck driver. With John Gregson, you didn't have to fantasize. Lo and behold, three miles out of London, a huge lorry cut in front of us. John got the car in control, pulled up beside the truck's cab, both vehicles going 60 MPH, looked up, and shouted to the driver, "That does it, you dangerous idiot, we're not inviting you to any more of our parties!"

We got back to London in time for a late dinner, and I resolutely kissed John goodbye at the entrance to my flat. I had an early call on Monday morning; he wasn't on call till after lunch. He was beginning to look as if he was going to suggest a nightcap and a trip back to Brighton, and I realized I wouldn't be able to resist the trip. So I quickly sent him home.

The next day on the set, John arrived with a little present for me. We cuddled in a corner, and I explained to him that I'd gotten to the set at 6:00 A.M. and I hadn't yet had time to think of anything appropriate for him. He kissed my ear and whispered, "Never mind. Open the little box."

In it was something I still have, though it no longer fits —a narrow gold *ankle* bracelet on which is engraved HEAVENS, ABOVE.

A decade or so later, I was doing another film in England, and I was watching the weather report when a map of England appeared on the TV screen. They had a report on the Brighton weather, and on the map they showed, Brighton was down in the southeast part of England, very near London, when everyone knew London was way up in the northwest. I almost called the BBC to tell them of the mistake in their map. Fortunately, something distracted me. A few evenings later, I was at a party at Jackie Collins's apartment, which was in a huge, elegant block of flats that faced Victoria Station. Laurence Olivier, who lived in Brighton and, I believe, had a *pied-à-terre* in this block of flats, was at the party. In passing, I mentioned that it must be very difficult to commute back and forth to Brighton when he was in a play. Sir Laurence looked at me rather quizzically and asked me how far I thought Brighton was from London.

"Well," I replied, "it may be faster by train, but it's a good seven-hour drive. Don't you remember the time in the mid-fifties when they had the big fund-raiser for infantile paralysis? I saw you there."

Sir Laurence looked startled and then amused. He asked me who it was who had driven me to Brighton the one and only time I'd been there. I told him it had been John Gregson. He said, with a very serious face, "You must have had a remarkable trip. For us ordinary folk, it's only forty-five minutes to Brighton from Victoria Station."

I stood there, stunned. For twenty years, I had thought

London was in the northwest part of England, facing the U.S., and Brighton was across England in the southeast corner, facing Europe. I think I've got it straight now. Well, no matter where it is, it was a lovely trip that lovely summer.

Back at the studio that afternoon, John had a scene with Peggy Cummins, so I was free. Sydney Box insisted I drive out to a country inn with him for lunch and to see his black-and-white cattle. They were the most beautiful cows I'd ever seen, carefully groomed and fat and batting their long eyelashes that looked as if they'd been curled. These beautiful cows really put to shame their poor American cousin, Elsie.

Sydney proudly explained at great length how much milk they produced, the calves they produced, how many cows to each bull. He knew so much about them, I began to suspect they were related. I couldn't even imagine why he was producing films when he loved producing milk so much. Some months after we began the film, these beautiful cows developed hoof-and-mouth disease, and, by the end of the filming, the British government made him destroy a great many of these cattle—which, outside of costing millions of pounds, almost gave the poor man a nervous breakdown. The picture was a contributing factor too. But it was a lovely afternoon, strolling through the green, green countryside of England. During that movie, at last I got to see the English countryside.

The shooting of the film breezed blithely along, and it was truly a glorious summer, different from the terrible winters I had spent there. I began to go to parties. There was a young actor by the name of Theodore Bikel, who was doing a play called *The Loves of Four Colonels* on the West End. Peter Ustinov, who had written the play, was also starring in it. Theo had been born in Mitteleuropa. His family had gotten out and roamed around other countries, then had gone to Israel, where he had had a career on the stage. Now he was living and working in London. Theo suddenly decided he was a guitarist and singer—he was neither at the time—and so, whenever there was a party, whether it was in somebody's home, a restaurant, or—once—on a houseboat on the Thames,

Theo would practice singing on his friends in *sixteen* languages and accompany himself on the guitar. His audience would slowly leave—I think the time on the boat, several people jumped overboard.

But now, Theo is a great concert performer and sells out Carnegie Hall and other large auditoriums all over the world. He also starred in one of the biggest Broadway hits of all time, *The Sound of Music*. But that summer he practiced his act on all of us. Well, what are friends for?

John Gregson had shown me where he lived on Hampstead Heath and all the pubs. Many artists, poets, playwrights, and actors also lived there. That summer I made one of the silliest real-estate mistakes of my life. One Sunday, my mother and I and the baby and our friends, the Nobles, were visiting George Coulouris on the Heath. Coulouris had been a well-known film and stage actor in Hollywood before he moved to London because of the blacklist. He had a cottage with a thatched roof, where he and his family gave us tea, and we talked about the plays, both classic and modern, that were on in the West End that season. George mentioned that the house next to his was for sale, and after tea he took us through the garden hedge and showed it to us. It had a thatched roof, too. The kitchen and dining room were on the basement floor; living room, study, and library were on the first floor; and lots of bedrooms were on the second floor. It had an attic full of tiny maid's rooms. There were fireplaces throughout the house, and beautiful vines covered the old brick on the outside. It also had a beautiful English garden, and it must have been about half an acre.

Mother quickly asked, "How much would it be to put central heating in this house?"

"To insulate it completely and put the most modern central heating would be about three thousand dollars," George said. "That house will probably go for about ten thousand pounds [about twenty-eight thousand dollars then]."

I looked at the elegant staircase and casement windows and pegged floors. It was a lovely, warm house, and for a few minutes there I tried to imagine myself living in London instead of New York. Rose, with her special

ESP, said, "Shelley, even if you don't live here, I know you'll be coming to England to do a lot of films in the future. You'll be spending a fortune on hotels, because I know you will be working in British films and on the West End."

"She's right," Mary Noble agreed. "This house is a fantastic bargain. We can furnish it inexpensively à la Portobello Road, and when you're not in England, I'll get you an estate manager who will rent it for you. It will pay for itself in time, and you'll have a lovely home on the Hampstead Heath."

I picked up the baby and held her. Peter Noble said, "Shelley, you can study speech here and perhaps in time maybe work at the Old Vic. Who knows, you might even get to be Dame Shelley Winters."

Why I make real-estate decisions emotionally I don't know. But I had refused to live in Italy with my daughter's father, Vittorio. My mind was set on New York. I seemed to remember Vittorio and I briefly discussing a London residence instead of Hollywood, because it seemed to be between Italy and New York. At that moment in time, I had more than enough money, but perhaps buying a house made me feel that I had to live in England and become British. I thanked George Coulouris and left that beautiful house and got in the car with my daughter on my lap.

I looked at the house from the car. It was in the center of a manicured lawn. The trees were artfully spaced and the greenest of green. It was altogether like a house in a dream. It wasn't the money. I certainly had the $5–10,000 I needed as a down payment. Why couldn't I have conceived of it just as an investment? I guess I just couldn't.

Mother got in the car and stared at me with disgust. We drove back to the flat. This house is now worth more than $2 million. I often think how perhaps my life would have been different if I'd bought that house.

Years later, when my daughter was about ten, Vittorio was in London seeing the theater with his third wife or fourth mistress, and he picked my daughter up at the Nobles'. I had just seen some glorious British play at the Old Vic, and when Vittorio walked in the Nobles' house,

I said something very bitchy to him and threw something at him. He didn't know why; he had no idea. Now he knows.

One Saturday morning that same summer, I got a call from my beloved Charles Laughton, who was opening a new play on the West End called *The Party*. He had not been on the stage for many years and was rather nervous about the whole thing. He asked me to come to the first preview. He didn't really like the play, but he mentioned that there was a redheaded young man who had a rather small part, and Charles wanted to know my opinion of him.

Charles Laughton, who was one of the most impressive actors I've ever seen on the stage—in *Galileo* and *Lear* —was completely wishy-washy in this unmemorable play. He closed it rather quickly after it opened to wishy-washy reviews. But the young redheaded boy electrified the audience almost the way Marlon Brando had in *Truckline Café*. The redhead's name was Albert Finney, and he was very young, and he had that powerful sexual electricity that one so seldom sees on the British stage or, for that matter, any stage.

After the play, I went backstage, and Charles introduced me to Finney. He had worked in the Liverpool Rep, and I believe he had come down to London just before the play had gone into rehearsal. I told my beloved teacher what I thought about the play. He agreed with me and said he longed to return to sunny California and his wife, Elsa Lanchester, and their enormous and glorious collection of Rubens paintings.

Charles suggested that Albert Finney walk me back to my flat, and that I tell the young man all about New York, and warn him never to go to Hollywood, and explain to him exactly what the dangers of becoming a movie star were.

Albert and I left through the stage door, and I felt rather awkward with this very talented, very young, working-class actor. He was rather threadbare and scruffy-looking, with the saving grace of freckles and red hair. He was carrying a large airline bag, and I asked him if he was so positive the play was going to close that he was already taking his makeup and things home. He smiled the most enchanting smile, which later became famous in *Tom Jones*.

"Miss Winters, I live out of this airline bag," he said. "Flats are so expensive and unavailable in London that I've been sleeping in my dressing room or at friends' houses. You don't have a spare settee that you're not using tonight, do you?"

I thought that was the fastest pass ever made, and I got rather angry. But it turned out that he was telling the exact truth. He was indeed existing in this manner. And when I returned to London a year or so later, he was the toast of the West End in a play called *Billy Liar,* and he was still sleeping in his dressing room and living out of the same airline bag.

It was late at night, and I remember we walked along the Thames and recited Shakespeare's soliloquies and duologues at each other. One I still remember. I had studied it with Charles Laughton in his studio in Santa Monica, and Albert had worked on it with an actress in some repertory company:

ALBERT: Ay me! for aught that I could ever read,
Could ever hear by tale or history,
The course of true love never did run smooth;
But either it was different in blood—

SHELLEY: O cross! too high to be enthralled to low.

ALBERT: Or else misgraffèd in respect of years—

SHELLEY: O spite! too old to be engaged to young.

ALBERT: Or else it stood upon the choice of friends—

SHELLEY: O hell! to choose love by another's eyes.

ALBERT: Or, if there were a sympathy in choice,
War, death, or sickness did lay siege to it,
Making it momentary as a sound,
Swift as a shadow, short as any dream,
Brief as the lightning in the collied night,
That, in a spleen, unfolds both heaven and earth,
And ere a man hath power to say "Behold!"

The jaws of darkness do devour it up:
So quick bright things come to confusion.

I was amazed. I said, "I didn't know I knew that duologue."

"My God, they really let Hollywood actresses study Shakespeare!" he said. "Your speech is pretty good."

He said this with a terrible North Country accent on purpose. We both started to laugh, and I stopped being the visiting star, and he stopped being the condescending West End prodigy.

We sat down on a low brick wall in Hyde Park. Finney took a hidden bottle of wine out of his jacket, and we drank the wine and began to tell each other stories about our careers. The one about me he liked the most happened sometime in 1947, when I was studying Shakespeare with Charles, who insisted I attend classes every single night, Saturdays and Sundays included. He had told me that that was the only way I could get rid of my Brooklyn accent and work in the theater. At that time, I was Universal's resident blonde bombshell and doing one of my innumerable Westerns, which, for the most part, only required long blonde hair, long skirts, low-cut blouses, and long hours of filming.

The head of the studio, Mr. Goetz, had called me into his office because the cameraman on my film was complaining that I had rings under my eyes which neither makeup nor careful lighting could erase. I explained to Mr. Goetz that I was studying speech, acting, and Shakespeare with Charles Laughton every night. Mr. Goetz looked confused and shouted, "Never mind. We don't do much Shakespeare here at the Valley lot, so you go home nights and sleep."

Albert laughed uproariously and asked me if I had obeyed my boss.

"Of course not," I said. "I just promised that I would."

Finney had such a mercurial charm that it took a while for me to become aware of his extraordinary intelligence and inherent dignity. I wish I'd caught some of that. In all the years I have known him, I've never heard anyone call him "Al." He's always "Mr. Finney" or "Albert." *Everyone* automatically responds to his artistic presence. All his friends—and, I think, the public—are very aware of his specialness.

That night so long ago, I walked hand in hand with this young actor, and as I looked at the lights reflected on the Serpentine, I was filled with happiness. I was sure that someday I would play great roles on the English stage, and my life and career would have purpose and dignity. So far it hasn't happened, but Albert Finney, who had a great and promising career on the London stage, became a big movie star with the film *Tom Jones*—unfortunately or fortunately, depending on your viewpoint.

That night as he walked me back to my flat, I carefully explained that I could not offer him my couch this night, as I had a baby in her crib, her nurse, my mother, and myself all occupying a small apartment.

"Never mind," he said. "I'll take a rain check."

As dawn came up over the Serpentine, I watched him walk, whistling through the park, headed for somebody's couch, his dressing room, or perhaps a park bench.

The film finished two days under schedule, no doubt due to all the fun we had making it. Near the end of the filming, Peter and Mary Noble and John Gregson and I were dining at the Caprice. I saw an elegant middle-aged Englishwoman sitting alone in a corner booth in a black silk dress and pearls and a diamond clip on her left shoulder and a sable cape. Her hair was simply and beautifully coiffed, and she sat there alone and serene, had her dinner and wine—and a brandy and a cigarette for dessert. She unhurriedly signed her bill and gracefully left. That woman has stayed in my mind all these years—how she was dressed, how she ate, her stylishness, serenity, and dignity, and how she had no sense of being embarrassed at sitting in a fashionable restaurant, eating alone. This of course was pre–women's lib. Though I have often seen men having dinner alone, this is almost the only time I remember an elegantly dressed woman eating alone in a fashionable restaurant. She belonged there. Although I have no idea who she was, she somehow has been a role model for me. But I don't think I've made it yet.

PART 2

*Shelley Fights for
Civil Rights,
Love, and Oscars*

7

When I returned to New York and finally got me and all my presents through customs, I headed for my little haven at the Meurice Hotel. I wanted to see all the new Broadway plays but my mother wanted to get back to her husband, my father Jonas, and Kathy wanted to get back to the tranquillity of California and get my baby's sleeping hours straightened out. So I put my entourage on the plane to California and I settled in for a week of studying and theater.

It was Friday, so I rushed to the Actors Studio to again get my life and career back on a serious track. It was a great session. Julie Harris did a scene from *Victoria Regina*. It was completely costumed, and the beginning of an impressive set was on the stage. Her performance was so powerful that it sparked in me a lifelong interest in Queen Victoria. I must say that Victoria, despite all the books written about her, doesn't seem a tenth as interesting as the portrait Julie Harris painted of her. But of course I am a Julie Harris fan.

When she opened in *The Member of the Wedding* on Broadway, I was lucky enough to have Harold Clurman, who was the director, invite me to the opening night. I didn't know Julie then and I had never seen her act before. I thought she really was a twelve-year-old playing this sad and lonely waif named Frankie Adams. That show and the performances of Julie and Ethel Waters have stayed in my mind as a pinnacle of theater acting. The audience didn't applaud after the curtain came down. We sat in silence for several minutes. We didn't want the play to end. We sat thinking about our own human condition and how childhood events victimize us. Two minutes later, we broke into wild applause, and, when the actors took their bows, we stood up and shouted, "Bravo!" When the lights went up, I was amazed to see that Julie Harris was a young woman, not a child. Harold Clurman asked me if I wanted to go to the opening-night party at Lee and Paula Strasberg's apartment and meet Julie, Carson McCullers, and Ethel Waters.

I was overjoyed. This was long before I knew the Strasbergs socially, and at last I would get to meet Lee and Paula Strasberg outside the classroom. They then lived in an enormous old apartment building, the Apthorp, on Broadway and Seventy-eighth Street. We arrived, and the apartment was jammed with the greats of theater and films—Alfred Lunt and Lynn Fontanne, Hume Cronyn and Jessica Tandy, Ruth Gordon and Garson Kanin. The writers, directors, and producers of Broadway were all there, paying homage to Julie Harris and Ethel Waters, but especially to Carson McCullers, who had written this play.

Harold Clurman brought me over to meet Carson. She was lying on a chaise lounge, fragile and staring into space. It was like meeting a frozen statue. Opening nights, the cast and producers and playwright usually go to Sardi's and wait for the reviews. As I watched Carson McCullers, I had the sense of a woman in absolute agony.

I'm sure there is no other art where the opinion of one man, in this case the critic of *The New York Times*, makes or breaks a career. Carson McCullers wrote one other play after that, but she seemed to have already had a stroke. Unable to move, she lay on the lounge and barely acknowledged the tributes that the actors, writers, and directors were giving her.

Lee Strasberg tried to make her hear that she was one of the greatest playwrights of our time. Paula Strasberg kept trying to give her brandy and sugar water, and she told me to rub Carson's feet, because Carson was practically in shock. I think that evening is the reason I have never pursued the career of playwriting. I've written several plays, including one that was presented off Broadway and was the beginning of Robert De Niro's career. I could not bear to inflict on myself anything like what I saw Carson McCullers go through that night so when my play, originally titled *The Gestation of a Weather Man*, opened in New York, I made sure I was filming in California.

That winter I saw a play that wasn't a hit but absolutely enchanted me. It was a poignant comedy called *Wedding Breakfast* by Theodore Reeves, whom I knew only as a television writer. In it were Lee Grant and that new actor Anthony Franciosa. There were only four people in it, and I resolved, there and then, I was somehow going to do that play in summer or winter stock. It took a big fight with Universal to get contractual permission, but I did do it the next summer.

I remembered I had seen Tony Franciosa perform scenes from *Wedding Breakfast* at the Actors Studio when it had been in rehearsal, and when I saw the play on Broadway, it confirmed my initial impression that Anthony Franciosa was a first-class actor.

One morning at the Actors Studio, I saw him do something from a play called *May Party for a Snowman*, which an actor, Mike Gazzo, was writing. Mike often sat way in the back of a huge fun bar and restaurant on Eighth Avenue called Downey's, which in the fifties became my second home.

May Party for a Snowman was about drugs and after a zillion rewrites became *A Hatful of Rain*. I would sit in the back of Downey's with the playwright, Tony Franciosa, Ben Gazzara, my wonderful young director friend Frank Corsaro, Frank Silvera, Harry Guardino, and Henry Silva, who was creating the role of a pusher called Mother. I believe that at these rehearsals, which lasted until four o'clock in the morning, the term "you mother" became synonymous with "you bastard" and went on to become a permanent part of our national slang.

Carroll Baker was doing the little part of the junkie's

wife, and, although the problem of drugs is openly discussed now, that was the first time I heard it as the plot and the theme of a play. I would sit in a corner, silent and enchanted, and listen to these talented and imaginative people improvise, and then the next night Mike Gazzo would bring in a powerfully constructed scene that would break your heart as the actors read it.

Everyone at the Actors Studio and in this very Irish bar called this group the "Actors' Mafia." I've never met a group of friends and theater comrades who were so inseparable. They lived together, ate together, and helped each other fill with cement the ratholes in their cold-water flats. They were the closest of friends, almost like brothers. It was a joyous and extraordinary experience to watch them. After the success of *A Hatful of Rain*, they somehow all became merely acquaintances, not enemies but not friends anymore. I think there was terrible anger when Mike sold the play to Twentieth Century–Fox and the film did not include many of the actors in their stage roles. They had all helped to create this piece, me included.

I was beginning to know Tony Franciosa quite well. Until very recently he had been working in Howard Johnson's as a short-order cook, and in between acting jobs he took a job as a CBS mail boy. He got to know the producers of live TV that way. The paying theater jobs were few and far between. Tony and I began having breakfast, lunch, and dinner together, but having just filed for a divorce from an *Italian* Italian actor, I could not see myself getting seriously involved with an *American* Italian actor. But I was so delighted in this young man's company that I began to think that perhaps in another life I must have been Italian. Tony was attractive and funny and talented and seemed to be so nuts about me that I got rather nuts about him. I could not tear myself away from New York.

One 3:00 A.M. on a warm spring night, we were walking back to the Meurice Hotel hand in hand. Tony was twenty-six and I was thirty-three, but he made me feel like a kid again. We skipped along the dark, silent streets of Manhattan and talked about doing a play together the following summer. Downey's stopped serving food at 2:00 A.M., and we were both getting very hungry.

"Does the Meurice have room service all night?" Tony asked me.

I knew that he knew that it did. He looked at me and said, "How about treating us to a Reuben sandwich and a couple of beers? I'm starving."

I guess I was starving, too. When we got up to my apartment, I remembered one of my suitcases, which I'd locked in England and for which I had then lost the key. I had yet to get it open, and it was an important suitcase. Meanwhile, out my window, dawn was coming up over the Hampshire House, and Tony began to try to make love to me. I gave him a most emphatic "NO" at certain limits. Finally, after he had chased me around my little apartment several times, he said, "Shelley, please tell me why you won't let me make love to you." In those glorious days, people didn't screw—they made love.

I looked into his beautiful blue eyes, and I had to tell Tony the truth. I began to weep with frustration as I explained to him, "Tony, I locked that suitcase in England. It's a very expensive one, and I've lost the key— and my diaphragm is in that suitcase."

He stared at me. Then he picked up the phone and ordered, "Two Reuben sandwiches, four bottles of Heineken, and a hammer and a chisel."

Room service sent those things up without a murmur, and I was never able to get that expensive suitcase repaired, but never mind, it was worth it. I came to realize that night why I love all things Italian. When Tennessee Williams has Blanche DuBois in *Streetcar* say, with the greatest of longing, "Young, young, young man," I know exactly what she means.

Despite many years of self-examination, I have never been able to understand my affair with and subsequent marriage to Tony. It was a kind of obsessive compulsion. Perhaps for me, the rejection and failure of my marriage to Vittorio was so deep that I was unconsciously trying to find a substitute. But Tony was nobody's substitute. I don't know how he was in other relationships in his life, but for us it was fun and fights and grand passion and low comedy. We did some of the finest acting we ever did in our lives together.

That warm spring we made love on the beach, love in the park, love on the Actors Studio balcony. Perhaps it was because Tony didn't have much money, and he didn't like me to spend my money on him. So there was nothing much else we could do together that was free.

The middle fifties were a happy time—the music, the restaurants, the theater. America was loved by the world, and maybe I was in love with love.

Now, with hindsight, I try to reexamine this compulsion and/or love affair with Tony Franciosa. It is still inexplicable to me. We were separated by a world of theater and film experience. We had completely different ethnic and religious backgrounds, yet the physical attraction was so strong that it was almost comical. We could not be in each other's presence without feeling desire and touching each other.

Several years later, when our marriage was at last breaking up, we had reached a point of almost hating each other. I was so disturbed that I was going to a psychiatrist. I spent the hour telling the doctor how wrong and destructive this relationship was for us. Tony was waiting for me in a car when I got downstairs. I got in the car, and we spit pure hatred at each other. Tony began driving crazily. He suddenly stopped the car somewhere on Fifth Avenue and pulled over to the side, looked at me with fury, and said, "Do you want to make love now?"

"Yes," I replied, and so we did. But that was still to come.

But, meanwhile, back in 1955, our love was new, fascinating, and, I guess, healing for me. When we weren't in bed, Tony and I were at the Actors Studio or at Downey's or at an inexpensive family-style Italian restaurant, the Capri. The food was delicious and inexpensive and our whole gang, the Actors' Mafia, hung out there. I felt like a kid again, and I behaved and dressed like one—full skirts and brown-and-white saddle shoes. I was no longer the glamorous Shelley Winters; I suddenly regressed with a vengeance. I forgot about my career, my home, and perhaps even my baby. I just talked to her on the phone. She sounded happy, and I certainly was happy. I would not return my agent's phone calls or Universal's. They put me on suspension, and I didn't care.

I remember one night sitting in Downey's about 3:00 A.M., as Tony and I often helped close it at 4:00. Ben Gazzara, who was in *Cat on a Hot Tin Roof*, was with Elaine Stritch, who was in some other hit show. Mike Gazzo and Kim Stanley and Marty Balsam were nodding over their last-call drinks. I had become expert at nursing green brandy stingers along for a couple of hours. One of my New York agents had managed to penetrate the instructions I had left with the telephone operator at the Meurice Hotel, and he left me an enormous financial offer to tour with any play I wanted to do on the summer-stock circuit. They offered me complete artistic freedom. We would start with Hinsdale, Illinois, the week of July 4, then tour all through New England and end August 14 in Westport, Connecticut. I could not imagine how he had gotten permission from Universal for me to do this, but I thought it was a great idea and decided that my company, Shellwin Productions, would produce the play. Right then and there in Downey's brown leather booth, I asked Marty Balsam and Tony Franciosa if they would do it with me. It was three o'clock in the morning, and they all stared at me in amazement.

"I am not drunk," I stated emphatically. "I am going to do *Faster, Faster* by Bill Marchant on Broadway this winter, and I think it would be best for me to begin getting used to live audiences again this summer."

Mike Gazzo kept mumbling about that play he was writing about drugs and how he had only twelve actors in it. I told him to shut up—in those days one didn't mention drugs on Broadway or especially in summer stock, and you certainly couldn't tour with twelve people. *Wedding Breakfast* had only four.

"Shelley," Marty Balsam said, "are you serious about this?"

Right then and there I made up my mind.

"Absolutely," I said. "I've been talking about returning to the theater since I signed that dumb seven-year contract, and now I'm going to find a way to make Universal let me do it.''

I then proceeded to order champagne for everybody, so they could drink to the revival of my theater career. Paul Newman came in with beautiful Joanne Woodward and joined us in our crowded booth. They were not married yet, and Joanne was driving Paul crazy with her dates with young Timmy Everett, a gifted actor and director who was later to set Broadway on its ear in Inge's *The Dark at the Top of the Stairs*. I ordered another bottle, and we all discussed the *Wedding Breakfast* tour thoroughly till closing time. Frank Corsaro offered to direct it. I don't know if we discussed salaries, but it all sounded like a big cooperative.

Paul Newman advised me that the best way to go from place to place on a tour was with bus and truck. That flabbergasted me. In the fifties, one did not rent trucks and buses easily; one had to buy them. But I was sure Jay Julien, my future lawyer and business manager, would solve the transportation situation. I knew the logistics were going to be a problem, because I was very lonely for my baby, and I resolved that I would take her and her nurse along on this impending tour.

Jim Downey announced that he had to close. It was 4:10 A.M., so Tony put his jacket around my shoulders, and we walked back to the Meurice Hotel. He seemed a little hesitant about something. It finally came out.

"Shelley, you haven't been on the stage since the end of the Second World War. The woman's role in *Wedding Breakfast* is very demanding. There's three acts, twenty scenes, six or seven costume changes. Lee Grant, who is a very experienced stage actress, would be exhausted after each performance. She would have to sleep between the matinee and evening shows."

In those days, nothing fazed me. I stopped right there in the middle of Eighth Avenue and looked deeply into his blue eyes.

"Tony, you are a very fine actor," I said sweetly. "But now I have acquired all the great training of Stanislavsky through my attendance at the Actors Studio. I know Lee

Grant was wonderful in the part, but I will be brilliant." Such chutzpah!

At that moment, we were almost run over by a garbage truck, which was grinding down Eighth Avenue. After rescuing me, Tony said doubtfully, "I'd love to act with you, but I hope we're up to it."

"Tony," I replied reassuringly, "I know you're up to anything, anywhere, anytime. So I will be, too."

I called Universal the next morning, ten o'clock Los Angeles time, and informed them that they must give me permission to do this play, or when my divorce from Vittorio was final I would marry a poor young actor, Tony Franciosa, have a lot of babies, and never have time to work for them again. My harried agent called me back in an hour.

"If you'll stay thin and come out and star in a film at Warner Brothers first, called *I Died a Thousand Times*, which is a remake of *High Sierra*, which Bogart and Lupino originally starred in, Universal will give you permission to do your summer-stock tour of *Wedding Breakfast*. But I can't imagine why a hot star like you would want to act in those tacky little theaters."

"Never mind," I joyfully told him. "Accept! I don't even want to read the script or hear the terms! But tell Warners I need two first-class round-trip tickets to Los Angeles, right away."

He then informed me that Charles Laughton wanted me to do a scene from *Night of the Hunter* with Robert Mitchum LIVE on the Ed Sullivan show. I then remembered that the sponsor of the Ed Sullivan show was Ford, so I astounded him by saying, "I will do this show if Ed Sullivan will give me a big blue Mercury."

"What's my ten percent," he asked, "a hubcap?"

But he was so glad that I had gotten off suspension that he arranged the whole deal just as I had requested. Universal got $200,000 from Warners for my services in *I Died a Thousand Times*. Universal had finally realized that I would not do their B pictures anymore, so they were just making a lot of money loaning me out for the rest of my contract. In those days, one of Universal's Abbott and Costello movies only cost about $400,000 to make, so one of my loan-outs financed half a picture for them.

With my new Mercury, I now had wheels to transport the cast around New England when we flew back from our opening engagement in Illinois. The Mercury turned out to be a coupe, but Tony and I, Marty Balsam, and Virginia Vincent, Frank Corsaro, Kathy, and the baby managed to drive from theater to theater for the next six weeks. The props and costumes and luggage were tied up on a rack on the roof. Not very elegant transportation for a movie star!

Shellwin Productions was the producer of this tour, and all my fellow actors started calling me "Miss Shell-win Prod." Especially when they got their paychecks.

One night, in Tony's arms, I told him about the two round-trip tickets to California and that I wanted him to meet my folks and baby, and then I told him a *big lie:* that Sidney Poitier, an old friend, had an apartment at the Chateau Marmont, and it would be empty for the five or six weeks I would have to be in California making the film. That would give him a chance to become acquainted with the geography of Hollywood, the studios, the agents, and the restaurants. I was sure that after a play or two he would be going out there to work a great deal.

In truth, I didn't know whether Sidney would be in or out of his apartment at the Chateau Marmont; but my desire for Tony was so intense that I couldn't bear to leave him for that period of time. I obviously didn't know what the hell I was doing. I planned to live in New York and I was luring him to California, but I didn't acquire that insight until some years later.

I do not know and can never know if Tony would have decided to become a film star or would have remained a happier, more fulfilled stage star if he hadn't taken that trip. What I do know is that there were performances in *A Hatful of Rain* in which the audience stood and yelled "Bravo!" at his brilliant acting. Nowadays he seems content to do television series. But then again, I just did a TV pilot and am ambivalent, to say the least, about sitcoms. Back in 1955 we thought of ourselves as artists, and money was not the goal. But now our whole society defines a successful life by how much money you've made.

The next morning I reported to the producer of the Ed Sullivan show with my tightest girdle, blackest dress, highest heels, and thickest false eyelashes firmly in place. I had to refute Walter Winchell, who had a column in the *Daily News* in which he had been slamming me about my sloppy appearance running around New York, and reminding me how my friend Marilyn always looked so gorgeous when she appeared in public. Little did he know that Marilyn was invisible when she wasn't wearing her makeup and glamour outfits. No one, but no one, ever recognized her.

Over the years, I've sometimes felt if I could just keep my mouth shut, I could be invisible too. I think people recognize my voice because of the Johnny Carson show. I know when I get in cabs in New York and give cabbies my address, they say, "Hello, Shelley," before they turn around. Oh, well, I guess it goes with the territory.

But that spring on the Ed Sullivan show, I did one interview in which I believe I was the quintessence of glamour and Robert Mitchum was the quintessence of manly movie-starrishness. It was quite a trick that Mitchum was able to do this so well, since I believe he was slightly tipsy. The hugeness of the Ed Sullivan Theater and all the live cameras whirling about terrified both of us. I got shrill and numb, so Mitch got a little drunk. Later on in the hour, when we quickly got into our makeup and costumes from *Night of the Hunter*, we were so befuddled by this live, live show that I stuttered, and they had to turn Mitch's mike up very loud in order to hear him; the millions of viewers across the U.S. could hear our stomachs rumble. We were so frozen with fear that when Charles Laughton, watching the show in Hollywood, saw our live performances, he was ready to knock our heads together. He couldn't believe that after all his careful direction we couldn't repeat for the live television cameras what we had already done on film.

Mitchum had "H-A-T-E" written on the fingers of one

hand and "L-O-V-E" on the other. During our scene, he held up the wrong hand to illustrate something he was saying. The audience of course laughed. I had done a lovely Southern, almost hillbilly accent in the film, but when I was doing this scene live for television, my St. Louis accent deserted me, and I lapsed into Brooklynese.

When we joined Tony for a drink after the show, I introduced him to Mitchum. Tony's only comment was, "You big movie stars need to work on the stage if you're going to do live television."

I said, "Listen, Tony. I've done live television and got an Emmy nomination for *Sorry, Wrong Number.* I've just never done a dramatic scene following a juggler before."

"Christ, I feel like I'm in fucking vaudeville," Mitchum muttered. "I ain't going to do that again." And he never did. When Mitch does television now, they do it with film cameras, and he gets millions of dollars, as he did for "The Winds of War," and "War and Remembrance." And his performance is indeed solid as a rock.

Ford delivered the blue Mercury to me, and I garaged it near the Meurice Hotel. Suddenly, it turned out that Tony had an offer of a live TV show in New York, and he could only join me in L.A. after my film had started. I asked him if he could drive me to the airport with all my suitcases. Tony mumbled something about not liking to drive in heavy traffic, and so we didn't take the Mercury; we took the movie-star limousine. I kissed him goodbye at the airport and realized I had only twelve hours to revert to Universal's blonde bombshell.

I flew west carrying almost the entire contents of F.A.O. Schwarz's toy store, hoping my baby would forgive me for having neglected her for two months. As I kissed and hugged her, she pointed to the TV and said, "Bad, bad." I will never know if it was a critique or a description of the scene she had seen me do on the Ed Sullivan show, which since the age of eighteen months had been her favorite TV show. Or maybe she was commenting on my absence.

8

My parents as usual were quite suspicious any time I stayed away from my baby and home for any reason other than work. When I told them of my plan to tour in one play that summer, then open on Broadway in the fall in a different one, they cheered my decision. They knew how unhappy I had been with the B pictures Universal was trying to force me to do.

My really important films were all done on loan-out. Universal at that time just wasn't doing any A films. When I'd signed that seven-year contract, I hadn't understood that Universal mostly did Westerns and program pictures. In the early fifties, theaters played double features—that is, two films, with the B picture as the second part of the double bill. Nowadays Universal is a different place, turning out films with $20 million budgets that are financially and artistically huge successes. Thanks to Lew Wasserman, the Universal tours for the public pay for their movie productions. Universal are also the biggest producers of television programs through their MCA company in California.

Television then was just beginning to make devastating inroads into the box-office attendance, and I was happy to have a serious, important film to do at Warner Brothers. The film studios, just as they had when sound was introduced in the twenties, were behaving like ostriches again and pretending that television was a fad that would go away.

I did not immediately report to Warners. I spent one of my long, four-day weekends at the Beverly Hills Health Club, Friday to Monday—my usual regimen of exercise, steaming, massaging, and fasting on fruit juice, losing about ten pounds and further ruining my metabolism, which I am still paying for.

My agent, Herb Brenner, and I appeared at Warner Brothers on Tuesday morning. I reported to the director of *I Died a Thousand Times,* Stuart Heisler, and he showed me the beautiful size-8 sketches for my wardrobe. My girdle was getting tighter and tighter, and I could hardly breathe. He suggested I get out of it. Then he had me watch the original, beautifully photographed, black-and-white *High Sierra,* starring Bogart and Lupino. When the lights went up in that projection room after we had watched this classic, I looked at Stuart and said:

"Why is Warners remaking this film? Why don't they just rerelease this great picture as is?"

My agent kicked me under the seat. My agent was getting 10 percent. Also, Universal was in financial trouble then and needed the $200,000, my loan-out price. Universal was paying me only $3,000 a week, when I worked, that is. In our present-day, inflated economy, $200,000 doesn't seem like much, but back then it was a tremendous price, considering the plunging movie attendance caused by free TV.

Herb quickly volunteered, "This one is a big color picture in CinemaScope. Jack Palance will star with you, Shelley. And Lee Marvin, who is a very good character actor, will be featured."

Then Herb rattled off some young persons' names like Dennis Hopper and Perry Lopez, who would play the rest of the gangsters. Mr. Heisler explained that we were going on location to Lone Pine, and we were just doing the interiors and the motel scenes at the studio, because my favorite director in all the world, George Stevens, was taking up most of the stages at Warners for *Giant.*

After a few days of script discussions, rewrites, and a

couple of read-throughs with my costars, we all left for the Lone Pine location—very lonely for me. I have done several Westerns in Lone Pine—adding up the different films, I must have spent at least a year of my life in the town of Lone Pine—but no matter how hard I try, I can remember nothing about it. It's some place up in the mountains, probably northern California, but it could easily be in Nevada or Arizona. I just don't seem to remember it as a real place. You know the way they try to make film sets look like actual places? It seems to me the art departments always tried to make Lone Pine look like a film set.

What I do remember is that the location was very rugged, as were the accommodations, and it was *cold*. My hair was very platinum, because the studio insisted I look as much like Jean Harlow as humanly possible, and, since it was a color picture, they had to bleach my roots every third day. I fully expected to catch pneumonia, having to sit with a wet head at four-thirty in the morning, and by the end of the film, I was sure my hair was going to fall out.

I would sit freezing by the telephone, while the peroxide was cooking, and attempt to call Tony in New York, where it was three hours later. He was doing this live TV show for ABC, and I invariably woke him up. He promised me he was guarding Universal's ticket with his life, and he would be in L.A. as soon as he could, and, if I was still on location, he would come up to Lone Pine.

This was the most platinum my hair had ever been in any picture. Nowadays, when I watch TV and see leading ladies with blonde hair and two inches of black roots, I want to kick my TV set. I know it's now the "in thing" to have two-color hair; why couldn't it have been in style in the fifties? Thank God I have strong, healthy hair.

There was a "wonder dog" in the film who seemed to have studied with Lee Strasberg. His motivations seemed clearer than any of the actors'. He could always repeat his actions exactly, and as many times as necessary. I never was aware of the trainer, who somehow managed to make himself invisible next to the camera. Although I'm not an animal person, that dog made friends with me

119

and saw to it that I somehow got through the filming at this lonely, rough location. I tried to buy that dog after the film, but the trainer just looked at me and laughed. He told me that this dog was the offspring of the dog that Farley Granger and I had starred with in *Behave Yourself* in 1949. That dog had completely stolen the picture.

Jack Palance spoke in such a husky, low voice that he was really scary. He was a huge, gentle man, but you sensed a tremendous anger in him. I had known him briefly around the Actors Studio, and of course we had worked together on *The Big Knife*.

I didn't understand his anger until I remembered how he had told me one day that Elia Kazan had promised him the role of Zapata in *Viva Zapata!* He was very elated about it and knew it was the break that would make him a superstar. I also remembered, some time later, meeting Jack in front of the Palace Theatre on Broadway. He had grabbed me and told me that Marlon Brando was playing Zapata. At the time, he was so disturbed and furious that I almost felt it was my fault. I had had nothing to do with that production and had only visited the set occasionally, because I knew Kazan and Marlon and Anthony Quinn and was interested in watching them work.

I felt that Marlon was the perfect Zapata, although Tony Quinn won the Supporting Oscar. Marlon had been nominated for Best Actor but had not won. The day after Tony Quinn won his Oscar, I was out walking along Beverly Boulevard. Tony pulled up in a car at the intersection of Beverly and Santa Monica Boulevards and yelled, "Hey! Look what I got, Shell!" He was holding his Oscar out the window. I bitchily replied, "But it's only the Supporting Oscar, Tony. I was nominated Best Actress Oscar for *A Place in the Sun*."

While shooting *I Died a Thousand Times*, I was very careful to congratulate Jack Palance on his performance in *Shane* and to talk about what a great experience working with George Stevens was. But it seemed to me that no matter what I said to my costar, his reactions always were weird and out of context in some perverse way. At first, I thought it was perhaps because he was playing a doomed gangster—he seemed so strange. But then it got so I never knew if we were in front of the camera or behind it.

Lee Marvin was a fine character actor then, and he was always full of fun and very intelligent, drunk or sober. Though sometimes loaded while we were working, he was always in control of the scene. He must have been British, because every night over martinis, after shooting twelve hours, we would meet in the bar and discuss nothing for hours. Lee Marvin was the most private person in the world. Years later, I again worked with him on a film called *Delta Force,* and he still was the same very private person. He had stopped drinking, and he wasn't half as funny as he used to be, but no doubt he was healthier and better off. A couple of years ago, when I read of his palimony suit, I was absolutely stunned that he had allowed that case to be tried in the press the way it had been. What he told me was, "If Michelle had asked nicely, I would have been of great financial assistance to her. Because she sued me, I would give her nothing." He took it all the way to the California appeals court and won.

Meanwhile, in cold Lone Pine, this tricky film location finally came to an end, and it seemed that everybody was drunk except the dog. In retrospect it was very stupid, because we did a lot of dangerous mountain climbing while shooting. Even though there were stunt men and women, Stuart Heisler insisted that the stars themselves do hazardous and difficult work. Over the years I got tendinitis in my Achilles tendon from that picture, torn knee cartilage from *Pete's Dragon* as a result of dancing in a tree and falling from it, a punctured left eardrum from swimming underwater in *The Poseidon Adventure,* and an injured back from *Order in Things.* I've just turned down a picture with Bette Midler, whom I've longed to work with, because I felt the scenes with her might be too dangerous. She's a great comedienne and actress, but she does jump around a lot.

When the company of *I Died a Thousand Times* finally

returned to Warner Brothers Studios for the interiors, I was overjoyed. But Tony was still stuck in New York. We had nightly phone calls, and I was acting as fast as I could, hoping to return quickly to New York with my family and start acting in live theater.

The scenes in the studio somehow seemed to get more difficult, if possible. Palance had the quality of a caged panther, and I was genuinely frightened of him. I stayed in my dressing room on the stage as much as possible and didn't talk to him.

George Stevens's film *Giant* was winding down, and James Dean would sometimes come and sit in my dressing room with me. He was convinced that Stevens hated him and felt his work was awful in the film. I kept trying to reassure him.

"If George Stevens didn't like your work," I said, "you would know it immediately. So, you must be great in the film."

"But Shell," Jimmy said, "he never talks to me and barely directs me."

I tried to explain that Stevens understood exactly how delicate the mechanism of the actor's psyche is, and he must be loving Jimmy's work in the rushes every night. If he wasn't discussing his characterization with Jimmy, it must be because Dean's performance was sensitive and extraordinary. I knew that George Stevens was always careful not to impose any extra burdens on his actors' psyches. If the director asks a talented actor to say one line in a certain manner, almost always the rest of the scene will go out the window and he will get that one line right. That's how delicate the mechanism of fine acting is. Great directors like William Wyler would sometimes just say, "Take one," "Take two," "Take sixty-five," "Take sixty-six," and on and on *until the actor himself* discovered what William Wyler really wanted and what was exactly right for the scene. All great directors know this. In *Giant* I believe George Stevens was having enough problems with the performances of Elizabeth Taylor and Rock Hudson and was concentrating on them.

But as the shooting of *Giant* progressed, Jimmy kept

showing up in my dressing room on the stage of the set for *I Died a Thousand Times*. I finally became aware that what James Dean really wanted from George Stevens was a surrogate father. I knew Mr. Stevens very well, and he would not play that game—I had tried it with him myself. During *A Place in the Sun*, when we saw the rushes, I would sit next to him on his left and Elizabeth Taylor would sit on his right. We would both sit so close to him that the poor man could only rest his hands on his knees. He was careful not to touch either one of us. He had too much respect for the art of acting and the art of film. George Stevens was so dedicated that, years later, he took the issue of cutting films up for commercial breaks on TV to the Supreme Court. He insisted that one would not butcher a Renoir or a Picasso—so great and classic films should be accorded the same respect. He did not win the case. Shame. All artists involved in filmmaking lost. I believe that films are the great new historical art of the twentieth century. Through this art, in the centuries to come, the earth's people will know exactly how we lived and worked and loved and laughed. Up to the nineteenth century we could only read about the people who lived on this earth.

At lunchtime, Jimmy would ride around the Warner stages on his motorcycle, doing fancy motorcycle tricks, or riding over the mountains in back of Warner Brothers. One lunch hour, when I was riding on the back of Jimmy's motorcycle, he insisted on taking me to the commissary by way of the Warner Brothers mountains. When my director, Mr. Heisler, saw us, he came to my dressing room after lunch and practically tore my head off.

"We are carrying heavy insurance on you in this film," he said. "If that boy wants to commit suicide, let him, but don't you ever dare get on his motorcycle again."

Jimmy had finished shooting his role in *Giant* but was still clinging emotionally to George Stevens and wouldn't leave the lot. I got a sharp note from Jack Warner repeating Heisler's instructions.

I laughed at my overprotective director, and at Jack Warner, but I respected their wishes and told Jimmy I would walk to the commissary from then on, though I had enjoyed the thrilling motorcycle rides.

Sometimes in life, you are in a situation that seems like Greek tragedy. You can see the end clearly, but you are powerless to change the onrushing events.

Something similar to the experience with Jimmy Dean happened to me a few years ago. *The Poseidon Adventure* had recently been released, and my friend Jack Albertson, who was my husband in *Poseidon,* was now doing a show called "Chico and the Man" with a very gifted young Puerto Rican–Hungarian comedian named Freddie Prinze. All the critics acknowledged that this boy was going to have a brilliant career and future.

Jack talked me into doing a guest shot for his show— the only time I've ever done a sitcom—and I did it with Jack and Freddie for a live audience and enjoyed it very much. The character I played, a Ms. Schrift who ran a bakery next door, was so successful on the sitcom that some months later, when I was working in Italy, I found out that Jack was having a running romance with her, talking on the telephone to the lady who owned the bakery; she was now a continuing character on "Chico and the Man." I was a big hit on TV, didn't even know it, and certainly wasn't being paid for it. I think all well-known actors' voices are now taken off the sound tracks of their pictures and put on some kind of computer and when they need to use your voice in something else they just take it off the computer and reconstruct the phrases and you're in a show you never did. My agent at last sent the producer of "Chico and the Man" and the head of the network a legal letter to either pay me or "cease and desist." They finally did the latter.

When I was rehearsing the actual "Chico" show, I got to know and like Freddie Prinze very much. He was also doing a Christmas show at NBC for "The Flip Wilson Show." One night after we had finished rehearsing I went over to Freddie's dress rehearsal. Flip Wilson had created a comedy sketch, satirizing *The Poseidon Adventure,* in which the entire cast swam across a flooded laundromat and escaped through a pseudo hatch in a washing machine. Being a girl who could never resist a challenge, when the TV cameras rolled, I joined the end of the line of actors and swam across in front of the camera and also escaped through their washing machine, mimicking myself swimming underwater in *Poseidon*—if you think this is convoluted, wait. Anyhow, my clothes got all wet from the suds in the laundromat, and, although the audience and crew were screaming with laughter, I was in a bit of a pickle as I was soaking wet, and my stand-in had my car. The prop men dried me off as best they could, and Flip Wilson lent me an orange terrycloth robe, which I still have.

Freddie Prinze said he lived near me and would drive me home in his new Stingray, which the producer of "Chico and the Man" had given him. So in my wet underwear, covered with the orange robe and my new mink coat, I got in Freddie's new fiberglass Stingray. After two blocks, I gasped, "The producers should have bought you a tank, Freddie, instead of a Stingray." The car had four loudspeakers, and he was keeping time to the hard-rock music with his brake foot.

Since it was Christmastime, the traffic was rough. Going over Barham Boulevard, we passed an open fire hydrant, and the brakes got wet. I instructed Freddie to go on the service road alongside the freeway. He ignored me and took the freeway. He was bragging about his New York driving and his new car and the fact that he, a New York City kid just out of the High School of Performing Arts, had learned to drive so quickly and so well. It was night, the freeway was crowded, and the brakes were wet, and of course we spun around twice. God must have been watching over us, because miraculously all the other cars on the freeway managed to avoid us.

"Freddie," I quietly said. "Get off the freeway at the first exit."

Which he then did. All the way to my house he kept telling me how great a driver he was, and how well he had handled the spin on the freeway.

When he walked me to my door, as soon as we got on my porch, I hit him as hard as I could with my fist. I was weeping with delayed shock and terror, and I said something like:

"Freddie, if you gotta go, *go,* but don't take other people with you."

And then I slammed the door in his face. A year later, Freddie was playing Russian roulette with a gun and "accidentally" killed himself.

Jack Albertson had nursed his career and taught him all his great lore of comic knowledge. I believe Freddie was like the son he'd never had. When Jack died a while later, whatever the physical reasons that caused his death, I believe it was a broken heart. Like Jimmy Dean, Freddie was a rare genius. I guess it all just happened for them too fast and too soon. To this day, when I work with young, talented actors or actresses behaving in a self-destructive manner, which often happens because of the prevalence of drug use, I want to scream, "Somebody do something." But you can't call the cops before something terrible happens, and now, like then, I feel helpless.

When Jimmy died I couldn't deal with it. One of my crazy subconscious notions is that I'm omnipotent and I keep thinking I can fix things for everybody. So if something terrible happens it means I wasn't able to fix it and so I don't want to believe it happened.

So I can't remember the exact minute or anyone telling me Jimmy was dead. I couldn't let it sink in until I got back to New York to the safety of the Actors Studio. Warner Brothers was being very quiet about it because they thought nobody would want to see a movie with a dead person in it and *Giant* was their big movie that year.

Anyway, back at the lot, *I Died a Thousand Times* crept along. One morning I was doing a dancing scene with a young actor, Perry Lopez, and Dennis Hopper cut in. We were doing the mambo, and we were having a final rehearsal before shooting. Suddenly, in the middle of my little scene with Dennis, one of the extras cut in, or so it seemed. As I prepared to bawl him out for doing something so unrehearsed, I looked at this handsome extra and realized it was Tony Franciosa playing a trick on me.

126

Tony had finally arrived in L.A.! I was overjoyed. I quickly introduced him to everyone on the set. In California he looked awfully young to me; somehow in New York he had seemed older. But I put this qualm firmly out of my mind. When we got to my dressing room after that scene was shot, and after we got through hugging and kissing, he gave me the script of the new play he had been rehearsing at the Actors Studio. The play was *A Hatful of Rain,* the play I had first seen him performing in, and Jay Julien had decided to produce it that fall in New York. In a letter, Jay wrote that if I liked the script and would agree to do it instead of William Marchant's *Faster, Faster,* they could get a theater from the Shuberts. I was so enchanted with Tony and the idea of going back to New York to live and act with him in a play that I agreed to talk to my agent immediately about this change of venue.

Stuart Heisler kindly gave me a long lunch hour, and I showed Tony around the enormous Warner Brothers studios in my brand new white Cadillac convertible with, of course, the top down. On the *Giant* set, we watched a scene that Rock Hudson and Elizabeth Taylor were doing, and then we watched Jack Warner and Solly Bianco, Warner's casting director and maybe his son-in-law, play tennis on Mr. Warner's private court in the middle of the studio.

We had a glorious lunch at the commissary and then, late that afternoon, I reported back to the set, which had now been moved to the back lot. We were doing a scene in some kind of tent, and it was a very dramatic scene. Tony had watched little films shooting around New York, and, of course, he had done live TV, but he had never seen the logistics of two or three big films shooting at once on a large studio back lot.

When I reported to the set, I suddenly found out we were to do the scene which I had been fearing throughout the shooting of the film. I think Mr. Heisler knew I was afraid of the scene, so he had not told me that we were going to shoot it that evening. It consisted of two pages of my character haranguing the ill-fated character that Jack Palance was playing. At the end of the scene, in a rage, he starts to choke me, and, as I write this, I can't remember whether he succeeds in killing me or not—and I ain't looking it up. Since I have played so many victim roles, I assume he succeeded in killing me. I must force myself to watch this film nowadays when it's on late-night television. They often play it at 2:00 A.M., but I'm still afraid to watch the end of it. I turn off the set when the cute dog is peering into the tent.

Tony stood on the sidelines behind some scenery and watched. Jack had been playing his character twenty-four hours a day for some weeks. We quietly rehearsed the scene, all except the last minutes. After two rehearsals, the cameraman informed Stuart Heisler that, even though it was a twilight scene, we were losing the light.

At that, the assistant director yelled, "Roll 'em," and Mr. Heisler said, "Action," and Jack and I began to act. Anyway, I was acting. Jack was very real and wonderful in the scene, tragic and almost inarticulate, and I believe I was at my nagging best. I remember the scene exactly —up to the point when Jack chokes me—then the next thing I remember is a nurse reviving me with spirits of ammonia and an ice pack on my neck.

It seems that Jack inadvertently had cut off my wind-pipe, and everyone on the set thought we were acting just great. Only Tony, who understood Method work, real-ized that somehow the character had become too real for Jack Palance. So Tony, on his first day in Hollywood, saved my life. He stopped the scene, and I believe he and Jack exchanged a couple of blows. But soon Jack was out of the character and couldn't have been more frightened or apologetic. The director called it "a wrap," and the studio limo immediately took Tony and me home, with the new Cadillac following, driven by a studio Teamster.

Sometimes when I recall this event, I think it was not possible, but it was in the assistant director's production report, and I had two black-and-blue marks on my neck for several days. In thinking about the whole shooting of this film, I sometimes wonder if Jack Palance was sending me sexual signals when we were on location. If he was, I didn't catch them because of my total involvement with

Tony—we were on the radiophone every night. Perhaps Tony's showing up on the set—young, handsome, and at the beginning of his career—made Jack very angry with me. But maybe I'm still overreacting to being choked and imagining the rest.

It turned out that Sidney Poitier really did have an apartment at the Chateau Marmont, and I had somehow convinced him to share it with Tony. Tony was very impressed with the Marmont's old and elegant Hollywood grandeur, so he pretended he wasn't, being an average New York street kid. Tony was so exhausted from the air flight, and I was so exhausted from having been choked by Jack Palance, that we just had a quick dinner at Schwab's drugstore.

After we had dropped off his suitcases at Poitier's apartment, we both felt frightened and strangely unsexy and confused at the turn "toward reality" our relationship was taking. New York had sort of been never-never land—the Actors Studio, staying up all night at Downey's, going to wonderful plays and musicals, and swimming at Coney Island. Now I was back in "my movie-star ambiance," and I had to explain to my mother, father, and daughter who exactly Tony Franciosa was in my life.

I tried and tried, but during the next six years—during our courtship, summer-stock tour, a year in a Broadway hit play, a year in California, and a couple of years of marriage—I never succeeded. They never understood our relationship. As a matter of fact, neither did I. And I still don't. And I doubt if Tony does.

Meanwhile, back at Warners, while I was finishing the film and on weekends driving Tony around Hollywood and its environs in my new white Cadillac convertible, the desk clerk at the Chateau began to think I had an apartment there too. The Warner Brothers driver who picked me up at 5:00 A.M. would look for me in front of my house in Beverly Hills, and if I wasn't standing there, he would try the Chateau Marmont. I was more often at the Chateau than at my house. I would sometimes go to work in my robe and bedroom slippers. I had other clothes in my dressing room on the lot. The transportation captain of the studio almost reported me to the Teamsters union because there were sometimes delays in finding me at 5:00 A.M. The assistant director would get annoyed with the driver, who, I must say, never squealed on me. If the Teamsters understand anything, they understand romance.

Hollywood seemed to make Tony very nervous, but we did go to a couple of small parties and some good restaurants when my agent or somebody invited us. I had to arrange this, because Tony had very little money, and in 1955 there was no plastic card and women just didn't pay the check. Oh, if those days would only return. It's not that I'm not for women's lib; I just still yearn for some of those perks the clinging woman enjoyed.

One afternoon when I had a day off from the film, we met Sidney Poitier at Lucy's for lunch. Sidney was shooting something at Paramount, and Lucy's was nearby. It was one of the most beautiful restaurants in Hollywood, and all the actors, producers, and directors from Columbia, RKO, and Paramount hung out there. It had an airy outdoor dining room all covered with branches and flowers, and it was surrounded by trees, and the food was some of the best I've ever had. I spent a lot of time, when I wasn't acting at the studio, calling people to get them to invite us to Lucy's. Tony loved the food there, too, and, although he wouldn't admit it, he loved gazing at all the beautifully dressed and elegant movie stars. So did I . . . I wonder where the Hollywood glamour has gone.

That day something happened that was symbolic of our whole relationship. We'd had an elaborate lunch with my agent, Herb Brenner, who was with the Music Corporation of America, which has been magically converted from an agency to the biggest television producer in the world. Perhaps we had too many mimosas (champagne and orange juice), but when we went out to the valet to get my new Cadillac, Tony gave the boy a dollar and got behind the wheel. I was a little confused by his action, but I meekly climbed in on the other side. He backed the car out of the parking lot and drove west on Melrose Avenue, which was the right thing to do. We'd had a very long lunch, and it was twilight. Six blocks later, I thought he should put the lights on.

"Tony, I think you should turn the lights on, and you're straddling the center line, so get more over to the right."

Whereupon Tony snarled at me, "Don't nag me; this is the first time I've ever driven a car."

Whereupon I said quietly and calmly, "Tony, please pull over to that empty space and stop."

He didn't do it. He drove up Melrose to Beverly Hills, pulled the car up in front of my house, and parked with the right front wheel on the curb. He grinned at me with his charming, sexy, boyish grin and said, "Hey, Shell, not so bad for the first time, huh?" Right then and there, if I had been sane, I would have shipped him back to New York. But I wasn't and didn't.

Frank Corsaro called from New York and informed me that *Wedding Breakfast* was booked to open in Hinsdale, Illinois; Binghamton, New York; Clinton, Connecticut; Westport, Connecticut; and Theatre-by-the-Sea in Matunuck, Rhode Island. I listened to Frank reel off all these summer-stock places and quaked. I hadn't been in front of a live audience for a long time. I had seen Tony in this very play the year before, and he and Lee Grant had been brilliant, but it was a difficult play, funny and sad. My character is onstage the whole time, except for six quick costume changes. But I summoned up my courage and told Frank that Tony and I would report for rehearsal as soon as I was done with the film.

I knew that if I was to attempt a leading role on Broadway in the fall, I had to have the experience of playing in front of a live audience first, because I knew unconsciously *then* and consciously *now* that the only real teacher an actor can have and must have is the *live audience*. Live audiences teach you timing, concentration, how to get laughs, how to stop laughs (you need to do this sometimes), and, by their restlessness or quietness or their coughing or silence, they teach you how and when you are effective.

The three-week rehearsal period was going to be a very difficult and concentrated time for me, and I again had to explain to my two-year-old baby that I would be leaving her for a month. As soon as the play opened in Hinsdale, Illinois, Kathy would be bringing her to Chicago to join me for the rest of the summer. The nurse and the baby listened very carefully as I explained this to them. Kathy nodded, and the baby put up her little hand in the air and made the bye-bye gesture. Over the years, that gesture has been engraved on my heart, and I often wonder when I have a 3:00 A.M. case of the dooms how different my life might have been if these career separations hadn't happened. *If*—perhaps the most pointless word in our language.

Before I flew to New York, my agent called me in to MCA, and we had a meeting with United Artists. It seemed that UA was financing independent pictures (independent of any studio), which was very unusual then. Since *Wedding Breakfast* was an insightful story about a summer romance, and since I, Tony, Marty Balsam, and a young comedienne named Virginia Vincent were doing this summer tour, it was suggested that I meet with a new, young, hot director by the name of Sidney Lumet, and perhaps, at the end of the tour, we would shoot the play in filmscript form, and I would be the producer.

United Artists would give me $600,000 for the cost of production (which would be like $2.5 million today). Sidney Lumet would frame the film by shooting in Grand Central Station—kids would be shown going away to summer camp with all their signs of different camps and then, in the fall, he'd shoot them coming home from the camps with the parents hugging and kissing them.

After many meetings with Sidney Lumet in New York, we all enthusiastically agreed to this venture. But, after working with Tony for eight weeks, I canceled the whole film and gave United Artists back the $600,000, which was the cost minus $7,000 for the two-day filming, which I had to pay with a personal check. I felt Tony was too unstable then to be able to handle the daily demands of a tight film-production schedule. If we shot over the budget, I, as the producer, would lose thousands of dollars. I don't know what happened to the film Sidney Lumet shot with the kids going to and coming home from camp;

I never saw it. Anyway, Sidney Lumet was so angry with me for canceling this film that he never hired me for any movie again, though I did do a TV show for him with Farley Granger.

Tony and I flew back to New York, he moved into the Meurice Hotel with me, and we started to rehearse *Wedding Breakfast* on the stage of the Belasco Theatre, which had been the home of the Group Theatre when I'd been an usher there at $1 per performance.

In the weeks of rehearsal, I came to know that Frank Corsaro was the best director I'd ever had since George Stevens. We rehearsed slowly and carefully, often improvising a scene to find the proper blocking. That means doing what is natural and easy in any given situation and making up the dialogue. Then we would learn the lines and fit them into the blocking we had discovered during the improvisations, in which we had only played our intentions. Only then did we learn the lines.

Frank allows for the creativity of the actor, in fact constantly demands and encourages it. There were only four actors in the play—Tony, myself, Marty, and Virginia. I was also the producer, so when we had an Equity meeting, I wasn't allowed to vote, but the other three actors elected Marty Balsam to be the Equity deputy, which meant he had to negotiate with me, Shellwin Prod. We discussed matters such as the actors' overtime pay, extra luggage, and costumes. I was pretty generous and lenient, and I the producer would often treat the entire cast, director, and stage manager to dinner. So, I was quite hurt when Marty the Equity deputy insisted that I the producer must pay the cast fifty cents a suitcase—travel expenses—between each summer-stock theater. Why should I do this, when all their luggage was on top of my blue Mercury? This wasn't fair to me, pro-union Shelley thought. During that tour, I rapidly became somewhat anti-union, but I'm happy to report that after the tour I recovered from this attitude.

9

When we opened in Hinsdale, Claudia Cassidy of the *Chicago Tribune* gave me the following review:

"In the first act of *Wedding Breakfast* Miss Winters wears a lovely organdy dress with pastel appliqué flowers, in the second act she wears a gold-colored housecoat, and in the third act she wears a nifty navy-blue travelling suit."

She then proceeded to rave about all the other actors' performances, implying that with a theater actress, instead of a movie star, the play would be wonderful. To hell with her; she ate her words when she saw me open the following winter in *A Hatful of Rain*, but how I wept that night at the Salt Creek Theatre in Hinsdale.

The next morning, I rushed to the airport and eagerly waited for the arrival of my two-year-old daughter and her nurse. I hugged and kissed her, and she was so excited she refused to take a nap. She had slept on the plane. It seemed to me that I had been away from her for years; actually it had only been three weeks. After much discussion with the nurse, we agreed that we would all go to the theater the next morning. I had a rehearsal there, and she would go to sleep early that evening, as she was again on California time, and I had an evening performance.

Since I had had less than glowing reviews, Frank

wanted to take me carefully through each scene, and since the other actors wanted *to work* for the rest of that summer, everybody concentrated on improving my performance. I had been frightened and lonely opening night and "unconcentrated." Tony had helped me as much as he could, but *Wedding Breakfast* was indeed a vehicle for a female star, and I had not been on a legitimate stage since World War Two. The Chicago audience was very polite, and they, too, admired my costumes and my courage.

The next day, my little girl watched the rehearsal with complete fascination. Kathy and I were amazed that a two-year-old could be so attentive and quiet for the whole first act. At the intermission, I brought her up on the stage, and she walked around the set. This set consisted of two apartments: on stage left, my Upper East Side apartment; stage right, Tony's Greenwich Village pad.

There were some grapes on a cocktail table that Tony ate as he telephoned me in my apartment on stage left. My daughter had been longing to taste the grapes, but she would not go through the imaginary wall and get them. She was in my apartment, and then she went backstage and pulled me along behind the scenery, and then she went into Tony's apartment. After that, I didn't give a damn what the Chicago critics said about me, because my child knew I had created the illusion that the play demanded. As we sat on the set in Tony's apartment, we began eating the grapes, and she listened intently as I tried to explain to her what the play was about. It was a rather sophisticated tale about a summer romance and difficult to explain to even a smart two-year-old.

Frank Corsaro suddenly yelled from the auditorium, "Please don't eat the props."

She jumped a half a foot, dropped the grapes, and started to cry. Frank picked her up and tried to comfort her, but she would not be comforted until he talked to her in Italian, and then she stretched her little hand out to him and said, "Some props, please." He gave her some grapes, and to this day, my daughter calls grapes "props." It's a family joke.

Thank goodness the next day was Wednesday, and Equity did not allow us to rehearse on matinee days. So Wednesday, between the matinee and evening shows, we all went swimming. By now Frank and the baby were great friends. She had sat through the matinee and watched the show in his arms. I don't know whether it was the presence of the two-year-old, but the audience suddenly realized they were watching a comedy. Perhaps I had relaxed and was playing the show in a lighter fashion. Or perhaps in my effort to try to make my child understand me, I was speaking more slowly and clearly, and the audience got the jokes.

We were sitting around the pool, and Frank was holding the kid in his lap. The actors began to have a violent discussion about the values of one of the scenes, whether that particular scene should be played for comedy or drama. I guess I was arguing with Tony, and a couple of minutes later I looked back to Frank for confirmation of my argument. My child had slipped off his lap and was under the water. She had had a few swimming lessons but did not know really how to swim yet. I quickly got her to the surface, and she obviously had not swallowed much water, but I was so terrified that I would not speak to anyone for a long, long time. I could not look at Frank. He apologized profusely and tried to explain to me that she had wanted to go swimming so badly and somehow his hands had gotten sweaty, and she had suddenly wiggled out of his grasp and slid into the water. I didn't talk to Frank Corsaro until our next stop, which was Triple Cities Playhouse in Binghamton, in upstate New York.

By the time we got to Binghamton, the show was running smoothly, and I was in control of my role and the play.

Now I would not allow my baby out of my sight. Fortunately, since I had a large dressing room in Binghamton, I had a crib installed, and during the matinees she would sleep quietly in my dressing room. By the end of the week, I allowed her and the nurse to sleep in the motel. I would put my makeup on at the motel, rush to the theater at 8:20, and rush back at 11:00 P.M. in my third-act costume. I had been so frightened at her sliding into the water that I couldn't take my eyes off her. Everyone tried to reassure me, insisting I was smothering her because of my fear, but this illogical fear lasted for a long time.

Marty kept explaining to me that Equity required that I be in the theater at 8:00 P.M., that I was not allowed to walk in the stage door at 8:20 in costume and makeup and walk on the stage and act, then walk out the stage door at the end of the play in costume. I was putting the other actors at a disadvantage, because they weren't sure that I was going to show up till the last second so they had no time to prepare calmly. This was one time when the management and union were in complete agreement. I just looked at them and said:

"I know if my child is backstage, she might cry and disturb the performance. But if you want me on that stage, I have to stay with her as long as possible and get back to her as soon as possible."

Since we were doing standing-room-only business, they had a choice of replacing me or accepting my unprofessional behavior. They accepted it. Tony tried to talk to me during intermissions, but I was suddenly cold and aloof with him. Maybe I was acting out something that had a psychological basis, but I didn't understand it, and he certainly didn't. It left him confused and worried about what our future would be.

At the end of the week, when we all got in the blue Mercury to go to the next city, the atmosphere was frosty, despite the ninety-degree temperature outside the car. Frank had had to go a couple of days in advance of the company to make sure the sets and lights were correct.

It was a long drive to the Clinton Playhouse in Clinton, Connecticut. Marty drove, and Virginia and Tony were in the front seat. Kathy and I and the baby were in the back seat; our luggage, the costumes, and personal props were strapped in trunks in a rack on the roof. We looked rather like rich Okies escaping the dust bowl of East Hampton.

When we got to the Clinton Playhouse, we found lovely accommodations. I had a little house with two bedrooms and a fireplace, and the rest of the cast shared nice houses. We eagerly showed up at the theater early for the "tech" rehearsals. Then our spirits plunged. The set was half built and unpainted, the lights were being hung, and the props and pieces of furniture were all over the empty theater. Frank Corsaro had been there a couple of days, but it seemed that the Clinton Playhouse staff consisted of 60 percent paying amateur apprentices and 40 percent lazy professionals. If there wasn't a part for them in the new weekly show, they swam in the lake or goofed off somewhere in town.

I thought this was the low point of my professional career. But I found out otherwise some years later. I was touring in a play entitled *Days of the Dancing* by James Bridges, then unknown but now a famous director and writer (*The Paper Chase; Urban Cowboy; The China Syndrome; Perfect; Bright Lights, Big City*). *Days of the Dancing* was a complicated show to tour, and Paul Richards, the director (who had been an actor in *A Hatful of Rain*), would arrive in each town about a week before the cast. But when we arrived in Myrtle Beach, South Carolina, Paul's face was very pale. The lady in charge of the Myrtle Beach summer theater took me, the star, and the entire cast to an empty field, and she smilingly informed us that this is where we were to put up the tent and build their summer theater. I can't remember exactly what I did, but I know that we did not build her theater.

Meanwhile, back at the Clinton Playhouse, we had a choice of helping those kids put up the set or not opening the show. I would have just as soon taken a week off; I was that tired of my one-week stands all over the eastern United States, but Tony and Marty, Virginia and Frank, and the nurse and my toddler dug in and helped. I got into overalls, and we worked until three in the morning, got the set up and the lights in place, and then I and my little family went to bed. I figured they could leave the set unpainted as far as I was concerned. My costumes were colorful enough for any stage. My child really helped; she handed us the right tools when we asked for them.

When I got to the theater about 2:00 P.M. the next day for the long-awaited tech rehearsal, the set was painted and the props were in place. The sofa was upholstered, and the actors were ready to rehearse from cue to cue very carefully since these young, inexperienced tech people needed the practice. We got finished at 7:30 P.M., with just enough time for me to have a sponge bath, set my hair, and put on my false eyelashes. Sometimes I feel I should be on a continuous summer-stock tour. I always lose twenty-five or thirty pounds between the Fourth of July and Labor Day.

The opening night performance started, the audience was wonderful, and the actors were very good. Heat never seems to bother me very much, but not so Tony—he was a sweat-er. I've known a few champion sweaters, like Elliott Gould when we did the play *Luv* together in summer stock. But Tony was a close second. It was a very hot summer night, and the theater was not air-conditioned. Suddenly, Tony made an entrance to do a scene in my apartment, and he was *completely blue*. Tony had been running from one side of the stage to the other, backstage from stage right to stage left, and he had been brushing up against the scenery backstage. The young apprentices who had painted the set blue had been told they had to size the set—a process whereby you paint some kind of clear stuff onto the flats to set the color so it won't run. They *hadn't* done it.

There I was on stage left, having to do a highly emotional scene with a completely *blue actor*. The blue of his apartment set had come off all over him. He did not know that he was blue, and I kept trying to give him hints. I kept saying things like, "Did you have an accident with a blue Chevrolet?" My ability to improvise had suddenly deserted me. He didn't know what had happened to him. He thought I'd lost my mind. I kept the scene going somehow, and finally he accidentally looked at one of his hands, which of course was blue, and then he noticed that, because he was sweating profusely, he was leaving a trail of blue water all over the stage. He glared at me as if it was all my fault and ran offstage. The audience was stunned, to say the least.

The young stage manager did not bring down the curtain. The audience just sat there in sort of a stunned silence. The next five minutes seemed like two hours. I sat on the stage and stared at the audience. Then I did a private moment about waiting for the phone to ring. Then I pretended that it had rung. I had an interesting long-distance conversation with my mother, discussing the summer romance that the play was about. Then I cleaned my apartment. There was no one in the wings. There was no stage manager (I later found out he was washing Tony off with turpentine). They had left me out there all alone with an SRO house.

I was just about to turn to the audience and say, "Would you all go home, please?" when my leading man came back on stage, and we somehow finished that evening's performance. All I was thinking about and praying about was that no one in the first few rows would light a cigarette; it was an old wooden barn of a theater, and the smell of turpentine permeated the entire place. Thank God, no one did.

I traipsed around New England for many weeks, playing with my daughter whenever I could, and the cast doing something or other. We finally got to the last week before Westport. We had Sunday and Monday off, as we were opening in Westport on Tuesday. I decided I must send my little daughter and her nurse back to California. She was getting fed up with *Wedding Breakfast* and the constant traveling. I drove them to the airport and told them I'd be with them in a week. During the entire summer, I had been distant and sexually remote from Tony. I still don't understand how it's possible to be a mother and lover at the same time, especially in small quarters. I know nowadays some women are able to do this, but I never could.

When Tony and I got back from the airport and settled into our little love nest at the Meurice Hotel, we made up for lost time. We stayed in bed for two days and sent out for sandwiches. We only went out to catch a concert in Central Park, but we could not concentrate on Beethoven. Tony knew all the isolated spots. I must have enjoyed it, but later I was ready to kill him. I was terrified, not of muggers (in those days), but of being arrested.

What headlines for a star! But we got through that week-end safely and drove to Westport early Tuesday morning. My skin was now glowing, my eyes were shining, and Tony was relaxed and happy.

Westport was the height of the summer-stock circuit. It was the *crème de la crème,* run by the Theatre Guild. It had a high standard of excellence, and all the greats of the theater, such as Helen Hayes, Noel Coward, and Lunt and Fontanne, played there or tried out their plays in the summer. I've played Westport many times.

Wedding Breakfast was a very slight, amusing bit of theater. I think it would have made a lovely movie comedy, but sometime during that week of playing, Tony and I had a terrible fight—I can't remember what about. He seemed almost beside himself with fury, so that was the historic week I canceled the movie, gave United Artists back the $600,000, and made Sidney Lumet very angry.

When we had been playing Hinsdale, Jay Julien, who was producing *A Hatful of Rain,* had sent me a telegram saying that I had to release him from my artistic approval of the script or the Shuberts would not reserve a theater for us, and we would lose the production for that fall. With some misgivings, I agreed to give up my artistic control and telegraphed my permission so that we would have the Lyceum Theatre. It made me very nervous to be in the artistic hands of the Actors' Mafia; I was beginning to realize that when Tony was in the throes of a role, he was, to say the least, undependable.

We had gotten very good press in *The New York Times* and the local papers, so lots of important theater people were coming to Westport to see our little production of *Wedding Breakfast.* Frank Corsaro was very proud of the way he had helped me develop my comic talents—as was I. The closing night of *Wedding Breakfast,* the audience was indeed illustrious, and the acting on the stage lived up to it, I hope and believe. All went swimmingly until the last few minutes of the performance.

It is the emotional high point of the play. My character has realized that it's just a summer romance. I must tell Tony's character that maybe we'll try it again next summer and see if there is any validity to our love affair.

Virginia Vincent, who was playing my young roommate, had a zipper up the front of her dress. In this scene, I was getting her dressed, putting her hat on, zipping her dress closed, and sending her off to marry Marty Balsam's character. As I was reciting my dramatic, tearful monologue, the zipper on Virginia's dress stuck somewhere below her belly button. And stayed stuck.

I tried to cover this theatrical nightmare by acting even harder, hoping to distract the audience from my dilemma and meanwhile trying to unstick the zipper. Since it was a very poignant part of the play, I was terrified the audience would catch on. Virginia's idea of helping me was to remove herself astrally: she just stood there on the stage with her arms akimbo and pretended she was somewhere else.

Suddenly the audience caught on, and they started to laugh hysterically, not like human beings but, rather, like hyenas. It was the wildest, most uncontrollable laughter I have ever heard in a theater. They were literally weeping with laughter. I guess the shock of me pulling that stuck zipper and trying to "Method-perform" emotional agony was too much for them. I kept stopping and starting and trying to get them under control. The more I tried the more they laughed. After what seemed like an hour of theatrical agony, I took a convenient safety pin and pinned Virginia's zipper closed, turned her around, and pushed her, not gently, into the wings. I then walked down center stage, waited till the audience got some semblance of control, and said:

"When she gets her zipper fixed, she's going to marry Marty Balsam's character. I then phone Tony in his apartment on the other side of the stage and tell him we will meet again next spring. YOU CAN ALL GO MAKE YOUR TRAINS NOW. THIS PLAY IS OVER." Believe it or not, I actually sent the whole audience home. They applauded wildly for five minutes and continued laughing as they left the theater. I, of course, was hiding in my dressing room weeping, but rather proud of myself.

What I found out later was that I had sent home the entire Theatre Guild, including Lawrence Langner and Theresa Helburn and most of the important producers and directors functioning in New York at that time. In the years to come, I was to do many plays for the Theatre Guild, but I never again sent an audience home. But before each opening night, Lawrence Langner would show up in my dressing room and say something pseudoserious like, "Remember, Shelley, they paid for their tickets, they are entitled to see the *whole* play that the writer wrote no matter what happens. The actors have to just keep going even if the scenery falls down."

"Yes, Mr. Langner," I would sweetly answer. "Of course, Mr. Langner."

Our tour of *Wedding Breakfast* ended. Tony took me to the airport, with Marty Balsam driving the blue Mercury. I reassured everybody that I would return as soon as the new script Mike Gazzo was working on for *A Hatful of Rain* was sent to me in California.

When Mike finally sent me the play, which contained 300 pages (the average play is about 110), Celia, the part I was to play, was almost nonexistent; she was more a part of the scenery than a human being. I sent Jay Julien another telegram, which said:

LISTEN FELLOWS I DON'T CARE WHAT TELEGRAM
I SENT BEFORE, UNLESS CELIA'S PART GETS BIGGER
AND BETTER, I'M NOT COMING BACK TO NEW YORK

So I spent the first week of August in Beverly Hills, taking my daughter on pony rides and playing with the young children of my girlfriends.

The Actors' Mafia obviously believed me, because, in about a week, I received another script of *A Hatful of Rain,* and Mike Gazzo had indeed written me a poignant and bigger role and had incidentally also improved the play.

One of the few cultural offerings that Los Angeles has is concerts at the Hollywood Bowl. On the afternoon of August 16, 1955, two days before my birthday, Arthur Laurents called me and invited me to see a young conductor, Leonard Bernstein, conduct the Los Angeles Philharmonic. I gladly accepted and spent the afternoon getting all dolled up. Arthur Laurents was a prestigious screenwriter and playwright, and we would most probably have box seats and the paparazzi would be photographing us.

We were going to have dinner after the concert, but, being one who can never enjoy anything on an empty stomach, I had a little dinner with my daughter and was just putting her to bed when my father, Jonas, phoned from the upstairs apartment, where my parents were now living.

"Shelley, can I come down and kiss the baby?" he asked.

The question amazed me, but I answered, "Sure, Dad, anytime you want. Come on down, now."

Arthur Laurents was ringing the doorbell, and, as I went out the door with him, I waved at my father, who was coming down the outside steps.

We drove to the Hollywood Bowl, and, as I was talking to someone a few feet from the box office, Arthur went to pick up our tickets. Suddenly, Arthur turned and said, "Shelley, there's a message for you here."

The woman in the box office looked at me and said, "Miss Winters, I'm sorry, I think you'd better go home. Your sister just called, and your father is dead."

I don't remember getting home. Arthur brought me into my house, where my mother and sister were sitting in the living room, weeping. They told me my father had come downstairs, gone into his granddaughter's room, kissed her, then turned around and walked back into my room, where he had died instantaneously of a cerebral hemorrhage. Well, it is written that one of the rewards of living a good life is a quick and painless death.

The next week passed in a daze. All I remember about my father's funeral is that somehow Vittorio Gassman was in Los Angeles and was a pallbearer. We had let the nurse take my daughter to stay at her home somewhere way out in the San Fernando Valley for a few days until after the funeral. Vittorio had rented a car and the air conditioning was broken, and as we drove far out in the Valley to get our kid, Vittorio, attempting to distract me, said, "I think, Shelley, we're going to have a fried baby.

August in the San Fernando Valley is like Dante's inferno." Then he quoted Duse, who'd died in Pittsburgh and in her final illness she'd said, "I don't have to go to hell. I've already seen the blast furnaces of Pittsburgh." When Vittorio and I had lived in the apartment from which I am now writing, he had studied Dante's *Inferno* with Valentina Cortese and performed it with her in Italian at my sister and brother-in-law's Circle Theatre. The audiences had yelled, "Bravo! Bravo!" although half of them didn't understand a word of Italian. We reminisced about this as we sweated that day in the heat of the San Fernando Valley. When we picked up our baby, he immediately washed her off with cool water as she hugged him. He told me to drive, and as we drove home to Beverly Hills through the arid valley, my daughter fell asleep in his arms. He looked down at our beautiful sleeping child and whispered in Italian, "*Stupida!* You couldn't stay married to me long enough to have at least another one?"

I pretended I didn't understand or hear him.

I was getting frantic phone calls from Jay Julien to report for rehearsals of *A Hatful of Rain*. I think I arrived a day or two late. It was terribly sad to have to leave my baby and mother and sister at this time, but that's something actors learn they have to do.

I had explained to my baby and the nurse Kathy that, as soon as the play opened, I would know if it was a hit or a flop, and, if it was a hit, I would leave the Meurice Hotel and get an apartment. I had four weeks of rehearsal and a tour of New Haven, Philadelphia, and Washington and then some previews in New York. Even now, as I write, I cannot believe what happened during this tour. But it all happened.

My kid was attending a prestigious preschool in California called Work-and-Play School and again I had to make the decision to leave her in a secure atmosphere or drag her around the country while I rehearsed and toured. It seemed best that I leave her. Vittorio was doing a film in California and my mother was so sad and lonely now.

10

The rehearsal of *Hatful* was either at the Plymouth or the Royale—I just know it was one of the theaters on Forty-fifth Street. It was a very long, hot summer. The first day that I arrived for rehearsal, I was exhausted and weak and sad. I came right from the airport and dropped my luggage off at the Meurice. I got yet another new script from Eddie Julien, the assistant stage manager, who was Jay Julien's brother. As I flipped through it in the taxi, I noticed it was again two hundred pages, much too long for a play, and consequently the part of Celia was smaller. But always being a cooperative actress, I shut up and started to rehearse.

We sat around a table and read *A Hatful of Rain*. Some of it seemed extraordinarily powerful. The actors were Ben Gazzara, Tony Franciosa, Frank Silvera, myself, Christine White, Steve Gravers, Harry Guardino, and Henry Silva was the pusher they all called Mother. Len Bedsow, the stage manager, read the stage directions for us.

Tony and I were again rather aloof with each other, I can't quite say why. He certainly wasn't responsible for my father's death. But I had been in the bosom of my family, and we had had a tragedy. I suddenly realized I was getting embroiled in another relationship, a serious one, before I really was free of my feelings for Vittorio. Our divorce would not be final for another nine months.

One day I remember I went to visit a drug ward with Ben Gazzara, who played my husband, Johnny. Tony didn't go, because he was playing Polo, the brother who does not realize what drug addiction is doing to his brother, or maybe Ben and I didn't want him to go. We visited this hospital in Spanish Harlem, and then we talked to the doctors. The appalling fact, they told us, was that there was only one percent cure in heroin addiction. One percent. Of course, now we have methadone and many other ways of treating addiction, but I'm not sure that there has been much improvement in the percentage of cures. At that time, doctors were recommending that they do what they had done in England, which was to make it legal. That way, if people were drug addicts, they would declare themselves such, and they would get a card and go to a pharmacy daily and get their drug supply, whatever the amount was. In this way, they would take the money out of the dope industry (they hoped). I often wonder if the United States had tried this experiment in 1955, if it might have worked to some degree and drugs would not be the blight they are now in the U.S.

After this gloomy research, Ben took me to Danny's Hideaway for dinner, and, as always, I remember everything I ate: shrimp, martinis, Caesar salad, steak, and cannoli. Ben could not have been sweeter or nicer, though I had always previously found him rather aloof and reserved. *Cat on a Hot Tin Roof* had made him a big Broadway star. He was still playing in it when we were in rehearsal, and he would leave the Tennessee Williams hit play when *Hatful* left town. During that dinner, for about five seconds, I wondered if I was attracted to Tony because he was playing the good brother, Polo. Ben was playing the rejecting husband, Johnny. Was I turned on to Tony because of his role? Polo tenderly takes care of his pregnant sister-in-law. Again I was wondering if I was mixing up my real life with my art. But this flash of insight only lasted for a few seconds. Ben and I had a lovely evening, but that was that. And I guess, at the end of the evening, Ben knew that I was, if nothing else, sexually attracted to Tony. We made jokes about it, and he took me home to my little hotel. In hindsight, maybe Ben wanted it that way, too. He had his hands full with a separated wife *and* Elaine Stritch.

So rehearsals of *A Hatful of Rain* continued. The experience was electrifying, ludicrous, fulfilling, horrendously frustrating—and I've waited over thirty years for a similar artistic experience.

Frank Corsaro was then an unknown off-Broadway director. He had been steeped in the traditions of Stanislavsky and Strasberg and the Group Theatre's method of work. He never just read a scene and then staged it, as directors do now in movies, theater, and TV. Starting from the first scene of the play, we improvised the scene, many times, and then we did the scene with the playwright's words, but we always kept in mind what we had found out about the characters' thoughts during the improvisations.

When I was younger, I had been lucky enough to study with Michael Chekhov. He had taught our class that actors properly trained could almost mystically send themselves onto the stage before a scene and then leave their presence on the stage after they left. Although I had done this exercise in that class of Michael Chekhov's, I had never experienced this particular phenomenon until the rehearsals and production of *A Hatful of Rain,* when Frank Corsaro got this Actors Studio ensemble to do this. The rehearsals were so fascinating that we all were loath to leave the theater; even if Frank was rehearsing scenes we were not in. We sat in the balcony and watched. We became a real family, and since Equity allowed us to rehearse only six hours a day, we would find all kinds of reasons to hang out together till we had to go to sleep.

The play is about Johnny, a young man who becomes an addict while in a military hospital recovering from wounds he has sustained fighting in Korea. This role was played by Ben Gazzara. When Johnny's wife, Celia, welcomes him home, she understands only that he is a strange and different man from the one who had gone to war. Polo, played by Tony, keeps trying to help his brother get back on his feet, giving him money constantly, which, of course, he uses for heroin. Frank Corsaro played the father, who, in the beginning of the play, arrives for a short stay with his sons and pregnant daughter-in-law, played by me. The father, of course, does not know that Johnny has become a junkie.

I have seen other actors play this opening scene, but none has ever reached the bizarre pain and humor that Frank Corsaro was able to get out of this scene. Father, son, and daughter-in-law sit around a table calmly drinking coffee, but under the rather banal lines is the tension of a desperate, dangerous junkie, who will steal and do practically anything to get his fix. During the improvisations, I was trying to keep the scene calm and happy, and, as we explored the scene, the coffeepot somehow became my enemy. Mike wrote this attitude into the scene. The audience laughed every time I opened my mouth and denigrated the coffee or the coffeepot. I couldn't insult my sick husband, my sweet brother-in-law, who was almost supporting us, or my father-in-law, who had come after the long war to visit, so I took my tension and anger out on this coffeepot. This was Frank's direction.

Frank went through the play, carefully illuminating the playwright's words, and sometimes even directing us to play in direct contradiction to these words, as people so often do in real life. And thus, this tragic, comedic theater piece slowly unfolded.

Although at this point, in real life, Tony and I were practically engaged, I suddenly could not sleep with him. He felt that way about me, too, I believe. I remember sitting in Central Park and looking at the water and sadly watching the boats and having this feeling of quiet, "impossible doomed love." There wasn't an analyst around at that point, so there was no one to tell us we were "acting out" the story of the play. The four weeks of rehearsals passed in a flash, and even though we would sit at Downey's till 4:00 A.M. and neck in the back of the balcony of the theater, we never slept together during the rehearsals of *Hatful*, despite that hectic, sexy summer of

Wedding Breakfast. I just could not betray my stage husband, nor could Tony betray his stage brother.

One scene in the play bothered Frank a great deal. At the beginning of the third act, Johnny's junkie pals invade the apartment (they usually hang out on the fire escape, stage right, outside the kitchen window). Johnny has stolen and sold Polo's car, but he owes Mother a great deal of money, and he needs his fix. This junkie scene managed to be both lethal and hilarious and it lasted about forty minutes. By the time it was over, people watching rehearsals had forgotten the story of the play, but when Frank tried to cut it, all the "Method actors" who were playing the junkies screamed bloody murder. Frank Corsaro, the director, Mike Gazzo, the playwright, and Jay Julien, the producer, decided to leave the play the way it was until after the New Haven opening. This decision was not a wise one. You have to remember that this was the first play ever done about drug addiction, and in 1955 this was a very shocking and taboo subject.

Finally, we all took the train to New Haven. For some reason, I had neglected to report to the costumers to get my two pregnant outfits. So, during my first morning in New Haven, I rushed to the maternity department of J. C. Penney and got two dresses, which I was to wear for the next year. They cost $16 total, which Jay Julien has still to reimburse me for.

The opening in New Haven was a disaster. The two balconies were full of Yale yuppies (then just called rich kids), but the curtain went up at 8:30 P.M. and came down at 1:30 A.M. The stark realism of the play was too much for that Yale audience. They did not think that "poor people," much less pregnant women and drug addicts, should be shown on the stage. They were used to Noel Coward. They behaved so badly during that opening night that the dean of the Yale Law School took an ad out in the New Haven newspaper apologizing for the behavior of his students that night. I couldn't read it because I cried continuously for the next twenty-four hours. I had never faced such a hostile audience. They booed and folded their programs into shapes of little airplanes and threw them. Can you imagine continuing to perform while this was going on? But Ben and Tony whispered under their breath, "Fuck 'em, Shelley. What do they know? Just keep going."

I was sure we would close the next night. But Frank called a rehearsal for ten the next morning and cut the play unmercifully—especially the junkie scene. The next night, to a half-filled house, we began to realize we were in a very powerful play. The small audience moved as close to the stage as possible during the intermission. You could hear a pin drop, they were so attentive.

Later that season, Shirley Booth, who was doing *Desk Set* by William Marchant (whose *Faster, Faster* I was supposed to have done), told me at Sardi's that *a whole* audience takes on the personality of one single person, and at each performance it will be a different person. She was telling me the absolute truth. If the play and performances are good, they will be attentive, but some audiences will laugh a great deal, some will weep a great deal, and some will squirm with embarrassment. It is a strange phenomenon, depending on the personality of the strongest person in the audience. The producers and most stage actors cannot explain it. They just keep wrestling with it at each performance and come to accept the fact that every audience is somehow different.

We played a split week in New Haven, business improving nightly, and then, closing night, Saturday, we played to Standing Room Only. Closing night, the actors and the playwright got standing ovations, and we the actors applauded that young audience.

The next day, Sunday, we moved to Philadelphia, where we were to play in an old and beautiful theater, the Locust. There were many shows trying out that season in Philadelphia. My old friend George Cukor was directing *The Chalk Garden,* a beautiful play by Enid Bagnold. Sometime during the tryout of that play in Philly, George quit and went back to the relative safety of Hollywood. Tryouts are horrendous.

A Hatful of Rain was a complex play of many scenes, and we were on the road to find out from the audience what scenes needed strengthening and what scenes needed cutting. I think one of the most exquisite forms of torture must be playwrights' experiencing out-of-town tryouts. Most of the cast was staying in inexpensive hotels, but the producer wanted me to have a suite in a fancy hotel. He felt I would be doing publicity and interviews, and, after all, I was the movie star in the play and was expected to publicize it. So I had a fancy suite, and Tony had the living room, which, of course, he never slept in. Somehow, as soon as we left New York, Tony and I were again crazy for each other. Philadelphia is the cradle and birthplace of our country, but somehow I always think of Philadelphia as a very sexy city. We got much better reviews in Philadelphia, and the public was very curious about this first play about drug addiction.

I began to have two major arguments with the director, Frank Corsaro, Jay Julien, the producer, and Mordecai Gorelik, the set designer. The set was in two sections: one a raked stage, slanting toward the audience, and the other, on stage right, was a platform, on which stood a dirty sink in a tenement kitchen with old, yellow linoleum. On stage left was the living room, which had an old chaise lounge and a frayed lampshade. The whole apartment looked as if it had never been cleaned. I felt strongly this apartment should look clean and show Celia's efforts to fix it up and make it as much like a home as possible.

The other problem was that I kept sensing from the audience that they couldn't understand why I didn't love and trust my brother-in-law, Polo, Tony's character. I was putting myself and my unborn baby's life in danger by staying with Ben Gazzara's character, Johnny. In the play, I don't know he's a junkie. I just know he is my husband, sick and stealing everything in sight. I kept trying to get Mike Gazzo to write a scene in which Johnny and I would talk about what our marriage had been before he had gone to fight in Korea. I wanted the audience to see why Celia is holding on to this man. She loves him so much and she keeps hoping the marriage will return to what it once was.

Mike Gazzo resisted all my attempts and would not give me the scene which I felt was so necessary to make my character and the play work. Nor would Mordecai

Gorelik allow the stage to be cleaned up. The fights about these two issues became gigantic, and even though my role of Celia kept getting bigger and bigger, I kept threatening to quit unless somehow my frustration over the audience's reaction was dealt with.

These problems were finally solved in the following fashion: the last week of our performance in Washington, Mike Gazzo agreed to give me the scene I requested, but he wanted it in the third act.

"Mike," I kept insisting, "through the whole play, the audience is sitting there wondering why I'm holding on to this sick husband who is so remote and dangerous."

Before our last performance in Washington, Mike wrote a beautiful scene about how Johnny and I used to make love on the beach in Rockaway when we were first married. Johnny was healthy and our love was new. Mike wrote it on toilet paper and threw it at me on the stage during a rehearsal and then left for New York. In my opinion, this scene made the whole play work.

The problem about the dirty set I solved in my own peculiar fashion. Opening night in New York, I made Tony go to Woolworth's with me, and I bought yellow shelving paper, a dark red lampshade, a cheap, nice rug, a patchwork quilt for the chaise lounge, a yellow oilcloth table cover, and a scrubbing brush and a soap pail. At six-thirty opening night on Broadway, I was down on my hands and knees with my hair up in curlers, scrubbing the kitchen side of the stage. Then I dusted and cleaned and redecorated the living room side of the stage. While I was doing all this, the propman came in and threw his hands in the air and said, "I didn't see it. I didn't see nothing." He was used to the Method shenanigans of the actors, but he had never seen a leading lady cleaning up a stage an hour before curtain. If the play had not been an enormous success with every critic praising "Celia's attempt at making a home in a tenement," I would have been sued by the scenic designer's union, the propman's union, the producer, the playwright, and, for all I know, the United Nations. All that happened was, the second night I got three dozen roses from Mordecai Gorelik with a note that said, "Sometimes the actors know more about a play than anyone else connected with it. They have a special communication with the audience." Jay Julien pretended nothing had happened. He was delirious over his first Broadway hit.

Meanwhile, back in Philadelphia, during our second week of tryouts, the show was beginning to have great form and substance. Tony and I didn't see much of Philadelphia because, when we weren't performing or giving interviews, we were in bed. I've often heard that men reach their sexual peak in their early twenties and women in their thirties, and, from my memories of Philadelphia, I can guarantee it's true.

We had finally realized that the play was *not* our real lives. Tony was the most endearing, tender, imaginative, and athletic of lovers. I swear, if sex were an event in the Olympics, Tony Franciosa would have been the captain of the team when he was twenty-six.

Suddenly, one night during a performance, Tony's face went white with pain. He managed to finish the act and then keeled over in the wings, holding his side and uttering muffled screams. I was sure it was my fault and had to do with all our lovemaking. When the ambulance got there, after a quick examination, the doctor said he thought it was kidney stones, and I was distraught because Jay Julien was physically preventing me from getting in the ambulance with Tony and telling me to finish the third act of the play. That night, there was a very long intermission and a very short third act. It was a testimonial to the actors and the play, since everybody understudied everybody else, which meant they changed their clothes and the stage manager came out on the stage and announced, "In the third act, the part of Polo will be played by Harry Guardino, Harry Guardino's part of Chuch will be played by Steve Gravers," and so on, all down the cast list.

I did not know what was the matter with Tony. I was sure it was appendicitis or something worse. As soon as the play was over, in full makeup and costume, I dashed to the hospital. I can't remember the name of it, but Grace Kelly's father was associated with it. At the information desk, they got me a wheelchair, because I looked so pregnant in my pregnant costume, and I had to keep insisting I was not in labor. I wanted to find Tony Franciosa, "my fiancé," who had been taken there from the theater in an ambulance. They kept trying to find what room he was in, but they didn't seem to have any record of his having been admitted to the hospital or what ambulance had brought him there.

I began to cry, the makeup streaking my face, and I phoned my sister in California, who was a nurse. I garbled out how the ambulance had taken Tony away from the theater and how he had doubled up in pain, and finally Blanche asked that I put the head nurse of the emergency room on the line. After Blanche talked awhile to the head nurse, the nurse turned to me and informed me that this was a city hospital and was so crowded that "my fiancé" was in the X-ray room for the night, as they couldn't find a bed for him, and he hadn't had the proper insurance papers when he'd been admitted to the hospital. She was rather sarcastic about "my fiancé" since she knew somehow that my divorce from Vittorio was still not final.

The nurse gave me the directions on how to find the X-ray room, and I began to wander around the huge, dark city hospital. For some reason, the elevators didn't work after twelve. I knew this was a city hospital and understaffed, but I have never seen such a dirty, empty hospital in my life. I was sure by now they had killed Tony. After lots of wrong directions, I finally found the room.

Tony was in a hospital bed in a corner among the X-ray machines and seemed out of pain but dazed. He told me that an intern had seen him, and they believed he had had a kidney attack, and they were waiting to see if he would pass the kidney stones before operating. They were giving him medicine to try to help him pass the stones. He also was getting a shot of Demerol every few hours for the pain. He didn't ask me question one about the play or how the performance had gone.

It was the beginning of October and was very cold, and this dirty X-ray room seemed to have no heat. They were understaffed, and all the nurses were running around with emergencies, and no one would pay much attention to me. So I covered Tony with my huge mink coat and got permission to give him little pieces of ice. He was very thirsty and they had refused to let him drink water. I sat there for the rest of the night, freezing and holding his hand. Whenever his pain got real bad, I would go try to find a nurse or intern to give him a shot. When the new shift came on at 7:00 A.M., I tried to use my movie-star pull and gave them a check for $300 guaranteeing his medical expenses, but there just didn't seem to be any beds. By this time I was paranoid and was sure they were not operating on him because his Equity insurance papers weren't available.

This was our final playing week in Philadelphia, and Saturday night after the performance I hired an ambulance and took Tony all the way to Mount Sinai in New York, where I knew the doctors. I got him a specialist in urology to see if he could get him to pass the kidney stones without an operation. I could not bear the idea that if he had to undergo an operation, he would of course miss the Washington run and the opening in New York. Jay Julien was on the phone, threatening to bring me up on charges at Equity, because I was supposed to be in Washington rehearsing. They were putting new scenes into the play, and I was sitting in New York at Mount Sinai Hospital.

Finally, on Tuesday morning, they had him in the operating room almost ready to operate, but they were trying some remarkable new procedure, which entailed a spinal block, and it worked. They got the kidney stones out without an operation. I gathered it was a very painful process. When he came down from the operating room and came out of the anesthesia, instead of asking about his medical condition, he said:

"Shelley, I'm okay now, so hurry up and get to Washington. You're going to miss the opening. I'll rejoin the show as soon as I recover from the anesthesia." Actors!

The doctor assured me he would be fine in a couple of days, and I did exactly what Tony suggested. Fast. I got to Washington in time for the rehearsal of two new scenes and opened with Harry Guardino in Tony's role. Ben

Gazzara, Shelley Winters, and Harry Guardino got rave reviews.

But poor Harry was so frightened at the opening in Washington that he could hardly get through the show. The next night, at the end of the third act, when the father hits his son Polo, Harry forgot the choreography of the punch, and Silvera connected with his jaw and accidentally knocked the poor guy unconscious. The audience was standing and applauding. Harry remained unconscious. I got a pitcher of ice water in the wings and poured it over Harry's face. He came to and was able to stand up somewhere around the fourth curtain call. Frank and I were able to hold him up while he took his bow.

A Hatful of Rain was a complicated production requiring sixteen stagehands. At every performance, the stagehands would each put up a dollar bet—at which scene something would go wrong. If we ever had a perfect show, the pool of money was to go to the next performance. In doing the play for over a year, the stagehands never had a perfect performance at which nothing happened, and this pool of money never went to the next performance. Method actors!

Even though I'd been a movie star for several years and had done several plays around California—including *Born Yesterday* in summer stock—I had never had the responsibility of a lead role on Broadway. The pivotal stable character in the play was Celia. I was on stage a great deal of the time. During the second week in Washington, I finally realized I was having trouble going from scene to scene without resting. When filming a motion picture, you have a chance to catch your breath while the crew are lighting the next scene. In the legitimate theater, there's no such thing as a break. Finally, Jay Julien got Stella Adler to come down to Washington to show me how to conserve my energy in each scene I was playing so I would have enough strength for the next scene in the act. This is something you must learn when you have a big role in an emotional play. The other thing Stella did was bring Tony Franciosa down with her on the train. The whole cast was overjoyed, possibly with the exception of Harry Guardino. But even Harry knew Polo was

Tony's part. He had worked on this role for over two years, developing it at the Actors Studio.

When Tony came up to my suite, he looked frail and pale. With tears in his eyes, he told me that he had had a very strange reaction to the spinal anesthesia he'd received at Mount Sinai. He could not sit or stand. If he did, he developed excruciating headaches, and they would not go away until he was flat on his back, on the floor or the bed or a sofa. I looked at him in stunned silence. I shakingly inquired if perhaps it wasn't something psychological or psychosomatic.

"No, Shelley," he replied. "It has to do with the liquid in the brain that is out of balance."

His doctor had assured him that, with a little time, everything would seep back into place, and the headaches would disappear, and he'd be able to stand straight again.

"But," he added, "I can't go back into the show till the headaches disappear or Frank figures out how I can play the role in a horizontal position."

He was lying on my living room floor at the time, which didn't seem to bother the bellhops bringing in his luggage. He could not even bear a cushion under his head. I got down on the floor next to him and kissed him.

"Tony, don't worry," I whispered. "I will keep this show on the road for a year, if necessary. You brought this script to me, and besides, I love you, and I will not open on Broadway without you playing opposite me."

He gave me a sad smile and said, "Would you please explain my physical condition to Jay, and I hope to God we can play some place after Washington, and I can go back into the play."

My phone had been ringing for about fifteen minutes, because Stella Adler and the entire cast were at the theater, waiting for me. There was a knock on the door and, when I opened it, there stood Jay, his face the color of the dirty snow in the Washington streets: sort of an ashy, gray white. Tony had had to come down from New York to Washington in a berth. Stella Adler had already told him that Tony could not rehearse that day or go back into the show that night.

158

We rode to the theater in complete silence. My jaw was clenched and, as we climbed out of the cab at the stage door, Jay said, "Shelley, you're my friend, but Equity will take away your Equity card if you keep twenty other actors out of work, and there will probably be repercussions in the Screen Actors Guild as well."

"You're my friend, too," I answered, "but there is no way that I will open on Broadway without Tony playing Polo. Since Stella Adler is here to help me, why don't we discuss this after the show this evening, and that will give you a chance to look around for a replacement for me."

Jay almost fainted as I marched into the theater and onto the stage. The cast and Frank Corsaro and Mike Gazzo and Stella Adler were waiting for me, and we started to rehearse.

Stella Adler was then, and is now, a great theater teacher. I had met her in Hollywood, and I believed she liked me. She had once given a dinner party for Vittorio and myself, when we were engaged, and she had tried to talk to me about my infatuation with him in the elegant powder room in her apartment:

"Shelley, at your young age, it's wonderful and almost necessary to have an Italian lover, but you must not marry them."

Of course, I had paid no attention to her advice. But now I needed all her wisdom, because I knew I was slowing down the play at some of its most pivotal scenes. Frank Corsaro explained to her at what points in the play I was having the most trouble, and we began to perform for her, scene by scene. She said nothing to any of the other actors—after all, she was being paid $500 *by me* to come all the way to Washington.

Over the years, I've always felt that, even given the inflation of the past thirty years, this was a very small amount of money for what Stella did for me. I am also still convinced that Jay was quite smitten with her, and that they were having a love affair. They may sue me for this, but these were the vibes I was getting from them at the time, and, being an authority on the chemistry of sexual attraction, that's what I felt (and I think that was the deciding factor that brought her to Washington to save Jay Julien's play).

In the middle 1950s Stella Adler was a knockout. A few years before this, I was sitting in the Copa at a table with Marilyn Monroe, and we were done up to the teeth. Lana Turner, at a nearby table, was at her most beautiful. Stella Adler made an entrance in a black satin gown with black egrets in her blonde hair. For the next hour no one in the Copa looked at us movie stars. Stella had such a dynamite stage presence.

As Stella coached me, I got a firmer hold on the character and was no longer exhausted at the end of an emotional scene. I became able to carry my energy over to the next scene. Stella rehearsed me through the whole play in Washington and watched several performances and did not leave until she felt I was secure in the role. Jay had managed to keep her there for a few extra days. Frank and she would huddle after each performance, then I would get pages of notes from Frank. I was beginning to get bravos when I took my bow. I did have the grace to take her and Jay out to a late supper at the most expensive restaurant in Washington.

Before Stella's arrival, I had been so distraught that, late one night, I'd slipped a note under Jay's door informing him, "I'm quitting the show." I hope I have learned by now that when a role has a great deal of rejection in it —as Celia's did—I sometimes act it out in real life, usually three times a production. This applies to movies as well as the stage. If the producer and director ignore me, I get over the middle-of-the-night dooms and go on working in a professional manner, but, I must say, I scare some producers who believe my momentary despair.

Harry Guardino got better and better in the part of Polo, and since Tony could now sit up to eat, he somehow got to the theater to see Harry's performance. How, I don't know. In my heart of hearts, I knew that Tony was different, funnier, and better. Anyway, I think I was better when Tony was on the stage. My apologies to Harry.

Finally, the weekend before we went back to New York, Tony was able to walk around the lobby. Saturday morning we went for a walk and even looked at the Lincoln Memorial and the Washington Monument. His headaches and dizziness returned right there, and he had to lie down on the steps of the Lincoln Memorial for a few minutes. Being Catholic and accustomed to praying, Tony, I believe, said a little silent prayer to Lincoln. I can't prove this, but many years later, Tony, who then was not especially political, went to Washington during the civil-rights movement and stood in front of the Lincoln Memorial with Marlon Brando and other stars to protest the treatment of our black citizens in America. I saw his picture in *Life* magazine; all the other stars were looking at the 250,000 people in front of them, but Tony was looking at Lincoln.

By the time we finished the run in Washington, Tony was able to take the train back to New York and sit up in the dining car. We arrived Sunday noon and went to the Meurice. There was a message from Jay that he wanted to have lunch with me alone on Monday. The set was being shipped from Washington, and our first preview was Tuesday. We were having a line rehearsal on Wednesday, another preview Wednesday night, and opening on Thursday. Tony was going to see the doctor Monday at Mount Sinai.

Even though Tony often had headaches when he stood up, he felt fine when he was horizontal. Since he couldn't think of many things to do when he was horizontal, I found myself horizontal much of that week, too. He told me that the doctor had assured him that sexual activity helped balance his brain fluid, and *I believed him*.

At lunch on Monday, Jay looked at me calmly and quietly and said, "Tony has not been in the play for almost three weeks—half of the Philadelphia run and all of the Washington run. Harry Guardino is wonderful in the part, and Thursday night when we open the show, I want you to open with Harry."

I sat silently for five minutes, examining my soul, my conscience, my libido, and my professional attitude.

"Jay," I finally replied, "number one, Anthony Franciosa brought this script of *A Hatful of Rain* to me. Number two, at your urging, he talked me out of doing William Marchant's *Faster, Faster*. Number three, he convinced me to give up artistic control of *Hatful* and trust that you and Mike Gazzo would see to it that Celia was a star role. Number four, if I had not agreed to taking out the artistic clause in the contract, the Shuberts would not have given you a theater. Five, you either open with Tony or you open with my understudy. Six, you can do what you want at Equity, but I feel that I have to do this for Tony. He may never get another chance to create such a great role on Broadway."

I never told Tony about this conversation. Now he knows.

When I got back to the Meurice Hotel, Tony had bought me a small bouquet of flowers and a very small bottle of champagne. The doctor had given him a clean bill of health and said he could start rehearsing the next day. I rehearsed his lines till we had to report to the theater.

Tuesday night Tony went into the show and gave a funny and moving performance. I was rather rattled, being afraid for Tony, but the audience kept us there for ten curtain calls. Stella had watched the show, and she made me stay in the theater until 2:00 A.M. while I ironed a man's shirt, which was part of my business in the first act. I had to do it exactly—the collar first, then the cuffs, the left sleeve, the right sleeve, the back, and then the front. I had to do it *a hundred times* exactly the same. If I made a mistake or did it differently, that time didn't count. She sat on the stage with a paper and pencil and counted exactly until 2:00 A.M. and made sure I could do it automatically. What she was teaching me, which I've remembered all my life, is that your mind and words and intentions cannot be free until you are unconscious of the props and don't have to think about them. This is as true on the stage as in real life. Frank had been calling me

"Paula Prop"; after that rehearsal, he never did it again. Props had always been my natural enemies, and I'd been avoiding them for years.

Jay called a line rehearsal Wednesday when we would normally have had a matinee. Frank went through Tony's scenes several times, and since all the other "understudies" had resumed their original roles, he had five pages of notes on our Tuesday-night performance. Frank's critiques did not agree with the ovations we had gotten from the audience.

"Forget it!" he shouted. "Two moments of the play Shelley still has not gotten right."

The first was toward the end of the second act. In a scene with Ben Gazzara, I feel the first twinges of life inside me. This fluttering feeling I remembered from my own pregnancy. It was like a faint tapping from the inside. I take Johnny's hand and put it on my stomach so he can feel his child alive and moving for the first time. Johnny's reaction is typical of a disturbed man. As I smile with joy, he grabs his hand away in fear and loathing and starts weeping. This is the first moment of the play that I face the reality that something is deadly wrong with my husband.

The second moment was at the very end of the play, just before the lights fade, with my husband shaking and weeping in my lap. I slowly dial the police and say, "I wish to report a drug addict." And then after a pause I cry out, "It's my husband! My husband!" That is the curtain of *A Hatful of Rain*.

Frank Corsaro rehearsed these two moments very carefully. And opening night, you could hear the audience weeping.

At the first matinee, I complained to the stage manager that I heard a strange clicking sound, like someone closing an outer door. After the intermission, he came back and said, "Shelley, when you don't hear that sound, start to worry. That's fifteen hundred purses being clicked open at the same second, as women reach for their handkerchiefs."

Opening night, we all left the theater after the flowers and congratulations and telegrams, and, as I passed a mounted policeman on the way to Sardi's to wait for the reviews, I jokingly said to his horse, "Hey, horsie, is this show a hit?" The horse answered me with a huge nod. Years later, after certain other opening nights, that horsie shook his head NO. But that night, I kissed him and went on to Sardi's. All the diners applauded and cheered us as we entered.

We all sat in frozen silence, waiting for the reviews to come in. Nobody said anything. Tony looked white-faced and shriveled, and Ben Gazzara had retreated into his real-life glass shell. I had complained about this glass shell to Frank many times during the rehearsals. On the stage, Ben had seemed to be talking to me through that glass bubble. All Frank ever told me was, "Use it. His remoteness and distance are what make it so heartbreaking for the audience."

As I looked around the table, I realized that all these young people, including the playwright, Mike Gazzo, had been working on this play at the Actors Studio for several years. Whatever the critics said in those papers that we were waiting for would decide their futures. If my reviews weren't good, I could just pick up and go back to Hollywood and continue my film career.

That isn't to say I wasn't proud of *A Place in the Sun*, *A Double Life*, *Night of the Hunter*, and *I Am a Camera*. But I was still under contract to Universal and owed them another picture or three. They had given me a year's leave of absence, but they were going to add it onto the contract, which meant I was under contract from 1948 to 1956 or '57. Nevertheless, that night sitting in Sardi's, I knew that, no matter what the critics said, I finally had to move my little family back to New York, and I resolved that the next day I would start looking for an apartment.

So, that opening night, I was praying silently that our notices would be good so that I would have a long run in *A Hatful of Rain*. All the Actors' Mafia, especially Tony, were putting drinks away as fast as they could, and no one but me was eating anything. It's probably the only meal I've ever eaten that I don't remember what it was. God, they were taking a long time to deliver the papers to us. Suddenly, apropos of nothing, I blurted out—to relieve the tension, I guess—"Well, Howard Hughes has to pay me a thousand dollars a month for the next five years, anyway." Tony looked at me queerly, as did the rest of the cast. I hurriedly explained my RKO deal with him for *The Treasure of Pancho Villa*. I don't think one actor sitting at that table believed a word of it.

Jay, who had been on the phone upstairs at Sardi's, suddenly came back, and he was smiling all over the place.

"What were the reviews?" we screamed at him. "Did you get them on the phone?"

He would not tell us. He ordered three bottles of champagne. He said a cab was bringing them up to Sardi's, fresh from the presses, and he would read them to us. We were all about to stick our steak knives into him when the reviews arrived.

Sardi's fell silent. Jay read them loud and clear in his best lawyer's voice. The reviews from the *Times*, the *Herald-Tribune*, the *Post*, the *Journal-American*, the *Daily News*, and the *Mirror* were unqualified raves for the play, the director, and especially the actors. They said things like, "The audience was riveted to their seats." They had not been so moved by a play since *The Glass Menagerie*.

Everyone started to cry and kiss each other. People were standing on chairs and cheering us. It seemed that a new playwright and a new Ensemble Theater, "The Actors Studio Company," had been born. This play had been created there. I suddenly realized, after about half an hour of people kissing me, that Tony had disappeared. I sent someone to look for him in the men's room, but he was nowhere in sight. His reviews had been wonderful. Ben Gazzara's had been the best, mine almost as good, and Tony's almost as good as mine. Since this was only Tony's second play on Broadway and his second night back in the show, I felt he must be delirious with joy, as I was. I thought perhaps he wanted to be alone, or had walked back to the hotel to call his mother and aunts and read the reviews to them.

When I decently could, I disentangled myself from all

the congratulations and took a cab back to the Meurice. I had a strange foreboding in my heart, but I didn't know why. As I walked down the hall toward our suite, I could hear things crashing, and there was Tony, stark naked, with sweat running down his body, screaming how terrible his performance had been, and it was somehow everybody's fault. Then he became inarticulate. What I was watching was sheer, out-of-control rage. Whether it was the kidney attack—me—Harry Guardino's performance—or the two years of working on this play, I didn't know.

By this time there were two bellhops standing behind me, watching. He had broken plants, and lamps, and chairs—almost everything breakable in the apartment was scattered and broken. I tried to interrupt, to quote to him the wonderful compliments Walter Kerr had paid him. *The New York Times* had written that he was the most promising and talented new actor to have appeared on Broadway in years. He sat in a corner and wept, and I suddenly got the eerie knowledge that he was still playing Polo and quite drunk. He could not stand it that Celia had rejected him and gone back to her husband, that his father hated him for giving his brother money, knowing that he was going to spend it on heroin. He kept quoting his subtext and his real lines from the play.

"But he fought in Korea," Tony kept muttering. "I didn't have to. He fought the war. I didn't have to."

Tony suddenly pushed us all out of the way, ran down the stairs and through the lobby, and continued running west.

A police car began following him and managed to catch him somewhere around Forty-ninth and Sixth Avenue. I knew that he was on his way to the Lyceum stage entrance on Forty-sixth and Seventh and was trying to get on the set to *change the ending of the play*. Of course, I can't know that for sure, but since I had exchanged so many thoughts with him on and off the stage, I believe I knew what he was thinking or trying to do. I managed to catch the police before they drove away, and they let me sit in the front with the driver. Tony was naked behind the cage, handcuffed and sobbing. The cops had recognized me and seemed also to know that we had opened in this antidrug play, which was already a big hit at the Lyceum that night. Times Square cops know everything. They found an old pair of Levi's and a sweater somewhere, and, before they took us into night court, they advised me to phone a lawyer and a psychiatrist as soon as possible.

I quickly called the Montgomery-something office, which was Adlai Stevenson's firm, and they gave me the number of a Mr. Paul Sherman, who handled night cases. I called him at home, explaining who I was, what the situation was, and that we were waiting in night court at 1:00 A.M. and we had to do *A Hatful of Rain* for the second-night critics *that very night*. In those days, the second-night critics were the ones who wrote for all the national magazines, the big important ones like *Newsweek, Time, Life, Look, Cosmopolitan, Ladies' Home Journal, The Nation,* and *The New Republic*. Mr. Sherman told me to wrap my head in a scarf, put on dark glasses, and stay in the phone booth until he got there. I also woke up a psychiatrist I knew, who knew the judge of this particular night court. Tony had disappeared. I didn't know where they had taken him, and I sat huddled in the phone booth for fear there was a roving reporter somewhere around the court. I was terrified that Jay Julien would read about this in the papers and take Tony out of the play.

Mr. Sherman finally appeared. I can't remember if I waited one hour or three or six, I was so distraught. When the woman judge finally heard our case, I explained to her about "affective memory" and how the actor substitutes parallel traumas of his/her own life. In rare cases, the actor sometimes gets lost in those acting exercises. How strange—my first film *A Double Life* was exactly about this problem. When Ronald Colman is acting out *Othello*, he brings his role and Othello's jealousy over into his real life and murders me, his waitress/mistress. The female judge listened, skeptically, to all of it.

When they brought in Tony, he was quite calm. He more or less paraphrased what I had told the judge. He said that despite the wonderful reviews, he had been somehow still doing Polo, even after the curtain came down. He had become so enmeshed in the tragedy of his character that he himself did not know what he was doing. The judge ordered Tony to Bellevue for a psychiatric examination and told him, that if he was released, he must see a psychiatrist on a regular basis. The judge looked at me shrewdly and said:

"See to it that your play ENDS when the curtain comes down."

Tony and I promised to do all these things from then on.

Seeing as who we were, it was a miracle that the press did not get hold of this incident. There were no reporters in Manhattan's night court that night.

Mr. Sherman and I sat on a bench outside Bellevue as dawn came up over the East River. Mr. Sherman stayed with me all night, and I began to remember some of the things that I had heard about the two years of rehearsals of *Hatful.* Eva Marie Saint had done my part at the Studio at the beginning, as the play was developed. The rehearsals became a little too wild for her, and she moved to Hollywood with her husband, Jeff Hayden. Then Carroll Baker did my role, but when Elia Kazan started the rehearsals of *Baby Doll,* she gladly left the play for the film. Paul Richards, a very fine actor who was playing one of the junkies, had told me that during one of the improvisations, when Polo confronts the junkies who are making an addict of his brother, Tony had picked up a crate of glass milk bottles—milk in those days was delivered in crates made of heavy metal wiring and heavy wood—and thrown it directly at him. Paul had managed to duck, and the box just grazed his head. If Tony had connected, he would have probably killed Paul with this heavy box.

I sat there on that bench on that cold November morning, no joy in my heart that I'd finally become a recognized, accomplished Broadway star. I was dazed from the events of this weird, unreal night, and scared that the newspapers or the producer would learn about what happened. I kept wondering why I, a relatively sane lady, just couldn't walk away from this obviously disturbed actor.

Was it the fault of his fatherless childhood? Or the rejection from his father in the play? Whatever the reason, I was connected deeply to a man who was now being examined for mental illness in that dark red city building called Bellevue.

"Shelley," Paul Sherman said, putting his arm around me, "I've been a lawyer for quite a while and a student of human behavior for longer than that. Some people can live with failure, but success terrifies them. Tony is perhaps one of them."

"Maybe," I said, and continued to stare at Bellevue through that long night.

11

And so the run of *A Hatful of Rain* began. The second-night reviews, which appeared in newspapers and magazines from all over the world, were as glowing as the opening-night reviews. The audience was as spontaneous and gave us a standing ovation.

The New York dailies had been so wonderful that when any actor made an exit, they would read their reviews again. Tony moved to the Hotel Bolivar, which was quite near my new apartment, and he began seeing a psychiatrist.

I had at last found a glorious apartment on Central Park West. It was huge and had a view of the park. I loved that building so much that I lived in it for the next twenty years, moving to three different apartments in the same building during that time. I guess during those two decades I had such fulfilling artistic experiences, and I made so many friends there, that with my magical thinking, that building seemed like the most secure and successful apartment house in New York. I never considered moving anywhere else. My apartment had a huge living room and dining room and an enormous kitchen and four bedrooms and bathrooms.

I called my mother and baby and the nurse, Kathy, and told them, "Hurry up and fly to New York. The play is a hit, and we have a lovely big furnished apartment right across from Central Park.''

I rented this beautiful apartment from Barbara Baroness McLane. It had pots and pans and linens, and the only thing I had to buy was a crib and a little carousel lamp to put in the baby's room. In a couple of years, I bought some of the Baroness's gorgeous antiques, and she turned over the lease to me.

My little family arrived on Sunday, my day off, and, to my amazement, my daughter, who was barely three, understood that, from now on, we would be living in New York and we would just visit California in the summers. When I took her up to the apartment, she immediately ran around the huge space and then became very quiet as she watched the carousel lamp go round and round. It is one of my most vivid memories—looking at her little face in the light of that lamp I prayed silently that I had made the right decision for her life.

My family acclimatized itself to New York very quickly, and I began to joyfully do my eight performances a week. I could write a whole book about the run of *A Hatful of Rain*, but the most important thing about the run of that play was the joy of acting with all those actors who'd been trained in the Method. No two performances were alike. The audiences were electrified and riveted, and I have waited thirty-five years for another theater experience like it. I'm *still* waiting.

During the very first matinee, I was doing the second-act scene with Ben Gazzara, downstage left. The scene consisted of me nagging him and trying to find out why my young husband had changed so much. During one of my lines, a young man in the second row suddenly said quietly, "Leave him alone!" I froze. Ben took my hand and whispered, "Keep going!" I kept on with the scene. After a moment or two the voice said loudly, "I told you, leave him alone!" I quickly went upstage, because if Ben wanted to continue the scene, I wanted to be as far away as possible from this disturbed young man. I wasn't brave enough to stick with the blocking. We continued acting, however, with me practically standing in back of Ben

Gazzara. This young man kept getting more agitated and talking to us from the orchestra.

It must have lasted only a few minutes, but it seemed like hours. I was really frightened. The young man, who I assume was a drug addict, could have had a gun or knife, and the play obviously disturbed him. Finally, the manager of the theater and two ushers got him out of his seat and out of the theater. For the next few performances, when we got to that scene, Ben was very puzzled by my new blocking, because I would always find a reason to stand in back of him or kneel behind some furniture.

All my adult life I'd fantasized about starring in a hit show on Broadway with my name in lights up on the marquee. At last I was living out my fantasy—so the following is still inexplicable to me:

For Christmas I'd given my daughter tiny roller skates, and I gave myself big roller skates. The first matinee day after Christmas, I decided we should both learn how to use them. I had been a crackerjack roller skater when I was a kid in Brooklyn, but I hadn't done it for a long, long time. When we got downstairs, I noticed there was a slight coating of ice on the sidewalk. It had rained the night before. That morning there were lovely icicles hanging from all the trees in Central Park, and the streets of Central Park West were shining with ice. I strapped only one roller skate on my child, but, remembering what a big-shot roller skater I'd been, I felt I could certainly handle two skates. I took no more than one step, and I fell, and I heard the ankle crack. I lay there on the sidewalk, gazing at the snow-filled sky, and wondered what the hell I thought I was doing.

Here it was, ten o'clock on the morning of a matinee day, and I had decided to teach my daughter to roller-skate on ice. The show was playing to standing room only, and I had visions of Jay Julien shooting me, as they did to horses. Somehow or the other, my mother got an ambulance; my ankle was X-rayed and then put in a cast. I took some pain pills and showed up at the theater as usual at half-hour, hoping no one would notice. I was in terrible pain, but I thought I could still somehow do the matinee. The assistant stage manager, Eddie, took one look and phoned Jay.

Jay rushed over, and we had a cast meeting about my cast. Chris White, a lovely young actress, who was playing one of the junkies, Putski, was my understudy and had had perhaps two rehearsals. I began weeping bitterly, feeling sure that I had destroyed the show. Jay just called another ambulance to take me home on a stretcher.

"Go home and rest until Monday," he said, "and then we'll either reblock the show and see if you can perform with that thing on your leg, or we'll have to close for eight weeks."

Ben Gazzara was very annoyed and reminded Jay that there were two stars performing in *A Hatful of Rain*. I couldn't get involved in the argument, because the men in the white coats were carrying me out to the second ambulance. I was sure they were taking me to the booby hatch, but all they did was bring me back to my apartment. My mother gave me some more pain medicine and, still arguing, I went to sleep. As I drifted off, I was still trying to figure out why I had done such a stupid thing.

Tony called me after the matinee and told me that when they'd announced that Miss Shelley Winters's understudy would be going on, half the audience had rushed to the box office to change their tickets or ask for their money back. This did nothing to cheer me up. I asked Tony how Chris had been in the role. Long pause.

"She's a good actress, Shelley," he said, "but, without you, there doesn't seem to be a play on the stage."

Perhaps I was selfish, but that was music to my ears and my leg stopped hurting. I thanked him.

"Don't worry, honey," he reassured me. "You'll be back in the show on Monday."

I didn't know how I could possibly do it, because the set was on two levels. But I resolved somehow to find a way to accommodate my broken leg. That Monday we had a lengthy rehearsal, and Frank Corsaro reblocked the whole play so that I could move slowly from room to room, and most of my scenes would be sitting down. That night, I put a long black knee sock over my cast, and I swear, after the first five minutes, the audience forgot about my broken leg. Except they did give me an ovation at the end of the show. I was resting in my dressing room when Joan Crawford came backstage.

"Well, Shelley," she haughtily informed me, "you were very powerful and had the entire audience weeping, but if I had a role with a drug-addict husband, was seven months pregnant, and had a broken leg, I could make the entire audience faint."

She then kissed me and added, "For God's sake, on opening night, when they say 'go break a leg,' they don't mean you literally do it. It's an expression of good luck."

She was right. But from that time on, when I was opening in a show, I warned people not to say, "Break a leg." At one point, Vincent Sardi put a sign above the bar saying, NEVER WISH A METHOD ACTRESS OR ACTOR GOOD LUCK BY SAYING GO BREAK A LEG.

The show was a joy to do, but some weeks we were sure it was jinxed. Eddie Julien broke his arm the next week. Then the week after that, Ben Gazzara jumped off the stage and left with the audience through the front lobby. I believe he beat them to the exit doors. His then-wife, from whom he was separated, had come in the backstage door of the Lyceum, and his girlfriend Elaine Stritch was up in his dressing room.

I used to get butterflies before I went on, and I had the habit of taking a swallow of rhubarb and soda to calm my stomach when the stage manager called, "Five minutes." I used to buy this in a brown bottle at Walgreen's drugstore. One day, I also bought nail-polish remover in a Walgreen's brown bottle. Sure enough, a day or so later, I took a swallow from the nail-polish remover bottle instead of the rhubarb and soda. Luckily, I spit most of it out, but at that performance the stage manager, Len Bedsow, was handing me milk. He stood in the wings, and every time I made an exit, or when someone else had a long speech, I would run into the wings and drink milk. Luckily there were no ill effects, but I think Jay Julien's hair turned gray during the first six months of *A Hatful of Rain.*

* * *

On February 14, Valentine's Day, which is my daughter's birthday, I decided she should have her third birthday party at Sardi's. I was hobbling on my cast, holding her little hand; the nurse held her other hand, and my mother made sure we didn't all fall down. We had twelve tots, all about three or four years old, including Tony's little nephew. In an hour, I realized that twelve tots could destroy Sardi's, and that day they almost did.

Then I had had this brilliant idea that we should all see *The Wizard of Oz*. Universal had arranged to show it for us at the Universal projection room. The lovely film started, and suddenly all the kids were terrified and crying. They could only stand about ten minutes of the film, so we had it shut off, and the exhausted mothers tried to get them under control again. They screamed and cried for two hours. I hadn't realized they were too young for it. That party turned out to be one of my less-than-great inspirations. Next time I saw Judy Garland, I told her about it.

"You have to be grown up to like *The Wizard of Oz*," she said. "I was terrified of it while I was making it, and I was sixteen."

Tony seemed very happy in *A Hatful of Rain*, and often we'd all go out afterwards and try various Italian restaurants. Unlike other shows I'd been in, this company hung out together.

Then suddenly, sometime in the middle of March, Tony had a very strange second act. He seemed to be somehow saying goodbye to me underneath the playwright's lines. Since that's not Polo's intention in the second act, I became puzzled and alarmed. When we came off the stage at the second-act intermission, Tony fainted in the wings. The theater doctor was close by, and his diagnosis was that Tony had had a couple of drinks and had passed out. Perhaps with my sixth sense, I somehow knew differently.

I ran upstairs to Tony's dressing room and found an empty bottle of Miltown in the wastepaper basket. I knew that that bottle had been full the night before. He sometimes took half a Miltown before he went on, to relieve

175

tension. I ran downstairs and begged Len to get the ambulance from Roosevelt Hospital. It came quickly. I told the young doctors that I thought he had taken a bottle of Miltown and washed it down with whiskey. I wanted to get in the ambulance with him, but Jay forcibly restrained me. I had to go back and do the third act. Again Harry Guardino took over the part of Polo, and Steve Gravers took over Harry Guardino's part, and so on, but the audience still stayed riveted to their seats.

As soon as the curtain came down, without taking my bows and still in makeup and costume, I took a cab to Roosevelt Hospital. As I went in the emergency door, I could hear the doctors slapping Tony awake. He had at last admitted he had taken the Miltowns. They pumped his stomach and got most of it out, and I stayed with him the rest of the night and gave him coffee.

That early morning, after he had safely gone to sleep, I sat there in yet another bleak hospital room and tried to understand why this role was so difficult for Tony. He was seeing a psychiatrist, he was getting bravos at the curtain, and his agent and producers were calling him with all kinds of offers. Was it me? I still don't know. He seemed to need and love me—I certainly did him. I now think perhaps I got involved with Tony so quickly so I wouldn't have time to feel the pain of the divorce from Vittorio. Perhaps Tony sensed this.

I knew that Tony had had a sad, sporadic relationship with his natural father. His mother and father had been separated when he was very young, and he had to go every week to his father's apartment to get the $8 check for child support. I knew he had been raised by his mother and two aunts. I felt that he cared for me, and I certainly cared for him, but there was something in the play that triggered this terrible anxiety in him, and having to repeat it eight times a week seemed almost too much for him. It took me a long time to face this fact.

My feelings about this were confirmed a few nights later, when he had come back into the play. In the fight scene with Polo in the third act, Frank Silvera, the father, taking off his coat, demanded that his son take off his coat and fight. Polo's lines are, "Come on, Pop. Forget it." But at this performance, Tony, in his role as Polo, suddenly departed from the lines and began to take his coat off in order to have a real fistfight with his father. Somehow, Frank Silvera avoided a fight and got him back into the play.

I began to talk to Tony about playing the role of Polo in a more superficial manner. At first he argued about it, but then he tried it out at a matinee. There were no more bravos, but he still got enormous applause, and he was able to relax and enjoy his dinner between the matinees and evening performances.

One spring day after the matinee, Tony insisted we have dinner alone. He handed me a little box with the dessert, and, when I opened it, I almost fainted. There was a huge emerald-cut diamond ring in the box. I stared at it. Either it was fake or Tony had stolen it. It was about three carats and a beautiful color. I looked at him in amazement.

With a trembling voice, I said, "Tony, where the hell did you get this? What did you do?"

Hurt and angry, he replied, "I got it in the wholesale jewelry district, and I'm buying it on time. I put $400 down on it. In a couple of years, I'll have it paid off. What's the matter, don't you want to be engaged to me?"

I thought it over and whispered, "We could *'be engaged to be engaged.'* Neither one of our divorces is final."

Tony had been married when he was very young. The girl was a secretary who lived somewhere in Greenwich Village. I think this was during his Howard Johnson period. They had been separated for a couple of years, and he had only just gotten a legal separation. He had not filed for divorce and I hadn't wanted him to.

"Tell me the name of the store," I continued whispering, "and I'll see if I can get the price reduced a little. After all, we'll be giving this shop a lot of publicity."

He gave me the receipt for the ring, and, at the next performance, I wore the ring pinned to the inside of my girdle. I knew this present was Tony's way of thanking me, and, besides, he knew that "all movie stars love diamonds." That night, I was quite sleepless and wondered if it really constituted an engagement. I was mad about him physically, but I had no intention of marrying anybody in the near future. But I was scared he would be very angry if I gave him the ring back. So the next day I hiked over to the wholesale jewelry district, found the shop, and almost passed out when they told me how much the ring was.

Tony was getting $750 a week in the play, which meant he was giving $75 a week to his agent, I didn't know how much to support his mother, and though he was having all his meals at my house, he was living in a hotel. So how could he afford this ring? I got the jeweler to reduce the price of the ring by $1,000. I told him to tell Tony that, because of tax reasons, he would only take $100 a week from him. I told the jeweler that I would send him $200 a week, but I swore him to secrecy, and I left him happy about the whole thing.

That ring became a big problem. We used to walk home at night from the theater, sometimes through the park, and even thirty years ago it was not very wise to walk around New York late at night with a big diamond ring on your finger. While performing, I was loath to leave it in my dressing room, and I'd pin it to my bra or panties, and a couple of times I dropped it during the show. I prayed that somebody would find it and return it to me after the act. Nowadays it rests in the vault at the bank, and every now and then I go and look at it. But it was a beautiful gesture, and I wore it for the next decade. I know, now as then, Tony's mathematics are as vague as mine, so when he left the show, the jeweler told him the ring was paid for. In the years to come Tony was to buy me many Tiffany baubles, but this engaged-to-be-engaged ring was the first and last one that I ever helped him pay for.

For a couple of months, everything seemed fine and happy, and then one night, during the second intermission, the pill thing happened again—this time with sleeping pills—and Tony could not do the third act. I at last had to face the reality that Tony could not do this play.

Whatever it was about *A Hatful of Rain* that made him act just great, there was something else in it that could destroy him. Sometimes during my 3:00 A.M. dooms, I would wonder if it was acting with me. But since I was so nuts about him this insight didn't last very long. We had an intelligent talk, and we agreed that he should ask Jay to release him from the rest of his contract.

I remember that night so well. Harry Guardino was doing Tony's role, and Tony watched him from the back of the theater. Afterwards, we walked to Central Park and sat on a bench. It was a cold spring. Tony put his arm around me, and we were both crying. It had been such a joy to act together.

"We'll work together again in a comedy," I said. "Remember all the fun we had in *Wedding Breakfast?* You'll see, Tony, we'll do lots of films and plays together." So far, we haven't. I doubt we will after this book.

Tony's psychiatrist suggested that he go to a hotel out on Long Island and stay alone and quiet for a month. That is what Tony did. We talked on the phone a couple of nights a week and for an hour on Sundays. When he came back to New York, it was summer. He looked great, and he was calm.

Sometime during this period, I heard that Elia Kazan was about to do a film called *A Face in the Crowd*. The scuttlebutt around the Actors Studio was that Andy Griffith was playing a sort of Huey Long character in it. I had been worried about the gossip that had resulted from Tony's having left the show before the end of the season. I called Kazan and asked him if there wasn't a part in his new film that perhaps Tony could do. I knew that Gadge thought very highly of Tony's acting abilities and had read his reviews.

"As a matter of fact, there is," Kazan said. "It's not the lead, but it's a very important part. I'll talk to Tony's agent about it."

The next day, Tony's agent called him and said, "You'll be leaving for the South in a month to be in Elia Kazan's new film."

In the world of the theater, to leave a show for a film was frowned upon, though it was acceptable in terms of a long career. But to leave a show without a job was unacceptable, and I felt this fortuitous role in a Kazan picture would save Tony's career. And so it did.

I next called my publicity man, Arthur Jacobs, in Hollywood and told him to release a story that would say that Tony Franciosa had been signed by Elia Kazan for a starring role in *A Face in the Crowd,* which would be the first of three important pictures he had signed to do for Kazan's company.

After Tony began to work in *Face in the Crowd* and Kazan saw his rushes, he insisted that Tony live up to his three-picture commitment that Shelley's publicity man had announced. When Tony saw the contract, he wanted to buy me another ring.

"Wait a minute, dear," I said. "Pay for the first one first."

In June, we all notified Jay that we were leaving *Hatful of Rain* July 1, which in those days was a run-of-the-play contract. Jay could not believe it—that, after only one season, we were all going to leave this Broadway smash that we had all worked on so hard to turn into a hit. Ben was leaving to do *Anatomy of a Murder,* and I was leaving just to accompany Tony to California. In those days I thought every show I did would be a smash hit, since this one was. That spring of 1956, I suspect I was thinking with some part of my anatomy other than my brain.

I rehearsed with a new actor for Ben's role, Steve McQueen. I believe he played a few performances, then Jay fired him. Steve rode around New York on his motorcycle, was charming, never punctual, and imitated Marlon Brando whenever he had a chance. In retrospect, I don't think Jay feels firing Steve McQueen was a masterful decision.

Jay hired Vivian Blaine to do my role, and, when I returned in the fall and went to see the play and saw her do my Celia, I got physically ill and had to leave the theater. Her interpretation was so different from mine— good but different. My reaction was violent; it was as if someone had stolen my soul. I had created the role of Celia, and I could not bear watching someone else interpreting her.

1

2

3

*W*hen we were roommates, Marilyn and I shared a mink coat and this bathing suit which we used for cheesecake photo sessions. After a decade, the mink coat lined a heavy black cloth coat. It came in handy walking down freezing Ninth Avenue to the Actors Studio.

*D*ylan Thomas, whom both of us cooked for, and who I didn't realize was a poet until he sent me funny postcards and *Portrait of the Artist as a Young Dog* with a loving autograph. I never thought I had a serious romance with him until I read his wife's book.

4

*M*y mother and father escorting me the afternoon before we dressed for the Academy Awards where I was nominated Best Actress for *A Place in the Sun*. I didn't win and my mother, without my knowledge, demanded a recount since the balloting is secret. She never could get them to do it.

6

5

*M*y wedding with Vittorio. I tore up all the pictures of the divorce.

*V*ittorio arrived in Beverly Hills when my daughter was two months old because he was contracted to *Hamlet* in Genoa and she was two months premature.

*J*immy Dean, friend, prankster, in the parking lot across the street from Googies, scaring us by revving his motorcycle. He constantly confused real life with acting and acting with real life.

*S*ydney Chaplin, friend, worthy opponent, tennis teacher, who taught me mostly how to have a wonderful time spending very little money as we rushed all over Los Angeles.

*M*y little girl learning about her father from the pictures in his "Amleto."

9

10

*V*ittorio and I pretending we're invisible to each other as we work in the same movie, *Mambo*, in freezing Venice, while the entire population of the city is discussing our divorce terms.

*J*erry Geisler, famous lawyer, escorting me to the California courtroom. Marilyn and I also shared Jerry Geisler.

11   12

*M*y beloved teacher Charles Laughton, who had to constantly remind me that I was a fine actress and not the tits 'n ass starlet that Universal kept forcing me to be. James Wong Howe made the lighting and the sets so eerie and poetic on *Night of the Hunter* that I think Mitchum and I did some of our best work.

14

13

15

*U*niversal didn't care about Oscars. They just wanted black lace stockings, and giving in to that is what I've been fighting all my life.

*N*ick Ray, a very fine director and the brightest, most educated man I ever knew. Marilyn dated him, too, and thought his gray hair was sexy.

*W*orking with John Garfield was a joy. He made me unconscious of the camera, but somehow made James Wong Howe get my prettiest angles. Despite serious directors constantly borrowing me for good films, Universal only wrote films for their blonde sexpot.

19

The Big Knife with Ida Lupino and Jack Palance was the movie version of the play by Clifford Odets. Robert Aldrich directed. Although it was a couple of years after Garfield's death, while working on this film I constantly thought about the way he had died.

Carson McCullers and Tennessee Williams, two of the greatest poets and writers of this century. It was my honor and privilege and good luck to have known them.

20

*S*terling Hay-
den testifying
for HUAC,
something I
never allowed
myself to hear
on the radio or
see on
television.

21

*M*y dearest
friend, Connie
Dowling, tell-
ing me not to
take my baby
to Italy.

22

23

*R*osie,
Shelley,
and baby
absorbing
British culture
and speech.

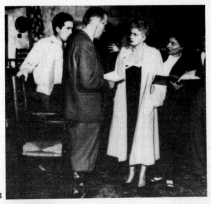

*W*orking with Wilfrid Hyde-White and Muriel Box in *Cash on Delivery*. When they spoke "Mayfair" my Brooklynese asserted itself and I was sometimes not sure what was being said.

24

25

*W*henever I see a film about Irish elves, I know it's true because I worked with John Gregson.

26

*H*ere I am "not eating" at a luncheon with Jane Russell and Mona Freeman so I would fit into my dress the next night when I was to be presented to the Queen.

*S*ome of the gang being shown around London. Left to right, Peter Noble, a latter-day Alan Ladd, Mary Noble, not backstage wife (she was in *Lolita* with me), blonde me, and Adolph Green who, though we went to the same drama school, has never written a musical for me.

27

*T*he prime of Laurence Olivier. I don't know and don't care who the lady was with him. It just wasn't me!

28

*S*ean Connery and the famous coat. I think I'm the only dame who ever got jewels or furs from this Scotsman. Some time right after this, Sean gave a press conference in which he announced he was directing me in a new play, *The Secret of the World*, and that we would film it together. I never heard another word about it. I never read the play. The coat is very shabby now but I can't bear to give it away.

29

30

*D*oing *Sorry, Wrong Number*, and no matter how dramatic the role I had to always look pretty whether I was listening to the planning of my murder, being strangled, whatever. My performance in this show, I'm sure, helped kill live television.

*R*eliving my adolescence and enjoying every moment of it at Coney Island with Tony Franciosa.

31

*W*hen Frank Corsaro directed rehearsals for *A Hatful of Rain* they were so fascinating we all were loath to leave the theater even if Frank was rehearsing scenes we were not in.

33

32

*J*ack Palance acting too realistically in *I Died a Thousand Times*. Thank goodness Tony was visiting me in California, understood, and stopped the scene.

*F*un and fights, writing late at night at Downey's, but Mike Gazzo finally wrote a great part in a great play for me in *A Hatful of Rain*.

*B*en Gazzara wanted me to rest my cast for the necessary eight weeks. But after two performances when half the audience left, he was glad to hold me as I hopped around the stage.

If this collage seems "furioso" it is nothing compared to the actual production. The audience always left the theater attacking the judicial and drug programs of New York City, New York State, and the Federal government. And this was 1956!

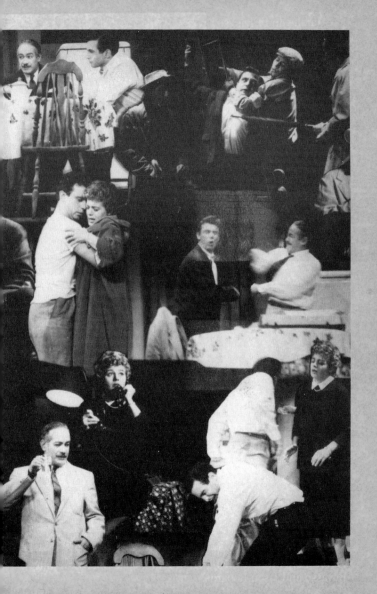

*N*atalie and Elvis, so young and happy, and looking forward to a life of artistic freedom and personal fulfillment together.

37

38

*H*ere I am proudly giving out the first Obie Awards to Julie Bovasso and Jason Robards.

12

I believe I felt guilty about Tony's nervous breakdown and having to leave the show. So that July, I gathered up my little family, and we returned to California. My engaged-to-be-engaged fiancé Tony Franciosa got a little suite at the good old reliable Chateau Marmont. I cared so much for him, I felt that if I used all my Hollywood know-how to get his career safely launched my guilt feelings would go away. So I began to drag Tony around to all the parties and posh spots of Hollywood. I never even went to see my agent or publicity man. I just thought about Tony and how to make him well and happy. Tony's agent, Stan Kamen of the William Morris office, was sure Tony would connect and so advanced him money to buy some clothes and to rent a car.

One afternoon, I took Tony to the famous men's tailor Sy Devore on Vine Street. He needed a sport jacket, slacks, and a dark suit. Tony spent an hour gazing at fabrics, unable to make up his mind. I had to take my daughter for a swimming lesson, so I left him there, and Sy promised to drop him off at the Chateau. When I met Tony for dinner at the Players, he was delirious with joy. He loved Sy's clothes, so he had bought thirty-two articles of clothing, including suits, jackets, slacks, and overcoats—I think about $6–7,000 worth. He looked so happy about it I didn't have the heart to tell him it was foolhardy.

He tried every one of them on for me when they were ready. He had never had a custom-made thing in his life —he'd just bought clothes off the rack, mostly at Barney's, which was an inexpensive store in those days. Then, I remembered my first days under contract, when I had done almost the same thing.

A couple of weeks later, we went to a Hollywood party at Jean Simmons's house. Her director, Robert Wise, was there, and they were talking about a movie called *This Could Be the Night,* to be filmed at Metro. The leading male role was a tough, charming young gangster from 118th Street, and Jean Simmons's role was of a teacher who converts this young man to civilization. Robert Wise had seen us in *Hatful,* and I can't remember whether I talked him into testing Tony or into just giving him the role.

I think *This Could Be the Night* was the best film that Tony ever did. He didn't yet know anything about his good camera angles, as he hadn't viewed any rushes, so he wasn't criticizing his looks. He was completely relaxed, funny, and charming, and Robert Wise got a wonderful kind of Cary Grantish performance out of him. Of course, when Metro called his agent, they said if they gave Tony this starring role, they wanted a three-picture commitment, "like Kazan had gotten." I was beginning to wonder if perhaps I shouldn't be an agent.

Later that month, I went to Fox to see the producer of the film *A Hatful of Rain.* Fox had bought the play. I can't remember the producer, but I sat and told Fred Zinnemann, the director, what a terrible mistake he was making in not hiring Tony to play the role of Polo. I seemed to have forgotten that I had been in the play, too, and had gotten rave notices playing Celia. Zinnemann explained to me that they were already in negotiation with Eli Wallach, but, as luck would have it, Eli Wallach's agent, Peter Witt, asked for a tremendous amount of money, whereupon Fox ended the negotiations and hired Tony to re-create his role of Polo. They of course insisted on a three-picture deal too.

I was deeply disappointed in not playing in the film version of *Hatful* the role I had so lovingly created in those long rehearsals, during the tour, and on Broadway. But when I read Tony's film script, I realized that they had foolishly transferred the locale from its tenement background to a middle-class housing project, and they had made the family middle-class Irish rather than lower-class Italian. Hollywood often does this with the purported intention of making the themes of screenplays more acceptable to the average American. It very seldom works, and they emasculate every play or book that they attempt this with. So the only remarkable thing about the film *A Hatful of Rain* was Tony Franciosa's performance. He was nominated for an Oscar.

During that summer, Tony and I got a little house at the beach, and Tony and my daughter became beach buddies. The first time my daughter saw the Pacific Ocean from the balcony of the little house, she looked at Tony and me and said, "My, what a big pool we got, Mommy!" Neither one of those kids had ever had a vacation on a lovely beach, with "Mama" seeing to it that they had dry clothes and sneakers and an ample breakfast, lunch, and dinner. We would roast marshmallows at night and sing songs, and, whatever Tony's problems had been that past winter, he certainly seemed fully recovered now. He loved Hollywood, and Hollywood loved him.

Before I had left New York, Cheryl Crawford, the distinguished and successful Broadway producer, had given me the script of a play called *The Girls of Summer* by Richard Nash, who had just scored a critical and commercial success with *The Rainmaker* on Broadway, starring Geraldine Page. I loved it in the first reading. Cheryl was planning to cast it with members of the Actors Studio, and Jack Garfein, a member of the directors' unit, would direct. Jack Garfein's wife, Carroll Baker, was supposed to play my younger sister, but something called *Baby Doll* got in the way. What the play is remembered mostly for is its opening trumpet solo of a haunting melody called "Girls of Summer," which was the first tune Stephen Sondheim ever had on Broadway.

I had not told Tony that I planned to return to New York in late August and start rehearsing this play in September. As it turned out, he would be shooting *Hatful* in New York while I was rehearsing, so I didn't think the separation would be too long this time. It didn't occur to me then to wonder, since I loved New York and I was planning to live and work there, why I was busily getting Tony signed up for films in California. But this would be Tony's third film, and he now had confidence in his comedic abilities and, I knew, in his soon-to-arrive movie stardom.

My film agent, who did not know I had already signed a run-of-the-play contract for *Girls of Summer*, kept sending me mediocre scripts. In fact, Universal kept notifying me that they were loaning me out to various studios, but I decided to ignore all these notifications, and I would let my lawyer and New York agent fight it out if necessary. As it turned out, they didn't fight my decision. They just added the time to my seven-year contract.

But the high point of all this happened while I was packing, and my agent called to tell me he was negotiating a new seven-year contract at Universal, for which I would get $1 million over the contract period of the next seven years and freedom to do plays and independent films. I was afraid to tell him that I already had a play contract, so I just said, "Herb, try to make it two million." I was joking, but he did just that. And when we finally sat in the office of Mr. Jaffe, the head of his agency, I tried to give many reasons about my artistic freedom to make Herb feel less upset when I refused to sign the new $2 million seven-year contract that he had so carefully negotiated.

That summer had been fun for all of us. Shirley Booth was touring in William Marchant's *The Desk Set*, so my old friends Bill Marchant and Alex Fondas were also at the Chateau Marmont, as were Sidney Poitier and Harry Belafonte. They were all busy making films.

When we weren't at the beach, we would swim in the Chateau Marmont pool, so my kid was becoming a crackerjack swimmer and diver. I took her everywhere with me—to the theater, to parties, to the studios, and to the Beverly Hills Tennis Club. I knew that soon I would be immersed in difficult, time-consuming rehearsals of a new play, so I wanted to spend every moment I could with her.

Tony finally accepted the fact that I had signed for this new play. We had been inseparable for almost two years, but I felt that now was the time for us to both take care of our acting careers, and he would return to New York and we would be together in five or six weeks. He drove us all to the airport with all our luggage (he still hadn't had time to get a license), and when I waved goodbye from the plane, I hoped that we could both do some growing up if our relationship was to continue.

Marilyn Monroe was on the plane, looking gorgeous, and she whispered to me that she had decided to move to New York permanently and, incidentally, she had invested $5,000 in my play, *Girls of Summer*. I was quite surprised by this information and hoped both decisions had been wise ones and would pay her glorious dividends.

When I reported for rehearsals the next day at the theater, everyone had set clocks back the night before, but my mother at midnight had set hers the wrong way (I'm still vague about which way you do set it). Anyway, I arrived at the first rehearsal two hours late. The entire cast of *Girls of Summer* glared at me. Richard Nash, the director Jack Garfein, and the producer Cheryl Crawford gave me the silent treatment. I didn't know what was wrong, because I didn't know I was two hours late. By my mother's clock over the stove I was on time. Finally Cheryl Crawford said, "Shelley, sit down. We'll have *another* reading of the play."

George Peppard and Arthur Storch began to read the first scene, and Pat Hingle whispered, "Kiddo, why are you two hours late?"

I looked at him aghast and said, "Pat, you're bananas!"

"You were supposed to set your clocks forward last night," he said, "not back." And then I realized what my mother had done.

The cast of *Girls of Summer* was mostly Actors Studio members but very young ones, and the play had neither the intensity nor the connection with social problems that *A Hatful of Rain* had. It's about two sisters who own a three-flat converted apartment house at the beach in Santa Monica, the younger one a ballet dancer, the older one (me) very protective of her. A construction worker in a rented red Jaguar picks the younger woman up coming out of ballet school and impresses her with his vacation flash. The older sister spends the summer trying to break up the relationship. She doesn't realize until the end of the play that she has done this so viciously because she is repressed sexually and is tremendously attracted to the construction worker herself. I think that was what it was about.

I rehearsed *Girls of Summer* for four weeks, and we took it on the road for six weeks, but I'm still not sure of its plot. In fact, I can't even remember the ending. The only thing I'm positive of about *Girls of Summer* is that about a year later, after it had closed, Hal Wallis, who had bought the play for Paramount, made a test of Elvis Presley for the role of the construction worker. Natalie Wood had seen the play and she tested with Elvis. She was to play the younger sister. I was in the projection room when they showed the test, probably because I had been aiding and abetting Elvis and Natalie's romance, and I had coached them in their test scene. The scene was wonderful. I never again saw Elvis do such a remarkable job of acting. I was sure that they would do the film, and I was hoping that I would re-create my role of the older sister. When the lights went up in that projection room, Elvis looked overjoyed and hugged Natalie. She and I both were so happy we practically cried. Then a rough, loud Southern voice in the back of the projection room said, "He's not going to be that kind of movie star! The money is in the music!"

Elvis, Natalie, and I froze. Hal Wallis turned to Colonel Parker and said, "But you made a deal with Paramount! We don't do big musicals here. MGM does them. We buy important novels and plays."

"Well, then he'll do a lot of little musicals," Colonel

Parker said, "like Crosby's and Bob Hope's road pictures."

I turned to Elvis, hoping he would argue about this important decision. He didn't open his mouth. He just looked at the floor. In retrospect, I realize it was the single most destructive decision that was ever made in regard to Elvis's career. He wouldn't argue with Colonel Parker about it. He just accepted the decision. I believe if he had worked with good directors and studied acting seriously and if that riveting sexual quality he had could have been shown on the screen in a dramatic role, he would have had a different kind of success. The only other actor I have ever seen who had that quality is Marlon Brando. Elvis could have been a serious dramatic actor, too, and still made money with his music, but who knows? He certainly would have had a happier and more fulfilled life.

During that period, Elvis would often come to my house, once bringing me a sack of manure for my dried-up lawn. He got his buddies to help him spread it over the lawn, and they would come and water it every day.

Natalie and Elvis's idea of being inconspicuous was wearing all white and driving a huge, convertible white Cadillac. Sometimes I would go to the movies with them. When we entered, I often felt we were the entertainment. They would sit close to each other, down front. I would hide somewhere on the side, but they gave off such an aura of success and happiness and fun that it seemed as if the projectionist had put a spotlight on them. The audience ignored the movie, stood up, and watched Elvis and Natalie. Finally, to get some privacy, Natalie forced him to go to the movies incognito. She taught him that the audience's reaction was very important and must be studied. I believe, after that romance, Elvis never again went into a movie theater unless he'd bought out the whole house.

Many years later, when I played Elvis's mother, Gladys, in a very good TV show, which was one of the few TV shows ever distributed as a movie, I was able to help Kurt Russell play Elvis very authentically—not just to imitate the musical legend but to get at the essence of this young, aspiring, yet sad man. During the time I knew him he would call his mother in Memphis at precisely 7:00 P.M. every single night.

I didn't start to work on *Elvis* until it had been shooting about ten days, and both Kurt and the director felt his performance was one-dimensional. I got Kurt to find the disappointments in his own experience that were perhaps parallel to Elvis's. It worked. He began to be so much like Elvis that one day when we were standing in front of a house in Pasadena, almost an exact duplicate of Graceland, two youngsters driving sports cars approached us from opposite directions. They were so engrossed in watching this seeming reincarnation of Elvis that they hit each other and, unfortunately, they had to be taken to the hospital in ambulances. I think they were both seriously injured. I hope not.

I had talked to Kurt about Elvis and his sweetness and aspirations for many days, and I believe he captured the essence of Elvis Presley in that film rather than just imitating him.

Tony was shooting the film of *A Hatful of Rain* in New York while I rehearsed *Girls of Summer*. The tour of *Girls of Summer* was noted for its constant rewrites and several changes of cast. Although the play had many beautiful things in it, what I noted then and later through many plays during my career was that when a playwright has the pressures of constantly rewriting, and the actors have to rehearse new scenes in the afternoon and then play a different one at night, and at the next performance try to put the new scene in, the result is often a shambles.

George Peppard, who played the serious boyfriend of my young sister, could not, during this period, walk and talk at the same time. I believe it was his first play, and I know later he became a very accomplished actor, but in 1956, when he was on the stage, he got a glazed look in his eyes and sweated. I don't mean he perspired, he sweated. When I see actors experience the profession of acting with agony, I often wonder why they want to put themselves through such torment. Of course, there are opening-night butterflies and the fear of the critics. But after a couple of weeks, when we feel secure in the role and that the live audience is out there responding—acting is a joy that nothing else, no other human experience, I believe, can touch. It is instantaneous and gratifying. When you've given a good performance, you're higher than anything else can make you. Unfortunately, in *Girls of Summer* it did not happen very often.

When we got to New York, Richard Nash had a rewrite of the first act. Cheryl Crawford, the producer, decided to have Clifford Odets redirect the play for a few performances. Clifford had an ear for human speech. He made us stop making the dialogue sound as if it was written in stone, and we began to throw away lines and develop comic timing. I don't think the play lost any of its meanings. I believe this approach enhanced its meanings. The audience began enjoying themselves, and it was altogether a different play from the one we had been performing up to then, and I began to have some hope for this, my second important play on Broadway.

By the day of opening night, a rehearsal was called for 9:00 A.M., and Jack Garfein, at the instruction of Richard Nash, redirected the play back to its deathless-dialogue performance. We worked until 8:00 P.M., and on that opening night I never even got to set my hair. I think it was the worst opening night that any group of actors ever had. All the laughs were out of the play.

I became so desperate over the lack of audience response that at one point in the third act I was trying to use an affective memory in a scene with Pat Hingle, and I got so confused that I did not know which version I was doing—Richard Nash's, Clifford Odets's, or my own life. I went up in the lines. Pat Hingle somehow got me back into the play, but the critics thought that I didn't know my lines. I knew my lines. I just didn't know which thoughts to use to produce those lines. I had been given completely opposite directions during the rehearsals of the last week. I believe *Girls of Summer* ran a couple of weeks longer to accommodate the theater parties, then closed.

A Hatful of Rain had been such a personal triumph and such an extraordinary theater experience. I believed, as

I said earlier, that every play I did after that would be a hit. This nonsensical, magical thinking got me into severe emotional trouble. I was devastated by the failure of *Girls of Summer*, and wished I had done some movies when I was in California that past summer. To make matters worse, Tony was shooting the exterior location scenes of *Hatful* in New York. I never went on the set with him, and he knew I was secretly suffering because I had not been cast as Celia in the film.

That winter, God and only God sent me a wonderful housekeeper. Her name was Molly Epps. She stayed with me until my daughter graduated from college, and when Molly finally left to get her own apartment, I was so devastated that I sold that spacious apartment on Central Park West for $43,000. I believe Meryl Streep lives in it now and bought it for $2 million. Well, real estate has never been my forte. I'm an actress, not an investor, and I buy homes, not houses.

That same winter I did some big TV show that made one of the sponsors, Macy's-Bamberger's, give me a huge stand-up refrigerator and a huge stand-up freezer. They were big enough to accommodate a ranch that employed a dozen field hands. I had never eaten frozen food very much, so I was rather stunned at seeing hundreds of gourmet steaks and chickens and lamb chops, which Macy's-Bamberger's supplied me with. When Vittorio came to New York for his daughter's fourth birthday, he looked at all this frozen food for about an hour. He kept opening the freezer door and looking at it. I do not believe they had frozen food in Italy yet. When he left to go to the airplane to fly home, he seemed quite angry.

"Don't you dare give that stuff to my child," he hissed. "You eat it if you want to, but I think it's dangerous."

To this day I do not think he trusts frozen food, and neither did Molly Epps, my housekeeper. I think she distributed it to various missions and church groups in Harlem, because I never got frozen food in my house—just fresh. My stomach and I thank Molly Epps.

Around this time, Edward R. Murrow asked me to do his famous show, "Person to Person." I was on the third floor of my building, so CBS had a huge truck outside with wires going to the cameras in my apartment. The cameramen went through my big apartment, interviewing Molly in the kitchen, me in the living room, my mother in the dining room, and my four-year-old child in her bedroom. She was very un-camera-shy and insisted on naming all the dwarfs from Disney's *Snow White*. Edward R. Murrow of course was interviewing us, but we just heard his voice as he was in the studio, watching us on the monitor. The experience was rather weird.

The wiring in that apartment was never the same after that "Person to Person" show. When you turned on a lamp in the living room, the light in my bathroom went on, etc. For years I called CBS and asked them to come back and fix the wiring in my apartment, but they never did.

When Tony finished his picture, he and I had had a lovely time in New York. He at last had a lot of money, and he took me to all the fancy restaurants. He also discovered Tiffany's and F.A.O. Schwarz, and at Christmastime he hired a professional decorator to decorate a huge tree. When my daughter came out at five or six o'clock in the morning, the living room looked as if Santa Claus had moved his entire stock to Central Park West. Tony had bought her about a hundred presents. They both spent the week between Christmas and New Year's opening them. At times I thought Tony was enjoying it more than my kid. I noticed that some of the toys were more appropriate for little boys than for little girls. I think everything that he couldn't have when he was a kid, such as a very expensive toy train, he bought that Christmas.

When he had to return to Hollywood to do *This Could Be the Night*, I felt very sad. With the exception of my show closing, this had been one of the happiest winters of my life, and I think it was somehow very important for Tony that *he* was working and *I* wasn't, and that *he* was making a lot of money and paying all the bills and I wasn't. It was that Christmas that he gave me diamond-and-sapphire earrings.

SHELLEY WINTERS

"The sapphires are for your blue eyes," he said, "and the diamonds are for diamonds."

I would spend hours explaining to Tony that his agent got 10 percent and his business manager got 10 percent and the government at least 20 percent, and that, although the figures he was getting for films seemed astronomical, he was really getting less than half that amount. But for a young man who had been working in Howard Johnson's just a couple of winters ago, the amounts of money seemed inexhaustible. He bought presents for his mother, his aunts, my mother, my housekeeper Molly, and anybody he could. He loved buying presents.

When Tony and I kissed at the airport and he got on the plane, he said, "Maybe we've been engaged to be engaged long enough. Maybe now we should just be engaged."

I kissed him to shut him up, and said, "Tony, aren't you still married to your first wife legally? So, let's talk about it when I get to California."

The plane took off, and as I drove myself home, my major emotion was frightened love. Why this feeling should appear after a sweet proposal I didn't know, and I just pushed it out of my mind.

During this period, I'd gotten to know Tony's mother and aunts quite well. His mother was a lovely woman and a great cook. She taught me how to make roasted peppers and other delicious Neapolitan dishes. I gather that she and her sisters had arrived from Naples thirty years ago. Their brother had met them at the boat. They had moved into the apartment they were still living in, where Tony had grown up, and his two aunts had gone to work for the Metropolitan Opera as seamstresses. Their brother took care of all their finances; they just turned over their paychecks to him. Before Tony left, he begged me to try to find a bigger, more comfortable apartment in a nicer neighborhood for his mother and aunts. I spent the next two years finding nice apartments for them. I finally figured out that no matter how nice or rent-controlled an apartment I found, they really didn't want it. They liked the one they were living in. They knew the priest and the church and the gangsters on the block. They felt safe on East 118th Street.

It took me a while to realize this. It happened one night when I took his aunts and his mother to the Metropolitan Opera. They had worked in the costume department of the Met for thirty years and had never seen an opera. Even though it was before women's lib, it seemed incredible to me in 1957 that grown women could be so dependent on the decisions of the menfolk in their family, but I finally understood they had been raised in Naples and had the mentality of the women of southern Italy. In the U.S.A. they lived as if they were still in Naples. Although they were intelligent and fun, they became frightened when they were away from all their male relatives on 118th Street. They seldom ventured away from their block. Tony's newfound celebrity and money scared them more than it delighted them. They had not yet seen him in a movie, and they were still suspicious of the reality of Hollywood.

I think they trusted me because I had been raised in Brooklyn in the bosom of a Neapolitan family who'd taken care of me when my parents were away. I understood most of what they said when they spoke Neapolitan slowly. They were happy, I believe, about my impending marriage to Tony and the fact that we were going to live in New York.

It took Tony and me two years to get his mother to come and visit Hollywood, and then the trip turned out to be a bit of a disaster.

My agent called me from Hollywood and said he was coming to New York and had something very important to talk to me about. I was hoping it was an important part in a distinguished film à la *A Double Life* or *A Place in the Sun*. We met in a very quiet restaurant on the East Side, and I was surprised when he explained to me that he would like me to do *A Double Life* on live television with Eric Portman. I couldn't imagine why.

"Herb," I said, "I could not possibly re-create the role that George Cukor so lovingly took me through, and it was the turning point of my career and made me a star.

I'm sure it would be too traumatic for me to try to do it again under the frenetic conditions of live television."

He then talked to me about my friend Marty Ritt, who had been blacklisted for a number of years since someone had named him. He was a fine director and had really gone through a terrible economic crisis during the past years. My agent, who was now representing Marty, explained that if I did *A Double Life* on live television with Marty directing me at CBS, Twentieth Century–Fox would feel he was safe enough for them to hire him, and it would get Marty off the blacklist. This is one of the crazy ways the House committee worked in those days.

I squirmed around and then said, "Can't we do something else besides *A Double Life?*"

"No, Shelley," Herb said. "That's what CBS wants."

I thought about it for a couple of long minutes and finally said, "Of course, if it will help Marty, who's a great director and has been my fellow actor since the days I first got into Equity, I will certainly help him get rid of the stigma of the blacklist."

I began rehearsing the following week, and, although Marty and I never discussed it, I knew he was very happy that I had agreed to repeat my role. Artistically, it was a nightmare. Eric Portman was a very fine actor, but he was not my beloved Ronald Colman. Live television is always difficult, especially when you have to make sure the right camera is following you, and that you're in the right light (or in the right closet).

At one rehearsal, Marty instructed me to come into my apartment, look around, turn on a light, and sit down. I came into the apartment, looked around emotionally, and sat down.

"No, Shelley," he said. "Just come in the apartment, turn on the light, and sit down."

I could hear him, and I thought I knew what he was talking about, but again I came into the apartment, looked around, and sat down.

"For God's sake," Marty said. "Why won't you turn on the light?"

To this day, I do not know why I answered him in the following manner: "Oh, Marty, I thought you meant my inner light.'' I guess I was so scared of repeating this role that I had gotten so much critical acclaim for that my acting gears had locked. I seemed incapable of acting and thinking at the same time.

We were doing this show in the new Brooklyn NBC color studio. I had dropped off my mother and Kathy and my little girl at some relatives' house in Brooklyn. I warned my mother not to let my child see this live show, as I am strangled at the end of it when Eric Portman recites Shakespeare's lines: ''Put out the light, and then put out the light: . . . I know not where is that Promethean heat/That can thy light relume.''

I was very glad when this live broadcast was over. It was a Sunday evening, and I climbed in the limousine quickly, knowing that I had done a less-than-brilliant job. We drove to my relatives' house, where my little family was waiting for me. When my daughter opened the door and saw me, she got a look of sheer joy and happiness on her face, and she hugged and kissed me so much that I knew she had seen the show somehow and had probably been traumatized by seeing her mother strangled on live television. I was furious and yelled at everybody. When I quieted down, they explained to me that the children had been in their cousin's room, where they'd been watching a children's show. Unbeknownst to the adults, who were all engrossed in *A Double Life*, the kids had turned on my show and watched it.

The whole TV show of *A Double Life* is a bad memory, but I am still glad that I was able to get Marty off the blacklist. With hindsight, it seems to me that all the people who appeared before the House Committee on Un-American Activities, whether they cooperated or not, had their lives destroyed to some degree.

I kept attending the Actors Studio, and Tony kept calling and saying, ''When are you coming back to California?''

My daughter was going to nursery school, my mother had found some ladies to play cards with, and my wonderful housekeeper, Molly, was not ready yet to uproot her life and come to California, so I had to find some reason for staying in New York. Perhaps the real reason I didn't want to go to California was that I couldn't face resolving my relationship with Tony. I believe I did a show for "The U.S. Steel Hour." Although I can't remember the name, I think it concerned a Polish wedding, and Pat Hingle and I starred in it. New York in those days was a mecca for serious actors—the Tennessee Williams–William Inge–Arthur Miller–Lillian Hellman playwriting renaissance was in full bloom on Broadway. Off-Broadway was just beginning to be a serious factor in the American theater; I presented the first Obies ever given, to Jason Robards and Julie Bovasso. Live television drama was in its heyday. When I'd get a case of the 3:00 A.M. dooms, I'd look at my big diamond engagement ring and try to think how I could be planning to marry a young man whose life for the next few years would certainly be in Hollywood. I knew that from here on I wanted to live in New York. The jet age had not yet arrived, and it was still a big deal, and exhausting, to fly back and forth. I resolved that I would discuss this with Tony during one of our 3:00 A.M. phone calls. I never did.

I stalled around New York until after my daughter's birthday, February 14. This time I gave her a party at home with twenty little nursery-school friends, and the only rambunctious thing that happened was that Alex Fondas, whose birthday is also Valentine's Day, knocked on the door, dressed as a huge white rabbit. Alex is over six feet tall and was then rather on the portly side. For the next couple of hours he had twenty little girls climbing all over him.

During that party there was another knock on the door, and in rolled a beautiful Steinway piano, tied with a huge pink ribbon and with a note saying, "Here's a grown-up present, from Tony." It was so sweet that I couldn't imagine how I could have planned a conversation with Tony that would no doubt upset him. When he called that night, he wished my kid a happy birthday, and then he told me later a wonderful TV script had arrived for me in California for the illustrious show "Climax." It was called "Don't Touch Me," and he had read this dramatic script and told my agent I would do it for $50,000; the going salary for "Climax" was about $20,000. Now Tony was agenting for *me*. He was busy doing his film and enjoying it, but I finally managed to promise him that I would be in Hollywood in about ten days to do this show and continue our engaged-to-be-engagement.

Sometime during this ten days, George Stevens called me from California, said he was coming to town, and asked me to go see the play *The Diary of Anne Frank* with him. Susan Strasberg had been playing Anne for almost two years, and I knew that Fox had bought the play for George Stevens to make into a film. My beloved George Stevens picked me up, and on the way to the theater I told him how happy I was that he was going to direct this poignant human document. I could not imagine what role I would play in this as all the women in it were much older than I, and I suspected I was too old to play Anne Frank—but not necessarily!

We saw the show and, alas, Susie Strasberg, who'd been in the play for two years, seemed a little tired and stilted. Stevens would not go backstage afterwards, and we went to Sardi's for supper. I tried to tell him how magnificent Susie had been when the play had first opened and that I knew it was impossible for an actor to play a role for two years and keep it fresh.

George, in his gruff way, said, "Shelley, stop selling me your friend! If I can get the financing to do this controversial film, I will have to get a *star* to play Anne. I think Audrey Hepburn is interested in doing it. If she gives me a positive answer, I will probably get the go-ahead from Fox, but, as yet, we do not even have a screenplay."

I was disappointed for my little friend, but I knew that was what Hollywood usually did, and I couldn't even yet admit to myself how heartbroken I was that I hadn't gotten to re-create Celia in the film version of *Hatful*. As it turned out, Audrey Hepburn withdrew from *The Diary of Anne Frank* because MGM had given her husband, Mel Ferrer, the chance to direct *Green Mansions*—if she starred in it. So Fox started a nationwide talent hunt to find a young Anne Frank.

A few months later, at a party at Lee and Paula Strasberg's house, I cornered Susie, and I begged her, *I begged her,* to send George Stevens a wire saying that she wanted to come to Hollywood, *without* her mother or father, and test for *Anne Frank.* She still photographed like a thirteen-year-old, and now that she had been away from the play for a while, I knew that she would make a magnificent test with Stevens directing her. I know the ego of film directors, and I am sure now as then that if she had sent that wire, she would have done a brilliant test and gotten the role of Anne Frank. But Susie was then involved in the first love affair of her life. Richard Burton and she were living in her parents' home in a little separate apartment and doing a play called *Time Remembered* with Helen Hayes. The lovers only had time for each other, and Susie could no more send that wire than she could fly. The thought of having to leave Burton for a day was more than she wanted to contemplate. I understood the power of first love, especially when there was such a strong sexual attraction between them, and I couldn't fault her. But I had seen her be so brilliant when *The Diary of Anne Frank* had first opened, that I've always felt sad that she was not the film's Anne Frank, with my apologies to Millie Perkins.

Sitting that evening with George Stevens in Sardi's, all I knew was that I was too old to play Anne and too young to play her mother or the other lady in it, and I had no idea why George had asked me to go see the play with him, but he finally said, "Shelley, when you were in your middle twenties, you convinced me you were seventeen and almost won the Best Actress Oscar for *A Place in the Sun.* Do you think you could extend your acting magic further and convince me that you're fifty and able to play Mrs. Van Daan in *The Diary of Anne Frank?* In the film it will be a much more powerful role than it was in the play."

I gasped as I stared at my idol. I knew he wouldn't let me do it with tricky makeup. He then showed me a picture of the real Mrs. Van Daan and said, "She was the strongest of all the people hiding in that attic. She lived through the concentration camp and died in an American ambulance on the way to a hospital."

Smiling through tears, I again said to him what I'd said when he'd asked to test me for *A Place in the Sun:* "Mr. Stevens, if you give me that role, you can photograph me any way you want to."

He said, "Shelley, will you gain twenty-five pounds to play it?"

"Fifty, if necessary," I answered.

He laughed and said, "No, but during the course of the film, which will probably take six or seven months, I would like the audience to see the group's starvation, especially in this woman, as she gives her food to her son and husband."

I didn't think twice. I just said, "Thank you."

I now felt comfortable about going back to California. Live TV didn't count much—the audience only saw it once, but it further solidified my intention not to do any cheap, forgettable films. I would wait for the distinguished *Anne Frank.*

13

I got to Hollywood April Fool's Day, which somehow seemed appropriate, and reinstalled my family in my Beverly Hills apartment. Tony was delirious with joy, because he had been offered a very important film called *Wild Is the Wind,* to costar with Anna Magnani and Tony Quinn, with his name, for the first time, above the title. My agent was still trying to get me to do Universal's B pictures, and I was turning the scripts down without even reading them, eagerly looking forward to working again with the great George Stevens.

Tony and I again rented our little beach house, and every morning he reported to Paramount and I reported to CBS. I cannot remember what that "Climax" television show was about. Tony could not have been more loving, intelligent, and sweet. I waited with longing and fear, expecting that any minute he would bring up the subject of turning our engaged-to-be-engaged relationship into a real engagement. I was very grateful that he was still legally married. When I would question Tony about where he intended to live, he would blithely answer, "Wherever you are—New York! California! Italy!" When I would ask him how he would manage to do this when he had signed for so many films, he would laugh and say, "Don't worry. We'll work it out!" But I knew that my daughter was going to go to school in New York.

I had already registered her there, and every minute that I wasn't working I wanted to be with her—not traveling around the world, trailing after a young husband. The problems seemed insoluble.

Sometime around this engaged-to-be-engaged period, I heard that Joanne Woodward, who had won an Oscar as Best Actress that year, had told her agent that she could only work in films that were located where Paul Newman, her husband, was working. She had decided that if they wanted a life together, his career took precedence over hers. This information astounded me, but over the years that is exactly what Joanne has done, and I know that she was offered many films that she turned down if they didn't coincide with Paul's locations.

But Tony didn't seem too worried about our living arrangements. Maybe he was assuming we would buy a house in my hometown, St. Louis, which is sort of in the middle of the country. He was enjoying the Chateau Marmont, and every night he would find a new and wonderful restaurant to try out, from Jack's at the Beach to Perino's, way down on Wilshire Boulevard. Since I liked to eat, as my readers have probably noticed, and George Stevens had told me I had to gain weight for *The Diary of Anne Frank,* I was enjoying all these fine restaurants. I remember asking Tony if he wasn't spending too much money on dining out.

"Yes, I am," he said. "Maybe if we bought a house and hired a gourmet cook, we would save money."

I stared at him, and then I either laughed or cried—I can't remember which.

I finished that "Climax" TV show, and Tony, who had been rehearsing his film *Wild Is the Wind,* regaled me with stories about Anna Magnani's broken English and wonderful talent. He started to pack to go on location in Nevada, somewhere in the mountains near Reno. Hal Wallis was producing this film, and Tony loved Paramount, mostly because they had a great barber and commissary.

While I was packing warm clothes for him, and trying to get him checked out of the Chateau Marmont, I remembered how Vittorio had once told me that he had rehearsed *Macbeth* with Anna Magnani, who was playing Lady Macbeth. Even though it was in Italian, it took him two weeks of rehearsals to realize that she had *never* read the play. She was improvising Lady Macbeth. She carefully explained to Vittorio that, after she improvised every scene, at the end of rehearsals she would then *perhaps* learn Shakespeare's lines in Italian translation. Vittorio had been so shocked at this that he had canceled the production. Tony and I, who were steeped in the Method, laughed and understood Magnani's rehearsal processes. Afterwards, I thought better of it and cautioned, "Tony, help her with her English! If she improvises, don't let her keep changing the lines or you're going to be shooting this picture forever!"

That night I took him to the airport. Paramount had rented a huge cargo plane to take the actors, the crew, and all the equipment up to the location. Tony and I kissed goodbye for five minutes, keeping the entire planeload of actors and crew members waiting. Some of them I'd worked with in my Paramount films *The Great Gatsby* and *A Place in the Sun,* and they hooted and whistled and kidded me till Tony and I let go of each other. I don't know why this goodbye seemed so permanent to me; Tony looked at me deeply and, catching the vibrations, became frightened by the intensity of my goodbye. I waved to all of them when the plane took off. And with sadness, and great relief, I drove back to my safe, unfashionable little duplex in Beverly Hills. Ambivalence, thy name is Shelley!

I finished my rehearsals of the CBS show, and Stan Kamen, Tony's agent from the William Morris Agency, came to see me often while we were shooting it. He was a darling guy, handsome, brilliant, and funny, and would obviously in the future be the head of the William Morris office. He was not only Tony's agent but his best friend, so I could not very well tell him of my hesitations about making my relationship with Tony more permanent.

I spent the next few weeks looking up my old friends, and the only one I could discuss my hopes and fears with was Constance Dowling. She was living in Bel Air now, and her husband, Ivan, had bought her a beautiful big house. They had three sons, and her life was busy and happy. Ivan was a successful producer and writer of science-fiction films. We would often have dinner with them, and my daughter would play with her sons. I kept trying to examine why I was so attracted to actors and what made it seemingly impossible for me to connect with a writer, agent, or producer, as Connie had—someone who would have similar interests, but who would be a more stable person for me to love. I felt lonely, and Tony would call me from location on the company's radiophone, but it was very difficult for him to get hold of it, since there was a whole company trying to use this one phone line after a long day's location shooting.

Early in May, after about eight weeks, Tony called me on that funny phone and said he was very lonely and I must come up to the location as they were about to finish shooting there in the next few days. The scenery was beautiful and he wanted me to enjoy it with him. I tried to tell him I didn't like waiting around locations, but the radiophone was disconnected. Stan Kamen called me a little while later and said he had arranged tickets for the following Saturday for us to fly to the small town near the location of *Wild Is the Wind*.

I knew that it was a rough location, so I stuffed a Valpac with a couple of pairs of blue jeans and boots and of course one beautiful nightgown. I explained to my daughter that I was going up to visit Tony for a few days, and she said, "Mommy, bring me back a present, a surprise."

Stan picked me up, and we went to the airport.

After we'd been in the air for half an hour or so and had had our morning coffee, Stan took a ring box out of his pocket.

"Shelley, this is for you," he said.

I stared at it, unable to take it. He opened the box, and there was a diamond ring in the shape of a wishbone, with many diamonds. I gazed at my handsome friend Stan.

"Darling, this is lovely of you," I said, "and I really like you, Stan. My mother and father adore you. We have the same interests. We're both Jewish. You'll be the head of the William Morris Agency soon, but I'd better think about this. Oh, my God! You are Tony's best friend!''

Stan looked at me in amazement.

''Shelley, what the hell are you talking about?''

I looked at the diamond ring and said, ''Stan, what the hell are *you* talking about? Aren't you proposing?''

Laughing, he said, ''No, Shelley. This is the wedding ring that Tony ordered from Marvin Hime before he left. This is for your wedding tonight.''

If I'd had a parachute, I'd have jumped out of the plane.

''Stan,'' I stuttered, ''what are you talking about? Tony's still married, and I don't even know if my divorce from Vittorio Gassman is final!'' (I knew damn well it was, but just.)

Stan looked surprised and said, ''Didn't Tony tell you about his plans for you two to marry today in Reno?''

''No, Stan, he didn't.''

''Well, I guess he wanted to surprise you. He established residence in Reno when he went up to location, got his divorce papers yesterday afternoon and the marriage license this morning. Shelley, you're going to get married anyway, and this is a very romantic way to do it, isn't it?''

As I write about this, my feelings of slow motion, dazed reality, and shock return. The only objection I could voice was: ''I can't do it! I haven't got a dress.''

Stan looked at me strangely and said, ''Shelley, you can buy a dress in Reno.''

I just looked at him in silence, saying nothing, and I remained silent the rest of the trip.

I think I was wondering how I could escape. Perhaps the plane would have a safe crash landing on one of the mountains, far away from Reno. But it didn't. When I walked out onto the steps, I looked down, and there was Tony in a beautiful dark blue suit with a carnation in his buttonhole and a blue tie and a stiff white shirt. I noticed that even his shoes were highly polished. I knew from the expression on his face that I would have to either marry him that day or get punched out.

Why he had arranged our wedding this way I still don't

know. Maybe he thought I would change *my* mind; maybe he was afraid he would change *his* mind. I'm not so sure that he wanted to get married at all. He just had gotten a divorce, and since he'd been married most of his young-adult life, perhaps he couldn't bear to be single. But I'm convinced that if I had refused to marry him that day, he would háve married Anna Magnani, or anybody. I don't think I said much. I remember smiling insanely as the publicity man on his film explained that Tony had gotten our marriage license in Reno, and all I had to do was sign it in front of the justice of the peace, who was also a notary.

I smiled. I smiled at everything and everybody.

"Shelley wants to go to a shop and get a dress," Stan said. "She can't get married in blue jeans."

I smiled and nodded.

The only store they could seem to find on the way to the justice of the peace was a J. C. Penney. I wouldn't let anyone go in the store with me, and as I walked through the store, I just kept on going until I reached the back entrance. The limousine driver and publicity man were standing in the parking lot. Tony and Stan were at the front door. So I decided I'd better get married. It seems funny now, but it wasn't funny then. I had been practically living with Tony for almost two years, and I believe I had been a solid influence in his life. True, he'd had a sort of nervous breakdown, but I was sure it wasn't my fault. Or was it? What I wasn't sure of was what he would do if I told him I wasn't ready yet for this marriage. He had obviously gone ahead with all these plans and for some reason had not told me about them. Perhaps it was too difficult to use the radiophone on location—I couldn't think of any other logical reason.

I bought a cotton dress with polka dots. The top was white with aqua polka dots, and the skirt was aqua with white polka dots. I asked the saleslady if they had a hat that would go with this outfit.

"Yes," she said. "There's a matching white cotton hat in the window with aqua polka dots."

She got it out of the window. The hat was rather burned by the Nevada sun, but that seemed appropriate somehow—I liked the fact that it was slightly scorched. I only wore this outfit at that wedding, but I kept it and looked at it for many years afterward. In fact, I only gave it away recently, when it came back in style.

I stopped at the shoe department and got a pair of white J. C. Penney high-heeled sandals. The whole outfit cost about $30. When I walked out into the parking lot, all done up in my J. C. Penney wedding finery, Tony was sitting in the limousine, and when he saw that I was really prepared to get married that day, he got the strangest look on his face. It seemed a combination of relief and fear.

He handed me a white orchid in a box that had been on the floor, and we all drove silently to the chapel of the justice of the peace. I do not remember any conversation. I remember looking at the marriage license I had to sign, and there it was: Shirley Schrift and Anthony Papaleo were getting married. Who were these people? I had no idea. Papaleo? I'd never heard that name. It seems Tony had taken his mother's maiden name when he'd become an actor, just as I had taken my mother's name, Winter. His father's name was Papaleo, and his mother's was Franciosa. But Papaleo was his legal name then, as Schrift was mine, so I signed the marriage license.

We all lined up in front of this justice of the peace, and suddenly this man started to pray some holy-roller religious service. Like a tobacco auctioneer, he hollered something like, "Brothern-sistern, we are gared here this holy day of such and such," and he was really screaming. It was the final straw. I began to laugh, hysterically. So did Stan. It was such a shock and really was pretty funny. This justice of the peace was also some kind of redneck revivalist preacher. Tony became red, very angry and, for a minute, I thought he was going to knock Stan's and my heads together, but someone got us some cold water, and we regained control. I guess Tony and I got married, but I don't remember a word of the ceremony after that. I had the strangest feeling, throughout the proceedings, that I was really marrying Stan, and maybe I was secretly hoping I was.

We drove into Reno, and we had some kind of wedding

dinner and took pictures, I think. The next thing I can clearly remember is Tony and me sitting at a blackjack table, playing, when suddenly the dealer turned over Tony's cards and my cards, facedown.

"You two are eighty-sixed," he said. "You can't play in Reno anymore."

Tony with his white carnation and I with my white orchid began to get very angry at the dealer. The gambling was distracting us from what we had just done. We yelled at the dealer, who shouted back, "For Chrissakes, you two have been drawing another card when you're holding a king and an ace! You've been doing this for the past five minutes. A king and an ace is the highest hand you can get in blackjack. It's twenty-one!"

I don't remember that wedding night at all. I believe we were in a luxurious suite in Reno, I in my expensive satin nightgown and Tony in more expensive silk pajamas. Somehow, we hugged each other and wept. For a long time, I didn't understand that we got married out of fear, perhaps fear of loneliness. Although I was quite young and Tony was even younger than I, perhaps we were afraid of being alone for the rest of our lives. I believe we weren't marrying with our love and strength; we were marrying out of fear. But there was no doubt, the next morning, for better or for worse, I was Mrs. Anthony Papaleo. Sunday morning, we wiped away our fears, stayed in bed all day and had elegant room service.

Very early Monday morning, I got up with Tony, and the driver took us to the location somewhere in the mountains. I sort of hung around while they were making him up. For an actress, there is nothing duller and more boring than watching someone else make movies. I sat on the sidelines and watched a scene he had with Anna Magnani and a brilliant dog, a Basque collie, who seemed to know his lines much better than either of the actors. For some reason, Magnani kept looking daggers at me. The whole set was buzzing with news of Tony's and my "elopement." I believed that Magnani felt it was rude of me to get married to her leading man during the shooting of her picture. By lunch, there were about twenty reporters hanging around the set.

Hal Wallis showed up for lunch and started to bawl me out. He wanted to know why I, an experienced, publicized blonde bombshell, couldn't understand that if we'd had a big wedding on the location, and given him proper notice, Tony and I would have landed on the cover of *Life*. He went on and on:

"How could you, who were so carefully trained by the Universal publicity department, do such a stupid thing? Louella and Hedda will never forgive you, and Walter Winchell will be Tony's enemy for life."

"Hal, shut up," I said. "I want to watch that dog act. I think I can learn something from it."

By late afternoon, I was tired of posing for pictures for the reporters and found a little hill to hide behind. When Tony finished shooting an hour or so later, he found me. He was carrying a bottle of cold champagne with plastic glasses, and trailing on a leash was a little Basque collie puppy.

"I saw how entranced you were with that trained Basque collie," Tony said, "so I've bought this one from the trainer. The dog in the picture is its mother and has a fantastic pedigree. It only cost two thousand dollars, and I think the kid will love it."

"You've already bought it? Oh, Tony, how can we keep a dog like this in a New York apartment? When it grows up, it's going to be big and strong."

"Come on, Shelley! It's a beautiful puppy, and bred to herd sheep. It will herd the children away from the Central Park West traffic. The kid is going to love it."

He was right, it was a beautiful puppy and smart as a whip. It was all black except for white paws, a white star on its forehead, and a white tail, and it was so endearing that I completely forgot my honeymoon blues. We had fun playing with it during lunch, and, when we got back to the set, I noticed Magnani had disappeared. Tony Quinn congratulated me and wished Tony good luck.

"You're supposed to do that the opposite way around," I told Tony Quinn. "Wish me good luck, and congratulate Tony."

Quinn gave me a kiss and said, "I know whereof I speak."

I suddenly remembered that, sometime around 1948 or so, I had gone to a bullfight in Tijuana, Mexico, with Tony Quinn. I was sure it was Tony Quinn—I know it wasn't Tony Curtis—but the only thing I remember, really, about that trip is seeing Cantinflas, the famous Mexican actor, fight a small bull. The pics were attached to long bread sticks, and I gathered that the whole bullfight had some kind of political and social meaning, which I never quite caught. And the little bull was so funny and brave that the crowd did not let Cantinflas kill it. It was a very light gray color. (Oh God, the things I remember and the things I don't.) The trip couldn't have been very romantic, because I had eaten a taco from a stand on a street in Tijuana. It was delicious, but I think Tony spent an entire Sunday night and Monday nursing me. *La turista* had struck with a vengeance.

After he left, and Tony got into the makeup chair, I said, "Why is Tony Quinn so grumpy?"

My young husband drew me down and whispered in my ear, "Magnani is stealing every scene they have. She's remarkable. And to get even, Tony is having an affair with her ugly English secretary/speech coach. In Italy, I think you're supposed to have an affair with your leading lady." I agreed, "It's only good manners."

I knew that if Magnani was really mad at him, Tony Quinn would end up a space on the screen. It must have been true, because in that picture you only saw Magnani and my handsome husband Tony. She obviously wasn't mad at him, at least until the very end of the picture, when we got married. Anna Magnani could act anybody off the stage or screen.

During the next few days of shooting, as I wandered around location with my new puppy on a leash, I did get the feeling that Magnani was mad at me. When I had lived in Italy, she had always been very nice to me, and I had adored her acting genius and her humor. Vittorio and I had been introduced by her, or almost. On my first trip to Italy, I had gone to the theater one evening with Frank Latimore and was sitting in a box. Magnani was sitting in the orchestra, dressed all in black, because Rossellini had just married Ingrid Bergman after a long relationship with

Magnani. She was in deep mourning, except for her bright red shoes. During the first act of a very dull play, she got my attention and pointed across the theater to another box, where sat Vittorio Gassman. She made an A-OK gesture with her thumb and index finger and winked at me. Only everybody in the theater could see what she was doing, and I pretended indifference. Vittorio showed up in my opera box during the next intermission, and although he couldn't speak one word of English in those days, we started a tempestuous romance that led to our marriage. Now, in retrospect, I have a feeling Magnani figured I owed her one—and thought it was very ungrateful of me, marrying Tony Franciosa while he was on a film location with her. Perhaps she was right.

Wild Is the Wind dragged on, and between lovemaking and gambling, Tony was getting very little sleep. But, I must say, it was a very interesting honeymoon, though I still didn't feel very married to Tony.

We got on the airplane chartered to bring the entire company back to Los Angeles for the interiors. I was quite surprised when we landed and Tony gave the chauffeur my address. I couldn't think why Tony wanted to bring his suitcases into my little apartment after the honeymoon. I had counted on him going back to the Chateau Marmont. I thought he was still going to live there. I was quite embarrassed when he walked into the house with his suitcases and the dog. My mother and daughter greeted me, and I quickly said to them, "Guess what— Tony and I got married up in Nevada!"

My mother paled and said, "You what?"

All I had to answer was, "Tony and I just felt like getting married."

My daughter looked confused and said, "Mom, what did you and Tony have to go and do *that* for?" Even at four, she was smarter than we were. When Tony handed her the puppy, she immediately named him White Feet.

There was plenty of space in my house, but Tony seemed to fill up every room. After a few days, we began to get crazy—it seemed so crowded. When he wasn't working, he was always on the phone. He had brought his entire wardrobe, which he'd had stashed at the Chateau Marmont, over to my house, and there were a few of his suits in everybody's closets. I couldn't quite bring myself to give him his own closet. When I began to complain, he shut me up by saying:

"Shell, as soon as I finish this picture, we're going to buy a big house with a pool and a tennis court."

I did not want to own another house in California, but I couldn't think of where to store all his clothes. Suitcases were all over the place, so I said, "Okay."

Tony would come home exhausted at 6:00 or 7:00 P.M. I would make him a wonderful Italian dinner—I had had a lot of practice cooking for my other Italian husband. I would cue him in his lines, and he would fall into an exhausted sleep. He would have to get up at 5:30 A.M., as the Paramount limousine picked him up at 6:00.

Toward the end of the filming, I began to notice that he was coming home later and later, and my spaghetti and veal scallopini were getting ruined. I asked him to phone me if he was going to be late so I could plan my cooking accordingly, but he seemed to be getting very forgetful. I rationalized that he was playing a large and difficult role. I would be a good little Italian wife, and I would have dinner with my child and get her to sleep. Then I would wait patiently until my hardworking husband got home, whatever the time, and then serve him his dinner.

Then I began to notice that Tony wasn't very hungry when he came home and didn't eat much. One night, about eight-thirty, I called Paramount. Somebody on the soundstage answered the phone, I identified myself, and the watchman or whoever said, "The company broke at six o'clock, Miss Winters." Then he stuttered, "I mean Mrs. Gassman. No, no, I mean Mrs. Franciosa."

"Miss Winters is fine," I said. "Thanks," I added, and hung up.

I sat still. I had to sit still. I was so angry that if I moved I would kill somebody. I called the guard at the gate at Paramount and pretended I was Tony's agent's secretary and asked if Mr. Franciosa had left the lot yet. The guard said, "Oh, yes, about six-fifteen. I believe the limousine had to drop Miss Magnani first."

I didn't think I was mad, except I got icy cold. And

when I looked in the mirror, I was white as a sheet. What was this crazy bastard doing? He had trapped me into marrying him just a few weeks ago, and now he was having an affair with Anna Magnani. I decided I wanted to know for sure—perhaps I could get an annulment *and* all his money. I picked up my award from the foreign-press correspondents. It was quite heavy, so it seemed an appropriate weapon. I stuck it in my purse and got in my car and drove to the Chateau Marmont garage.

I left my motor running and got into the elevator. I stopped the elevator one floor below the penthouse. How I knew that Magnani had the penthouse, I do not know—maybe it was ESP, but I knew. I walked very quietly up the stairs to the penthouse. I silently turned the knob on the door; it wasn't locked. Those ignoble adulterers had been so confident they'd left the door unlocked! I pushed it open.

There were Magnani and Tony on the gorgeous living-room couch, stretched out, kissing. I must admit they were clutching their scripts in their hands too, but I figured that was just a safeguard.

I started to scream, "*Puttana* [whore]!" and other appropriate Italian curses. I started to chase Magnani around the couch and then around the suite with my heavy weapon. Tony did not even try to grab me. He had seen me enraged before, so now he sat very still. He had decided if anyone was going to get killed, it was not going to be him.

I stumbled, and Magnani managed to get out the door, whereupon I proceeded to chase her down the steps of the Chateau Marmont. Somewhere around the third landing, she looked back at me, and we both started to laugh, hysterically. We sat down on the landing, and when we could control our laughter, she whispered:

"*Stupida!* Don't laugh. He kill us both if you laugh! Be jealous and scream. Otherwise, he kill us!"

She was very wise, but I was still laughing.

"Anna, it's crazy," I said. "The only thing I can hope is that I have caught some of your great talent by osmosis. Maybe it works that way."

"Whatever," she said, and slapped me. "But for God's sake, *scream*. Come on, chase me!"

So, I began to chase her again, laughing and crying at the same time. When we got to the garage, she jumped in her car, narrowly avoiding hitting mine, and sped down the hill. I stood there, laughing and crying, thinking that Anna Magnani was very smart. If Tony felt two female movie stars were laughing at him, given his Italian temper, he might easily become so enraged he'd kill us both. But if two movie stars were jealously fighting over him, his male ego would be inflated, not to mention anything else.

I was leaning against my car, laughing so hard my stomach hurt. As soon as Magnani left, Tony came bounding out of the garage elevator after me. He had combed his hair and straightened his tie and clothes. I covered my face and pretended à la Stanislavsky that I was weeping bitterly. He tenderly took me in his arms.

"Shelley, darling, how can you behave like this?" he said. "I was only helping her with her English."

"In a horizontal position?"

"For God's sakes, we were just rehearsing a scene in the picture."

He put me and my award (now minus the plaque) in the passenger seat of my car, and he got in the other one. He started to drive swiftly toward the beach and, strangely, all I could think about was that he still didn't have a license, and I hoped no cop stopped us. When we got to the beach, he told me how much he loved me, how deep were our friendship and artistic bond. In a daze, I agreed with everything he said.

For the rest of the filming, Tony came home at 6:15 P.M., and neither one of us ever mentioned the Chateau Marmont again.

In the wee small hours, I knew that Tony, let loose among the beauties of the silver screen, was like a kid in a candy store, and I knew I never could keep him on the straight and narrow nor, in fact, demand any semblance of faithfulness. I just resolved to get myself back to New York and solve the problems of this hasty marriage there.

* * *

Sometime during my marriage to Tony Franciosa we went to a Cannes Film Festival. I can't remember exactly what year it was but it was during the fifties. Toward the end of the festival we were invited to lunch at Pablo Picasso's home. There was a long, narrow table in a sort of flower-covered screened-in porch. Many famous international actors and directors were at this lunch.

But glory of glories, I was seated to the right of Pablo Picasso. Tony had been seated down the table to the left. I think that Ava Gardner was sitting opposite Tony. But I didn't notice or care since the greatest painter of our century was talking to me and I was answering him in garbled Spanish, French, and Italian. He knew a few English words, but I really don't know what language we spoke. Somehow we communicated, perhaps with gestures and songs.

We compared the arts of acting and painting. He told me that the message of the painter or writer or actor will be received by each member of the audience or viewer depending on his or her life premises. It was a new idea for me and a very profound one.

He asked me about Vittorio Gassman. I told him that we were divorced, that we had had a beautiful little girl, and that I now had a new husband. He looked down the table at Anthony Franciosa and changed the subject.

He told me about his boyhood in Spain and I told him about growing up in Brooklyn and the boys I had known who had gone to Spain to fight Franco in the Abraham Lincoln Brigade. I described the sad block party we had for the so few of them who had returned, after the Spanish democracy had fallen. Even the small children on my block then knew about Hitler and Mussolini. We all understood that Spain was a rehearsal for the coming world war. He listened to me closely as I described with gestures how I yearly visited *Guernica*, his greatest painting, which was then in the Museum of Modern Art in New York. (That painting depicts the fall of Guernica during the Spanish Civil War, in case some acting student reads this.)

After the delicious French-Spanish lunch we were all invited to see Picasso's new work and then out to a yard to a sort of outdoor lithograph studio. While we were watching him work, on what seemed like an antique lithograph machine, I became so entranced by the remarkable experience that I completely forgot Tony's existence.

After we viewed many of Picasso's new, magnificent works he presented me with what I thought was a lithograph. He signed it and wrote something in French on the back of it. He then rolled it up and handed it to me. He had written in French, "For the young artist, who indeed understands The American tragedy."

When Tony and I divorced, this was the only thing in our apartment he wanted, but Picasso had given me the lithograph and I would not give it to Tony for love or money.

Just a few years ago, an art director from the Plachon Theatre in Lyons was having cocktails at my New York apartment. He looked around my apartment and said, "Miss Winters, you have done very well financially in Hollywood, haven't you?" I asked him why he thought so, and he said, "*Mon dieu,* you own a Picasso." I laughed and told him it was only a lithograph, even though Picasso had signed it. The picture was in purple, yellow, and black. It was a drawing of a young boy and a little girl sitting on the floor drawing on a piece of paper. The shadow of a large purple woman leans over protecting and embracing both of them. In the lower left-hand corner there were Roman numerals in various colors.

"I'm sorry, Miss Winters, but you have an original Picasso crayon drawing. He does various drawings before he paints and the Roman numerals are in different colors—Picasso uses that code, depending on which color is predominant in that drawing. This must have been his final drawing because the oil painting of this drawing hangs in Rio de Janeiro and this purple is the predominant color in it."

That night in Cannes after this famous lunch, Tony was very angry with me. He went out all night and got very drunk. The next morning he had quite a hangover and a terrible cold, but he still insisted that we go on to Venice, which was part of our tourism plan. I had told Tony all about the freezing winter of beauty and agony I had spent in Venice, when I had been working with and divorcing Vittorio.

We took the *rapido* to Venice, then took the gondola from the station to the Danieli Hotel. By the time we got to the hotel Tony had a 103° temperature. When the doctor arrived the next morning even I knew Tony had a bad strep throat and was very, very ill. The doctor, a German who I suspected wasn't a real doctor but had just stayed in Venice after the Second World War, didn't seem to have any penicillin and just gave Tony aspirin and something to gargle with. Some time during the next three hours a huge American warship pulled up in the canal outside of my hotel window. Tony was shivering so hard his head was bouncing off the headboard.

I picked up the phone and ordered the operator to connect me with the American warship. I yelled so loud, she somehow managed to do this. The operator on the boat connected me with the ship's hospital.

I screamed, "During the Second World War and Korea I entertained at many, many naval installations and on many huge ships and now my husband is dying."

"Who is this?" a male voice inquired.

"Shelley Winters," I wept.

"Stick your head out the window," he said. I did and almost fell out the window into the canal. Obviously the ship's hospital faced the Hotel Danieli.

"Be right there," the voice said.

In about two minutes a naval-officer doctor arrived with two sailors carrying a stretcher. They took Tony, but wouldn't let me go aboard. In two days he was back at the hotel, well and healthy.

In 1986 I was aboard the S.S. *Kennedy* for the fireworks display celebration. I personally thanked Admiral Abrams for the Navy's saving Anthony Franciosa's life thirty years ago.

The admiral said, "You're welcome, Miss Winters, but I was only ten years old at the time."

Even Lillian Gish thought it was inappropriate and she was at least ninety-one.

Meanwhile, back in Beverly Hills after the Magnani

incident, Tony behaved as if nothing had happened, and in the next days began to drag me all over the hills, looking at houses. I usually could stop that by suggesting we go shopping, much to the disappointment of the Beverly Hills real-estate ladies. One Saturday, Tony took me to see a house—in fact, he insisted on it—that was on North Palm Drive, in the so-called Golden Triangle, across the trolley tracks, on the expensive side of Santa Monica Boulevard. In the last thirty years these houses have escalated in value, from about $80,000 to $3 million. The realtor told us that it was the estate of Donna Reed and her ex-husband, who'd died some months before, and it was a gorgeous, completely furnished house. She was right.

The real-estate lady who was showing us the house never shut up. Finally I asked her to go out to her car and let us look at it by ourselves. It had an enormous center hall with a beautiful curved stairway, and a glass wall behind which orchids were cultivated, and it opened directly to a glassed-in family room that faced an enormous pool, beautiful grounds, and a guest apartment above the garage. There was an endless living room, a dining room, a breakfast room, and a kitchen big enough for a restaurant. To the left was a beautiful paneled office, and both the living room and the den-office had fireplaces. The family room, which faced the patio, had an indoor-outdoor stone barbecue. The curved staircase led up to four plush bedrooms. The whole house looked as if it had been immaculately cleaned, and everywhere you looked there were glass and silver, huge sofas, antiques, linens, and television sets. It looked as if no one had ever lived in it, and it had a kind of museum quality, except I knew that death had lived in this house for a long time. When I asked the real-estate lady, she admitted that the man who had owned it had died of cancer, after a lingering illness.

I got out of the house into the sunshine as quickly as I could. I had to face the fact that Tony was crazy about the place. It was his fantasy—living in a mansion in Beverly Hills. He wanted the house so badly that he wore down my objections, which, after all, were totally unrealistic and nonsense superstition. I knew you couldn't catch cancer from furniture, or indeed from anything.

But it seemed, if we wanted the house, we had to go to court on a certain morning and make a bid. It was part of the man's estate. I tried to get Tony to agree to let a lawyer or one of our business managers do it, but he didn't trust them. We had agreed to go only up to $80,000, which meant we had to put down only 20 percent. I knew I could afford it, but I wasn't sure Tony could, given the way he was spending his money.

To this day, I am so sorry I gave in and agreed to go bid on the house. It was stupid. For some reason, when people see movie stars they are sure they are millionaires. Anything that *they* might want is eminently desirable and very valuable. My foreboding proved correct. When the bidding started at $50,000, which was like $200,000 now, it quickly escalated up to $85,000. Tony went up to $90,000, while I shook, and somebody else bid $100,000. I pinched him hard. With hindsight, I know this house is now worth $3 or $4 million, but back then $100,000 for a house I never planned to live in seemed disproportionate.

As we left the Los Angeles courthouse, Tony was red with anger. He wanted that house so much, and I think he would have gone up to $150,000. There were a lot of reporters waiting for us as we walked to the car. Suddenly, some photographer aimed his camera at us.

"Don't you dare take that picture," Tony said.

"I can take any goddamn picture I want," the photographer replied.

With that, Tony grabbed the camera and broke it. The photographer hit him, and he returned the punch—I think that is what happened. Before I knew it, Tony was being held by two policemen, the photographer was lying on the ground, and I was shouting, "I'll get Jerry Giesler," who was then the most famous criminal lawyer in Hollywood. What Tony did not understand is that if you are a public figure, anyone can take a picture of you, as long as he stays a certain number of feet away. I had tried to yell that at him during the skirmish, but he was too angry to hear and my advice came too late.

I guess they booked Tony that afternoon, and his trial was set for some time after he finished his film. Stan Kamen put up Tony's bail, and we all drove silently home. I could not believe that my troubles had been so compounded. I had developed the idea from long, habitual thinking that I was always the guilty one, that I could have somehow prevented this. It was like living through my father's arrest for arson all over again, and I was terrified.

When we talked to Giesler the next day, he was very reassuring after he questioned Tony. He was sure all the cameraman wanted was money, and the most Tony would get would be a warning and maybe a year's probation, because it was his first offense. The trial was some months later. During this period, my poor Tony was very subdued and would play out in the garden with my kid, but he didn't want to go anywhere. It was as if his magic balloon had burst.

About this time, I got a very interesting script based on a novel of John Steinbeck's called *The Wayward Bus*. Ivan Moffat, who'd been one of the writers on *A Place in the Sun*, sent me the book. I had a couple of meetings with Charles Brackett, who was going to produce, and I was very tempted to do the film, if I could squeeze it in before rehearsals started on a new play. I had received this play from my New York agent. It was almost poetry, and it was called *The Saturday Night Kid*. The writer was a young playwright by the name of Jack Dunphy, a wonderful poet and an insightful writer who was a friend of Truman Capote's.

In the midst of these decisions, Tony was sent the script of *The Long, Hot Summer*. Jerry Wald, the producer, asked me to read it too, saying there was a part in it he would like me to play. Tony was overjoyed. He felt at last we would work together again, and perhaps we would re-create that special magic we'd had in *A Hatful of Rain*. We began to talk about ourselves as if we were the latter-day Alfred Lunt and Lynn Fontanne. Hollywood seems to encourage this kind of delusion—maybe it's the hot sun and the smell of the night-blooming jasmine.

I liked the script, and I felt sure Marty Ritt, who had just started at Twentieth Century–Fox, would make an offer to my agent and/or Universal. So I turned down *The Wayward Bus* and waited eagerly for a chance to go to Louisiana with my husband and have a real honeymoon while acting gloriously into the sunset. I notified my New York agent that I would do *The Saturday Night Kid* after *The Long, Hot Summer*. Lo and behold, the film was never offered to me.

Marty Ritt, or Twentieth Century–Fox, or whatever the powers that be, decided that they wanted Lee Remick in this role. I hid my disappointment, and since Tony so much wanted me with him, and he was so thin and nervous because of his impending trial, I agreed to go on location with this film in New Orleans. I had never been there, and I was pretty sure that no one in the cast would know that I had thought I was going to be in the film. It turned out that Paul Newman and Joanne Woodward did know and were especially nice to me.

I began to think they hadn't hired me because Lee Remick was so young. I believe I was thirty-two and skinny, but I felt sure I had gotten too old already. I kept my thoughts to myself and helped Tony with his role. We had lovely quarters to live in, and I hoped he could forget for a while about his trial. I talked to the William Morris office almost every day. They were trying to settle the problem by paying the photographer some money, but he seemed to be very vindictive and would not retract his charges and wanted Tony to go to jail. I think he felt that this case would make him famous. I did not tell Tony this.

I even got the photographer's home phone number from Jerry Giesler's secretary, and I tried to call him from Louisiana but couldn't reach him. I called his editor and tried to tell him that Tony had had a nervous breakdown a year earlier, and God knows what jail would do to him. He couldn't have cared less. So I stopped trying and phoned Jerry Giesler.

I don't remember much about New Orleans, except one strange evening when Paul and Joanne and Tony and

I went to a Creole bar in kind of a rough section of town. It had wonderful Cajun food, and of course I remember the shrimp with remoulade sauce. We had some wonderful drinks, and then I looked around and noticed that the bar had a raised stage behind it, about four feet above our heads. I was having some lovely dessert when I suddenly realized there was a cage to the left of the stage. I stood up to see what was in the cage. A woman was in the cage, wearing what seemed to be animal skins. I sat down and asked Joanne, "Is this a strip joint?"

"I don't think so," she said. "They have great Dixieland jazz, and some kind of floor show that everybody's talking about."

A few minutes later, the very good band started to play discordant, wild jazz. A rather tough-looking gangster type got up on the stage and opened the cage. This woman came screaming out, sort of dancing wildly and doing a strip. She had gray hair with streaks of red in it, but she had strange, apelike gestures and movements. She was pulling off the animal skins, and I was shocked at this apparition, as was everybody at our table. She seemed to strip down to just panties made of leather. She had a squat, muscular, very good body. Suddenly she stopped dancing and started to insult and spit at the audience. She spoke a strange kind of patois and was screaming like a banshee.

A huge bartender in the pit in front of the stage got up on the stage, and he was brandishing a cat-o'-nine-tails. The rest of the bartenders were trying to get her to shut up. Then somehow the huge bartender whipped her back into the cage. The whole experience was deeply disturbing and horrifying to me. The dancer was obviously a retarded creature. I never went to New Orleans again.

We got out of that restaurant quickly, and the rest of *The Long, Hot Summer* became a long, hot blur for me. I couldn't wait to get back to sane New York or even daffy Hollywood.

14

I can't remember the exact dates of the following, but somehow it was like living through my father's trial again, when I had been ten years old and he had been unjustly tried for arson. Jonas, the believer in the American Dream, was convicted and given ten to twenty years, and he served a year and was stabbed while he was in prison. My mother managed to get him a new trial, which completely exonerated him. Often in the following days, I didn't know if I was living in the present with Tony or if I was a traumatized child reliving the nightmare of seeing my father sent to prison.

Long Hot Summer was shooting its interiors, but Tony was given a day off to appear at his trial. Jerry Giesler had carefully talked to Tony about whether he had ever gotten into trouble with the law before.

"Of course not!" Tony had said.

Giesler hoped that since this was the only time Tony had ever been arrested, the judge would perhaps give him a not-guilty verdict by reason of extenuating circumstances of provoked harassment. The day of the trial, I sat in back of Tony and kept smiling encouragement. The judge came into the court, and he said, "Would Mr. Franciosa and Mr. Giesler approach the bench?" He immediately asked Tony if he'd ever been arrested before.

"No, your honor," Giesler said. "This is a first offense."

The judge picked up a yellow paper and asked, "Weren't you arrested and convicted of stealing a sewing machine in San Francisco and then trying to pawn it in 1950?"

Tony got a confused look on his face while I and Jerry Giesler gasped.

"Not quite," Tony answered. "I was doing *Detective Story* in San Francisco in 1950, and I was doing research on the role of the burglar. So I wanted to get the feeling of what it was like to steal something and be terrified while you're trying to get rid of the evidence."

The Los Angeles judge looked around the court and said to Jerry Giesler, "I don't believe this. I thought I'd heard everything."

I prayed that Tony would shut up, but he went on, "The judge in San Francisco understood my motives completely and gave me a year's suspended sentence and probation."

Giesler's eyes glazed over. The Los Angeles judge pounded his gavel, and sentence was pronounced.

Giesler immediately made a motion for an appeal. Tony stood there, stunned. I guess I was crying. *I* could believe that Tony had totally wiped out this experience, but I didn't know if anybody else could believe it. I had never heard him mention that he'd once done *Detective Story*. I'd never known he'd been on the West Coast. I thought *End as a Man* had been his first play, in 1953.

Tony and I went back to our little beach house. I think the only way we could survive was to pretend that he wasn't awaiting a new trial and/or perhaps sentencing. Jerry Giesler felt sure that if Tony had to serve time, he could get him transferred to the honor farm and reduce the sentence to ten days in jail. He had talked to the judge in chambers and—miracle of miracles—the judge did understand something about Method acting and more or less believed that Tony had stolen a sewing machine as research.

He was still guilty, but there were some mitigating circumstances. When I relayed this information to Tony, he didn't seem to listen. I told him that Robert Mitchum had once served thirty days for possession of marijuana, and while everyone had thought that it would destroy his career—in fact they had thought it would destroy Hollywood at the time—in some way it had made Mitchum a more glamorous figure. Tony smiled at me rather wistfully.

"Well, maybe marijuana is glamorous, but stealing a fifty-dollar sewing machine is pretty crummy. I think if I had stolen a Rolls-Royce, I would have been a big shot. This way, I'm a *pisher*."

I took him in my arms and tried to comfort him. We were on the balcony of our little beach house. He got out of my embrace and said, "I got to go down and play with my buddy. We're building a sandman." My kid seemed to sense that Tony was in some kind of trouble. She was too young to understand what was going on, but sometimes, when he was lying on the beach, she would come over and pat his face, and she would bring him glasses of water and little shells. She was learning to read, and Tony would play a game with her. He would pretend he didn't know how, and she would teach him to read. Even at four years old she was very studious, a little teacher.

In the midst of all this, Tony got the script of a film that I think is one of the best ones he ever did. It's a classic now. The name of it was *Career*, and it was based on a big off-Broadway hit by James Lee. Giesler told Tony that he could stall either a new trial or his sentencing until after he had done this film. It was not a long schedule, but it was a wonderful role. Joe Anthony was to direct the film and Shirley MacLaine, Dean Martin, and Carolyn Jones were to costar, and, although Tony was nominated for an Oscar for *Hatful*, I have always felt his acting in *Career* was his best.

Audrey Wood called me the following morning and told me they were going to try out *The Saturday Night Kid* in Westport, and if it worked there they would bring it to Philadelphia and then open it on Broadway. It would be directed by a talented young director, George Keathley, and they were looking for a star to play opposite me. They already had Joe Wiseman to play the third character in the play. We had a long family huddle, and Tony decided he would stay in California with my child and mother, Kathy would look after them, and I would go back East for the tryout of this play.

Tony then said something very strange to me. We were walking along the beach.

"Shell, if I go to jail, I want you to stay in New York. I don't want you to come and see me in there. As soon as I get out, I'll fly to New York or Philly and join you."

I started to protest, but he got very calm and grown-up, and he reiterated:

"You are not to come and visit me in jail. I have talked to your Mom, and I know the terrible trauma you had when she took you to see your father in Sing Sing. You are to stay in New York and not come near me if I have to go to jail."

Even now, when I think about it, I start to weep. He was so sensitive and intelligent, I could not understand how his behavior sometimes was so irrational. I believe when the Bible talks about the sins of our fathers, it means those things that our fathers have unknowingly inflicted on us as children. Perhaps we never fully recover from them and spend our lives expiating them. His father had left his mother when he was an infant. Tony's childhood was spent with his mother and spinster aunts, and he only saw his father on terrible Sundays when he had to pick up that $8 child-support check. I know that his mother, who of course was Catholic, would never give Tony's father a divorce—till she was hit by a car, the year before I met him, and she needed money for the hospital. Tony was obviously caught in this struggle of hatred and recrimination all his young life. I guess as an adult he acted out the hatred that his life situation must have generated in him as a child. This is amateur psychoanalysis, but I think some of it is accurate.

I saw that Tony absolutely meant what he said about my not visiting him if he went to jail, and I finally agreed with him. He reported for work on *Career*, and it was a great filmmaking experience for him. Joe Anthony, who was a stage director too, had made Paramount agree to three weeks of rehearsal before shooting the film. What a luxury! And since they knew that Tony was basically a stage actor, I was sure he would be magnificent in this role. So I packed my ever-present suitcases, and this time my little girl and Tony took *me* to the airport. I hadn't minded my gypsy life when I was in my twenties—I had done one-night stands with plays and Universal tours all over the country with films, but now I had a lovely big apartment in New York, and my idea of a vacation was just to stay home and polish my furniture and play with my child.

We were to start rehearsals in New York, but they had not yet cast the other leading role. *The Saturday Night Kid* is about a woman who gets into what she thinks is an empty cab, which turns out to be occupied, but she is obviously hysterical and wet from the rain, and inarticulate. The man in the cab is a photographer, and he takes her up to his studio in Chelsea to get her calmed down and find out where she's going. It is midnight on a Saturday night. The weird, twisted cab driver crawls all over the skylight and around the outside of this loft, trying to guess or see what his passengers are doing. As the play unfolds, you find out that the woman has killed her husband. He abused her for years, and she finally hit back when he beat her, and, unfortunately, she had a scissors in her hand. The play is about victims.

The photographer is mature and kind, and he realizes the terrible trouble this girl is in and tries to help her remember what happened. The play was in beautiful prose and had a powerful, eerie quality about it. Jack Dunphy was truly an artistic descendant of Tennessee Williams. As the producers were negotiating with various actors for the difficult role of the photographer, I was haunting the plays on Broadway. I walked over to Sardi's to have a quick supper, and Sidney Poitier was alone at the bar. He joined me for dinner, and I told him about *The Saturday Night Kid*.

He asked if he could take the script home with him, and he would call me the next day with suggestions. He called me the next morning and said, "Shelley, is there any reason why the photographer couldn't be black?"

I sat holding the phone and was stunned and excited. What a wonderful idea! It gave another dimension to the play: there was no earthly reason why the passenger couldn't be a black man. I quickly told Sidney to phone his agent, and I would phone the producers, Roger Stevens and Audrey Wood.

I was delirious with joy—what an exciting play this would be! This was the very beginning of the civil rights movement, and how wonderful it would be to show on the stage a kind, educated black man who helps an uneducated, violent white woman. After the first five minutes, their color would have nothing to do with the reality of the terrible human dilemma.

I quickly called Audrey Wood and told her that Sidney loved the play and would like to do it. She sounded excited, if a little hesitant, and said she would discuss it with Roger Stevens and George Keathley, the director, and possibly Truman Capote.

I'm still not quite sure what really happened. I was told that Sidney had had a sudden picture offer and could not do the play. After we had been in rehearsal for a couple of weeks, I found out that that was not true. The director, George Keathley, who was from the South, felt that having a black actor in this role would distort the play. I was ready to kill him. I would have walked, but I knew if I did, Equity would suspend me. I could not believe that that man was so shortsighted. It would have deepened the play and emphasized the compassion of one human being for another caught in a terrible situation. The lascivious cab driver, played by Joe Wiseman, would have demonstrated the puerile, prejudiced curiosity of the uneducated white man.

We should have at least had a reading of the play with Sidney, but Audrey explained to me that George was a hot young director, and they had to stand by his decisions. She agreed with me that the play would indeed have been enhanced by Poitier playing this role.

But they had cast a wonderful actor, Alex Nicol, opposite me. Alex was an Actors Studio member and was a rising star in both theater and films. We started rehearsals in the Morosco Theatre. I loved that theater, and whenever I walked through the long, covered alley to the stage door and put my right foot over the doorstep, I felt like a true star of the theater. They've recently demolished the Morosco to put up a huge crappy Marriott hotel. I can hardly believe it. Doesn't the hotel industry know that if they demolish all the theaters, there will be no tourism in New York? There's certainly no other reason to come to New York these days, and no tourists will come stay in their hotels.

Alex Nicol was a very mature, *menschie* guy (for an actor). He was great fun and lovely to act with. We tried out the play in Westport for a week, and although the critics mentioned flaws in the structure of the play, they praised its lyricism and all the performances. Joe Wiseman had received great reviews that said he was the quintessence of evil. After Westport we had a hiatus of a couple of weeks while Dunphy rewrote and while the Broadway set was installed in the Locust Street Theatre in Philadelphia.

During these two weeks, I went back to New York and redecorated my apartment, and my mother and my daughter and her nanny arrived. Tony had finished *Career*, but he immediately went into a film at MGM called *Go Naked in the World* with Gina Lollobrigida and Ernest Borgnine. Since Tony had been making such prestigious films, I couldn't think why he wanted to do this picture, which seemed one of Metro's routine melodramas. Tony usually discussed his films with me before he accepted them, but he was already a week into shooting when he phoned me about it. I called Stan Kamen, and he told me that Tony was able to put off his sentencing another few weeks by doing this film. I understood how frightened he was at the idea of going to prison, even if it was the honor farm. (Mitchum had told me all about this farm, supposedly honor.)

When Tony and I talked long distance, I tried to discuss this with him, but he was into denial and just pretended he was having a wonderful time and didn't have this fearful problem hanging over him.

I left for Philadelphia, and my mother promised me that she would come on Saturday night with my kid, and on

Sunday, my day off, I would show my little family the Liberty Bell and the beautiful and strange museums all over Philadelphia. Before my daughter was ready for kindergarten, she had seen the children's museums in New York, Los Angeles, Philadelphia, Indianapolis, and Washington. She seemed to have developed a special affinity for museums and to this day sees every exhibit that the Met has to offer.

The producers booked me into a suite in the fanciest hotel in Philadelphia, as I had to do the eternal interviews and publicity to ensure good box office. When I arrived, the director was waiting for me in the lobby of the hotel with an entire new script of *The Saturday Night Kid*. I of course had memorized and performed the old script in Westport. We had a week of rehearsals and then we opened. When there are only three people in a play, all the characters talk a lot. I studied the new script, and we rehearsed in the lobby of the Locust Street Theatre. The set was so complicated that it took two days to light it. But when we finally saw it, it was breathtaking.

The play was in lyrical prose, and the set was stylized and surrealistic. One half of the stage was an enormous skylight slanting toward the audience at a sharp angle, and the rest of the stage consisted of many kinds of photographic equipment. At one point in the second act, Joe Wiseman falls through the skylight. This stylized drama was quite a jump for Shelley's realistic Method acting. Alex and Joe had great patience with me and helped immeasurably, but I was having a fight to the death with the director. One New Year's Eve, when the Actors Studio was giving out its annual awards, I got one for the Actress Most Able to Resist Direction. Keathley didn't seem to care much about motivation; he just wanted us to stand in the right place for the lights. He was very concerned with the "picture" on the stage.

Opening night in Philadelphia, we had the Theatre Guild subscription audience, but we had gotten so many new scenes and lines, and the lighting of the show was so complicated, that we often felt like puppets. So opening night was rather a shambles.

Toward the middle of the play, when I finally realized

I'd murdered my husband and I was emotionally distraught, I never could seem to get myself into the place the director wanted me to be for the lighting effects. I seem to remember being deep in the throes of anguish as Alex Nicol pushed me around the stage until he got me into the right light.

Our reviews were less than brilliant, but by second week I finally pulled everything together and, with the help of the timid young author, I got hold of the part, and it became a joy to play.

The two producers and director issued sighs of relief, and we began to have wonderful performances and ten curtain calls a night. Jack Dunphy kept doing rewrites, which we would rehearse in the daytime and then try to put into the play that evening. The only performances that I really enjoyed were Wednesday and Saturday matinees because, thank God, Equity would not let us rehearse on matinee days, and I could give my brain a rest and just act.

One Friday morning, we were given a wonderful new scene for the third act. We rehearsed it all day, as we were to put it in that night. It was about ten pages of new dialogue. The audience was attentive and involved, but there was a man in the first row who had his feet on the orchestra rail and was fanning himself with a program. It was driving me crazy. It split my concentration, which was never the firmest during tryouts, and at the intermission I got the stage manager to go down into the orchestra and talk to him. We started the second act with the new scene. My concentration scattered, because I could still see the man's feet on the stage and see him fanning himself with the white program in the dark theater. I kept blowing my lines, and finally I could stand it no longer. I turned to the man and said:

"Look, mister, we came to Philadelphia to try out a new play. We're putting a new scene in tonight, and your damn feet are on the stage and you're fanning yourself with a program—it is driving me nuts! Would you please stop fanning and take your feet off the stage?"

The entire audience applauded, but I had broken the cardinal rule in the theater: I had shattered the "fourth wall." I had lost the audience, never to get them back during that performance.

And wouldn't you know, the same people from the Theatre Guild who'd seen me send an audience home in Westport a few summers before, when I was doing *Wedding Breakfast*—Lawrence Langner, Theresa Helburn, and Philip Langner—were sitting in the Locust Street Theatre that night. They had come in from New York to see the new version of their *Saturday Night Kid*. When the play was over, Alex Nicol, my friend, grabbed me and said:

"Shelley, if you ever talk to the audience again, I'll break your neck! You can't knock them out of the play like that and ever get them back."

In a meek voice, I promised never in my life to do it again. That night in the dressing room, the entire Theatre Guild looked at me amazed. All Lawrence Langner said was:

"When you were in *Oklahoma!* ten years ago, did you ever send the audience home?"

Of course I hadn't, but all I said to Mr. Langner was:

"Yes, of course! Even sometimes when I'm in a movie, and they don't pay attention, and they're eating too much popcorn, I turn from the screen to the audience and send them home."

"I believe you," he said, looking at me with a wry smile. "I know it's not technically possible, but I'm sure you've figured out a way to do it."

Many years later, Woody Allen made a movie called *The Purple Rose of Cairo*, in which an actor jumps off the screen and talks to Mia Farrow. Perhaps he'd heard about my performance in Philadelphia.

The next night, the closing notice went up. I was distraught. Jack Dunphy had finally given us beautiful rewrites, which clarified the problems of the play's exposition. The play came together, and the audience began to love it. I begged Roger Stevens and Audrey Wood not to close it and just bring it into the Morosco for a week of previews and the theater parties.

They said it was too much of a financial risk, and that

it was too esoteric for the average playgoer. I believed the New York critics would have loved it. I could not bear to see them destroy that beautiful set. I was sure that some producer, in a season or so, after Jack Dunphy had had a chance to rewrite again, would bring this powerful play into New York, and perhaps Sidney Poitier would do it. I would not let them destroy the set and burn it, which is what they usually do when a play closes out of town.

I therefore personally paid to have the set taken to a warehouse, and I paid for the storage rental for three years, hoping someone would rescue this beautiful play, and that it would somehow get born on Broadway. It never did.

Christmas was approaching, but on December 7, which is always a day of infamy for me—I remember so vividly the Japanese attacking Pearl Harbor—I got a long-distance phone call backstage. Tony told me he had been sentenced to thirty days at the honor farm, and, with good behavior, he could possibly get out in fifteen days.

I begged him to let me come to California so I could visit him.

"No," he said. "Stan Kamen is going to bring me anything I need."

But I heard in his voice the same shame that I had heard in my father's voice. We talked until they called half-hour, and when we hung up, we were both weeping. I knew that the hardened criminals who were in this so-called honor farm would treat Tony badly because he was a budding movie star, and I talked to Giesler and Stan, and anybody else I could think of, to see if he could be isolated from the other prisoners. Stan called me back after he'd talked to the warden of that facility and said the only other choice was to put him in solitary confinement—they didn't have special accommodations for movie stars. When I see how the press hassle Sean Penn and Madonna, and how they sent him to the prison hospital, I really feel for her and understand the pressure cooker they are living in. Part of the phrase *pressure cooker* is press.

* * *

Unfortunately for me, during the filming of *Night of the Hunter,* Mitchum, who had just gotten out of the same honor farm Tony was in, had told me about the reality of that place. Recalling that my father had been stabbed in prison, and knowing how dangerous Tony's nervous system was, I was terrified for him.

I cannot remember whether Tony served ten days or thirty days, because the time seemed interminable to me. When Tony got out, Stan drove him to the airport, and he took the red-eye to New York. I met him at La Guardia, but I hardly recognized him.

His usually ruddy complexion was gray. I think he had lost about twenty-five pounds. He seemed somehow shrunken too, as if his height was less and his frame was somehow smaller, and he seemed to be unable to communicate. When we got home to Central Park West, he went into our bedroom, took an hour-long shower, put on his bathrobe, sat in a corner, looked out the window, and would not talk to anyone. It was like reliving the time my father came home from Sing Sing.

I had been seeing a psychiatrist in New York, a wise and wonderful woman, and I called her and told her the condition that Tony was in. She got him admitted to the Neurological Institute, where he spent Christmas and New Year's. When he came home after ten days, he seemed much better, but not fully recovered. He seemed ashamed to go out, just like my father. He thought everyone was talking about the "criminal." I somehow again began to feel that everything was my fault. I tried to deal with the reality of the moment, and did everything I could think of to cheer Tony up.

To begin with, we began to go to the Actors Studio on a regular basis, and to see wonderful plays. We had a belated Christmas party at the end of January, and I invited all his friends and his family, who loved him, and mine too. There were no publicity men around. Tony had four films opening in New York—*This Could Be the Night*, *A Face in the Crowd*, *A Hatful of Rain*, and *Wild Is the Wind*—and he and I began to be invited to very classy parties. Suddenly Tony realized that the experience in prison had not hurt his career, and now he was a genuine movie star.

He didn't buy thirty-two suits this time, just a fancy tuxedo, and a Tiffany diamond-and-sapphire bracelet for me. He wanted to buy a car, but I convinced him he should wait until we got back to California, as I already had a convertible Cadillac in a very expensive New York garage.

From all our nights together on the New York party circuit, one special elegant party sticks in my mind. It was February, and Joe Levine was celebrating the opening of some picture and the forming of his new company. It was being held at a prestigious new restaurant, the Four Seasons. I was thin and beautiful, decked out in my sapphires and diamonds, and Tony, looking much older, was masculine and handsome in his new custom-made dinner jacket.

I even let him hire a limousine, although it seemed a dreadful waste to me that, while we were at a party for four hours, the driver would be sitting in front of the Four Seasons, getting paid. All the producers and directors in this beautiful restaurant made us feel as if we were very hot properties and were saying complimentary things about our work. We sat down in the center of the restaurant, next to a large pond full of water lilies and gardenias. It was the most beautiful room I had ever seen.

I felt lovely and loved and talented. Then Tony began to circulate around the room, mainly talking to other glamorous young actresses, and I began to feel deserted. Someone across the pond was trying to catch my attention. I finally put on my glasses and looked. It was Sir Laurence Olivier. I almost fell in the pond. He was mouthing lovely compliments and drinking silent toasts to me with his champagne glass. I did likewise with my champagne glass. I began not to miss Tony at all, even though I was sitting alone at a table for two. Then (glory of glories) Laurence Olivier wrote a note and put it on a lily pad and pushed it toward me. Nobody saw it but the entire restaurant.

I think I was blushing, but I retrieved the note. He'd written, "Do you think I'll ever catch you between husbands?"

It was then that I remembered that the first time I had met Olivier was at a New Year's Eve party at Sam Spiegel's house right after the Second World War. He had just come out of the British air force. We'd had a couple of lovely dances, and I kept talking about my then-navigator husband, who had returned from Europe and Africa to Chicago. Olivier had gently teased me about how patriotic I was, because I wouldn't dance too close—especially with Laurence Olivier.

The next time I met him was some years later at MGM. I'd just given birth to my daughter, and Vittorio was shooting a film called *Rhapsody* with Elizabeth Taylor. Larry walked me to the MGM commissary, and we were talking about my Shakespearean studies with Charles Laughton. He complimented me on having lost my Brooklynese speech. I told him I longed to work on the West End, especially in a Shakespearean production.

He told me that George Bernard Shaw had talked about sex as "the fire that propagates the world," and he said, "Shelley, if you can ever stop getting married and procreating, perhaps you could concentrate on a West End career."

That night at the Four Seasons, as I read his note, I realized he remembered my words. He had just done *The Prince and the Showgirl* with Marilyn Monroe, and I gestured to him to come over to my table. He walked around the restaurant, and he looked so handsome and dignified that I could almost see his crown from *Henry IV*. When he sat down, he poured us both some more champagne, and when I questioned him about the experience of working with Marilyn, he got a blank look on his face and said:

"Oh, I remember that Marilyn now. That was the cute little girl who was your roommate. She came into your apartment once when you were showing me the lights of Hollywood."

I gagged on my champagne.

He continued, "She is so talented. Can't she function without her mentor-bodyguard Paula?"

I suddenly remembered how George Stevens had treated Montgomery Clift's coach, Mira Rostova, during *A Place in the Sun.* He never acknowledged her existence, even when she got her hands in front of the camera while she was instructing Monty, ruining a take. She might as well have been an invisible cockroach, the way George treated her. I was sure Olivier had treated poor Paula Strasberg the same way.

I changed the subject and said, "Oh, yes, I gave you a lift to the Beverly Hills Hotel from one of Hedda Hopper's cocktail parties, and you wanted a nightcap."

We stared at each other. I remembered that he had sat on my little balcony while I gave him some sobering-up coffee. He seemed to want to stay, but I was so in awe of Laurence Olivier that my normal sexual appetite was frozen. As we looked at the lights of Hollywood, Marilyn opened the door. I had neglected to put out our signal that you shouldn't come in, a glass milk bottle. She had stood there frightened while I introduced her to Laurence Olivier, and he graciously kissed her hand. I dumbly phoned a cab to take him to the Beverly Hills Hotel.

That night at the Four Seasons, we were talking about my friend Marilyn again, and he took my hand and said, "Shelley, as you get older, you realize you only regret the things you didn't do."

We both laughed, wistfully I think. And then he said, "When we began rehearsing the film *The Prince and the Showgirl,* I wish I had remembered meeting Marilyn that night so long ago, but she looked so different in London, I didn't realize it was the same girl."

"I'm sure she remembered," I said.

"Maybe," he replied. "But she didn't mention it. Perhaps if I had remembered, we would have had a better relationship during the film."

I had not as yet seen the film, so I didn't know what he was talking about. When I saw the film, I knew. But here I was in this glamorous restaurant with the great Laurence Olivier holding my hand and reminiscing about our not-so-casual meetings over the years in Hollywood.

"Have you ever been to the Actors Studio?" I asked him.

He carefully said, "No, but I would like to see the New York home of the Method."

He told me that his exposure to the Method was limited to Stanislavsky's *An Actor Prepares*. When he was playing in repertory in Liverpool at the Liverpool Rep, Ralph Richardson had gotten hold of a copy of *An Actor Prepares* in English. Each actor in the company got to borrow it and had to read it quickly. They were performing one of the long Shakespeare history plays. The whole company could tell which exercise an actor was up to in the book—use of place, sense and memory, use of objects, or substitution—by the way he performed that night.

Suddenly Larry and I were aware that an ominous presence was hovering over our table. It was my young husband, Tony, looking rather wrathful. I said something stupid like, "Oh, Tony, I want you to meet my longtime friend Laurence Olivier."

Olivier stood up. Tony gave me a queer look and shook Larry's hand, and said, "Very pleased to meet you." Larry said something elegant, and then I think he decided he'd better not leave us two honeymooners just yet. He sat down, forcing Tony to sit down, and, with all his elegance, he told us both how brilliant we'd been in *A Hatful of Rain*. We both glowed.

"Mr. Franciosa, the morning papers are not out yet," he said, "but I think you've been nominated for the film of *Hatful*."

Tony got a dazed look on his face.

"Thank you," he said. "Thank you, sir!"

Larry said, "Shelley, how dumb they were not to have you re-create your role in the film. If they had, Zinnemann would have perhaps gotten a director's nomination for the film as well."

With that, he walked away. Tony and I just stared at each other. Then I hugged him, and I knew that everything was okay now. He would forget about the terrible months of trials, appeals, sentencing, and jail. He had been nominated by the American Academy of Motion Picture Arts and Sciences for an Oscar.

In a little while, all the producers, directors, writers, and stars at this party were congratulating Tony. He was so happy he could not eat the delicious dinner that they served in a little while, so I ate mine and his.

We drove home through the snowy park, and I told Tony he would be getting many great film offers now. An Oscar nomination was good for ten years of choice roles and escalating salaries. The phone was ringing when we got into the apartment, and his agents and friends and relatives were calling him from California and Spanish Harlem, where his family still lived.

The next morning was an Actors Studio day, but Tony was too excited to go. I tried to convince him that everyone at the Studio would want to congratulate him, especially Lee Strasberg. After all, *A Hatful of Rain* had been created at the Actors Studio. But Tony told me that he had an appointment with Marty Jurow, who'd once been his agent and now was going to be an important producer. It seems that Marty Jurow had gotten letters of intent from Tony and Anna Magnani and, with those, he was able to raise the preproduction monies to buy Tennessee Williams's *Orpheus Descending*. Marty was coming by to talk to Tony at twelve o'clock. I kissed him and warned him not to sign anything unless his agent and/or lawyer saw it first, even though I knew how anxious Tony was to film this wonderful Tennessee Williams play.

I got very dressed up and put on an elegant mink hat, eyelashes, a black coat with a mink collar, and my low-heeled boots. That day I met Marilyn Monroe at Columbus Circle on Fifty-seventh Street, and we brave Hollywood actresses walked all the way down Ninth Avenue to the Actors Studio on Forty-fourth Street. Marilyn commented that it was always easier in New York to stay in shape, because you walked everywhere.

It was still eerie for me when people would recognize me and not Marilyn. She had her invisible cloak on. No one bothered us. Just occasionally a nice New Yorker would say, "Hi, Shelley!" and go on. Marilyn had her hair covered in her old turban and was wearing her rimless clear eyeglasses, and so she was invisible. I guess her old black coat made everyone think she was my maid or something.

That morning the Actors Studio was jammed. Everyone had come home from Christmas holidays, and the place looked like a meeting of the Screen Actors Guild. Lee Strasberg waited until everyone calmed down, and he began to talk to us about the need and the responsibility we had, to try to create a national theater in America. Every civilized country in the world has a government-supported national theater. Other governments understand the need of their people for the culture and poetry of the times to be expressed in the theater.

The only time in the history of America we had a publicly supported theater was during the Roosevelt years, when we had the WPA. It was one of the ways he dealt with the Great Depression. That theater enriched our national life. Orson Welles's Mercury Theatre produced actors, writers, and directors who invigorated the theater and films for decades. Strasberg's dream was the creation of such a theater, a repertory theater which would do all the great plays of Eugene O'Neill, Tennessee Williams, Saroyan, Odets, Miller, and Hellman. Their plays were done in repertory in every language all over the world, but very seldom could you find them on or off Broadway. The prohibitive financial structure of Broadway made it impossible.

I was sitting in the second row, saving a seat for Tony if he should come. When I looked behind me, Laurence Olivier and Tony Richardson were sitting to the right of the auditorium. Marilyn was sitting in back of me, but I guess Laurence Olivier was in mufti too, and they didn't recognize each other or something.

During this session, we saw many scenes and exercises about the use of objects. Lee was stressing how important the props and/or furniture are to an actor. For instance, if an actor is reading a newspaper that says EARTHQUAKE IN INDIA, he holds the paper in perhaps a casual way. But if, as he reads it, he sees a town mentioned where his brother is working, he then holds the newspaper entirely differently. How important are the inanimate objects we use in our daily lives, and how telling is your handling of one of those props—a paperweight that belonged to a dead father, a book that belonged to a beloved teacher, pearls once owned by someone you loved.

We saw two scenes that day that illustrated profoundly how important the use of such props is, how they affect an actor's imagination and the content of the play that he is doing. Perhaps we had all sensed this as part of our craft, but we'd never understood the power of using them until Lee demonstrated in this exercise that day how it could change your characterization and the very soul of the part you were playing. There were forty or fifty members of the Studio there, and about twenty acting observers, all professionals who made their living acting, writing, or directing.

After sessions at the Actors Studio, we would all go to the Greasy Spoon, an aptly named coffee shop, which was between Eighth and Ninth Avenues, and is now the locale of the New York Improvisation. I followed Marilyn down the stairs of the Studio, but she didn't make for the front door. She went to the ladies' room in the back. I finally followed her in and asked her if she wasn't coming to have a hamburger at the Greasy Spoon.

"No, Shelley," she said. "I'm staying in the ladies' room until I'm sure Olivier and Tony Richardson have left."

I asked her if the shooting of *The Prince and the Showgirl* had been that rough. She blinked and smiled and said, "English actors are ashamed of their feelings and hate the idea of exposing themselves with our Method work. They prefer to act with technique."

I knew she was right, for the most part, but when those actors who have developed their brilliant exterior technique finally allow themselves to work deeply, it is an astonishing experience to watch them. I told her about Ralph Richardson and Celia Johnson, but she just smiled sadly and asked me if I'd seen *The Prince and the Showgirl* yet. I told her truthfully not yet.

"Never mind," she said. "Wait till you see *Some Like*

It Hot. It's high comedy, but I think I create a real person and a funny lady in it.''

I told her I was sure she did. Other actresses were crawling all over us in an effort to get to the toilet, but we stood our ground by the washbasin and kept talking.

"You know, Shelley, you're sort of in *Some Like It Hot*," Marilyn said.

I looked at her with amazement and said, "How?"

"Well, it's pretty difficult to relate to two men dressed in drag and in full makeup and pretend they're girls. Paula Strasberg told me to use 'substitution' and pretend they were my dearest friends, like the girlfriends I never had. So, Shelley, I pretended Tony Curtis was you and Jack Lemmon was you, too. I just pretended I was talking to you and put your face over their made-up, silly faces. I think it worked great.''

I kissed her and turned around and made for the Greasy Spoon. Laurence Olivier and Tony Richardson were sitting at the counter, drinking coffee. I joined Ben Gazzara, Janice Rule, and Will Hare and surreptitiously made sure my eyelashes were on straight and my lipstick had not faded. In a little while, Olivier came over to me.

"Shelley, we are having the last run-through of *The Entertainer* with just a stage light and chairs before we leave for Boston tonight," he said. "Would you like to come and see the run-through?"

I replied, "I would love to."

"Well, get to the Cort Theatre by two-thirty," he said, then he and Tony Richardson left the Greasy Spoon.

I swallowed my greasy hamburger, the specialty of the house, and I dashed to the phone and called Tony, asking him if he would like to see Olivier do a run-through of *The Entertainer*. He told me he was talking with Marty Jurow, and he sounded rather strange. He was still receiving telegrams and phone calls congratulating him on his nomination.

It had begun to snow, and he promised that when my kid came home from nursery school at three o'clock, they would both go sledding, across the street on a little hill in front of my building in Central Park. She was still very much a California baby and loved the snow, which she hadn't yet seen until this weekend. I told him I would be home in a couple of hours.

"Don't sit too near Laurence Olivier," he warned.

"I'd love to sit near Laurence Olivier, especially on the stage, but so far I'm just sitting in the audience."

When I got to the theater, the actors were talking to Tony Richardson. I quickly took a seat about ten rows back, in the middle of the orchestra. I had expected to see other members of the Actors Studio in the theater. I'd assumed Tony Richardson had invited everyone, but I seemed to be the only person in the orchestra. I sat quietly and felt that my blonde hair looked awfully blonde. I didn't want to distract the actors.

Suddenly sitting next to me was Alfred Ryder, a distinguished actor and a member of the Studio, who at that time was married to Kim Stanley.

"What are you doing here?" he whispered.

"Olivier and Tony Richardson asked me to come to this run-through," I whispered back. "What are you doing here?"

He told me he was Olivier's understudy. I knew he was a very fine actor, but if Olivier was sick, everybody would ask for their money back.

"I know it's silly," he said, "but according to Equity, he has to have an understudy. I love watching the rehearsals, and I need the money."

Tony Richardson jumped off the stage, nodded to me, went upstairs, and sat in the front row of the mezzanine. The metal folding chairs on the stage represented the set and the furniture and various tables, doors and windows. The stagehands' union will not allow the actors to use props during rehearsal unless six of them are paid, so actors have to work with what they can.

The play started, and Joan Plowright and Brenda de Banzie were extraordinary. About ten minutes into the play, Olivier made his entrance. *The Entertainer* is about an aging vaudevillian in some English seaside town, trying to keep going in the face of various adversities. Olivier was brilliant and quite funny.

In one scene, he begins to weep, and I could see from my seat that they were real tears. Alfred and I were very entertained by his mercurial, brilliant performance, but we were not moved with feelings of either pity or identification. Olivier suddenly stopped, came down to the footlights, and, in a projecting voice, addressed Tony Richardson, up in the mezzanine.

"Tony, could we please start from the top again? I want to try something."

"Of course, Larry," Richardson said, "but you know we are having a dress rehearsal in Boston tonight. They've already got the set up." This was a strange, un-British, undisciplined request on Olivier's part. I felt the rest of the actors go into a sort of shock, and Alfred, sitting next to me, grew rigid.

Olivier had been doing *The Entertainer* for a season in England, and I believe had also toured the provinces with it, and he was to shoot the film the following summer.

Laurence Olivier stood quite still, thinking. Then he walked over to the proscenium and began to touch it and look at it in a strange way, almost with hatred. He had taken off his glasses and put them away, and I got the feeling that he could not see very well without them. For a second, as he leaned against the proscenium, I was afraid he would fall off the stage. He seemed to be a little drunk, but he hadn't been drunk when he'd started the rehearsal. He suddenly hawked and coughed like a very old man and spat on the proscenium. He stood there and watched the spittle run down. He walked into the wings and the stage manager said, "Let's start again."

I thought I knew what he was doing. However fulfilling the theater had been for him, as with every other actor, it had cost him a great deal, perhaps his whole family life. In some ways he must have hated what it had cost him. This love/hate relationship in the theater is something all actors understand. All actors have had the experience of having the curtain go up and you know you cannot stop until the play is over—whether you have a terrible cold, pneumonia, a 104-degree temperature, or you're having a miscarriage, or your real mother has died an hour before, *you have to finish the play*. You lie to yourself and the audience, but you finish the play, and it often fills you with self-loathing.

The run-through started again, and all the actors were somehow quieter, and in some strange way funnier, certainly realer. Ten minutes later, an old music-hall actor walked out on the stage—no more the brilliant Olivier, but a sad, defeated, almost embarrassing actor with a North Country accent and bleary eyes. Alfred and I sat there stunned. We had the sense we were no longer watching acting but the real thing, almost like watching a documentary. The other actors were sparked by this performance, and their performances were completely different from the first time we had seen them. When it came to the part of the play when Olivier had cried real tears, he didn't cry, but Alfred and I found ourselves weeping. That act was one of the most thrilling things I had ever seen in the theater.

At the end of the act, Olivier put his eyeglasses back on, walked over to the proscenium, took his handkerchief, and wiped off the spittle. He turned around to Tony Richardson and said, "All right, Tony, what do you think?"

Who would have thought that Sir Laurence Olivier needed reassurance? There was a pause, and Richardson said, "Well, let's just finish the play and we'll discuss it later, Larry. After all, we're opening in Boston tomorrow night."

Olivier needed the reassurance of his director, to be told to continue doing what he was doing. His use of the object, the proscenium, and what it meant to him had changed and improved his whole interpretation of that role. However, that endorsement was not forthcoming from Tony Richardson at that given moment, due to the stressful situation of having to open the play with a new set the next night in Boston. When the second act started, there was, once again, brilliant, mercurial Laurence Olivier on the stage, but the powerful interpretation of the defeated vaudevillian was gone.

I crept out of the theater and got into a taxi. Olivier had that morning seen Strasberg and members of the Studio demonstrate "the use of an object," and he had effectively used the proscenium of the theater as his object. I resolved again, then and there, to only go to Hollywood to do fine films, and no matter where Tony's life took him, I would stay in New York or hopefully someday London's West End and work in the theater.

Some months later, when I read in the press that Larry and Vivien Leigh were divorced and he was marrying Joan Plowright, a brilliant, very Method-oriented young English actress, I wondered wistfully, What if—if?

When I got back to the apartment, I was anxious to tell Tony all about this experience with Olivier, and that he mustn't dare miss any more sessions at the Studio. I opened the door with my key and walked through the hall to the living room. I started to rattle off all this information about the remarkable acting I'd just witnessed. As I began to run down, I noticed Tony was with a former William Morris agent, and they weren't paying any attention to me—they were just sort of staring at each other. Then, right in the middle of my story, Tony got up and walked into the bedroom.

Silence. I asked the agent if something was wrong. He asked for a drink. I got us both some Scotch, and I again had a fearful premonition. This agent was now becoming a producer. He had acquired the property of *Orpheus Descending* by procuring both Tony Franciosa's and Anna Magnani's letters of intent. This is how he financed the acquisition from Tennessee. He explained to me that when Meade Roberts, who transcribed all of Tennessee's plays into films (and not much else), had finished the screenplay, Audrey Wood had somehow given the final script to Marlon Brando, "by accident."

Marlon wanted to do *The Fugitive Kind*, as *Orpheus* was now called, and the agent had just finished explaining to Tony that if he had Marlon, he would get many millions to make the film. Since he had helped Tony's career when he'd been an agent at William Morris, Tony had agreed to relinquish any claim on the film property.

I didn't know whether to stab him or punch him out. Tony had just recovered from a terrible experience, and I knew this artistic betrayal from someone he respected and admired would devastate him. I knew if the agent really had Marlon Brando, any opposition would be self-defeating and frustrating. Brando was big box office, and that is the reality of the film industry. So I just asked him how much money he had given Tony.

"Well," he said, "when I got the financing for the film, I was to give Tony one hundred and seventy-five thousand dollars. But Tony has waived all rights, and he has also agreed to waive the financial obligation of my company to him."

"I'm sure you misunderstood Tony," I sweetly said. "In any event, I don't waive my eighty-seven thousand five hundred dollars. You know there's community property in California."

He looked aghast. I continued, "If you want me to discuss the entire problem with Marlon, I would be happy to do so. I think he would love to know how he unwittingly took a role away from a young Studio member who was just beginning his career, after you had used his name to get the option from Tennessee."

His face got ashen. He knew that if I discussed this with Marlon, it might wreck the whole project.

"The check for the full amount will be here in a couple of hours," he said as he left.

And so it was.

I went into the bedroom, and Tony was again just staring out the window. The nurse was pulling my child on a little sled down below.

"Never mind," I said, putting my arm around him. "Marlon and Magnani will hate each other on sight. I know them both, and the picture will stink."

And so it did.

I never saw it. To this day I feel it is disloyal to Tony for any member of the Actors Studio to go and see that picture. It got dreadful reviews and just about destroyed Magnani's career in America. Marlon walked through it and all but told the audience he was doing it just for the money. When any of my acting students do scenes from *Orpheus Descending* they automatically get bad critiques from me; I still hate it so.

Tony and I continued our round of parties and theater and good restaurants. In a couple of weeks, I was notified by my agent that George Stevens finally wanted me to come to California to start rehearsals and costumes for the role of Mrs. Van Daan in the film version of *The Diary of Anne Frank*. I wept with joy. (The filming had been delayed a year before they got a script and cast.)

I was so glad I hadn't done any B pictures since *Hatful*, and now I had a chance to be in this distinguished film that would not only give me a great acting role, but a chance to be part of a most important historical document.

Suddenly, Tony was offered the chance to play the title role in *Goya*, a big-budget film to be made in Rome by United Artists. He was ecstatic, too, now—he would be starring with Ava Gardner, on his very first European film. He was going to Spain first to do research about this great painter. We spent the rest of the time in New York at museums and bookstores. Tony was reading everything he could about Goya. I suddenly remembered my friend Mickey Knox, a Paramount actor who lived in Italy now and as he was bilingual, did translations and dialogue coaching. I found out when I phoned him that his Spanish was pretty good. He agreed to meet Tony in Madrid, and I got Tony's agent to have UA hire Mickey as dialogue director for the film and help Tony with his role.

I did not do any research on *Anne Frank* except for reading and rereading her diary. I knew I was in George Stevens's capable hands, and he would tell me everything I needed to know about this Dutch-Jewish woman who was hiding in Anne Frank's little attic.

Thinking of Holland, I suddenly remembered that, at the very beginning of my career, I'd done a musical film called *Knickerbocker Holiday*. It was a film based on the Broadway show in which Walter Huston had made "September Song" so famous. In the research I had done for that role, I had learned a great many facts about the Dutch people—how strong and courageous they are and what infinite patience they have. They build fields that they will never see, just their great-grandchildren. First they build dikes to keep the ocean away from fields they're building. Next, they drain the sand. Then, they take out the sand and bring dirt to the fields. This takes many years of drying and hauling. Their great-grandchildren will grow things on these fields. These facts I remembered as I read the role of Mrs. Van Daan. They gave me a quiet strength of purpose about the Dutch when I played her. Everything in life is valuable, and I had done this research in 1943 for a Hollywood musical.

In the next week, Tony and I prepared for yet another career separation in our rocky marriage. We went to the airport, this time together, he to fly to Spain and I to Hollywood. At the airport, he said something sort of strange to me:

"I'm so very glad you've got this role with George Stevens, but I can't help wishing you were going with me."

This statement certainly added to my ambivalent feelings. I reassured him as best I could and told him what a great director Henry Koster was, and that Ava Gardner always had the best cameramen and crews. She was an MGM baby on loan, and they always took very special care with her films. We kissed goodbye and then flew to the opposite ends of the earth.

I sat in the plane and carefully read the film script of *Anne Frank* again. And then I reread Anne Frank's *Diary of a Young Girl,* with its introduction by Eleanor Roosevelt. I thought of all the things I'd done during the Second World War, and how I had carefully pushed away all knowledge of the concentration camps until the end of the war. My then-husband, who was a navigator, had hinted at them, and our family had missing relatives who, we found out later, died in the concentration camps.

I tried to imagine what it was like, hiding in an attic with the Nazis prowling around Amsterdam, looking constantly for the hidden Resistance fighters and Jews. It was beyond my actor's imagination. These people hid in this little attic for more than two years. They could not make any noise. In the daytime, they were afraid even to use the toilet. They were almost afraid to breathe during the day. Their attic was above a grain store, and the entrance to the attic was a hidden stairway behind a bookshelf.

I spent almost six months on the set of *Diary of Anne Frank*, which was that attic, exactly reproduced on the soundstage at Twentieth Century–Fox. George Stevens made the set so real that it was almost unbearable. He would turn the heat up in August if we had to swelter. He would turn the air conditioning on if we were doing a winter scene and we would all sneeze and freeze.

When we started shooting the film, Stevens had all the adult actors come to a projection room. He showed us the films his unit in the Special Services had taken of the concentration camps. His Army unit had been the first into Dachau. Watching those horrendous films possibly made me play that role so that I won the Oscar, but I believe shooting that film scarred me for life. I can never read or watch anything about the Holocaust. It is beyond human comprehension that human beings could do such a thing to their fellow beings. We saw a color film of piles of bodies, some dead, some alive—babies, children, mothers, men—the bones in the crematorium, and the dazed, walking skeletons that were barely alive when the American army arrived. The soldiers took as many as they could back to the hospitals.

I could not comprehend it. The Nazis had destroyed millions of Jews and many millions of Resistance fighters, Negroes, Gypsies, Communists, Catholics, Poles, Frenchmen, Czechs, Russians, and Yugoslavs. I could not comprehend it. To this day I'm not sure that I have dealt with it. What kind of sickness invaded the German mind that they could slaughter children and babies—these millions of noncombatants? We in America cannot really understand this kind of malevolent hatred. We can just hope that this disease has been eradicated from the face of the earth.

The day we started shooting, there was some kind of problem concerning Darryl F. Zanuck's request concerning the type of camera to be used. It seems that Twentieth Century–Fox had patented a new camera system called CinemaScope, in which the film had to be projected on a huge curved screen, and the powers that be at Fox were insisting that George Stevens photograph this picture about people hiding in a little attic in CinemaScope. We did not shoot that first day.

It seems CinemaScope was going to be Hollywood's answer to television, which in 1958 they were still pretending would go away. If people were watching pictures on a small little box, they were going to entice them away from that free little box with a huge horizontal screen. While CinemaScope was great for photographing Niagara Falls or Westerns or any outdoor spectacle, it was not very useful when photographing actors' thoughts and feelings.

Stevens sat on the set for two days. When the assistant director asked him what he was to do, Stevens said, "Think, like I'm doing." His thinking drove the executives crazy, because shooting this film cost about $50,000 a day. Stevens and his cameraman, William Mellor, suddenly decided that this attic needed vertical beams to hold up its roof, and that's what they did—they arbitrarily put these beams wherever they needed them on the set to make the film seem small. They were not placed in any realistic positions. They were just moved to different positions in each of the scenes. They gave the audience the feeling of this tiny attic, even though it was photographed in CinemaScope. This saved the film's subsequent release on television and cassettes. Even when you saw it on the gigantic CinemaScope screen, you had the feeling of watching a small cramped attic.

I was on the set eight hours a day, whether I was in the scene or not. I sat as close to Stevens as I could—to hear him talk to the crew and actors. I was now wise enough about acting and film to know that I had another chance to work with a true genius. I wanted to learn everything that I possibly could about his techniques. I hoped that one day I would direct films; I'm still hoping. At one point in the filming, it was about 8:00 P.M., and they were still on the stage doing a scene that I wasn't in. Stevens saw my rapt face taking in everything that was happening, from the construction crew to the sound department to the lenses that Mellor was using to his rehearsing the actors. He suddenly turned to me and said, "Shelley, I bet if I asked you to sweep up the stage, you'd do it."

"Yes, I would, Mr. Stevens," I replied. "And I told Mr. Cukor that, too."

The little girl that they had chosen to play Anne Frank was a seventeen-year-old model by the name of Millie Perkins. She had a sweet childlike innocence, the gift of seeing beauty in every situation, and an optimistic attitude about everything. From Anne Frank's writings, we know she herself must have been like this. Millie was very worried that she knew so little about Jewish traditions or history, so I rather took her under my wing and tried to help her as much as possible. I gave her books to read, and talked to her about what the religious background of Anne Frank must have been. Like most American Jews, this German family was completely assimilated, or so they thought. Otto Frank had been a high officer in the German Army in World War I. Before the advent of Hitler, the Franks had thought of themselves as more German than Jewish, so all of it now seemed very comprehensible to the little Catholic Millie Perkins. They were people comfortable in their religion and not obsessed by it.

The first shooting day, the third one on the schedule, we shot the scene in which all the people arrive in the attic, and the Van Daan son, played by Richard Beymer, takes the Jewish star off his coat and starts to burn it. Jews were required to wear these yellow stars once Hitler came to power. The boy was getting rid of that stigma as soon as possible. Suddenly I remembered something from Anne Frank's diary and, although I knew that when you transfer a book to film something has to be lost, I didn't want this lost. Without realizing it, I yelled, "Cut!"

I thought George Stevens was going to throttle me. He looked like he would. I was shaking, but I stood my ground.

"Shelley, you're not even in this scene," he thundered.

Then I told him I remembered that in the diary and

play versions, when the boy starts to burn his star, Anne tells him that it is really David's star—King David of the Old Testament. The shape of the shield that he took into victorious battle was the shape of the Jewish star, and it's not what the Nazis have turned it into—a mark of shame. That is the original meaning of the Star of David.

George Stevens stared at me and then he yelled, *"Ivan Moffat!"* He was the writer who had assisted Albert and Frances Hackett, the playwrights who had also written the screenplay. Ivan had been working on this screenplay with George for so many years that he was slightly dazed. George Stevens called a ten-minute break, and they all retired to his trailer to examine what had been accidentally cut from the play and the book.

I was frozen with fear, but I had remembered these few lines from the play and they were so powerful for me because, when I was a little girl in the early thirties, I had worn a gold Jewish star proudly, all the time. It was a pin I had won at the Jamaica Jewish Center for the only subject I ever excelled in, the history of the Jewish people. To this day I remember the Pioneer Hebrew songs that I learned in my Brooklyn grammar school.

When Stevens came out of the trailer, he had new pages for Millie and Dick Beymer. He twinkled his eyes at me and gave me a pat on the head. In a few minutes, I watched him reshoot this scene in which Dick starts to burn his Jewish star, and Anne Frank whispers to him, "Don't do that. After all, it's David's star—the shape of the shield of his victorious army." This little moment in the film is extraordinary—the two terrified Jewish children, who are hiding from the Nazis, remembering their heritage of the powerful King David. I will always be proud that I had the courage to stop the filming and see that that moment was restored to the film.

The picture progressed day by day in the most fulfilling way an actor can work. Tape recorders were then the size of large TV sets. George Stevens, who'd hated sound since its inception, understood that music affected each actor most powerfully and personally, so whatever emotion he needed for a scene, he would reach next to his chair and push a button, playing that actor's personal tape. He had recorded a tape for each actor of the sounds and music that affected him most powerfully in various emotions. He would play the tape sometimes right through an actor's dialogue, and then edit the music out in the cutting room.

George claimed that silent pictures had spoken in an international language, and that the invention of sound had diminished rather than enhanced motion pictures. I think he was right.

After every tense scene, George Stevens would put on a raucous rendition of "The Purple People Eater" to make us all relax and start fooling around, so we would forget the tenseness and often the agony of the scenes. I recently did a children's picture for no other reason than that it was titled *The Purple People Eaters*.

Stevens had insisted that I gain twenty pounds to play Mrs. Van Daan. He knew that the weight made me look older. I obliged by gaining thirty pounds.

I got a wire from Tony that said he was flying home for the Oscars, since he had been nominated for *Hatful*. It was either the last Monday of March or the first Monday in April. So I immediately began to lose weight so that I would fit into one of my beautiful evening gowns, as I knew we would be photographed from all angles during the Oscar telecast. I wore a coat, fortunately, in the scenes of *Anne Frank* that were shot in the weeks before that Oscar telecast, and I had no close-ups. We had the luxury of shooting the film exactly in sequence. Stevens was concentrating on Mr. and Mrs. Frank's scenes at the beginning of the filming and did not notice until the Friday night before the telecast that I had lost weight. I spent the next Saturday and Sunday in the Beverly Hills Health Club steam room and lost another fifteen pounds.

Tony arrived that Saturday night, and we hugged and kissed, and I told him that Stevens had given me the Monday night of the telecast off. I was so anxious that he should win the Oscar that the whole event is rather a blur.

I only remember sitting to the right of him, looking at my handsome young husband, who was almost comatose and beyond speech during the whole Oscar-cast. I have no idea who won that year. I just know that Tony didn't.

When the presenter came out to announce Best Supporting Actor, she announced some other actor's name when
the envelope was opened.

Tony just held my hand tightly, and we both tried to
smile for the TV cameras. We did not even go to the
Oscar party. We went home, and then he caught the red-
eye for New York and then a plane to Italy.

When I reported back on the set Tuesday morning,
having gobbled spaghetti and ice cream all Monday night,
Stevens took one look at me and said, "Your back is to
the camera until you gain back the twenty pounds you
lost last week!"

So if you ever see *Anne Frank* on television, notice
that during the entire Hanukkah scene my back is to the
camera. When I gained the weight back, he did my close-
ups for that scene. There was no way to fool that lovely
fox, George Stevens.

After Tony had left, I had the feeling he hadn't even
been there. His trip had been so fast. I had not really
talked to him about his film or for that matter anything
else. But his film was supposed to end long before mine,
so I knew that he would be back in a couple of months
and then we would have a long talk. I must admit that
during the glorious six months' shooting of *Anne Frank* I
did not think of Tony very much. Out of sight, out of
mind. I was creating a great role in a great film.

One day about four months into the shooting, George
Stevens announced to us that we were having lunch with
Mr. Otto Frank, the real Anne's father. He had never
seen a production of the play; it would have been too
difficult a thing for him to do. In fact, it was rather courageous for him to come and watch some of the filming
that afternoon.

We all had lunch with him in our costumes, shabby,
smelly wartime Dutch clothes. He looked around the
table at all the actors who were portraying his friends and
family. He was trembling, and he had tears in his eyes.
He was a tall, stately gentleman, with a fringe of white
hair, and he had an erect, soldierly carriage, and he was
very intelligent.

He looked at Millie Perkins for a long time—she looked quite a lot like the real Anne Frank. We went on with the lunch, and we all tried to let Mr. Frank know how welcome he was, and how much we respected his child's famous diary about his family's ordeal.

After lunch, he came on the set again and watched me do the scene in which the rest of the people in the attic find out that my husband had been stealing food. Ed Wynn, who played the irascible dentist, was very sad and funny. In the scene, I am defending my husband, played by Lou Jacobi, against all the other people's attacks. Joseph Schildkraut, who was playing Otto Frank, calms us all down and warns me to watch my husband from then on. I try to argue, "No one seems to understand. My husband is bigger than everybody else, he needs more food, and he suffers hunger more violently."

Stevens had a way of almost shooting the first rehearsal, when you hadn't yet planned anything, and your reactions were very spontaneous and unexpected, maybe not at all what the writer or director had envisioned. Stevens would get this on film, and then he would rehearse the scene for hours to make sure he got all the values and interpretations he wanted, and then he would shoot the scene again. He would often use a great deal of that first spontaneous master shot. But then he would have the two-shots and the close-ups to orchestrate the scene with when he edited the film.

Otto Frank sat and watched us for several hours. After my close-up, I went over to him and sat down. He smiled at me and said:

"I believe, Miss Winters, you will get the Oscar for this picture."

"Why?" I asked, amazed.

He patted my cheek and told me that I was very like the real Mrs. Van Daan, and I had her courage, silliness, and compassion.

"Mr. Frank, if I win an Oscar for *The Diary of Anne Frank,* I promise I will bring it to the Anne Frank Museum in Amsterdam."

He smiled and said, "That would be a very difficult thing to do, wouldn't it, Shelley?"

I equivocated. "Yes, but I'll keep it for a little while, and then bring it to the museum."

And that's what I did. It took me a decade of thinking about it, and I had gotten another Oscar, but when I was doing a film, *That Lucky Touch*, in Brussels, my black housekeeper, Molly Epps, reminded me of my promise to Otto Frank, and I said to her, "Molly, I'm going to *Brussels*, not Amsterdam."

"Look at the map," she said. "They're very close to each other. You can go there on a Sunday."

Molly was making sure that though I was fighting for civil rights I kept my obligation to Israel and the people who had died in the camps.

So I sadly packed my very first Oscar and took it to Brussels with me. After I had been shooting *Lucky Touch* for a month, on my first Sunday and Monday off, I got on the train to Amsterdam and found the Anne Frank Museum and went up the steps to the museum office. When I handed the Oscar to the woman in charge, she seemed very confused. She said something that struck me as very strange:

"Mr. Frank will be here in a few minutes."

This was a dozen years after he had watched me play Mrs. Van Daan. I said to the lady that I had thought that Mr. Frank lived in Switzerland now.

He walked into the museum, and now he was a very old man of eighty-five. I handed him the Oscar, and he said, smiling:

"It is almost a miraculous coincidence. I only come to this museum twice a year, for about an hour. You know this is the real house we hid in.

"Shelley, hundreds of thousands of young people go through this attic every year, and they will love to see the Oscar you won for the role you played in Anne's *Diary*. How did you know to come today?"

I said, "I didn't know you would be here."

By this time, we were surrounded by teenagers from every country in the world.

He paused, looking around. "Sometimes I think God is punishing me by letting me live so long. Every day I think how foolish I was to believe that the countries of the world would not let Hitler expand. I brought my spice business from Berlin to Amsterdam, and I felt safe for my family. I was so sure Hitler could never take Holland.''

The young people around us were listening avidly and translating to each other in their own languages.

"They all died," Mr. Frank said. "All my family and friends. I was the only one that lived.''

The lady curator of the museum guided us into a private office. A very young man suddenly said, "I'm a cub reporter from AP in Sydney, Australia. This is a very important story. Miss Winters and Mr. Frank, couldn't I come in with you and talk about it?''

"Of course," Otto said, and led him into the office. For the next half-hour, we explained to this young man about how we had first come to meet, and often we would tell this kid what questions to ask. But he got the whole story right, and I guess the AP liked it, because it ended up on the front page of every newspaper in the world the next day.

Mr. Frank showed me through the museum, and I was stunned by what an exact replica the set had been of the Anne Frank house. By then, the Dutch had requisitioned another house next to it, and both were now called the Museum Against Intolerance. There was an exhibit in the other house about what was going on at that time in Chile. It was terrible, and I could not look at the photographs.

That night, as I took the train back to Brussels, I remembered everything about the shooting of *Anne Frank,* my most important film. I recalled that as the picture had progressed day by day, we came to know, from Stevens's careful direction, that we were indeed in a great classic. Time has proved it so.

The determination of this great director was further demonstrated at the beginning of the picture when he needed to bring the camera below the ground floor, where the spice store was located, then up on the second and third floors of the attic. Bill Mellor could not get his camera low enough for the scene in which the burglar breaks into the spice store. This shot was very important to the audience because, right at the very beginning of the picture, they must understand the logistics of the building where the people are hiding. That day when we went to lunch and were all gathered in the commissary, Stevens came over to our table and said to stay put until he sent for us. We dawdled over our coffee and no dessert, then suddenly we heard what sounded like a bomb. We all became very frightened and ran back to the stage. We found out that Stevens had gotten tired of appealing to Darryl F. Zanuck to dig a place for the camera below the stage floor. Zanuck had stalled and stalled. So that day, Stevens just dynamited the stage. He had been in the Special Services during the war and knew exactly how to carry out precision blasting and demolition. I resolved then and there never to cross him.

This excavation he put to wonderful use. In the scene in which we all are sleeping and we suddenly hear someone in the store in the middle of the night, the camera in the pit followed the figure up the stairs. Stevens would not tell us in advance what was going to happen in the scene, and, when we first hear the burglar, we become still and frozen. The dentist that Ed Wynn played has gone to the bathroom, and we do not know if he has heard the thief or not. The burglar, hearing Ed Wynn's footsteps, gets frightened, runs from the shop, and leaves the front door open and flapping in the wind. Otto Frank must go downstairs and lock it. The camera follows this desperate night errand while we all stay in the attic, holding our breath, praying that a Nazi policeman doesn't see the open door and catch Otto Frank.

I remember another special scene in which one of the Dutch women who is helping to hide us brings us a small radio. At this point we are able to listen to the "Voice of America." Underneath all of the hopeful announcements, we realize that Hitler's troops have spread all over Europe. Though we think that the children don't understand, we know that if he wins, we are without hope. But Otto Frank will not let us dwell on this. As time passes, we finally hear that the tide of war is reversing. We become hopeful again.

I learned something about acting that I was to use for the rest of my life. When you act deeply, relating to the traumas that you have buried, you reawaken fears and feelings that float around you after the scene is over. After one special, exhausting, terrible day, when we filmed the scene in which the people in the attic are peeping out a high window and watching the Nazis round up Jews, Stevens used that horrible double siren the Gestapo trucks used—two short blasts in different keys. To this day I cannot bear to hear that sound, which they now use on many ambulances and fire engines. When I hear it, I still get cold with fear.

When we did that scene in the film, after it was over, I went to my dressing room to take off my costume, which was by now much too big for me. I lost twenty-five pounds during the shooting of the film, exactly as Mr. Stevens wanted me to do. As my sweet hairdresser, Ruby, took the pins out of my hair, I suddenly turned to her and said:

"Ruby, I know you hate me. You're really anti-Semitic, aren't you?"

Ruby had worked with me through many pictures, and of course she didn't understand that I didn't know how to deal with the feelings of fear I had evoked in the scene. I was transferring them to her.

"My God," she said, "I've worked on ten pictures with you! I know this is a very unattractive hairdo, but Mr. Stevens wants it this way. It makes you look like a fifty-year-old woman. What am I supposed to do?"

She started crying. On every other film I had done with her, she had made me look as beautiful as possible. Suddenly I remembered it was only a picture, it was not reality, and I snapped out of the fear that the scene had evoked in me. She finally seemed to understand. But for the rest of the shooting of *The Diary of Anne Frank*, she looked at me a little suspiciously as she sized me up.

That night, driving home in my car, I finally fully realized, maybe for the first time, that Tony could not differentiate the scene and the reality when he evoked his feelings of fear. Fear induces a terrible feeling of weakness, so he pivoted into anger and hatred. These are stronger and easier emotions to deal with.

In the years to come, I was lucky enough to be connected to a woman psychiatrist in New York who was able to explain to me how nature buries our traumas, but if they result in antisocial behavior, they must be looked at and worked through. I have had many problems in my career, but I have been able, I believe, to have the insight most of the time to prevent destructive behavior. I know some people think I'm temperamental, but I have done one hundred films so far, and about fifty plays, and I think I was only able to do such an enormous amount of disciplined work because I was able to handle this occupational disease. I call it traumatitis. This disease of acting is one of the main reasons so many artists become alcoholics or drug addicts. I think this psychiatric knowledge prevented me from following either of those routes. The only addiction I have is food, and I think I more or less have this under control now. If Tony reads this book, I can tell him that I have found through the acting classes I teach another way of working, sort of extending my Stanislavsky research. It was developed by my friend Eileen Aiken through her studies with Lee. It's called Keen Observing and Personalizing. It is not so traumatic to the psyche.

Tony had been sending me very strange letters and cables. I can't remember the exact wording in these communications, but, in essence, he said his film was in terrible trouble and he was having a terrible time of it. If I was a good wife, I would walk off the film of *Anne Frank* and join him in Italy and help him. When I read between the lines, I realized that he was doing a film called *Goya*, and Ava Gardner, although in the same film, was making one called *The Naked Maja* (the name of one of Goya's famous paintings). I would call Tony on Sundays, and he did indeed sound awful. His film was two months behind schedule, with no end in sight. I promised I would fly to Rome as soon as Stevens released me.

The end of our film was, of course, when the Nazis

know we are hiding there and they come up the stairs to get us. Stevens had me sitting in a low chair, waiting, clutching my old fur coat and a huge bundle of silly possessions. My straw hat is carefully on my head, and I am wearing my white gloves and sensible shoes. How does one dress to go to a concentration camp? He had let me pick out what I would wear. My face is indeed ravaged by those months of starvation and agony. I had deep rings under my eyes, and I did not need any makeup. Stevens put the camera on me and said:

"Shelley, you are brave. You reassure everyone in the attic. You are a courageous woman."

He talked to me while the camera was turning, and then he put on the tape machine—Hitler talking to his storm troopers, a long, insane speech—and Stevens kept saying to me:

"Listen, but you are courageous. You reassure the others."

I think this is the scene that won me the Oscar, but I would not like to do it again. The very last scene of the film is one in which the Nazis are coming up the stairs to the little secret garret where Anne Frank and my son are —above the main attic. She is looking into the blue sky, and she says that maybe peace won't come for a long time, but despite everything, she has to believe that people are "really good at heart."

The day the film ended was both joyous and sad. We had been a tight family—Millie Perkins, Joseph Schildkraut, Gusti Huber, Ed Wynn, Lou Jacobi, Richard Beymer, and myself. Somehow we did not want a wrap party. Millie Perkins brought me a little present. She was only seventeen and on the first day of shooting some idiot had said to her, "You are representing the eight million Jews who were killed in the concentration camps." Millie turned green. I took her to my dressing room and told her to forget what that person had said to her. Anne Frank knew nothing about the impending Holocaust. Millie was a lovely actress and she's worked through her adolescence, girlhood, and womanhood. We were to do two other films together and become close friends.

A few nights later, Stevens took us all to dinner at

Chasen's, but the night the film ended I went to some big function for Israel bonds at a big hotel. Present were executives of the motion picture and music industries, especially Capitol Records, and I remember the audience was racially and religiously mixed. I can't remember my speech, but I know that I said:

"Who knows when you or your children or grandchildren will need the country of Israel?"

This was a rather shocking thing to say in America in 1958, but I think the audience understood that I had just completed *The Diary of Anne Frank,* and it made them all think of the horror that had happened in Germany, until then one of the most civilized countries in the world, a culture that had produced people like Beethoven, Schiller, and Goethe. Anyway, that night they bought millions of dollars' worth of bonds. That night, the ten-year-old country of Israel needed those investments very badly.

15

At times in my life I have felt like the synthesis of the comedy and tragedy masks that one associates with the theater. I can only describe the next episode as "from the sublime to the ridiculous," but I only have this knowledge in retrospect. After *Anne Frank,* I rested for three days in New York. I had planned a week, but Tony called me one middle-of-the-night, and he sounded so distraught, and almost hysterical, I had to promise him I'd take the next flight to Rome.

On the plane, I thought about all my flights to Italy— all the trips because of my marriage to Vìttorio and many Italian-American productions. I should get an award of some kind from Alitalia. I personally put them on the map in the 1950s. Through all the publicity, negative and positive, that my adventures engendered, I'm sure I increased Italian tourism no end.

It was a long flight in those days, and as I was arriving in Rome at some ungodly hour, I didn't bother to change into my glamour clothes. I arrived in blue jeans, my now-brown hair tied back with a rubber band, and no makeup. I got off the plane and slowly walked down the steps.

I immediately thought there must have been some terrible international crisis that involved somebody else who was coming down the stairs in back of me. There at the airport were at least fifty photographers, and newsreel

263

and TV cameras were on top of vans. Reporters began to
yell at me in several languages. I kept looking back at the
airplane, thinking someone like a premier or president
was on this same international flight. We had stopped in
London and/or Paris while I had been sleeping, and my
guess was that someone very important had gotten on the
plane.

As always, I was carrying various bundles with me—
presents, Tony's summer clothes, an overnight bag of
medications, jewelry—the things that I did not want sent
through in my suitcases. Suddenly a limousine drove up
to the plane, and Tony opened the door and gestured me
to get into the car, quickly. I did not understand any of
the questions that I finally realized the reporters were
screaming at *me*. I hastily climbed in the car, and we
drove off the airfield.

"Tony," I screamed. "My *suitcases!*"

"Never mind," he said. "Someone from the movie
company is picking them up. He's at the hotel waiting for
your claim checks."

Now I looked carefully at Tony, even though the limousine was quite dark. He again had that shriveled-up
look. My handsome husband was no longer six feet tall.
He seemed to be about five-six, which was about my
height. He looked as if he weighed less than I. His clothes
swam on him. He had weighed about 190 pounds when
he'd left Hollywood. Then I remembered that when he'd
gone to the Oscar show, he'd looked quite thin—but he
hadn't had this *shriveled* thin look. I suddenly knew I
was back in my role of Mama Winters. I wasn't being
met by my young handsome husband; I was being met by
a sick, frightened son.

Tony put one arm around me and then put a beautiful
big velvet jewel box in my hand. He looked at me, smiling
strangely, waiting for me to open it up.

"Go ahead," he whispered. "Open it up."

I apprehensively did so. There was a beautiful Bulgari
pin in the shape of a seashell, with rows and rows of
diamonds, cabochon light and dark sapphires, and matching earrings. Bulgari has more beautiful and more expen-

sive jewelry than any other jeweler in the world, and I know jewelry.

"For God's sake, Tony," I cried. "What did you do now?"

He got very angry and said, "What do you mean, 'What did I do?' I bought you a present from the most famous jeweler in the world, Bulgari, and you don't even say thank you. You just yell at me."

"Thank you, Tony," I said, and then was silent for a moment. I put my arm around him and his head on my shoulder. I realized he was trembling.

"Tony, if you don't tell me what you did, how can I get it fixed?"

I still don't know why I so automatically accepted this mother role. I guess I had slipped into it during the past four years.

Tony didn't answer me. He was asleep. The studio driver had been watching us in the mirror, and he said to me in Italian:

"Signora Gassman, that's the first time Anthony has been to sleep in three or four days. I think it's better to let him sleep, because we work tonight all night."

I whispered back to him in English, "My name is Signora Franciosa. Are they doing the exteriors?"

"No," he replied in English. "We work on the stage, but Signora Ava Gardner only work from sundown to sunup, so everyone must be up all night."

I could not believe what I was hearing. I asked him, Wasn't it too expensive to shoot at night?

"Yes," he said, "but she don't care. We are now two months over schedule and they want to finish the picture fast."

I wanted to ask him more about this long delay in the filming, but I was afraid of waking Tony. We got to the Excelsior Hotel at 7:00 A.M. Rome time, but the chauffeur drove us into some mysterious back entrance. Although I had stayed at the Excelsior many times, I had never known about this entrance. I realized suddenly I hadn't even had to show my passport at passport control or to the hotel concierge.

It was difficult waking Tony and getting him up to the

room, but Vito, who was the driver, practically carried him. In the elevator, I realized Vito had been my driver during the terrible days of shooting *Mambo*, when I had been in Italy for six cold months and was preparing to divorce Vittorio, whom I was acting with in the film. I quickly pushed this memory away. I thanked Vito, and the last thing he said to me was:

"See if you can get Anthony to eat something. He hasn't eaten anything for a long, long time, just wine."

I thanked Vito for putting Tony on the bed and gave him my claim checks. He was going back to the airport to get my luggage. I decided not to question Tony right then and there. I just ordered bacon and eggs and hot milk for him. He was awake and staring into space. He was staring out the window at the American flag on the flagpole at the American embassy. His expression was one of longing.

The breakfast arrived. I began to talk to Tony about all the film scripts that had been sent to the house in California for him, accompanied by offers of $200,000 per picture. I had some of the scripts in my suitcases, and I told him how Louella Parsons, Hedda Hopper, and the reporters on *Variety* and *The Reporter* had written stories about him. They all said he should have won the Oscar for *Hatful*.

I was telling him all the good news I could think of, because he obviously was in despair. When I showed him pictures of my little girl and me playing on the front lawn of the house in Beverly Hills, he began to cry. I decided that he needed ten hours of sleep. He began to eat almost without noticing and to tell me about all the delays and difficulties they had been having with the script. While he was talking, I popped a big red sleeping pill into his mouth. Without even thinking about it, he swallowed. He washed it down with the hot milk and just kept on talking. I got him back in bed, and he was asleep in five minutes.

Tony was always handsome, but asleep he was beautiful. As exhausted as his face looked, he still resembled a sleeping David. I wondered if he had had time, in the months that he'd been in Italy, to go to Florence and see the one and only, real *David*, the great statue by Michelangelo, which I consider the eighth wonder of the world. I used to kid him that he had a Venus girdle, just like the statue of David. That is a ridge of muscle where the leg fits into the torso. It's very beautiful, and only young men have them when they are athletic and lovely. Tony had kidded me back and said the first thing he would do in Italy is check out this story of mine about David's Venus girdle.

Looking at Tony sleeping awakened all my maternal instincts. So far, he had taken many positive steps in his career, but many of his acting experiences had been abortive. He had managed to overcome the problems, but whatever was happening on this film, whatever its name, was killing him. I knew the months of painstaking research he had done on Goya, and how he had felt this film was the opportunity of his life—to play this historic, great painter. I unpacked my suitcases and decided to go out for the Italian weekly magazines, which were sold in the kiosk across the street from the Excelsior.

Down in the lobby, I carefully looked around. There were no reporters that I could see outside the door. I went across the street and bought an armful of newspapers and magazines and then returned to the lobby, sat in a corner, and ordered coffee. As I began to look at the magazines, I thought I'd better have a brandy. All of them carried stories reporting my arrival in Rome *"to arrange a divorce or annulment"* from Anthony Franciosa, and the big question was: Which movie star was Tony going to marry after the divorce—Anna Magnani or Ava Gardner? Some of them speculated that perhaps Shelley and Vittorio Gassman would remarry. I sat there stunned. I was mad and sad and glad, in that order.

My Italian was a little vague, to say the least, but I managed to read through all the stories. Magnani had had the class not to make any statements to the press, but Ava Gardner obviously had a full-time publicity man working for her. She had repeatedly given out interviews about Tony's and her plans and romance. She had also had time to go to Spain and fight a small bull with some renowned matador and get her face scratched by a bull's horn in the process of learning bullfighting. I wondered if

Tony had been dumb enough to get in the bullring with her. It seemed obvious how he'd spent the days with Ava Gardner—especially lunch hours. And perhaps at night he had helped Magnani feed her cats in the Coliseum. I had heard that this was one of her pet hobbies. She had once said to me:

"In peacetime, Italians feed the cats of Rome, and in wartime, the cats feed the people."

There were pictures illustrating all these conflicting activities my husband had gotten involved in. There were glamorous and sad pictures of me with captions referring to me as Signora Gassman. This was no contradiction to the Italian readers, however, since many of them had not recognized my divorce from Vittorio Gassman, much less my second marriage. The whole thing was rather funny, and that's how the Roman press treated it. I must say, they were treating poor Anthony Franciosa as the victim in all this—being torn apart by three movie stars. It was indeed a Pandora's box, and I wondered how I could close up this box and get Tony back to health and the safety of New York—before I divorced him in California.

I went back up to the suite and took a shower and lay down on the couch with a pad and pencil and tried to map out my strategy. If Tony felt as bad as he looked, he had to get out of this film and back to his psychiatrist in New York.

About 4:00 P.M., the phone rang. It was Frank Kaufman and Lou Lerner, the William Morris agents in Rome. I told them to come up and then made sure the door to the bedroom was closed. These two young men eyed me warily. They saw the Italian papers on the floor. I promptly told them off in a whisper and added that I was going to call Stan Kamen at William Morris in Hollywood and tell him exactly how they'd taken care of one of their new and valuable stars.

They panicked and explained that Ava Gardner was willful and kept rewriting the script, and the director, Henry Koster, could not control her. When she had heard I was coming to Rome, she'd notified Koster that she would only shoot at night, and the set had to be closed to everyone, especially the wives, sweethearts, and agents of her fellow actors.

I ignored this information. I had brought the script of *The Story on Page One* for Tony. This was to be an original Clifford Odets film, directed by him, and with a great cast of actors, including Rita Hayworth, Mildred Dunnock, Gig Young, Alfred Ryder, Sanford Meisner, and Hugh Griffith. Since Tony had already done his contractual three films for Twentieth on his original commitment, his salary was now open for negotiation, and I had asked them for $250,000 for this picture.

Kaufman asked me why I was negotiating this deal and not William Morris, and I whispered back:

"While I was working at Twentieth Century–Fox on *Anne Frank,* in the last week of shooting the head of casting stopped by my stage and mentioned this Clifford Odets package. I asked him if there was a part for Tony in it, and he said, 'Yes, the lead.'

"I told him, 'You know, he gets $250,000 a picture now.' The casting director got pale but he handed me the script to bring to Tony in Rome."

In those days, $250,000 was like $1 million. Kaufman and Lerner stared at me. They knew that Tony meant a great deal of money for the William Morris Agency, and they had not been able to protect him or his role in this bollixed-up picture he was doing.

Then I said, "Incidentally, Hank, Tony has two months of overtime pay due him. He usually sends his checks to me and I deposit them for him, and our business manager pays William Morris their commission."

The two young agents now turned green. One of them said, "Since the picture is so delayed and a great deal of the delay is Tony's fault, he agreed to waive his overtime money."

I started to laugh. It was *Orpheus Descending* all over again. They didn't know that's why I was laughing.

"Well boys," I said, "if you and William Morris want to waive your commission, that's okay with me. But as you know, there's community property in California, so if you want Tony to finish this cockamamie film, you'd better have a complete U.A. check here in dollars, not lire. Have it here before he reports to work tonight or he ain't going.''

Mr. Lerner stuttered something about how they had advanced Tony $20,000 to buy a Facel Vega. Now it was my turn to stare.

"A *what?*" I asked.

I thought they meant a house or an island in the Mediterranean called Vega. They explained it was a fancy sports car that Tony had his heart set on. In those days, spending $20,000 for a car was unheard-of. A Rolls-Royce cost about $15,000. I was ready to punch them out. Tony had driven around Stage 11 at Fox for his driving test, and a man from the motor vehicle bureau had given him his license. He had been driving a rented Chevrolet with automatic shift up till then. So the first car he buys is a $20,000 racer, a Facel Vega. He would have to ship the damn thing back to the United States, if he didn't kill himself in it first. I was so angry I asked them to leave. I vowed if I could find out where the car was— after making sure it was not at the Excelsior garage—I would secretly sell it.

I hid all the Italian newspapers. A certified U.A. check for $160,000 arrived just as Tony awakened. When I showed it to him, it cheered him up considerably. But he still seemed very worried that his artistic disagreements with Ava Gardner had cost the company money.

I ordered dinner as I reassured him. He ate a large bowl of pasta, a steak, a salad, and a large banana split. The entire hotel seemed to be pleased that Tony was having this large meal at last. The cook came up to the room to make sure he liked everything. He obviously was a favorite of the staff. I wondered how he communicated with them. Maybe they spoke Neapolitan. He certainly knew all the curse words in that language.

As he dressed, I felt he seemed cheerful enough for me to try to find out how he was planning for our future. It was difficult to get his attention, because he was avidly reading *The Story on Page One*. He was riveted to the Clifford Odets script. I took out the newspapers, shook them in front of his face, and quietly asked:

"Tony. Are you in love with Anna Magnani or Ava

Gardner? Do you want your freedom so that you can make a life in Italy or Hollywood? I'm not angry, dear. I just want to know."

Half of me wanted him to say he was in love with one of them, and the other half of me was afraid he would say so. As always, during the years that Tony and I were involved with each other, when I zigged, he would zag, and when I zagged he would zig. He took me in his arms and said:

"Shell, you leave me alone for six months at a time. I'm not a very strong person. I only want to make a home with you, your kid, and our future children. I've been stupid and foolish, and I can't wait to get the hell out of Rome."

With mixed feelings, to say the least, I kissed him and sent him off to work. As he went down in the elevator, I called Vito the driver and whispered to him to come back for me at nine o'clock and not to tell anyone. He said O.K. but he sounded frightened. I sat on the balcony, looking at the flag at the American embassy, and planned how I could get Tony out of this mess, help him finish the picture, and get him the hell back home as quickly as possible. I hoped that he could go on with his analysis and have some understanding of himself. He was ruining a very promising career, and I hoped he wouldn't jump into another marriage or relationship if we did get a divorce, which was highly probable. But the first thing on the agenda was to finish this damn picture.

I mapped out my strategy. First I put on a very loose girdle, then I took one of the small pillows from the sofa, stuffed it into my girdle, and pinned it in place. I dressed carefully, making my clothes look like maternity clothes, and even though it was hot, I put on a loose coat. I knew that the Italian reverence for motherhood would see me through the next difficult hours.

How I evolved this diabolical scheme I have no idea, but it worked. When Vito returned, I got in the car and told him to drive to the studio. He looked more frightened.

"Never mind," I said. "Nobody will send me home."

Vito drove me to the studio, and when I got out of the car, he noticed that I had suddenly become pregnant.

"Bravo, Shelley!" he said, laughing. "United Artists will thank you. This is the only way this film will ever finish."

I told him to write a letter about this fiasco to the head of the Italian film company. I was only interested in disentangling Tony from these Roman ruins, and I didn't care whom I had to lie to to do it. As soon as I walked onto the set, the crew rushed to get me a comfortable chair, a pillow for my back, a stool for my feet, and a glass of cold water. It was a very hot night, so they put a fan directly on me. But they still all called me Signora Gassman. Some of the crew had worked on *Mambo,* and most of them certainly had worked on films with Vittorio Gassman.

Tony was in makeup. I took off my coat and waited. Tony came out of the makeup room, did a double take, and then took a long look at me. He rushed to my side, kneeling on the dirty stage floor, and he began to kiss me.

"Darling," he said, "why didn't you tell me? I would have walked out on this loony picture and come to you."

At first, I thought he was going along with my gag, but then I realized he truly believed that I was six months pregnant. He had seen me at the airport coming down the steps, he had seen me in the car before he'd fallen asleep and when he'd awoken in the hotel, but he must not have taken a real look then. Well, I'd had a robe on in the suite, but was he so dazed from the sleeping pill I'd given him that he believed that this was the first good look he'd taken at me—and I was pregnant?

Ava Gardner came out of her dressing room, looking like a goddess. Indeed, like the naked Maja. I remember exactly what she wore. She had a tightly fitted brown velvet period evening gown on with a bustle and bare shoulders. Her hair was done in a high French knot, and she had a Spanish comb on the right side of it. She had a yellow diamond necklace on and brown lace gloves, and she was carrying a long lace Spanish fan. I can still even smell her perfume. It was Tabu.

She gazed at this religious still life of the pregnant wife

squatting on a chair with the husband's arms around her. You could hear a pin drop on the soundstage, where about two hundred workers stood, watching. I wondered if she would try to order me off the set. No fool she. Even when she was angry, she knew the Italian crew would brain her if she insulted an expectant mother. Tony shakily got to his feet, and Henry Koster appeared magically at Ava's side.

"Shelley, don't pull that crap!" Ava hissed. "You haven't even seen him for nine months."

"Ava darling, Tony was home for the Oscars," I said. "He was nominated, remember? But then, you wouldn't know about the rules for participants in Oscar telecasts, would you?"

She looked as if she wanted to kill me, but she walked over to a makeup table, grabbed a handful of cold cream, and smeared it all over her face—her eyelashes, her hair, everything went. Henry Koster took charge and yelled:

"It's a wrap! We're rewriting the script. So we're finished in Rome. We now go on location and work in the palace near Naples."

He turned to Tony and said, "Mr. Franciosa, you have a week off. You're not involved in the exterior court scenes. For God's sakes, go somewhere alone with your wife and stay away from reporters."

I kissed Henry Koster and took the dazed Tony by the hand, and, with his wig and makeup and costume still on, we left the stage and got back in the limousine. Vito held the car door open for us, and as we got in the car, Mickey Knox yelled:

"Hi, Shelley! Congratulations! I'll bring his stuff to the Excelsior."

I think, up till that moment, Mickey had been hiding behind Ava Gardner. I said nothing in the car. I did not know how to tell Tony, who was so overjoyed at the prospect of becoming a father, that my pregnancy was fake. I still couldn't believe that he had not noticed, that morning when I'd arrived, that I wasn't pregnant. I decided to wait till the next morning. When I don't know what to do, I stall.

When we got safely back to the suite, both phones

were ringing. Tony started to answer one, and I put my hand on it.

"Tony, we are not going to talk to anyone," I announced with great authority. "Tomorrow morning we are driving to Naples, then taking the boat to Capri."

Suddenly Tony was transformed.

"Great!" he said. "We can drive my new car! I forgot to tell you—I bought a wonderful, gorgeous new Facel Vega. I got a great buy on it. I know you'll love it!"

When he went into the bathroom to take off his makeup, I rang the concierge and told him that we were receiving no calls and to just take messages. I also told him that if he saw to it that we were not disturbed till 7:00 A.M. the next day, he would get five thousand lire (about $50). I decided if I could get Tony to Capri for a few days, I could extract him from this Roman quagmire, and perhaps he could get well enough to finish the film. So I decided I would ride in that Facel Vega to Naples.

I asked the concierge what was the quietest and most luxurious hotel in Capri, and he told me the one that was on the top of Anacapri.

"Make a reservation for a suite for a week," I ordered, "starting tomorrow, for Mr. and Mrs. Franciosa [the concierge too was still calling me Signora Gassman]."

When Tony came out of the bathroom, I quickly took off my maternity outfit and returned the pillow to the sofa. Tony laughed and cried at the same time, but he didn't seem too devastated by the idea that I wasn't really expecting. He knew that I knew that he was not ready to be a father.

"But you looked pregnant in Hollywood."

"I was fat for *Anne Frank,* stupid."

"You'd better take that pillow to Naples," he said, "for when I have to work in the garden of the palace. We're filming the last scenes in the film. Yes, I think you'd better wear that pillow if you're planning to come on the set."

"Darling, to get you safely home to New York, I'll wear anything!"

At least I'd gotten him out of Ava Gardner's clutches, or so I thought. The next morning, I read that Magnani had flown to Hollywood with dignity and denials and just one comment:

"Miss Winters is such a Method actress that I'm sure she can conceive all by herself." (It sounds funnier in Italian—she compared me to the Immaculate Conception.)

All our urgent problems seemed solved, except I had no desire to make love with Tony or anybody. I had not really seen him for six or seven months, and I had been a faithful and good wife, but my sexual appetite had disappeared. At night I would disappear into the bathroom, pretending to take a long, hot bath, and do my specialty of Crying Under Water. I think I had learned this trick for *A Place in the Sun* or *Night of the Hunter,* and, later in life, I used it in *The Poseidon Adventure*.

One night, when I finally heard Tony breathing deeply, sound asleep, I came out of the bathroom. I sat on the balcony in my unromantic flannel nightgown and gazed at the lighted flag on the American embassy. I wondered when and where and how I would ever have a relationship with a mature grown-up man. Why did my inner script keep me loving men I had to take care of? Why did I keep repeating this silliness and marrying men with whom I knew no real marriage or partnership was possible? Just the act of marrying seemed to satisfy me. I know now I was avoiding any real marriage. I married men whom it was not possible for me to even live with, and I resolved that when this marriage ended, I would never get married again. So far, I've kept that resolve. It's like a baseball game: three strikes, you're out. I knew that Tony had behaved foolishly, but he was more destructive to himself than to me, and I had married him with my eyes wide open. I had known his wonderful loving nature, but I had certainly seen his destructive behavior before I had married him.

Only in retrospect do I understand that by continually helping him I was enabling him to remain a child. Now I think I understand that his neurotic behavior was perhaps the result of my emasculating him in some way—my power, my celebrity, whatever. And in his neurotic behavior he was fighting back.

I went to sleep on the sofa, and woke up at dawn. By the time Tony awakened, I had us both packed. At the last minute, I looked at the little pillow on the sofa and decided I'd better pack it, just in case I had to see Ava Gardner again. When Tony awoke, I had breakfast waiting for him, and his Facel Vega, whatever that was, was out in front of the hotel. I got us out of Rome as if Hitler was in the suburbs. He wasn't, of course; just the entire world press, wanting some more stories about our rocky marriage.

When I saw his $20,000 Facel Vega, I almost didn't go. It was silver gray, and it looked as if it was ready for the Indianapolis 500. But Tony drove very carefully and slowly to Naples. I think every time he took the car above 35 MPH I screamed, so he had to creep along. At one point, I thought he was going to open the door and tell me to get out. But I knew this car could go over 150 MPH easily. I managed to keep us alive until we got to the ferry for Capri. I told him you were not allowed to take cars to Capri (big lie). I had been there, and I knew how steep and narrow the little roads all over Capri were.

There was someone from the production office waiting for us in Naples. Tony had to report to the production office immediately and get his new pages and schedule before we left. He wanted to stay at the hotel in Naples for that night. I was adamant—I didn't want to be anywhere near where Ava Gardner might be. While he went up to the production office and I was chatting with the assistant director, Ava got off the elevator, looking gorgeous as usual and surrounded by her entourage—her makeup man, hairdresser, publicity man, and assorted bullfighters. She was all smiles and friendship.

"Isn't it great that I was able to get the film shortened?" she inquired. "We'll be through in a couple of weeks!"

I smiled, too, and said, "Ava, it's just great!"

Then she astounded me by saying, "My friends know

a great Spanish restaurant here in Naples. Why don't you and Tony join us tonight?''

I luckily had on my raincoat and I had quickly stuck my hands in my pockets and was holding it away from my flat stomach, but she did not even look down. I thanked her and explained that Tony and I were going away for about a week, as he didn't have to work. We weren't even registering at the hotel in Naples. Then she began to look angry.

"Where are you going?" she asked. Which was none of her goddamn business.

"It's a secret," I said, and then, out of the corner of my eye, I began to notice reporters and photographers jumping out of the woodwork. In fact, her personal photographer was lining up his camera to get a shot of the two of us. I think they got one shot just before I ran for the door.

The production limousine drove us back to the dock for the boat to Capri. It was a silent trip across that beautiful bay, but there was such tension between us that I looked at Vesuvius receding in the distance and was sure it was going to erupt. When we finally got to Capri, it was beautiful and fragrant, and the flowers were in bloom all over the mountain. Back then, the Bay of Naples was clean and clear. You could see the rocks and pebbles on the ocean floor. We finally took a cab up the circling narrow road to Anacapri, which is on the very top of Capri, where our hotel was. By the time we got there, Tony was grateful that I had not let him bring his Facel Vega.

They showed us to the most romantic suite of rooms I have ever been in. Balconies overlooked all the other little islands that surround Capri. We could see Vesuvius and Pompeii. There was another large island in the distance. I asked Tony to look at the map and tell me what it was. He blithely informed me, with great assurance, that it was Sicily. I believed him until twenty years later, when I went to Ischia for the mud treatments and explained to the concierge that I wanted a motorboat in a few days to take me to Sicily to receive the David of Donatella Award, which is Italy's Oscar. The man informed me that it would take a month to take a motorboat trip to Sicily. Tony had misinformed me that Ischia was Sicily.

We stood on that little balcony and watched the sun setting in the west in glorious colors. With the scent of those beautiful flowers around us, all my anger against Tony evaporated. Magnani and Gardner were sexy and beautiful and famous women. I guess you can't leave a kid in a candy store and tell him not to taste the sweets —or so I rationalized.

The management of the hotel had left us a wonderful bottle of French champagne, blue candles and ripe fruits. We reminded each other that we'd never had a real honeymoon—we'd both been so busy with our careers. So that night and for the next few days we had our delayed honeymoon. All we did was eat, sleep, make love, sun on our terrace, and swim in the clear Mediterranean.

There are two famous rocks off Capri, and we crawled all over them and dived. Gracie Fields owned a restaurant on the beach, and we lunched there every day from 1:00 till 4:00 P.M. They served some marvelous wine from Gracie's vineyard, and you could only drink it on Capri because it didn't travel—if you tried to take it to the mainland, it would turn to vinegar—sort of like my marriage. Tony began to look healthy and handsome again. As we strolled through the little squares all over Capri, he was forever buying me little presents from the boutiques that seemed to be all over the place, even in the caves.

The first Saturday morning we were there, the phone rang. Tony was out on the balcony, working on his tan and, I think, sleeping. I picked up the phone and wondered who, besides the assistant director, knew where we were. For a second, I was afraid that it was someone in the States ringing us. I had told the operator to screen all our local calls, but, for whatever reason, she had allowed Miss Ava Gardner to ring through.

Ava sounded high and happy and said, "After all, we're both Hollywood babies. Shelley, we should all have fun together! Why are you being so old-fashioned?"

She announced she was coming to Capri that afternoon

with her entourage and said we would all have a great time together.

I got very quiet and said, "Ava, I grew up in Brooklyn with Murder Incorporated as my playmates. You see, I went to junior high school with these men. Ava, I swear, if you so much as set a foot on Capri while my husband is recuperating, I'll put a contract out on you. I believe those men have connections in Naples."

I paused and then said in a deadly serious voice, "Ava, you know I mean it."

I guess she believed me, because she did not show up on Capri. I didn't play all those gangster molls in B pictures for nothing.

When I bawled out the operator, she told me that the press were down in the square, waiting for my meeting with Ava Gardner. In those days, I believed Ava notified the press before she went to the bathroom. She lived her life on the front pages. I guess during that period I did that too.

I took my little pillow, pinned it back to my girdle, and put on a very loose blouse. I left Tony sleeping on the balcony and took an Italian net shopping bag. The hotel taxi drove me down to the square. I'd hardly had time to get out of the cab when I was surrounded by reporters. In English and Italian, they were screaming questions about my relationship with Ava Gardner and her relationship with Tony. I stopped them all with a *"Sta' zitto* [Shut up]!" and I made the following statement:

"I wish here and now to apologize to Miss Ava Gardner for scarring her face. I really didn't mean to do it. I hope it isn't serious, and that the plastic surgery works. When a woman is expecting, she sometimes gets irrational, as you all know from your own families."

The reporters were busy, nodding and writing, and it seemed that a hundred cameras were photographing me. I continued:

"I know Miss Gardner is a professional and has been working very hard to make this great film, *The Naked Maja,* a monument to her extraordinary acting career. Although when Tony left Hollywood he was doing a film called *Goya.*"

When I decided to be bitchy, I made it in spades. But she had practically destroyed Tony's health and sanity. From the things Tony had told me about the film, I knew she had destroyed that too. She had screwed him literally and figuratively. She had changed this biographical film of Goya so much from the original script that it was un-recognizable—it was now about the model instead of the painter.

This little ploy of mine finally shut Ava Gardner up, and she'd leave us alone, I hoped, for the rest of the filming. She knew now if she made any more statements to the press, I would come up with something that would embarrass and humiliate her and perhaps destroy her beautiful goddess image. Publicity implying that she'd been in a cat fight, and another actress had managed to scratch her up, would hardly enhance that image. The press may have known that she had really gotten those scratches from a pseudobullfight, but they chose to believe my imaginary version. If you ever see *The Naked Maja*, and, for Tony's sake, I hope you won't, notice that they only photograph one side of Miss Gardner's face through most of the picture.

The reporters ran to phone their newspapers, and I quietly toured the square and bought Tony some goodies. When I got back up to Anacapri, I decided not to tell him about my run-in with the press. I knew I had found a way to shut Ava up, with her constant destructive publicity. If I was lucky, he wouldn't read the newspapers, since they were in Italian. I think he knew that he had had enough publicity for quite a while.

He was studying the script of *The Story on Page One*, as he was to start rehearsals with Clifford Odets as soon as he finished this pizza picture and returned to Holly-wood. He knew what a great playwright and theater person Clifford Odets was, and he knew it was a wonderful opportunity for him to reestablish himself as the fine actor he was. That night we decided to have dinner on our balcony, and the waiter brought the blue candles and flowers, and we had some of the best food and wine we'd ever had. Tony, who rarely smoked, took out an ornate, heavy, webbed gold cigarette case. He opened it, and it was empty.

"Shelley," he said, "do you think you could make a compact out of this?"

I looked at it. It was marked 22-karat gold. The inner side of the top had obviously been engraved and then erased by a not-too-skilled jeweler. I looked at it for quite a while and said, "Well, Tony, if your relationship with the naked maja is as erased as this engraving, I would love it."

That compact is now in the vault, with all the other jewels. Maybe when this book comes out, I'll have a garage sale.

The rest of that week was indeed idyllic. The only discordant note was of my own making. One afternoon, while Tony was talking to some Italian movie director around the pool of Gracie Fields's hotel, I wandered off to one of the boutiques. I looked at a bikini in the window and decided I ought to have it. I tried it on, and, as I gazed at myself in the mirror, I started to weep. Gaining twenty-five or thirty pounds for *Anne Frank* and then losing them had not helped my figure. I resolved that as soon as I got back to New York or California, I would exercise every day and shape up for *any* glamorous role which might be offered to me.

When I had played a dowdy teenager in *A Place in the Sun,* it had not hurt my career, even though the president of Universal, Mr. William Goetz, had said to me, after we'd seen the film in the Universal projection room, "Well, if I had known Stevens was going to have you look like that, I wouldn't have let you do the picture."

After that wonderful film, Goetz quickly got me back into my blonde-bombshell image again. So I thought perhaps I ought to brighten and skinny up to make sure that America didn't think I really looked like Mrs. Van Daan. In those days, stars seldom played character roles, and I guess I was as much a victim of that thinking as anyone else.

Not so long ago I received a bad review in *The New York Times* in a film I wasn't even in. When Bobby De

Niro opened in *Raging Bull,* Vincent Canby accorded him a glowing notice, but the last line of his review said that the only thing he objected to was Mr. De Niro gaining all that weight and losing it, and that Bobby had been influenced by Shelley Winters, who'd done the same thing with as little effect. Mr. De Niro won an Oscar for that role, as I did for *The Diary of Anne Frank.*

Sunday we sailed back to Naples, and Tony reported to the production office of *Goya,* now officially called *The Naked Maja.* I kept looking at Tony out of the corner of my eye, and I didn't know whether it was the prospect of doing a picture with Clifford Odets or the fact that I had brought him some semblance of family commitment, but he was steady and calm and making jokes again.

He just wanted to get the film over with, because he really understood it was past saving. He was just hoping that it would open and close quickly because, in those days, when you were unfortunate enough to be in a turkey, it would quickly disappear and not haunt you on television, and there were no video cassettes then. By that time Tony had made so many good films, some of them as yet unreleased, that I sincerely felt this one miscalculation would not hurt his career. I reassured him of this fact *every* day at 6:00 A.M. while he had his breakfast coffee but, when he had a difficult scene, he would still insist that I come to the studio with him and sit by the camera and watch what went on.

I compromised and some days got to the set around lunchtime. Henry Koster never understood why he couldn't get a shot in his camera until 11:30 A.M. on those days. Tony would stall till he made sure that I approved the scene. I would rub my nose, which was the signal to go for a take. Henry Koster one day caught me at it, and all he said was, "Would you please arrive on the set earlier, like 9:00 A.M. Just you. Then we'll get this damn picture done sooner."

I had seen some of the rushes the first day in Naples, and I understood that Tony had played each scene before I arrived on a high emotional pitch, not realizing that when you put all these scenes together, Goya would be hysterical throughout the picture. So I got him to under-play and relax and be his own charming self in some of the final scenes. Ava Gardner was gorgeous and rather aloof, and there was a very handsome bullfighter, who spoke no English, sitting on the other side of the camera.

So the last days of *The Naked Maja* were relaxed and congenial. When the last shot was in the camera, none of the crew wanted to have a wrap party. They just wanted to go home. I rushed upstairs and started packing for Tony and me. He called me and said he was looking at the rushes with Henry Koster and making sure there were no additional exterior shots, and we would leave the next morning, as he didn't want to drive to Rome at night.

It sounded odd to me, because we had planned to leave Naples that night. Rome was only an hour and a half's drive, and we had decided to get the car serviced in Rome and then drive it to Paris. We could then put it on a boat at Cherbourg bound for New York.

Tony's rushes were taking a long time. I sat and read all the literature I could about the Facel Vega. It was a French car, and the instructions were in French, but I sat there studying them. What I figured out was that it had a Chrysler motor, and it was a racing car with a French body. It could easily go about 190 MPH. I couldn't imag-ine what Tony was planning to do with this machine in California. It was now about 8:30 P.M. I didn't think I was getting angry, so I ordered dinner for two, took a shower, and, when room service arrived, I signed the check and ate the dinner.

I was feeling fine, except every time I ate a course I threw it up. It was now 9:30 P.M. No phone call, no Tony. I resolutely decided I would give him the benefit of the doubt and chose to assume that perhaps he and Koster were having a few drinks. But I found my finger dialing Ava Gardner's suite. No answer. I did the only sensible thing I could think of—I took two sleeping pills and a glass of wine and was quickly unconscious.

I woke up stretched out on the bed, and Tony was dead asleep on the couch. I decided I would not discuss his late dinner until I got to London or the U.S.A. I somehow couldn't just take a cab to the airport and fly home. Our marriage was zigging and zagging again, but I'd lost interest in the game and just wanted to get home.

I took a shower, got dressed, and went down for breakfast. Then I went out and sat in the Facel Vega. I do not know whether it was an hour, half an hour, or three hours, but Tony came barreling out of the hotel with our suitcases, and he got in the car. We had nothing to say to each other, and the tension was as strong as the Naples sun. I looked at him in the car mirror and he indeed looked as if he'd been partying most of the night.

I had bought a map of the road from Naples to Rome. It was not yet the superhighway with no speed limit that exists in Italy today. The curves of the road along the beach were difficult, so Tony could not go too fast. But at several points I broke my vow of silence and had to say, "For God's sakes, Tony, slow down!"

Somewhere just past Castellammare, which is a beach with black sand, I realized he was hung over and in a state of mind that made it dangerous for him to drive. So I tried to have a normal conversation with him and discuss our trip. I talked about Cannes and our drive through the south of France to Nice, and about how it would be fun to put the car on a ferry, after we had seen Paris, and drive through the English countryside to London. I rattled on, not meaning a word of it, but he began to visibly relax and slow down. He was saying something sweet to me, and suddenly the car rolled over in slow motion into a ditch and landed on its roof.

It is quite true that when you're in an accident, your life passes before your eyes. That rollover seemed to take an hour, and every mistake I had ever made in my life appeared on a CinemaScope screen on the roof of the car.

I think I was lying on the roof of the car, thinking about why I was staying in this destructive marriage, when someone began to scream at me in Italian. A hand reached in, rolled the window all the way down or up, and pulled me out, while this young, strong man continued to scream. Someone must have pulled Tony out, too.

They dragged us away from the car, in case it was going to explode, and we sat down on a big rock. I looked at the smashed car and eagerly waited for the moment that it would explode. It didn't. Then I began to laugh hysterically. I noticed that my hand was bloody, and I didn't know whether the blood was from my hand or head, which I was holding. I laughed and laughed until an Italian ambulance came with an Italian doctor and they gave me an Italian shot, which knocked me out.

I don't remember much after this. I think I woke up in some Italian hospital, looked out the window at the ocean and the black sand, and wondered who had painted the sand black. I was completely without will. Perhaps I had a concussion. The next thing I remember was waking up in the Savoy Hotel in London and wondering why the Thames didn't have black sand.

How I had gotten to London I just didn't know, or care. I just knew I was closer to New York. I got up and began to walk around an elegant two-bedroom suite. Tony's clothes were in the other bedroom, but I wasn't quite sure who Tony was. I went back to my bedroom. I knew I was angry at something, but I couldn't remember what. So I got all dressed up and went out.

It was quite chilly and rainy on the Strand in front of the Savoy, and I got a cab and said, "Harrods." At that time there was a Christian Dior boutique in Harrods, and I accidentally wandered into it. I immediately bought a heavy black wool dress and three Christian Dior suits, black, gray, and brown. I still have them in my closet, hoping I'll make size 10 again. I just gave one to my secretary, who is a size 8, and it fit her. I don't think I was size 8 when I was *born,* but perhaps I had gotten very thin between Castellammare and London.

The saleslady was very nice, and luckily I had a lot of traveler's checks in my purse. I discovered they were signed Mrs. Anthony Franciosa. I surely didn't know who that was, but I signed them anyway. I told them to send the clothes to the Savoy and walked out onto the King's Road.

The sun had come out, and I felt happy and free. I passed by the Jaguar Ltd. showroom, and a sleek gray-

and-black Jag was in the window. It was a gorgeous car, sedate and respectable, a really heavy, safe, large family car. It was stable and roomy and beautiful. So I walked into the showroom and bought it. A man with striped trousers and a cutaway and a flower in his buttonhole wrote down my order. He looked like a best man.

"I hope it's a nice wedding," I said.

"Yes, Miss Winters!" he said. "Certainly, Miss Winters!"

"Please send the bill to Mr. Anthony Franciosa % United Artists at their London office," I said, signing the bill of sale.

"Certainly," he said. "And you know, Miss Winters, if you drive the Jag around London for a while, when you ship it home on the boat you can bring it into the United States as a used car, and the import duty will be minimal."

"Thank you," I said. "Can you suggest a boat?"

He looked at a card and said, "The *United States,* which is your fastest ship, is sailing Friday."

"How convenient," I said. "And what is today?"

He looked at me a little suspiciously then and said, "Tuesday."

"Good," I said. "It sails from London to New York Friday."

As I started to write it down, he said, "No, it sails from Southampton. It makes the trip in three days."

"Thank you," I said. "Can you make a reservation for the car and me?"

"Gladly," he said.

I walked quite a while, and I suddenly realized I was at Hyde Park Corner, and there were a lot of men and women making speeches. I stood listening to the orators haranguing the crowd about Algiers. I thought I ought to go home, or back to my hotel, but I couldn't remember which hotel it was.

I borrowed a shilling from a bobby, called the Dorchester from the corner phone box, and asked for Miss Shelley Winters. I usually stayed at the Dorchester when I was in London. The operator recognized my voice and said, "Miss Winters, I believe you're staying at the

Savoy this trip." She didn't seem to think it was strange that I didn't know where I was staying. After all, I was an American.

I took a cab back to the hotel, and, since I had no more English money, the doorman paid the cabbie for me. I walked into the lobby, and I had no idea what number my room was. I proceeded to the desk and asked for my key.

"Yes, Mrs. Franciosa," the concierge said, "here it is."

"That's the wrong key," I replied. "I'm Shelley Winters. We're not married. If we are, we're getting unmarried."

The concierge looked a little dazed but nevertheless handed me the key. When I got to the suite, Tony was there, waiting, with an elegant lunch. I sat down and began to eat. Every once in a while, I stared at him. I asked him nothing.

"Are you feeling better today?" he asked.

"Fine," I replied.

"Would you like to go to the theater tonight?"

"Fine."

"Do you want to see your friends, Peter and Mary Noble?"

"Fine."

The lunch was delicious—potted shrimps, rare roast beef, Yorkshire pudding, haricots (fancy string beans), salad, and trifle for dessert. I suddenly realized I was starving. No wonder I was a size 8. I think I got back to a size 10 during that luncheon. Tony wasn't eating much. He just sat there watching me, looking rather scared.

"Aren't you hungry?" I asked.

"No," he answered, "I ate a late breakfast." So I ate his lunch, too.

I was beginning to get a dreadful headache, and Tony realized it and brought me some medicine, a glass of water, and a very convenient ice pack.

"I think I'll have a nap now," I said.

"Are you sure you want to go to the theater tonight?" he asked.

"Fine," I said, and went to sleep.

That night we went to the theater, and I think I saw *Look Back in Anger*. It seemed an appropriate play for the mood I was in. We met my chums Peter and Mary Noble, and they could not understand why I hadn't phoned them.

"Peter!" I suddenly piped up, "I bought a Jaguar! Can I have it delivered to you? And can you drive it around London until Friday? And then drive me to Southampton, where I and the Jag are going to take the *United States* back to New York?"

"You're doing what?" Tony asked.

I just looked at him and said, "By the way, you're paying for the Jag. United Artists is deducting it from your salary. I have no idea how much it is."

Peter quickly said, "Sure, Shelley, I'll take you to Southampton."

"Are you sure this is what you want to do?" Mary asked.

"Of course," I replied, and dropped the subject.

I believe after the theater we went to dinner at the Caprice restaurant. Tony looked dazed and sad, and my friends seemed sad. They had never met Tony before but knew we had only been married a couple of years.

We talked about our friend Farley Granger most of the evening. He seemed a safe subject. On the way back to the Savoy, Tony took my hand and said, "I'd like to go back on the *United States* with you, because I have to go to Hollywood in a week or so."

"Fine," I replied. "See if you can get a cabin."

On the drive down to Southampton, and on boarding the boat, I was only concerned about my Jag. It was beautiful and stately, and every once in a while I put my gloved hand out the window, like the queen, and waved at imaginary crowds. When we got to the boat, I almost didn't let it board, because they explained to me they had to cover it with grease and tie it down in the hold. I became agitated. Peter reassured me that the United States Lines shipped cars to America all the time, and they knew how to take care of them.

When Tony and I reached our cabins, I found they were adjoining. I don't know who had told them we wanted adjoining cabins. I locked the door between our cabins, but I was polite to Tony.

It seems we did not have to dress for dinner the first night, and when we went up to the dining room we met some old friends, Ilya and Ruth Lopert. He was the European head of United Artists, and she was a fun lady who knew a great deal about art films, since they owned several art houses in Europe and America, including the Paris Theatre opposite the Plaza Hotel.

The *United States* was a fast and marvelous ship, and I can't understand why it discontinued its run to Europe —I hope I had nothing to do with this decision. I spent the next three days walking around the decks and never going down to the cabin if I could help it. After the first night, Tony never came back up on the deck. He was seasick and stayed in his cabin for three days, and I gambled with his traveler's checks. I think he was afraid of me, with good reason. I think he thought I might push him overboard accidentally. If I could have, I would have. I seemed unable to divorce him, so at that point murder seemed the only solution. We were locked into this destructive relationship. It demonstrated itself in weird happenings. At one point in the voyage, we came very near an iceberg, and I wasn't a bit afraid of it. I just sat up on the deck and looked at it. After the disasters I had been through, it seemed inconsequential.

When we docked in New York, I stayed by the ship until attendants took the Jaguar off and cleaned it up enough to drive it uptown. I drove. Tony sat next to me in silence. Somewhere around Forty-second Street, I asked him where he wanted me to drop him.

"Do you really want this kind of publicity now?" he asked. "If I register in a hotel when you're in town, we will have all the columnists calling us, and they'll rake up all the crappy notoriety we had in Rome."

I was trapped again. I kept driving.

"Don't you have the Cadillac in the garage?" he asked.

"Yes," I said. "Now I have a Cadillac and a Jaguar in the garage, and you can't drive either one of them until you learn how to drive."

He said nothing. I think he was hoping that since he

had bought me a Bulgari pin and earrings and a Jaguar, I should forget all about his escapades and the car accident. I didn't forget, but I put all of it on hold for a while, to forestall any more scandal.

When we arrived at my apartment on Central Park West, I gave the doorman the keys to the car—and got in the elevator to return to the security of my mother, child, and Molly Epps.

The sleeping arrangements at Thanksgiving were a little odd. I slept in my bedroom, Tony slept in my mother's bedroom, and my mother slept in my child's bedroom. Molly cooked a gorgeous Thanksgiving dinner. But the relationship between Tony and me was strained; even though I had some of my chums from the Actors Studio to dinner and his mother and aunts, it was a rather solemn meal. I was arranging never to be alone with Tony, and perhaps he was doing the same with me.

Between Thanksgiving and Christmas, I almost relented, and Tony and I were sitting in our living room and having drinks. I was cuing him in his lines for *The Story on Page One*. As I headed for the bathroom, the phone in the bedroom rang. I picked it up. It was Lauren Bacall.

"I've been waiting for Tony for an hour," Lauren said angrily. "I'm sitting in Danny's Hideaway alone. Where the hell is he?"

"Lauren," I replied, "you're complaining to me because my husband is late for a date with you?"

"Well, dear," she said, "if your husband doesn't respect your marriage, why should I?"

"You're absolutely right, Lauren. He'll be there in a few minutes. Look for a man with a bandaged head."

When I returned to the living room, I knew Tony had been listening on the extension. His face had once again turned the familiar greenish-white color it assumed in moments of crisis.

"Let's not discuss it," I said. "Just go keep your appointment. I think I'd rather have this Christmas and New Year's alone with my daughter, mother, and Molly. I'm sure you'll have to start rehearsing in California, *now*."

* * *

It turned out to be a lovely Christmas. With Tony's departure the tension vanished from the house, and I took my kid sledding and ice-skating in Central Park. My little family had a wonderful Christmas. Tony had again bought out F.A.O. Schwarz, and half the store was delivered on Christmas Eve. He had bought me a three-strand pearl necklace with a sapphire heart as a clasp. I had the necklace for quite a while, but I didn't wear it till I somehow managed to lose the heart clasp and replaced it with an antique diamond one. I wondered if he'd given the same present to Lauren Bacall.

I rather dreaded New Year's Eve because I didn't have and didn't want a date. But when I attended the Tuesday session at the Actors Studio between Christmas and New Year's, I found my fellow actors decorating the Studio with balloons and confetti and was informed that I had to make a contribution to the rip-roaring shindig they were planning for New Year's Eve.

It was a "not-for-profit" affair just for the Studio members and their kin. And it was a costume bash. You were to come as the historical actor or actress you most admired. Luckily, years before, when I had seen Laurette Taylor in *The Glass Menagerie* in Chicago, at the start of its pre-Broadway tour, Tony Ross had taken me backstage to meet her and, after we had talked a while, she had given me an extra of the nightgown she wore in the show. It was too long for her, and she did not want to destroy the silk by hemming it.

I still have that nightgown, and nowadays I'm wondering if I have the courage to do that role in Tennessee's great play. Recently, when I was doing a film with Geraldine Page, I asked her if she didn't want to play Amanda in *The Glass Menagerie*. Her answer was, "Unfortunately, or fortunately, I saw Laurette Taylor in that role. I don't think I have anything to add to that."

I have felt the same way about this great performance, but I was so depressed that night of New Year's Eve that I felt Laurette Taylor would have wanted me to cheer up in her nightgown. I think she worked her magic. I went to the party, and I suddenly pivoted over and remembered I was an accomplished, acclaimed actress, I had almost won the Best Actress Oscar for *A Place in the Sun*, and I had done the great film of *The Diary of Anne Frank*, which would soon be released.

At midnight everyone kissed everyone else. Geraldine Page, Rip Torn, Ben Gazzara, Julie Harris, William Inge, Marty Balsam, Barbara Harris, Arthur Penn, Anne Bancroft, Harold Clurman, Maureen Stapleton, Cheryl Crawford, Jane Fonda, Anne Jackson, Eli Wallach, Burgess Meredith, Walter Matthau, Paul Newman, Joanne Woodward, Estelle Parsons, Franchot Tone, and Arthur Miller were there . . . and Marilyn Monroe.

Conrad Janis had a banjo band, made up of actor-musicians who played loudly and badly. We drank some strange punch, which I found out later was composed of inexpensive wine and vodka and fruit juice. Around 2:00 A.M., we all bundled into a strange assortment of furs, ranging from squirrel to sable, and taxied up to Lee and Paula Strasberg's apartment. Susan and Johnny Strasberg were there, as were several of Lee and Paula's older and more dignified friends and relatives.

We all sat around the floor until dawn, listening to Lee's opera and symphony records. He and Harold Clurman and Clifford Odets were arguing about and discussing their varied and conflicting memories of their Group Theatre days. We sang old songs, and despite the chaos going on in Hollywood with the advent of television, the New York theater was still flourishing, and that early morning of 1959 Lee made us all feel like accomplished stars of the theater. Maybe it was the weird punch.

Sometime during the night, Julie and Harry Belafonte had arrived, and I was overjoyed to see them. I was a little drunk, but Harry began to tell me that he had bought an insightful new book called *Odds Against Tomorrow*, which he was doing with Robert Ryan and Ed Begley, to be directed by Robert Wise. The story concerned three bank robbers, but it was really about white and black hatred, and its theme was the fact that if American minorities didn't hang together, they'd all hang separately.

I sobered up. "Harry," I said, "what a wonderful idea!"

"Well, Shell, there's a very good part in it, although

not very big, and it's Robert Ryan's mistress. It's sad and funny, and I would love you to do it.''

I told Harry I would love to, but I was sorry I could not go to Hollywood for quite a while.

He and Julie looked at me strangely, then Harry said, "You don't have to. It's going to be shot in New York City and upstate.''

"Thanks, Harry," I replied. "I'll do it.''

Harry asked, "Don't you want to read the script first?''

"No. If you and Robert Ryan and Ed Begley are acting in it, and Robert Wise is directing, and I can stay home in New York, I'll do it.''

Harry laughed and said, "I'll send it to your apartment tomorrow.''

nor very big, and it's Robert Ryan's mistress. It's sad and funny, and I would love you to do it."

"I told Harry, I would love to." Jim Lister, maybe I could run out to Hollywood for quite a while . . ."

He said once looked at me strangely. Then Harry said, "Now that I have to . . . it's more to be said to me." You clip and upstart.

"Thanks, Harry," I replied. "I'll do it."

Harry asked, "Want you want to read the script first?"

"No, if you and Robert Ryan and I'd those who're doing it," and Robert Ryan who is directing, and I can stay home in New York, I'll do it."

Harry laughed and said, "I'll send it to you at your home tomorrow."

PART
3

*Appropriate
Winters*

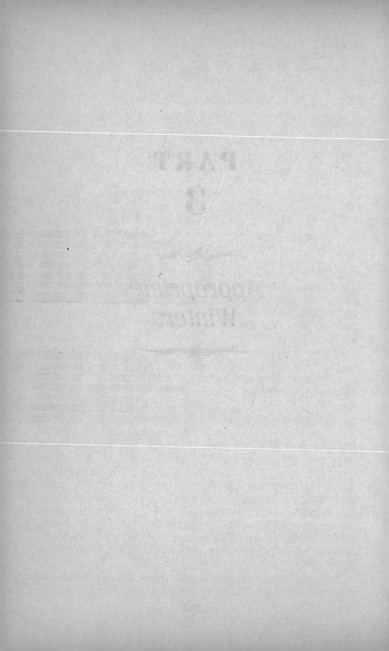

16

We rehearsed *Odds Against Tomorrow* in rehearsal rooms in a lovely building in lower Manhattan. The best part of rehearsing there was that Ratner's, a famous dairy restaurant, was on the ground floor of the building. After the first day, Robert Ryan would meet me there every morning for breakfast. I had known him not-so-casually in Hollywood in the late forties. In fact, I believe Marilyn introduced him to me during the shooting of *Clash by Night*. I had asked her who the handsome man was when I'd seen a still of them together. He looked about thirty-five.

"He's lovely," she said, "but he's awfully young."

My young friend was still fantasizing about Zero Mostel, Lee Strasberg, or Albert Einstein. I never knew her to be attracted by a young man. If they weren't fifty, they were kids, as far as she was concerned. I guess Marilyn was always trying to replace the father she'd never known. Sometime around '49 or '50 I sort of accidentally had breakfast at Schwab's with Bob Ryan. There wasn't an empty booth, so he sat with me. Now here I was having breakfast with him again at Ratner's in New York, and we were reminiscing about our young Hollywood days.

Robert Wise was an extraordinary director. He had directed me in *Executive Suite*, an original and sensitive film. He carefully orchestrated Robert's and my scenes. The essence of our scenes is that he is my live-in lover, just out after a long stretch in Sing Sing, and I have waited for him. I am the manager and hostess in a hair-dressing salon and make pretty good money.

As an ex-convict, of course he has great trouble finding a job. I stupidly keep reassuring him that I love him, that he mustn't worry about working, and that I'm making enough money for both of us. My reassurance further emasculates him. His desire not to be financially dependent on me gets him involved in this foolishly planned bank robbery. He knows almost from the beginning that it will fail, but he feels so impotent with me that he goes along with the dangerous plan.

When we began to shoot the interiors, we used a movie studio somewhere on the Upper East Side of Manhattan and the old Astoria studios. Bob Wise was shooting the film as much as possible in sequence, so we worked at the studio in the beginning of the filming. Then the company moved upstate for the locations of the robbery and, after four weeks of exteriors, we came back to the studio.

Tony had been calling me once a week, Sundays, at a set time. We were cordial on the phone and discussed our various films and financial matters, but did not talk about when we would see each other again.

It was a bitter cold winter, and the studio we were working in had been there since silent-picture days. As always when filming, there seem to be long delays in lighting, mix-ups in schedules, camera equipment doesn't show up, the generator blows up, and script changes are made. Bob Wise and Harry Belafonte, who was one of the producers, would stop shooting to look at the film. It had to be very carefully edited because of the complications of the plot—three men involved in a holdup who hate each other. So Robert Ryan and I would sit in our little set of a cheap run-down flat that was sort of an apartment-hotel. We would talk about the theater, organic farming, where Hollywood was going in this age of television, anything but what we were really thinking about. If I remembered correctly, Bob had been rather a heavy drinker when I'd known him in my early Schwab days, but you never could tell if he was drunk. He would just grow very quiet after eight hours of steady drinking. The only time I suspected he had a hangover was when he had two beers at breakfast.

He had also smoked a couple of packs of cigarettes a day, but it seemed, during the shooting of *Odds Against Tomorrow*, that he had completely reformed. Well, almost. One cold, snowy late afternoon, when we had been waiting since 7:00 A.M. for them to finish a scene with Ed Begley and Harry, I told Bob all about my sad, hasty marriage. We were snuggled in our set bedroom, preparing for the love scene we were about to shoot.

In the scene I'm rather sexually aggressive with him, and he is withdrawn and rather off. I mean, that's what the script required. That afternoon, after hearing my sad tale, Robert was at his most reassuring and loving. But I guess I still had some stupid notion in my head about being faithful to Tony. I told Bob about some of my marital problems in Italy. He became annoyed with my sexual reservations.

"What's going on?" he said. "Shelley, you're being faithful to Tony, and he's faithful to all the leading ladies of the Screen Actors Guild?"

I began to laugh hysterically so I wouldn't cry. Then we noticed Robert Wise was standing in the hallway, watching us. He's quite an elegant gentleman, and he murmured:

"Shelley, Bob, that's wonderful preparation, but I think you've got your motivations backwards."

I'm not sure we ever straightened it out, because every time I've seen that film, I've thought we made all the political points of *Odds Against Tomorrow* quite well, but the human points seem rather blurred.

The film went over schedule a couple of weeks, but United Artists didn't object too much, because they were already planning that it would pay back its negative cost on black-and-white television, which of course we didn't know at the time.

Sometime toward spring, after we'd finished *Odds Against Tomorrow*, Harry invited me to meet someone at a sort of symposium at his house. When I got there, I realized there were young intellectuals from every college newspaper around the Eastern seaboard; Marty Peretz was the only one I really knew. He was doing graduate work at Harvard, and he was then Max Lerner's researcher. In the years to come, I got to know Marty very well as we worked together in many civil-rights organizations. He is now the publisher and editor of *The New Republic*.

We all sat around on the floor of Harry's enormous living room on West End Avenue, and in a little while an unassuming, very calm, beautiful young black man came in and sat down at one end of the room.

Harry introduced him simply, and explained that Rev. Martin Luther King had just come back from India, where he had studied the nonviolent tactics of Gandhi, which had gained India's independence after centuries of British oppression. Everyone in that room became uplifted and full of purpose. The truth, the warmth, and the optimism Dr. King radiated touched everyone who heard him that night. My life suddenly seemed to have a different meaning after I listened to that remarkable man. I stopped worrying about which movies to do or what Tony would or could not do. I pivoted back to being a woman who was conscious of her own humanity and responsibility to her brothers and sisters.

Rev. King talked about Rosa Parks, the black woman in Montgomery who'd been too tired to walk to the back of the bus. Her feet hurt her, and she refused to go to the back of the bus, and so she started a revolution. I remembered when I was in *A Hatful of Rain* this event had occurred, and we had had a little television set in my dressing room, and the whole cast, when they weren't on the stage, had stayed glued to it. This seemingly unimportant incident had grown into a shining beacon for black people all over the world. The Montgomery bus boycott had started a new revolutionary movement toward civil rights and real equality for all minorities.

Dr. King had the most forceful and spiritual beauty of any person I have ever met. You felt honored just to be in his presence. During the coming weeks, I came to know Martin Luther King and his wife, Coretta, quite well, and when the film *Anne Frank* opened on Broadway, he asked me if they could take me to the opening. Tony was still in California, and we were still playing the game of living on opposite coasts whenever we could manage it, so I was very grateful that I had such distinguished people to take me to the opening of my important film. Without my telling him, Dr. King understood that although I was married, I was alone. I thanked him and said, "Of course," and invited Harry and Julie Belafonte too.

Working in the civil-rights movement gave me a new confidence in myself and a self-esteem that I had never had. In fact, that spring I wrote my first play. It was called *Hansel and Gretel in the Oven,* and Patty Bosworth and Tom Wheatley performed it at the Actors Studio. It was the first play ever, to my knowledge, about homosexuality and the tortures of a young actor trying to hide it. The day it was performed, the Studio was filled with important writers and directors, including Jerome Robbins, Israel Horovitz, and Arthur Laurents.

I wasn't aware that I was doing something revolutionary by writing about this subject. For me, the play was a human problem—a young boy and a young girl, both fledgling film actors, who are caught in the agony of their public life and their hidden private life. The play was sad and funny, and all the members of the writers' group in the Studio congratulated me and assured me I had a wonderful future as a writer—I must just stick to it. In years to come I was to write many plays. The only one that was good enough to be produced off-Broadway was also one that I had started at the Studio, called *The Gestation of a Weather Man*. By the time it got to off-Broadway, at the producer's insistence, I found another title: *One Night Stands of a Noisy Passenger*. It was three one-act plays involving six different people. The first took place during the Second World War in New York, and Sally Kirkland and Richard Lynch performed it. The second took place during the Korean War and the blacklisting in Hollywood, and the setting was Paris, and Will Hare and Joanna Miles did it. The third one was with Diane Ladd and Robert De Niro. The play ran for a week, and the fledgling Robert De Niro was acclaimed in every magazine and review. The play did pretty well, too, but it was undercapitalized, and it didn't have time to find its audience. I was so bitter about this off-Broadway experience that I have not written another play, even though the theater critics gave me great encouragement.

What do you know . . . I was having a wonderful winter in New York, alone with myself. I didn't need a man as a crutch. I'd gotten great reviews in *Anne Frank*, and I was writing and really becoming friends with my little girl. Somewhere around this time, my agent phoned me and asked me if I would come out to Hollywood and have discussions with the Columbia executives and Philip Leacock, the English director, about a film called *Let No Man Write My Epitaph*, the sequel to *Knock on Any Door*. I refused to come for initial discussions. They had to come to New York to talk to me.

I was rather pleased with this offer for the wrong reason. When I was quite young, I had been under contract to Columbia for very little money. After a year, they had dropped my option, and the casting director, Max Arnow, had told me I just wasn't cut out for the movies —I wasn't photogenic, didn't understand the camera and my voice was all wrong. So now I told my agent to make Columbia pay a lot of money, and I had to have a definite artistic involvement in the film. When I read the script, I was pleased. It was about a young woman who tries to raise a boy alone in a slum, and there are wonderful characters helping her. I finally had to fly out to Hollywood, and it was okay, because the day after I arrived, Tony had to go to New York, to discuss a play, I believe. This time I drove him to the plane with relief. We didn't talk about *anything*.

The discussions in casting for *Epitaph* took about a week, and I convinced Mr. Leacock, who was a dream, to cast James Darren, Burl Ives, Jean Seberg and Ella Fitzgerald. He also cast a friend of mine, a wonderful black actor by the name of Bernie Hamilton, who played a legless beggar. When I had directed *Thunder Rock* during the war, although Bernie was a sailor in the U.S. Navy, he had come to an audition. His audition was so good and I had encouraged him so much that, after the war, when he got out of the Navy, he reported back to me. I sent him to the right teachers, and he has had quite an illustrious career in Hollywood. He was the first character actor to break the color line, getting cast in parts that had originally been written for whites. Since there were so few opportunities for black actors in American films in those days, Bernie also became something of a Christmas-tree tycoon: He sold Christmas trees on the holidays to make sure he had enough money to support his family during the whole year while he waited for acting jobs. Bob Mitchum had done this too during the early part of his career.

Epitaph is about an unmarried young woman who becomes a prostitute in order to support her young son and eventually becomes a heroin addict. Mr. Leacock ordered me to do as much researching as I could about this terrible social phenomenon.

There was a strong role of a pimp, an evil, sexy and handsome man. I had seen George Scott at the Actors Studio and on the stage with Judith Anderson in some strange play, and he had electrified the audience with his villainy, so I put up a losing battle with the powers that be at Columbia to try to get him this role.

They felt that George Scott was not enough of a name at that time to be hired for this film. Well, six months later, when *Anatomy of a Murder* came out, he proved that *I* should have been running Columbia.

I was having a lively time in Hollywood with all my California pals that I hadn't had a chance to see in the past couple of years. One day when I was having costume fittings at Columbia, I met Marilyn in the executive dining room where we had never gone when Harry Cohn was president of the studio. She told me I simply had to come to the Twentieth Century–Fox commissary the next day. Nikita Khrushchev, the premier of the Soviet Union, was coming to Twentieth Century–Fox to have a conference with Darryl F. Zanuck about some big artistic exchange program, and then Khrushchev was going to Disneyland. I thought my beautiful young friend was hallucinating. I said something like, "Marilyn, can I have one puff of that before you throw it away?"

"Honest, Shelley," she said. "I have it right. I think it will be fascinating to meet Nikita Khrushchev in case our films ever play in Russia."

"Marilyn, I think your films are already playing the Loew's Moscow."

"Come on, Shelley. You keep talking to me about Stanislavsky. Wouldn't it be great to go there and see the Moscow Art Theatre? Sort of get the Method from the horse's mouth?"

"That's a date, kiddo."

We giggled about what we would wear, and I went home and called Arthur Jacobs, the publicist, and said, "Is it true that Khrushchev is coming to the Fox commissary tomorrow?"

He told me, "Yes, it's true, and if you want to go, I'll clear you with the FBI and arrange for you to be there. But, Shelley, you have to be on time."

"I promise," I said. "I promise, I promise."

What followed was a most bizarre series of contradictions. I got to the Fox commissary the next day at ten minutes to twelve. I think the entire commissary was surrounded by the California National Guard, and there were Secret Service men all over. In these days of *glasnost* it's hard to describe the rabid anti-Russian feeling that existed in Hollywood. It was very nerve-racking. I obviously had been okayed by the FBI. They seated me at a table for three halfway from the dais. I'd barely sat down when Judy Garland joined me. There were shrimp cocktails on the table in front of both Judy and me, and we both felt compelled to eat. We were both so nervous. But just then, over the loudspeaker, came a screeching, military voice:

"Please do not touch any food until Premier Khrushchev and his party are seated. Their motorcade is approaching the Twentieth Century–Fox gate."

Judy and I looked at each other. We felt this whole day

304

was highly improbable. Even as I write this, I feel it couldn't have happened, but it did.

Judy and I began to hold hands, and our hands were like ice.

"Oh, my God," she said, "suppose he falls down or something? We'll be in an atomic war."

"Judy, stop scaring us. Just like every other movie fan in the world, he wants to see the movie stars, but I can't think what he'd want to talk to Darryl F. Zanuck about."

The voice over the speaker system then said, "The premier of the Union of Soviet Socialist Republics and his party are approaching the commissary." Marilyn still wasn't at our table. And then I noticed that my ever-late friend was being escorted through a side door, by two burly Twentieth Century–Fox guards, to a front table to the left of the dais. Everyone stood up, and I began to feel that I was having some weird dream. Why, or how, could the head of the Communist Party of the Soviet Union be coming to Twentieth Century–Fox, the entertainment center of American capitalism? All I could think of was that perhaps the entire North American continent was somehow in jeopardy, or maybe, just maybe, this could be the beginning of the two superpowers living in peace in the world. In 1959, at the height of the Cold War, that seemed impossible and highly improbable.

During the next couple of hours, Judy was pale as a ghost and obviously felt the same tension that I did. It got so bad we could not wait for Khrushchev to be introduced, and we secretly and ravenously ate our shrimp cocktails. Khrushchev arrived. He was a plump, rather grandfatherly-looking man with a plump, grandmotherly-looking wife, and, if I remember rightly, two large teenage children. They all looked like farmers from around Cleveland, not Russia. Their clothes looked as if they came from Sears, and I could not believe this was the ruler of all the Russias.

"The Star-Spangled Banner" was played, and we all sang, and then, believe it or not, they played "The Internationale." In the Twentieth Century–Fox commissary! You understand, the influence of the blacklist was still being felt. Judy and I broke into hysterical laughter, and we stuffed our napkins into our mouths. The whole event was so unlikely. As soon as "The Internationale" was over, we sat down, and we didn't wait for the illustrious guest to eat. We devoured everything in sight—lettuce, rolls, and anything we could grab. That afternoon passed in a blur, but I remember the highlights.

We had steak béarnaise, which was the tenderest I've ever had, elegant vegetables, and some kind of potato puffs with air in them, and I've never had them before or since. I guess Zanuck's personal chef catered this lunch. We had some kind of ice-cream cake, and at each place was a different-shaped ice cream, and flags with the hammer and sickle or the stars and stripes. I never thought I would ever live to see the hammer and sickle on the Fox lot. So many people had lost their jobs and been blacklisted in the movie industry for even hinting that something like socialized medicine could be adapted to the American system.

We had elegant wines and champagne, and Judy and I had second helpings of everything, including the wine. I think we were projecting the magic thinking that if we ate and drank a lot of everything, nothing terrible could happen. Sometime during dessert and brandy, after a flurry on the side of the commissary with Walt Disney, a Russian interpreter came to the dais and whispered something in Khrushchev's ear. Then Khrushchev got up and made a very long and angry speech, in Russian of course. Judy and I were terrified. We were thinking of sneaking out the side door Marilyn had come in and getting the hell away from Fox as fast as we could.

After Khrushchev had wound down, Zanuck came to the microphone and said:

"Walt Disney has informed us that he does not think that Premier Khrushchev and his family should go to Disneyland this evening, as he cannot guarantee their safety."

Why Walt Disney couldn't close his damn Disneyland to the public for a couple of hours and take Khrushchev's family through it, I'll never know. I've often suspected that Disney was the reason for the next Cold War crisis, the Berlin Wall or something. I got very angry at Walt

Disney's lack of diplomacy. Even I know you catch more bees with honey than vinegar. Dumb dumb dumb.

To make the day's faux pas complete, the entire commissary of about five hundred stars, writers, directors, producers, and cameramen were traipsed over to the largest of the Fox stages. John Foster Dulles was whispering in Khrushchev's ear, but the premier was still red with anger. When we got to the stage, there was the set of *Can-Can*—an imitation theater and proscenium complete with theater boxes. Then, for some reason, Mr. and Mrs. Khrushchev were put in one of those little imitation gilded stage boxes, which I was sure were made of plywood and would come crumbling down at any minute.

The chorus of *Can-Can* and Shirley MacLaine proceeded to do the can-can, complete with showing their backsides in lace panties and black stockings and throwing their skirts in the air with their petticoats over their heads. All I could do was pray.

"What do you think will happen if that gold theater box breaks?" Judy whispered. "The Khrushchevs between them look like they weigh quite a bit."

All I could answer was, "I hope we have our defensive submarines encircling Russia. If they fall through that box, the world might be destroyed."

I could not imagine what idiot had arranged this. The can-can number seemed endless. When it finally was over and the premier and his wife came down safely from that stupid box, the entire audience heaved a sigh of relief and applauded. All the stars of *Can-Can* lined up in a row to be introduced to Khrushchev—Shirley MacLaine, Frank Sinatra, Maurice Chevalier, Louis Jourdan, and Juliet Prowse. Khrushchev stopped to chat with Shirley, and she evidently asked him what he thought of the can-can. He turned to the microphone someone carried and said something very loud and stern in Russian. When translated it turned out to be:

"Humanity's face is more beautiful than its backside."

He kept shaking hands so we all relaxed, but when he got to Maurice Chevalier, he ignored his hand and the introduction and walked right past him. What an insult.

Willie Wyler, who was standing next to Judy and me, whispered to our astounded faces:

"Chevalier was a collaborator in Vichy France during the war. He performed for the Nazis. Zanuck may have forgotten it, but Khrushchev and the Russian people never will. Too many of their people were murdered by the Nazis."

Khrushchev hurriedly started to leave, but stopped to talk to Marilyn for a minute with his translator. She gave him her sexy smile and wiggled and said something in Russian, but nobody translated it, and we couldn't hear it. Later I found out that she said it with her breathless voice, and the translator got it. But Khrushchev obviously understood her intention, and he got a big smile on his face. He then marched off the stage, trailed by his family and the diplomatic corps of both countries. He got in his limousine and drove back to the L.A. airport with sirens screaming. I have always felt that Marilyn may possibly have prevented a third world war by at least making Khrushchev leave Twentieth Century–Fox with a smile on his face. In the years that followed, I have read very little about Khrushchev's Hollywood visit. At times I've thought I dreamed the whole thing, it was so embarrassingly terrible, but I've researched it, and it really did happen.

Sometime later that week, I saw Marilyn at Chasen's Restaurant, and I asked her what she had said to Khrushchev.

"Natalie Wood speaks Russian fluently," she said. "She taught me a few words."

"Really? What did you say? Tell me in English."

" 'We the workers of Twentieth Century–Fox rejoice that you have come to visit our studio and country.' " She then whispered it to me in Russian, in her sexy voice, and I agreed it sounded great.

I was notified by my agent that the script of *Let No Man Write My Epitaph* needed a rewrite. Willard Motley had not approved the final draft so far, and I could go back to New York for a while. He was surprised when I reacted to this information with sadness. He thought it had something to do with the money, as all agents do.

"Shelley," he said, "they're paying you for this time you've spent doing costumes and script changes and casting. You're on salary."

"It's not that, Herb. It's too complicated to explain."

I wanted very much to get back to my child, my mother, the Actors Studio and all my friends in New York. I hoped I could squeeze in some kind of theater for the month or so that I had before the film started. But Tony and I had not really lived together since the fall of '58, and here it was the spring of '59, and he was in my apartment in New York. I could not very well tell him to go back to California or move to a hotel unless I wanted to file for divorce and suffer the publicity that would result. Maybe it was just a rationalization, but I really didn't want any more of that publicity. So I decided to pretend that nothing serious was the matter, to treat Tony like an old pal and what would be, would be. Again, I hoped that we were both more mature and could proceed with our lives, whatever our decision was, in an adult, dignified fashion.

I returned to Central Park West, and Tony seemed to have changed. He was great friends with my daughter now and had been taking her to her school and even picking her up at the bus at 3:15 P.M. Nothing he could have done would have made me forgive him more quickly than this. I thought, Well, perhaps we could be kinder to each other and try again. Perhaps Tony had had enough of playing the bachelor in Hollywood, which I believe he had done with various leading ladies. Perhaps I had gone along with it in a masochistic fashion, gritting my teeth and hoping he'd outgrow this behavior.

During this period, Tony worked on scenes from a play by Tennessee Williams called *A Period of Adjustment*. The original script, which I still have in my files, was called *A High Point Is Built on a Cavern*. It's about two couples. Both men were in the Korean War and have now returned to civilian life and are making a lot of money. During the course of the play, they all worry about who's sleeping with whom and don't notice that their house is slowly sinking. It is built on some kind of fault and there are little tremors and earthquakes, but they ignore this problem and only concentrate on their sexual frustrations. I think this was the most political of Tennessee's plays. It very accurately depicted American society in the late fifties.

Somewhere around this time, Julie Belafonte called me and said, "You know, David Susskind has this program which is broadcast from someplace in New Jersey called 'Open End.' And he has various celebrities discussing all kinds of subjects. Well, *The New York Times* Sunday has a full-page ad, taken by some far-right group, claiming it is a letter of Abraham Lincoln's. In this letter he supposedly says the Negro is inferior.

"My husband, Harry, and Sidney Poitier are going on this program to refute this Ku Klux Klan gobbledygook, and Harry would like you to be on the program with them."

I answered, "I would love to, Julie." Then I must have taken temporary leave of my senses, because I asked, "How about Tony? Could he be on the program, too?"

At that point I should have understood that Tony was very confused politically. He was very warm and understanding and helpful about racial issues, but his span of concentration was not too good at any time, and though I had given him a lot of books and articles on civil rights, at that point his only reading was film scripts and plays.

I asked Julie if Martin Luther King and his wife Coretta could come to dinner before the broadcast, as my housekeeper, Molly Epps, who was a sensational cook, had asked me if she could meet Martin Luther King "anytime, anywhere."

Julie said she'd see and call me back. When she did she said, "They'd love to." The next few days, my apartment was in a whirlwind. I had a large dining room, and every piece of furniture and silver and all my dishes suddenly became as beautiful as if they were in a palace.

The night that the Kings came to dinner, Molly outdid even herself. Since she kept me on a diet, she had never, ever cooked such an exquisite gourmet meal for me, although she had worked for me for many years by then. The Poitiers were there, and my little daughter. We had a wonderful time and a great deal of fun. Afterwards, all the adults went down and piled into the limousine, and Martin Luther King and his wife had to go to a rally. Dr. King wished us luck and said, "Watch out for that Mr. Susskind. He is very tricky, and although he's a very liberal man, he needs to have controversial programs." I *thought* we were listening to Dr. King. But obviously I wasn't paying enough attention.

We got to the television station in New Jersey, and we had a long, wonderful discussion about civil rights, and Harry and Sidney were brilliant. The Lincoln letter that this fascist organization had put in *The New York Times* had never been authenticated. But that was only the jumping-off place for our discussions. After two or three hours of open discussion, it was getting near midnight. That's why the program was called "Open End." We were all rather weary, and Susskind turned to Tony, who had taken no part in the discussions up until then and was checking out his hair on the monitor.

"Do *you* agree with what Lincoln said in this letter?" Susskind asked him.

Tony sleepily answered, "Of course I agree with Lincoln. I think he was the greatest president we ever had."

Sidney and Harry froze. I jumped in with, "David, what Tony means is that if Lincoln ever wrote such a thing, he probably meant that, just as people coming out of concentration camps are inferior in schooling and nutrition and physical stamina, so the Negro, coming out of slavery, was often undernourished and uneducated."

Tony said, "Yeah, David, that's what I mean."

This was maybe the most embarrassing moment of my entire life so far, and Tony wasn't even aware anything had happened.

Sidney and Harry, with fire in their eyes, ended this "Open End" program, and said we all had to get back to New York, and the four of us climbed in the limousine and drove over the George Washington Bridge. Tony had no idea he'd said anything wrong. Somewhere around the middle of the bridge, Harry said, "Shall we open the door and throw him over?"

"Yeah," Sidney said. "Stop the car."

"What's wrong?" Tony asked. "What did I do?"

Sidney looked at me. "When he gets home, Shelley, explain to him, and I don't know where you should start, but try to educate him. He is now living in 1959."

When we got home, I started educating Tony, and stopped being mad at him. I realized that there wasn't much he could have learned on 118th Street in New York or in Hollywood. I guess I must have done a good job, because some years later I saw him on TV at the Washington Monument with Marlon Brando and other important public figures taking part in the civil-rights March on Washington for Jobs and Freedom. Tony did many strange things, but he was good at heart and had the endearing quality of putting his money where his mouth was. I think Tony always felt that if it was deductible, such as charities or worthy causes or loaning money to fellow actors, you would come out ahead in your income tax. I'm sure the years have taught him it ain't so. There has to be income to deduct it from.

Some weeks later, I again was watching Susskind, and he had one of the cruelest shows that I have ever seen on television. He had five ladies in their forties or fifties who had no idea why they were on this show together and were trying to figure out the common denominator that had brought them together on the air. They were all from middle-income families, and they lived in suburbs around New York—Staten Island, New Jersey, Queens, Westchester, and Bronxville. They were attractive ladies, most of them blonde. As the show progressed the viewer became aware that they all had two children each. Suddenly Mr. Susskind forced two of the women to admit that their sons were homosexual. As this "Open End" show continued the other three women came to realize, or think, that perhaps their sons too were homosexual. They obviously loved their sons very much, and it was indeed a shock to them, and to me as I watched it, to be put through this on the air, in front of so many people. Remember, this occurred long before the consciousness-raising which brought us civil rights, women's liberation, and the movement to end discrimination against homosexuals.

* * *

I was very angry with Mr. Susskind for a long time. A couple of years later, I had occasion to get even with him on television. I was on the Johnny Carson show in New York, publicizing some film or other, and the show was still ninety minutes long in those days. Susskind was to be the third guest. David Steinberg had been rapping with Johnny when I was introduced, and I forget what we talked about, but, as sometimes happens, we were all on a roll, setting up jokes for each other, and so the program was hilarious. Johnny, being the consummate showman he is, forgot about Susskind until the last ten minutes of the show, and then he reluctantly ended this hilarity and brought Susskind out.

Susskind was furious, and he made the grave mistake of saying to me, after he'd said hello to Johnny, "Shelley, you really are a monumental yenta, aren't you?"

I answered, "Of course, David, and who is the young blonde yenta in the makeup room with you? Your latest wife? What happened to the old one who put you through law school? And I know why you're mad at me, David—because I helped Bob Kennedy become the senator from New York. You've had thousands of hours of air time, and you could not be elected dog catcher, could you, David?"

Those were just the nice things I said to him. For the next ten minutes, Johnny Carson refused to go to commercial. As his director, Freddie de Cordova, tried to get him to put the commercials on, Carson recognized this was a historic moment on live television. He refused to cut away from me and Susskind, who was now holding his arms and hands up, as if a boxer were pummeling his head. David Steinberg was rolling on the floor with laughter. I didn't care. I felt Susskind, may he rest in peace, had been asking for this for a long time.

Some years later, when *Look* magazine printed pictures of the three most powerful moments in live television history, they printed pictures of Ruby shooting Oswald, the hundreds of Vietnamese people clinging to an American plane as it took off, and Shelley Winters murdering David Susskind live on Johnny Carson.

17

It was spring 1959. Tony's and my marriage seemed calm and relatively happy, but we were still avoiding living with each other. Tony went somewhere to do something, and I started working for the not quite yet Reform Democratic Committee. The 1960 election was not so far away, and Tammany Hall had had a reactionary grip on the Democratic Party for more than a hundred years. Bentley Kassal, and other young lawyers and politicians, contacted me to come to tea to meet Eleanor Roosevelt. Bentley Kassal was single.

I was overcome with joy. I had adored Eleanor Roosevelt since my childhood. During the Depression, I was told that when I had gotten a hot lunch in school it was thanks to Mrs. Roosevelt. As children do, I decided that she was *really* in the school kitchen, cooking it herself. No matter what anyone told me, I refused to believe any differently. I had read her "My Day" column all through my childhood and adolescence. Even now, I feel if only I had met her earlier in my life, I could have believed in my brains and been a congresswoman instead of an actress. *If*—the saddest word in our language.

Anyway, at long last, I was to meet her. It was a memorable meeting, with many New York civic leaders and the new progressive factions of the Democratic Party. Tammany Hall's influence was declining in New York, and I became immersed in both local and national politics. I remember the day I met her backstage at a huge theater on upper Broadway, where I was helping organize the program. Some celebrity, who was to have made a speech, had not shown, and someone said, "Shelley, can you talk for a few minutes while we regroup?"

"No, I really don't think I can." I was paralyzed with fear.

Mrs. Roosevelt, who was standing a few feet from me, walked up and put her arm around my shoulders and, in her lovely, schoolteacher voice, said, "Nonsense, Shelley! You're what we call an 'emotional Democrat.' You're a little weak on facts, but your heart is in the right place."

With that inspiration, I went out and talked for five minutes about conditions then prevalent on the West Side of New York—the tenements next to the big luxury apartment houses, the landlords who turned off the heat at night in freezing weather, the inflation that was eroding our buying power at the A&P on Ninety-sixth Street. I can't remember exactly what I said, but the audience gave me a huge ovation. When I came off the stage, Mrs. Roosevelt pinned a funny little gold donkey to my collar. I still have it and will always treasure it.

Tony was in California, doing "Heaven Can Wait," a live television show for "The Dupont Show." It was stressful to do these shows, because you rehearsed for two or three weeks, and then they photographed it like a play. It was like an opening night.

Since Tony and I were still zigging and zagging, our marriage was happier when we both lived on opposite sides of the country. Tony managed to stretch out this television job for a couple of months, and I helped him stretch it. I began to understand that Tony was calmer and worked better away from me.

One Sunday morning, Frank Corsaro came for breakfast, and while he was concentrating on playing with my kid, he surreptitiously slipped me a script. It was a play called *A Piece of Blue Sky*—by *Frank Corsaro*. I never knew that Frank wrote, although I knew what a great director he was. When I asked him about his new medium, he answered, "The play of yours I saw at the Actors Studio, *Hansel and Gretel in the Oven*, inspired me. If you like my play, perhaps we'll do it in summer stock, and then maybe bring it to off-Broadway."

I replied, "Oh, my God, Frank, I have a commitment at Columbia to do *Let No Man Write My Epitaph*. It's by Willard Motley, and it's the sequel to *Knock on Any Door*."

"Don't worry, Shell. Where there's a will, there's a way. We'll work around your commitments."

That night, I read his play. It was powerful—about a family during the Depression, and the wife, who would be played by Marian Seldes, makes friends with a hotsy-totsy lady upstairs, played by me, who has a very disturbed husband. He's unable to find a job, and is slowly becoming impotent and suicidal. My character falls in love with Marian's husband, played by Al Morgenstern. The entire tenement and block, played by Sudie Bond and others, who were very like the witches in *Macbeth*, turn against them.

The play was funny, and it had the quality of a Greek tragedy. You knew that these two people, caught up in the poverty and desperation and loneliness of the Depression, would be condemned and destroyed by the morality of their neighbors. Their doom was inevitable, but all through the play, you hoped that they would somehow escape this fate, because of the funny and endearing quality of the lovers.

All the actors who were to be in it were accomplished professionals, most of them Method-trained, and I looked forward to another great experience like the kind I had had in *A Hatful of Rain*. When you rehearse and perform with an ensemble that has been trained by Lee Strasberg, the joy of acting is one of the greatest things in the world. You exchange thoughts and feelings without words, and the audience always hears you and understands.

We started rehearsing in May, and we were to open at the North Jersey Playhouse in Fort Lee, New Jersey, which was run by an unassuming, sweet gentleman by the name of Robert Ludlum. I had worked often in his theater, and Mr. Ludlum always kept everyone calm and collected, especially during the tryout of a new play. He lived in a modest little frame house, and he had a lovely wife and two children.

Years afterwards, when I saw all these spy and mystery best-sellers written with viciousness and intrigue and blood, I knew there must be two Robert Ludlums in the world. I mean, I was positive that my sweet stage manager and producer from Fort Lee could not possibly be this author. I saw Robert Ludlum on television recently, and he was indeed the same. Mysterious and deep runs the heart of man—perhaps because he always had to be so mild and logical with his actors and playwrights, he vented his darker side in his novels.

I began to study Frank's play. When I wasn't doing that I spent every spare moment with my daughter, who was now six, and a very grown-up and wise six. My mother, Kathy the nurse, Molly the housekeeper and my daughter all decided that I had to come home every night while I was in Fort Lee, Mineola, and Westport, as they didn't want to traipse around again after me in stock. All those places were more or less commuting distance from New York, so I readily agreed.

We began to rehearse at the Actors Studio, and Frank took us carefully through each scene. The cast became a close family. When you have a joyful theatrical experience, you become very much a real family. Marian Seldes and I became fast friends, and a couple of years later, when we were both divorced, she and her little girl moved in with me and my little girl.

Al Morgenstern was a joy to act with. He had two children, and he was a very *menschie* guy. For some reason, the responsibility of his family rested always completely on him. He was also a great driver and would drive us back and forth from our performances. He lived in the Village, and so when we came over the George Washington Bridge, he would drop me off on the Upper West Side and take the car to his home. We became fast friends, and we got to know each other's problems. He was the first person, outside of my psychiatrist, with whom I was able to discuss my strange relationship with Tony.

He often brought his little boy, who was about six, to the theater, and his boy and my little girl would draw pictures in the dressing room and watch us from the wings during the matinees, and Al's calm humor would keep the children occupied through the long performances. I used to watch Al from the wings when I wasn't in a scene with him and wonder, *why the hell, if I had to marry an actor, couldn't I pick a mature, calm, handsome man like him?* Was I so disturbed that I could only relate in negative situations? This longing for stability was wonderful for my role; I was playing a fanciful sort of flapper, and although she's in her early thirties, she still lives in her glorious high-school days of the 1920s. She will not acknowledge the deep trouble her husband, played movingly by Gerry O'Loughlin, is in.

The audiences loved the play. We did standing-room-only business everywhere we played. Sudie Bond, who was a little wispy redhead with an ugly/beautiful face, was enchanting on the stage. She never got to be in big films, but she established a company called the Paper Bag Players, a children's theater, and although Sudie died very young, her theater company lives on and is quite famous. She had one successful comedy series that I know of, and she was genuinely funny. I was so glad when she was able to make some real money at last. It was the "Flo" series, and she played Polly Holiday's mother.

Marian Seldes has had more hit shows since then than I can count, including *Deathtrap* and *Equus*, and has never missed a performance. She's on Broadway almost every single night of every season. I found out later that she is the daughter of the critic Gilbert Seldes and has a master's degree in theater. She never especially liked the movies and did not do many films. We are good friends, and now we both teach. Acting with her was a delight, and I hope I get another chance to do so.

The three weeks of playing passed very quickly, and we kept hoping against hope that we would be brought to

Broadway. But, alas, Broadway, even then, was getting financially prohibitive. If perhaps I could have gone right on with the play and opened it, then we could have moved the set from Westport and had a run off Broadway. But I had this film commitment to Columbia, and I had done the costumes, and they had cast the people I had recommended. The director had had many meetings with me on the rewrite of *Let No Man Write My Epitaph*, so I had to go to California.

I really hated to leave this play, and at the last minute we were told by Henry Weinstein that in the fall we would be doing it on Channel 13's "Play of the Week." We would then have at least a kinescope of the show. We had a sad party in Downey's, and we all kissed each other goodbye and said we would see each other in the fall to do the show on television. Meanwhile, I paid to have the set stored in Westport, in case some producer wanted to open in the fall. Someday, I have to figure out how much I've spent in storing sets of plays that I loved and hoped would not die out of town, but would be born again and have their proper life on Broadway and then in films. Maybe *A Piece of Blue Sky* didn't get done because it dealt with a very sad time in America. We were in the end of the rich fifties, going into the glorious sixties, and nobody wanted to remember the terrible thirties. The sixties turned out to be not so glorious, but we didn't know that yet.

My daughter was in a very good school, and they would no way allow me to take her out in the middle of a term. This time I had to make the trek to California all by myself. My mother, my housekeeper, my nurse, and my child would join me for the Thanksgiving and Christmas holidays.

During the next ten years, there was a sign in my hallway that my daughter had drawn which said "Welcome home, Mommy" on one side and "Goodbye, Mommy" on the other side. When she got to be an adolescent, she would put the "Goodbye, Mommy" sign facing me when I got off the elevator and the "Welcome" sign when I was leaving. It was her little way of reminding me of my absentee motherhood. I know she had my mother as a loving grandparent until she was fourteen and Kathy, her nanny, until she was nine, and Molly until she came home from college. But I still feel guilty and bemoan the fact that I did not spend more time with her when she was young.

But in the fall of '59, I wasn't aware of how much I was missing of my child's growing up. I reported to Columbia, and they told me that the film would not start until November 18, and we would be rehearsing for two weeks before that with all these gifted performers. This was unusual, and it would give me time to do some research about the drug addiction of the woman I was playing.

Tony and I now felt very strained with each other after we had had a long or for that matter even a short separation, but he seemed to be in good cheer and was talking about buying a house again. I kept stalling, not only because of the memory of the first house we'd bid on, but because I knew I was going to live in New York, and I did not want any big houses with servants and swimming pools that I would have to take care of in California. I had already seen that with the kids in California, the role model was the best surfer—in New York, where it was cold and got dark early, the role model was the kid with the highest marks. Scholarship was the highest achievement, and the one thing every kid sought. I was determined that my kid would achieve all the academic honors that I had missed. She did—at Harvard.

I didn't tell Tony this plan of mine again. He knew it. How we were going to have a marriage, with me living in New York and him living in California, we never discussed. Just about that time, our accountant notified us that we'd gotten our 1958 tax return back from the government, and attached to it was a letter from the IRS, which said, "Even for movie stars, if you're married, one partner cannot live in New York and the other one in California. You have to be domiciled in the same state." I believe they just let us submit separate and new income tax forms for 1958. I began to understand that for Tony, his idea of a perfect life was to be married, but to live as a bachelor.

The day we had to go to downtown Los Angeles and explain our different tax return to the examiner was difficult and I had a strange feeling that he was pitying us, despite all the money we were making. I guess he realized from examining our various jobs that we had hardly spent any time together since our marriage in '57.

That night we had to meet Aaron Rosenberg at Chasen's Restaurant. Aaron was Tony's producer on *Go Naked in the World,* the film that he had just completed with Gina Lollobrigida and Ernest Borgnine. He was a lovely man. He had been a famous football player and despite, or maybe because of that, he was a very good film producer. We thought he wanted to meet with us for dinner that night to offer us a film. We quickly downed two martinis each because we were edgy from the day with the tax examiner. Aaron began to explain, with great care, that MGM wanted to redo all of Gina Lollobrigida's close-ups in *Go Naked in the World* and that he needed Tony on the set to feed her the lines and cues. The problem was that she could not speak English very well then, and she seemed to be more occupied with how she looked than with her acting. Her performance, consequently, was disjointed, and they couldn't release the film for that reason. They were hoping to get her back from Italy by saying that they wanted to rephotograph her and make her look even more beautiful. Chuck Walters, wonderful at directing women, would be brought in to work with her. The way the film was, they would have to have somebody else sync her voice, which was what she was used to in Italy, but American audiences weren't accustomed to that. Tony seemed to understand everything Aaron was saying, and he agreed with it all. The film had been finished for two months, and so far, MGM had been unable to release it. Obviously they were hoping to recoup their investment in this way.

The Franciosas were invited by Columbia to attend a very fancy shindig at Romanoff's. In those days, one did not arrive at a fancy affair in blue jeans or leather. One spent the entire day getting ready to be photographed by the magazines and newspapers of the whole world.

Twentieth Century–Fox was giving the party to introduce Hollywood to Sophia Loren, and Sophia Loren to
Hollywood. This was obviously the decade of the Italian
movie starlets. In fact, when my short hairdo became
fashionable, it was referred to as the Italian cut, even
though my lovely Universal hairdresser, who was thoroughly American, created it. The press loved my hair,
but Mr. Goetz, head of Universal, said I looked like a
chrysanthemum. He liked long blonde hair. When I'd
been married to Vittorio in Italy, I had of course met all
the Italian movie stars and starlets and they'd all begun
to cut their hair short like mine and Marilyn's.

Sophia was just beginning to play big roles then, and
she had been fascinated by all my Hollywood stories. So
now I thought I should go to Romanoff's and make her
feel welcome, and she would see a familiar face. Besides,
the food was always great at Romanoff's.

My handsome flatmate, who incidentally happened to
be my husband, was quite depressed that he didn't have
another film starting immediately. But I knew there
would be a lot of beautiful women at Romanoff's, and I
was sure that would cheer him up. We sat at a big table
next to Sophia, and she was exquisite. She looked happy
and gorgeous, and she had on a stunning gown that
showed a great deal of her lovely bosom, all that the
traffic could bear, in fact. The dinner was a buffet, and
after we had had a couple of drinks, Tony said, "I will
get dinner for us, Shelley."

He picked up the napkin and playfully put it over his
arm. Once, somewhere, Tony had been a headwaiter.
Anyway, he picked up two plates and two big silver serving spoons and began to deftly serve up a little of everything that was on this huge buffet. He was dexterously
wielding his two silver spoons when Jayne Mansfield
walked up to look at the buffet, a couple of feet from him.
She too looked gorgeous, but the front of her dress was
cut lower than safety would allow, and as she leaned over
to sample some of the goodies, one of her beautiful
bosoms fell out of her décolletage. Tony looked at it,
hypnotized, and started to go for it with his two serving
spoons, with which I, terrified, was sure he intended to

put her titty back in her dress. I screamed, "Tony!" before he could accomplish this little feat. He spun and looked at me, and I signaled, "Don't you dare do that—just come back to this table!" He got quite red but came back to our table. A waiter served us our dinner.

The next day I noticed, looking through the newspaper, what was to become a famous still—Sophia Loren, who was so well endowed herself, was looking at Jayne Mansfield's bosom, as Jayne leaned over her at the table when she was introduced. When Tony saw this still, he said, "See! You shouldn't have stopped me. No one would have noticed. And Sophia would have thanked me for dishing that titty back in Jayne's dress."

In today's society, this does not sound so sensational, but these were the last days of the glitz and glory of the old glamorous, pseudoproper Hollywood. That evening at Romanoff's would come to be known as the Battle of the Bosoms. Alas, Romanoff's is gone, and Jayne is gone, but the memory of all the fun we had is still with me. Jayne and I got to know each other in New York when she was doing *Will Success Spoil Rock Hunter?* and she was just great and enormously funny in it. I never could allow myself to ask Jayne to observe at the Actors Studio, though the idea occurred to me. Marilyn was attending the Studio then and Jayne was doing a satire on Marilyn in *Will Success Spoil Rock Hunter?*

When I started the film *Let No Man Write My Epitaph*, I hadn't had much time to do the research on the physical process of drug addiction, but I hoped I could squeeze that in before we got to *that* scene. When we had done *A Hatful of Rain* my character had been the unsuspecting wife of an addict, so then the less I had known about the subject the better. Things moved too fast now, and I had one of the most embarrassing moments of my entire career during the shooting of that film. Somewhere in the middle of the film, after a long, terrible fight with my very young son, James Darren, who is beginning to suspect I'm a drug addict, I lock myself in a bathroom. I'm in serious withdrawal, and I have managed to get some heroin from my pimp, played by Ricardo Montalban. (In those days, Ricardo wasn't so choosy about doing only family-oriented films.) I pour the heroin into a spoon, put a leather belt around my arm, holding it tightly with my teeth, melt the heroin with a candle, and then take out a hypodermic syringe. This shot was being done with the camera on a huge crane, and it took several hours to light it. My acting was just great, I thought. But when I came to the part about getting the melted heroin into the syringe, I took off the top of the syringe and poured it from the spoon into the top of the tube. Philip Leacock, who had been patience itself, shouted, "CUT!"

All two hundred special-effects men and crew members and actors on the set froze, and this English, gentlemanly director got down from his perch on the huge camera crane, walked up to me, and carefully said, "Miss Method Actress, you did the research for this role about heroin addiction?"

"Of course, Mr. Leacock," I answered, having the grace to blush.

"You saw an addict fill his syringe from the spoon that way?"

I began to sense something was wrong, and then I noticed that the crew were doubled up in silent laughter around me. I looked at the heroin spoon and the syringe with some confusion. Mr. Leacock gently showed me that what I had been doing was impossible. He put the needle into the phony melted heroin and sucked up the fluid through the needle. All I could think of to say was, "Well, maybe addicts in New York do it differently."

Of course he knew I was trying to get myself out of a tight place. I had never seen anyone give himself a fix. In *Hatful* Ben Gazzara had given himself a fix but I was offstage. Nonetheless, I should have researched this role while I was in New York, and I hadn't because I'd been so busy with Corsaro's *Piece of Blue Sky*.

I continued shooting *Epitaph*, and the director got me a technical adviser who was a doctor who took care of drug addicts, and from then on, I believe my performance improved. We even went back and redid some of the earlier scenes, showing how my character had become addicted and how she deteriorated.

One morning about ten-thirty, I was rehearsing a scene with Ella Fitzgerald, who acted as beautifully as she sang. I was called to the phone. It was a frantic Aaron Rosenberg, asking me if I could possibly get Philip Leacock to shoot a scene that I wasn't in, and could I come out to MGM? They were sending a car for me.

I put Mr. Leacock on the phone, and, after listening to Mr. Rosenberg for a couple of minutes, he said yes, he could shoot a scene other than the one he had just rehearsed with Ella and me. I don't know what he explained to Ella, but as she walked me to my limousine, she said, "Shelley, there's plenty trouble in the world, and when you grow up in Harlem, even when you get out, the troubles come with you."

I remembered that Tony had grown up in East Harlem, but how would Ella know that? Of course, she had followed our tempestuous marriage on the front pages of the world's press. Ava Gardner's publicity man had made sure of that.

By the time I got to MGM, I was shaking. Chuck Walters and Aaron Rosenberg met me in front of the stage door. I knew Chuck from my musical-comedy days at MGM. He was a very beloved director to all the actors who had ever worked with him. Like George Cukor, he was famous for getting wonderful performances out of women. Chuck Walters's lip was bleeding, and his right eye was turning purple and yellow. A car from the MGM hospital arrived, and he said, "Shelley, don't be upset. I'm going to the hospital now. I'll be back on my set after lunch."

Aaron Rosenberg held my hand and explained what had happened. It seems they had done the first retake with Gina Lollobrigida, with a piece of the matching set behind her. Chuck finally got a take that he liked, and the sound man said he understood her English, and the acting was quite good. Then Chuck yelled, "It's a print!" As everyone was preparing to move to the next set of the next retake, Tony stood up and hissed, "Wait a minute! She gets a second chance to improve her work—what about me?"

Chuck looked at him in amazement. Aaron Rosenberg

was called down to the set, and he again, sotto voce, explained to Tony that they had told Gina they wanted to make her look more beautiful, and they only wanted to reshoot her close-ups. They did not have the set for the backgrounds of Tony's close-ups and, most important of all, he was very good in the picture, and they didn't need any retakes. Tony didn't seem to understand, and he was adamant about not doing the next shot unless he got a chance to improve his performance, too.

I did not know what to do. I called New York from the stage phone and spoke to Tony's psychiatrist. He told me to make sure Tony wasn't drinking, give him a Librium, and talk about something else until he was calm, and then see if he could understand what realistically was going on. The psychiatrist would call him during the lunch hour in his dressing room in the Star Building at MGM.

I walked over to Tony's *little* stage dressing room. When Tony saw me, he was hostility itself.

"You're shooting your own picture," he yelled. "Why are you here?"

"I'm off until after lunch," I lied. "I came over to have lunch with you, dear."

I think he believed me, because he took my arm, and we walked off the stage. His body was shaking and wet. He was that strange white-green color he became when he was just under hysteria. As we walked to his "star" dressing room, he told me that they were pulling a number on him again as in *The Naked Maja*. They had promised to let him do his close-ups over again. He believed they were now just protecting Gina's role and making it her picture, as they had with Ava Gardner on *Naked Maja*.

I listened, and when we got into the dressing room, he seemed to get calmer. I asked him if he would like a Librium. As he was thinking about it, I got a glass of water, and when he opened his mouth to answer me, I popped the Librium into his mouth and gave him the water, which he had to drink or choke. He began to laugh and almost choked on the water.

He said, "That's what you did to me in Italy with the sleeping pill."

"Yes, Tony," I said. "I did."

I distracted him with funny stories and ordering lunch. He still felt that Aaron Rosenberg and MGM were screwing him and redoing the film to tilt it over to Gina Lollobrigida and Ernest Borgnine. Somebody had told him, he said, that they had redone Ernest Borgnine's close-ups, too. I didn't argue with him. After we had lunch, he lay down to rest.

I held his hand and said, "You know, Tony, on a big color film like this, when they have to reshoot and get the sets out of storage, it costs about a hundred thousand dollars a day."

"So what?"

"Don't you remember when we had dinner with Aaron at Chasen's, and he explained to us that they were unable to release this film, *Go Naked in the World*, because of Gina's performance and her lack of understanding the English language? Don't you remember that dinner, Tony? Aaron has told me that your performance is wonderful, that if the picture gets good notices you'll get another nomination. They don't have to redo your close-ups, Tony."

I think he finally heard me. He put a hand over his eyes and began to cry. Then he clung to me.

"I don't know what I'm doing," he said. "I just don't know what I'm doing. I think I'd better go back to New York quick and get to my doctor again."

"All right, Tony," I said. "As soon as my film is over, we'll do that."

He still clung to me like a baby, and I realized I was weeping, too.

In a little while, his psychiatrist called, and Tony spoke quietly and coherently and told him he would be coming back to New York as soon as I was finished with *Epitaph*, and in the year to come he would do only live TV in New York and continue with his psychoanalysis.

I stayed for the next two shots, which were retakes of Gina. Tony just fed her his lines and helped her as much as he could. That morning he had put on all his makeup and the correct clothes, and now he realized how silly it was, because the camera was pointed over his shoulder and onto her. He resumed the character he played in the film.

While they were changing the lights, Gina came over to me and said hello. Thank goodness she still did not understand English too well. She thought that the whole morning had been the result of a fight Tony and I had been having. She whispered in my ear:

"Why do you keep marrying Italian actors? Italian-American or Italian-Italian? Why don't you marry a nice Yugoslav businessman, like I did? They take care of you!"

Tony was trying to treat the whole morning as a joke, but when he took a good look at Chuck Walters's face in the light, he walked away from the set for a moment.

"Tony," I whispered. "Next time you feel like punching out a director, could you make it Otto Preminger? He's a great director but a real bastard. I saw him almost destroy Marilyn on *River of No Return*."

Tony went over to Chuck Walters and, in tears, apologized profusely. I left and I knew that the rest of the day would be okay.

Aaron took me to the car and said, "Thanks, Shelley. Columbia has only phoned a dozen times."

I instructed the limousine driver to speed back to Columbia in Hollywood as fast as he could. I finished the scene with Ella Fitzgerald by nightfall. While Ella and I were waiting for them to change the lights for our close-ups, I told Ella something of what had happened that morning. She took my hand and sang a little song for me while we were preparing for the next scene. It was the spiritual "Nobody Knows the Trouble I've Seen." That scene was so haunting and good that Philip Leacock asked her to sing all through the rest of the picture, even while we were waiting for the crew to change the lights. She did, and sometimes they left her voice on the sound track. It improved everybody's performance, and it certainly helped the audiences' understanding of this ghetto film. To this day, when I teach young actors, I make them play music that is meaningful to them as preparation for a scene.

I'm very proud of that film, although I only see it late

at night on television. It was one of the first films to cast black actors as just human beings who happened to be black. The parts they played did not necessarily have to be black people, but when I had discussed the casting with Philip Leacock, he had eagerly accepted my suggestion about Ella Fitzgerald and Bernie Hamilton. In the earlier Willard Motley film, *Knock on Any Door,* although it had been set in a ghetto, it had not had any black actors in major roles. I am not quite sure how Philip Leacock got this casting decision past the Columbia brass. As I drove home that night and thought of Ella Fitzgerald singing that song, I drove very carefully and prayed, "God, please let me get out of this marriage before something terrible happens." I'm not sure God was listening to me. I guess it was something I had to do myself—find my own strengths to do it.

I thought I had handled the episode at MGM very well, but the next day I had a dreadful reaction. I had an outdoor scene with Burl Ives, out on the Columbia back lot. I'm sitting in an old-fashioned two-door coupe, about to get out of it. Burl approaches me to reprimand me for the neglect of my child, my son. I close the car door, and have a three-page scene with Burl through the window of the car. We rehearsed this scene for an hour, and it was rather an emotional one, then we finally began to film it. The director said, "Action!" And we began to play the scene.

When I shut the car door, I realized my hand hurt, but I continued doing the scene until I had come to the end, and the director said, "Cut!" I had slammed the car door on my hand and hadn't even realized it. I just said, "Burl, please open the door."

When they took me to a hospital and X-rayed my hand, we found that I had no broken bones, but the ligaments and cartilage were crushed, and I had to finish the film with my left hand hidden in some way, usually in my pocket. I had not felt the car door slam on my hand. I must have been in a rather comatose condition during the shooting of the end of *Epitaph*.

That Christmas and New Year's were spent in California. My little family joined us in Beverly Hills. Hollywood was still glamorous and we went to lots of parties and premieres and nightclubs. Even then, I never especially felt as if I was part of the "in" crowd. I had a lot of noncelebrity friends. They were directors, assistant directors, and production managers and writers, and they had been my friends in New York and then in Hollywood.

But Tony had made lots of celebrity friends, and suddenly I found Judy Balaban Kanter calling me for parties. She was married to Jay Kanter, who was a big agent at MCA now. He was Marlon's agent in Hollywood.

I had known Jay when he had been Marlon Brando's gofer in about 1950. In fact, once in 1949 or 1950 Marlon had taken me to a big party at Norman Mailer's house. Marlon did not have a suit and I insisted that he wear one to the party, so he borrowed Jay Kanter's suit. And since Jay was rather diminutive, and Marlon was rather muscular, he looked pretty strange.

I had not seen Jay Kanter for quite a while and was surprised and happy that we were rekindling our old friendship. His wife, Judy, was the daughter of Barney Balaban, president of Paramount, and Judy and Jay had two lovely little girls. Judy was not really a pretty girl, but she had beautiful red hair and a gorgeous body, and she was very chic and vivacious.

The Kanters had a beautiful house on Rodeo Drive, on the right side of the Beverly Hills trolley tracks. One day, Judy insisted on showing me a spectacular house that was priced way under the market value and right across the street from her house.

"Tony has already seen this house," she said, "and loves it. It's only seventy thousand dollars for this huge Beverly Hills mansion with tennis court and swimming pool."

I wondered if Judy was taking up real estate on the side. Since her children were in private schools there I could not very well explain to her that I didn't want my daughter raised in Beverly Hills. I just tried to discourage Judy's house-hunting for Tony and me. Tony was rather annoyed that I did not want to buy this mansion, but before it could develop into a *cause célèbre*, I made reservations for all of them to get back to New York and relative safety.

I believe that New Year's Eve we went to one of Sam Spiegel's famous New Year's Eve parties. I rather wandered off by myself that night, at the beginning of the new decade, and sat in a cabana across the pool, and at midnight I watched all the people in the living room and on the terrace kissing. I think I was saying an absolute goodbye to Hollywood. I knew that from then on, whenever I would make films, I would try to make them in New York, Europe, or England, or anywhere in the U.S. except Hollywood. It wasn't Hollywood's fault; it was mine.

Epitaph still had a couple of weeks of shooting, but since my daughter had to be back at school right after New Year's, my Mom, my nurse, and my little girl, with Tony in charge of the safari, returned to New York. I wandered around my California apartment and had a terrible case of the postholiday blues. I knew Tony and I were married in name only now but he still seemed unwilling to discuss a permanent separation. In truth we were both afraid to discuss it. At that point, I don't think Tony was crazy about being married to me—he just didn't want to be divorced. It was true of me, too, I guess.

Tony's family life had been so fragmented while he was growing up that he seemed to be clinging to this substitute family he had with me.

In New York Molly was cooking wonderful meals for him, and my mother and Kathy the nurse took very good care of all his needs. I began to realize from our long-distance calls that when I wasn't there, they all got along just great together. But perhaps that was just my blues.

I was working every other day, as they were doing scenes with James Darren and Jean Seberg. She played the educated, beautiful girl who was offering my son a better life out of the slums. *Epitaph,* as I write about it, seemed to have the same plot as *A Place in the Sun,* except now I was sort of playing Anne Revere's part.

In the midst of all these woeful thoughts, my phone

rang. It was cocktail time, and I had no cocktail party to go to or anybody to have cocktails with. Twilight has always been a sad and lovely time for me, especially at the beach, but in Beverly Hills, even before the smog, it made me feel sad. I had to answer the phone, as I was the only one living in my apartment at that point. I said hello, and a husky voice, with a Scottish accent, said, "Hello, Shelley. Guess what? I have finally made it to Los Angeles." It was my Scottish chum, Sean Connery. He explained to me he was doing a film at Disney Studios called *Darby O'Gill and the Little People*. I think Peter and Mary Noble had told him about my rocky marriage. So to cheer me up, Sean immediately started to tell me all the London gossip and news. His manner was so lovely and funny that he got me out of my doldrums. After he made me laugh for ten minutes, I finally asked him where he was. He was in some strange motel in Burbank, near the Disney Studios. They had taken him there straight from the airport, and he had been working on his film nonstop for over a week. I informed him that he wasn't in L.A. yet—he was in Burbank.

"I was beginning to suspect that," he said. "This city is so huge, it confuses me and the steering wheel on the car they rented me is way over on the left, which as far as I'm concerned is the wrong side. Could you possibly come out and pick me up? I'll buy you drinks and dinner."

Long pause.

"Is your husband working? Perhaps we could meet him somewhere after his filming."

I informed Sean that my husband was back in New York. He sounded relieved, probably having read of Tony Franciosa's various bouts around the globe. "Well, you can at least pick me up and we'll go someplace elegant for dinner."

I told him I would, and proceeded to put on my sexiest outfit and longest eyelashes. I hadn't seen Sean for a number of years, but he had done some films in England and some important TV work, and he was getting quite well known in Europe.

I got into my white convertible Cadillac, the third one

I'd had since *A Place in the Sun,* and drove out to the desolate Walt Disney Studios, then in the middle of nowhere. Sean was waiting in front of his lonely motel, and when he got in my car, I again realized how manly, mature, and magnificent he was. Now all his muscles were suntanned. His self-deprecating humor and whimsy made me eager to show him Hollywood, Beverly Hills, and Los Angeles, the way he had shown London to me.

During the next couple of weeks, any day we both weren't filming, I took him to the Farmers' Market, Grauman's Chinese Theatre, the Hollywood sign, and Schwab's. I even managed to teach him how to drive on the right side of the road with a left-side steering wheel. Even before he got a Los Angeles license he was a better driver than I, but I still insist I'm a wonderful driver *when I concentrate.*

Some decades later, when I was doing *Poseidon Adventure,* a policeman trailed me as I was rushing to get to the Johnny Carson show, also in Burbank. I had a black wet suit on and flippers, having just come from my underwater swimming lessons. The motorcycle pulled me over at the intersection of Hollywood and Highland. The policeman made me get out of the car, and he just stared at me in my outfit. I got my registration paper and license out of my purse and said, "Okay, officer, just give me my ticket. NBC will pay it. I have to get to the Johnny Carson show right away."

He looked with amazement at my license and said, "My God, they really gave you a license!" And then he gave me a lecture, which was mainly about how he had enjoyed my work for the last couple of decades, and he didn't want to have to scrape me off the highway. I should understand that I somehow did not have the proper reflexes for driving an automobile. He had been following me down Sunset since Laurel Canyon, and I had been changing lanes every block.

"Would you promise me to try not to drive unless it is an emergency?" he asked.

I promised.

Then he escorted me all the way to NBC and did not

give me a ticket. A decade later, the same policeman stopped me, but, thank God, my secretary was driving.

But back in the decade, on that Friday night, when I picked up Sean, he got in the driver's seat and said, "I'm not sure yet whether I can drive on the right side of the road, but I'm going to drive anyway, since we're going all the way out to the beach on Sunset."

He drove with his best authoritative James Bond manner, although he wasn't to play that role for quite a while. . . . But he was already practicing it on me. I sat quietly as we drove along the most exciting and beautiful winding stretch of road on earth, Sunset Boulevard. Sean told me we were first going to a barbecue at Ella Logan's house. I don't quite remember why he knew Ella Logan. Maybe she was singing the songs for *Darby O'Gill* since she had been so fabulous in *Finian's Rainbow*. I knew her from the Hotel St. Moritz. I had had an apartment there when I'd done *Oklahoma!* on Broadway in '48 and she'd done *Finian's Rainbow*. I had gotten trapped in the elevator with John Gielgud and their little dogs and Dorothy Parker.

I was a little nervous about going to a Hollywood barbecue with this handsome young actor, because I didn't want any more publicity. But since Tony was probably going out with Lauren Bacall in New York at that moment, I said to myself, "The hell with it."

We arrived at Ella Logan's house, which was off a huge circle in the middle of Sunset Boulevard, just past Brentwood. The circle and Ella Logan's house are no longer there, but that was one of the happiest nights I had ever spent in Hollywood. Dorothy Parker and many of the other wits of the Algonquin Roundtable were there. I remembered that there were many fine writers, musicians and cameramen who managed to live in Hollywood not on the front pages.

Of course, I remember the menu too. It was the first time I'd ever had barbecued chicken that had been marinated in honey and soybean sauce, with little crusts of garlic. There was some kind of exotic Spanish rice, arugula salad, and champagne with fresh peaches floating in it for dessert.

I realize that most people remember events and then the food they had. I remember the food and then the event. I guess taste is a sense that also comes under the heading of sense memory. A very strong one for Shelley.

It was a witty and delicious evening and Sean, who usually drank beer, only drank wine. He told us amusing stories about his adventures in Disney's world. He said that there were large areas of the studio which seemed to be fenced off—he thought maybe for secret U.S. government work. We all said "Nonsense" but two decades later, when I did a film at Disney's studio, *Pete's Dragon*, I found out that Sean's stories were absolutely true.

It seems that Disney had developed scuba diving for the U.S. government during the Second World War. He had developed a technique so that a stuntman could breathe through an oxygen tank strapped to his back for some film stunt while swimming in deep water during a special effect in a film. Although Disney was doing only family-oriented, animated films in '60, he was still developing war techniques for the government, right in the middle of Hollywood. I've often wondered if Sean went back to England and reported to the British government whatever he saw at the Disney Studios. Well, they're still our allies, I think.

We had a wonderful time at that party. I had forgotten all the highly intelligent artists who worked in Hollywood. I had forgotten how much they liked me and how much I liked them. I had been too immersed in my career and neurotic marriage. We ate and drank, danced the tango and rhumba, played funny games, and somewhere around 2:00 A.M., Sean got me back into my white Cadillac.

Soon I noticed we were still going toward the ocean on Sunset. Why weren't we heading back to Burbank? After a short struggle with my still-married conscience, I didn't ask Sean where he was going. He parked on a cliff overlooking the turbulent Pacific, and I began to tell him about the nonsensical relationship I was involved in. Sean said something very wise to me at the end of my tangled story:

"Shelley, you're a very strong woman. And although Tony obviously seems to be attracted to strong women, perhaps he secretly is longing for a quiet, meek young girl who isn't an actress and treats him like he was God. Most actors eventually want that. You helped him become a better actor, but you constantly challenged his ideas and values. You insist that he think like you do, be politically progressive like you are, be a movie star like you are, and if he is constantly comparing himself to you and your accomplishments, he has to be unhappy with you."

Perhaps these were not Sean's exact words, but that was the subtext of what he said to me. This was the first time I really faced my responsibility for the dilemma that Tony and I now found ourselves in. I didn't know whether to thank Sean or punch him so I decided to kiss him, which seemed to be the easiest thing to do. We did not come back to Hollywood till Monday morning, to our respective films, and I can't remember exactly where we stayed in Malibu, but the food was great, as was everything else.

I finished *Let No Man Write My Epitaph* and started packing to get back to New York. I don't know why I can't leave clothes in both New York and Beverly Hills. Perhaps it's some weird fetish—I like to drag ten suitcases back and forth across the country, as a matter of fact, all over the world. Oh well, Elizabeth Taylor drags thirty. Maybe it's because no place really feels like home. So we take everything with us, just in case.

The evening news came on as I was packing and they were announcing the Academy Award nominations. I was nominated for Best Supporting Actress for *Anne Frank*, just as Otto Frank had told me I would be. Sean arrived a little while later, carrying a bottle of champagne and flowers. When he opened the door, I was sitting in the middle of the floor, crying.

"What are you crying about, for God's sakes?" he asked. "You're in a magnificent film, and you're probably going to win the highest award any actor can receive."

"Sean, I cannot possibly take Tony to the awards. If I was sure I *wasn't* going to win, I could have him come back and attend the awards with me, but suppose I win? He'll be happy for me, but, for some reason, I think he will be hurt and resentful, because he didn't win for *A Hatful of Rain*. I attended the awards with him that year, and he took it very badly. He just went out to the airport and got on a plane."

"Never mind," Sean said. "That was quite a while ago. He's done a lot of films since then, and why don't you cross that bridge when you come to it? Perhaps you'll be divorced by the time the Oscar-cast rolls around."

I had no answer. Sean took my many suitcases out to the car, and I was thankful he had once been a lorry driver. He still had the muscles to swing all those big heavy suitcases into the back of the car. We drove out to the airport, and Sean managed to drive with one hand and hold my left hand with the other. What a weird predicament. When I should have been overjoyed that I had been nominated for the second time for an Oscar and had a good chance of winning, I was sad and frightened.

When I got to the airport, I asked Sean if he wouldn't want to stay at my house in Beverly Hills, since Disney had put him in that lonely motel.

"That would make a great story for Louella Parsons," he answered, smiling. "She'll say you have given up Italian actors, and now you've switched to young Scots teamsters."

"You're not so young, Sean. I know that you know that we're exactly the same age."

I got on the plane, and I knew Sean would put my car back in my garage and probably walk back to Burbank. After all, it was only ten miles, and I knew he wouldn't spend the money on a cab and he didn't know the proper buses at night. Oh well, the best way to learn a city is to walk through it. I believe Sean was a jogger long before it became fashionable. Anyway, he was a great athlete.

I sat up on the red-eye all night, rather sleepless. I believe they still had berths on the planes in those days, but they cost $100. Even though I was making a lot of money, $100 then was like $400 now, and I could not see my way clear to spending that much money for one night's sleep (Sean's influence, no doubt). Later in life, there were some nights when I'd gladly have spent $1,000 for a good night's sleep.

When I got to my apartment in New York, no one, *but no one,* mentioned that I had been nominated. I was in the kitchen with my daughter, my mother, Molly, Kathy, my temperamental blond cocker spaniel and Tony, having an early breakfast. I wanted to see my kid off to school before I went to sleep. I began to think perhaps they had not watched TV or seen a newspaper yet. Or maybe I had imagined my nomination—and Sean's flowers and champagne.

When Tony took my daughter down to the school bus, Molly, Mom, Kathy, and the dog all kissed and congratulated me.

"Mom," I said, "doesn't Tony know I've been nominated?"

"He came in very late last night," Mom said, "and perhaps he doesn't know yet."

It made me sad to realize that everyone in the house, including my child and the dog, understood Tony's competitiveness, perhaps better than I did. I went into the bedroom, took a shower and my sleeping pill, and finally fell asleep.

The next day, everything was as usual. But Tony and I went to the Actors Studio and then everyone started congratulating me; finally he did too. Perhaps he had just found out about it that cold February morning.

I saw some of my fellow actors from *A Piece of Blue Sky,* and Gerry O'Loughlin told me that we were about to kinescope or film the play. Henry Weinstein had told him we would rehearse a week on the set at the Astoria Studios and perhaps film or tape it with three cameras, the way Lucille Ball had just begun to do in "I Love Lucy." I didn't understand exactly what Gerry was talking about, but I thought it was a great idea.

When I got home that afternoon, my agent called to congratulate me, and he thought I ought to come back to

L.A. immediately and do interviews in newspapers and on TV about *Anne Frank*—in other words, electioneer for the Oscar. I told him that I was only campaigning for Adlai Stevenson that winter and I was filming *A Piece of Blue Sky* with three cameras for Channel 13.

"What are they *paying* you for that?" my agent asked.

"I believe everyone's getting the same—a thousand dollars, for a week of rehearsal and shooting."

His shriek almost came through the telephone. "Shelley!" he yelled. "Stop being a dunce! You've just been nominated for an Oscar and will probably win. It's an important and prestigious picture. For God's sakes, stop doing *crap!*"

I got very angry, and said, "Herb, those B pictures Universal puts me in are *crap*. This is a wonderful play by my lovely director friend Frank Corsaro that I performed in all summer. For God's sakes, why didn't you come East and see me in it? Perhaps you could have sold it for a movie. It's one of the best parts I've ever done, and I'm going to do it with my friends."

Herb said, "I give up," and hung up.

We immediately began to rehearse the play again at the Actors Studio. Henry Weinstein, who had produced the summer-stock production, was still trying to raise the money to do this play on Broadway. But no one in the late fifties was interested in investing money in a play set in the Great Depression. Everyone was making a lot of money, and the whole world loved the U.S.A., or so we thought. So Henry was unable to finance it.

In a week or so, we started to rehearse on the set in Astoria. We shot the play in three days—an act a day, and it was a great experience. I have always regretted that this play did not get born on Broadway and then made into a film. In *A Piece of Blue Sky*, you see what happened to the Depression babies, and you understand why the next generation had to have more things and more money and more security. The young people of the fifties produced the affluent dropout frustrated society of the sixties, which in turn produced the yuppy callous kids of the seventies and eighties. I think every generation has to examine its immediate economic history to understand what is happening to it. I believe that is one of the true functions of the theater.

I was spending every moment I could away from shooting to be with my kid. Her birthday was in February, and she informed me that she wanted ballet lessons for her seventh birthday. Silly me, without asking her doctor, called Julie Belafonte, and she told me the name of a teacher who had a class of little girls. I began to take her to lessons three times a week. If anyone reading this book has a child or grandchild who's under eight, don't let her take ballet lessons. Till a child is eight, her bones can't take the stress.

When Oscar time rolled around, which I believe that year was the first Monday in April, I took myself out to California, and since I wasn't at my slimmest, I had a lovely black off-the-shoulder dress made, with a small waist, under which I wore a waist cincher, and a full skirt with a petticoat. It had a lovely white collar all around the shoulders, and I thought I looked simple and elegant, as befitted a serious actress of films and stage.

I found out Twentieth Century–Fox had made me a glamorous white satin evening gown too. They had made it on a canvas figure exactly my body when I was a size 10. When I went to the studio to try it on, I was sure my friend Marilyn had designed it. It had a halter neck and was backless, cut on the bias, and slit to the thigh. I got into a very tight girdle and I squeezed into the dress. I thought it looked sensational. I thanked the very famous designer at Twentieth and took it home. That night, when Herb Brenner, my agent, came to get me to take me to the Oscars (going with your agent to the Oscars is like advertising you're alone and have no man in your life), I made Herb photograph me with the very new Polaroid camera. We shot me in both evening gowns, and we almost missed the Oscars while I studied the photos to see which one I looked thinner in. The black off-the-shoulder won. The other was more glamorous, but I looked like a bad imitation of Marilyn in it.

Herb and I got in the car, and my fur stole got caught in the door. When we got to the Pantages, I could not get out of the car. I had been a presenter two or three times at the Oscars, but the last time I had been nominated was in 1951, when I had been nominated Best Actress for *A Place in the Sun*. I had gone with Vittorio and my parents. I was positive that I was going to win, because Ronald Colman, the previous year's winner for *A Double Life*, came out to present Best Actress. I was sure when he opened the envelope that he said Shelley Winters. He said Vivien Leigh, but I heard Shelley Winters. Vittorio had had to tackle me in the aisle as I prepared to walk up to the stage.

Thank God there had been no TV cameras present in 1951, but now there were TV cameras all over the place. I think I was comatose, but I remember Army Archerd interviewing me in the lobby and telling me that the Las Vegas odds were in my favor and he was sure that I was going to win. But at that point my ears weren't open.

We got into our seats, and I noticed that the scaffolding for the TV cameras was all on the left side of the theater. Our seats were on the right side, about the third row. That year, *Ben-Hur* won almost everything, and all the people from *Ben-Hur* were sitting on the left side of the auditorium. The show opened with the award for Best Supporting Actor, which meant that the award for Best Supporting Actress would come way down at the end of the evening.

Nothing is as captive as the audience at the Oscar presentations since the advent of TV. You must be in your seat by five-thirty, and the show often goes on till eleven-thirty. If you want to get up and go to the bathroom and the camera catches you, you will ruin the whole show. Somewhere toward the end of the show, after having watched numerous people on the left side of the auditorium get up and accept their awards, I said furiously to Herb, "I cannot stand this agony anymore. I obviously am not in a seat that a winner would be sitting in. The TV cameras couldn't possibly get to us. Let's go."

With that, I put on my stole and started to trudge up the aisle. Louella Parsons was sitting on the aisle, two rows in back of me.

"Go sit down," she hissed, grabbing my stole. "This is *disgraceful!*"

I pulled my stole away and kept walking up the aisle. Just about then, Peter Ustinov came out, and, as I got to the back of the orchestra, he announced the winner of the Best Supporting Actress Oscar. I didn't hear him. I just kept walking. Somebody grabbed my arms, turned me around, and said, "It's you, foolish! You've *won* for *The Diary of Anne Frank!*"

Herb had been running up the aisle trying to catch me, and he said, "Shelley! You *won!* You *won!*"

I stood frozen. I whispered, "Are you sure?"

"Yes," he said. "Go! *Go!*"

I don't remember walking down the aisle or going up the steps. I think I flew to the stage. Standing in front of the mike, I began sobbing. I guess I thanked Mr. Stevens, the Hacketts, the studio, God, and Otto Frank. It's all still a daze. Since that show was live TV and there was no kinescope, I'll never know exactly what I said.

Suddenly I was standing backstage beside Simone Signoret, who had just won Best Actress for *Room at the Top*. Oh God, we both had exactly the same dress on—black jersey, off the shoulder, cinched in at the waist, with a full skirt. We both realized simultaneously that we had picked the most flattering gown for the "fuller figure."

"Shelley," she said, laughing. "I think you and I make size ten go out of fashion tonight."

While we were taking pictures backstage for the world press, Yves Montand came up to her. She looked in his eyes and said in French something which I understood because I knew a little Italian, "*Chéri,* you will win next year."

I just stood and looked at her. She squeezed my hand, and I knew I had done right to leave Tony back in New York. She had been married to Yves Montand for many years, and although she was something of a feminist, even back then she still felt the need to reassure him.

I was so obviously alone. She whispered in my ear, "Where is Mr. Franciosa?"

"In New York," I answered.

She smiled and said, "Wise, wise." The photographers

pushed Yves Montand out of the shot. They just wanted Simone and myself in the shot with our Oscars.

I didn't go to the Governors' Ball that night, though I should have. I went home and my mother, daughter, and Tony all called me to congratulate me. I promised I would bring my little gold statue home the next day. The academy could engrave it later. After I hung up, I wondered why I hadn't gone to the party with Herb. I felt a bit like an artistic Cinderella. Perhaps I was oversensitive, but I felt that I didn't want hundreds of reporters asking me where my handsome actor-husband was, and why he hadn't been with me when I'd won my Oscar. I could say he was sick, but I couldn't very well say he was working, because the news services could check that one out.

I took the plane home to New York the next morning. When I got off at Idlewild, there was Tony, waiting to greet me at the foot of the stairs. I took the Oscar out of my makeup kit, came down the stairs, and kissed Tony so that the photographers could get a lot of pictures of the happy couple greeting each other in New York as the wife brings home her Oscar.

When I got home, I found that Tony had bought me an entire barful of Tiffany glasses—very heavy, huge water glasses, old-fashioned glasses, and wine glasses, and heavy glass ashtrays and an ice bucket. They were all crystal and handcrafted by Tiffany. His present confused and dismayed me. Although I thanked him profusely and I knew he loved to go shopping at Tiffany's—why was he furnishing our apartment further, if we were both unconsciously, or consciously, thinking about separating and eventually divorcing? I didn't pursue it.

As I write this now, I have just accidentally broken the last old-fashioned glass from that set. The heavy ashtrays have survived, as no one is allowed to smoke in my house.

We all looked at the Oscar, and my kid teased me with, "Mommy, I don't think he will fit into my doll's baby carriage." Tony had given her a $500 reproduction of the big English baby carriage which Universal had had imported from England for her. I suddenly took a good look at my child. She was pushing her expensive doll carriage around the room and she was LIMPING. I carefully inquired why. I found out that she had hurt herself in her ballet class—rather seriously. I was ready to knock everybody's heads together. Just because I had flown to California for a couple of days to get an Oscar, couldn't they all keep their eyes on my child? I picked up my daughter and went into my bedroom and wept. She comforted me.

"Mommy, it's nobody's fault," she said. "The doctor said I wasn't to have ballet lessons until I'm eight years old. My bones are too soft. Okay? It doesn't hurt much. I just cannot run around for eight weeks."

I asked Kathy if what she'd said was true.

"Yes," Kathy confirmed. "We have to keep her as quiet as possible for a month. She mustn't go back to school until after Easter."

I knew my bright child was loving school, and now I had to keep her out of school for three weeks.

Easter was approaching, and although I had just come back from Hollywood, Tony had organized a trip to California for his mother. Since I liked her so much, and felt I could show her around Hollywood properly, I agreed to go along. I guess I felt it would be better for my kid, since she could not go to school, to come to California and sit in our garden, and I could drive her around in the convertible Cadillac, and she wouldn't be so bored.

In a few days, a huge limousine picked us all up, with my two months' worth of luggage, and then we picked up Tony's mother in Spanish Harlem. She was so happy and excited that it lifted all our spirits, and Tony and I began to be very nice to each other. We were almost like a family again.

When we got to the airport, Tony very efficiently picked up our tickets and checked our luggage, and I wandered over to the newsstand to get magazines for all of us. I bought the usual *Time, Life, Newsweek*, and *Cosmopolitan*, and then I did one of the stupidest things I've ever done in my life. I bought *Confidential*. I wish I hadn't.

18

On the way out to California, sometime after lunch, while everyone was napping, I opened the *Confidential* and started to read that scurrilous magazine. There in black and white—and, possibly, red—was the following:

"Tony Franciosa and Judy Balaban are quite an item. Judy, who is helping Shelley look for a house, does not remember what happened the last time the Franciosas looked for a house. Tony slugged a photographer and eventually went to jail. We wonder if Jay Kanter and Shelley Winters are going to move into this new house with all their children."

It went something like that. I took the magazine to the rest room, tore it into small pieces, and flushed it down the john. It didn't matter. It was engraved in blood on my soul. Sometime during the trip, I managed to sit down next to Tony. I had been pacing the aisles. Suddenly I wasn't mad anymore. All I felt was relief. I quietly told Tony about the item, and, since we were on a plane, nobody could yell. At first he did exactly what men usually do: denied everything. I waited until the denials petered out and then I calmly answered that I hoped he was serious about sexy Judy.

"Tony, she has two small children, and since we're going to eventually get a legal separation and then a divorce, let's try to plan it and do it quietly with as much dignity as possible.''

Tony just stared at me for a long time. Finally I spoke: "Do you love her, Tony? She's a young girl. She's not an actress. Perhaps you won't feel competitive with her, and maybe you can make a better life with her?"

After a long time, he answered me with another question: "Shelley, how much money do you think her father has?" Perhaps he was kidding, and trying to make a joke about the whole *Confidential* thing. But I was stunned. Tony was making a great deal of money and didn't need any of Barney Balaban's money. Was he so insecure that he felt all of his money and fame and acting talent would disappear, or was this just one of those stupid things you say out of confusion? But suddenly I realized *it was no longer any of my business*.

"We'll discuss this after your mother leaves," I said quietly. "Let's try to give her a good time, since this is her first visit to California."

As soon as we got to Beverly Hills, I started organizing and packing overnight cases for the trip to Palm Springs. I informed the household that, rather than have the kid get exhausted on a long sight-seeing trip to Palm Springs, it would be better if she stayed in Beverly Hills. There is a large swimming pool at the Racquet Club in Palm Springs, and it would be very frustrating for her if I didn't allow her to go in it.

My mother decided to pass on the trip, too. She wanted to get her apartment upstairs in order. During the winter, she had hardly ever been in it; she had been trailing around with me and my child.

As I was getting our swim and tennis things together, the phone rang. It was Judy Balaban Kanter. She ostensibly wanted to discuss the house that was still for sale across from hers on Rodeo Drive. In retrospect, I wish I had bought the damn thing. It was $70,000 then and is probably worth $3 million now. But at that point I wasn't capable of thinking about investments. I took a breath and said quietly, "Judy, if you ever call here again, I'm going to do something truly terrible to you. I'm going to give you Tony."

Long pause. I guess she realized I had seen the item in *Confidential*, but the gutsy redhead answered, "Never mind, Shelley. I've already got him."

I giggled hysterically as I got in the Cadillac. Tony asked me what I was laughing at. I couldn't explain. I just kept laughing. Perhaps I was laughing to keep from crying. Tony, his mother, and I drove to Palm Springs the Friday before Easter Sunday and we registered at the Racquet Club. We had a lovely dinner that evening. Saturday dawned hot and dry in the desert. There was some kind of important tennis tournament that we began to watch even before breakfast. It was about 10:00 A.M. Many Pimm's Cups began to circulate around the tennis courts. They contain gin, ginger, ice, and a stick of cucumber and are served in a large metal mug. I didn't have any, nor did Tony's mother. I just ate the cucumbers in Tony's drinks. We watched through breakfast and lunch.

After Tony had had about six Pimm's Cups, I took his mother away from the endless tennis and showed her some of the tourist sights around Palm Springs—the Indian reservation, the tramway up the mountain—and I pointed out all the houses of the movie stars. Her trip was complete because when we went to the Palm Springs drugstore, she saw Frank Sinatra and Liberace in the flesh. And then I introduced her to Annette Funicello. By the time we finished our tourism, Tony's mother was convinced that the movie colony was composed only of Italian movie stars.

When we got back to the Racquet Club, Tony was quite drunk, but I managed to get some coffee into him, and we all went to dinner. During dinner, I became aware that Tony was very angry at his mother, and she was angry with him. Perhaps they were speaking Neapolitan, but I couldn't quite follow the argument. It had something to do with why Tony's father had left his mother when he'd been an infant.

I managed to get Tony into his twin bed before they came to blows. Sometime later that night, I awakened and he was weeping in his sleep. I got out of bed and sat in a chair, looked at the desert moon, and I watched Tony's face until 4:00 A.M.

When we awakened rather late Easter morning, he had blacked out anything about the night before. I didn't pursue it. I called his mother to ask her to join us for breakfast. The operator gave me the room clerk who informed me that Mrs. Franciosa had ordered a limousine, in the middle of the night, and it had taken her to the Los Angeles airport. I guess she didn't know there was an airport in Palm Springs.

I was stunned, and all I could think was, "I wish I was that Mrs. Franciosa instead of the Mrs. Franciosa I am." Then I realized she was Mrs. Papaleo or whatever. Only then did I realize that she had taken back her maiden name. Her married name was Mrs. Papaleo, as was mine. Anyway, that was what had been on my marriage license, which now I was going to tear up.

When Tony found out that his mother had flown back to New York, he became wooden. He wanted to drive back to L.A. immediately. While I was packing our things, I asked him if perhaps he didn't want to stop at the beautiful Palm Springs Catholic church for the Easter service. Perhaps it would make him feel better, and he could call his mother when we got back to Beverly Hills and make it up to her.

He looked at me strangely, and I realized he was still angry. I decided I'd better shut up or he would substitute me for his mother. I didn't say a word the rest of the trip, but, as we approached L.A., I remembered that I had forgotten to buy my daughter an Easter basket.

I asked Tony to stop at a candy shop or drugstore so we could buy my kid a chocolate bunny or an Easter basket. He did not answer me; he just kept driving fast. I asked him twice. He just went faster. Remembering the drive from Naples, I shut up.

How ambivalent Tony was about my daughter became very clear to me many years later, right after my mother died. We had her safe-deposit box opened. I discovered a letter in it from Tony to me. I can't remember which coast it was sent from, but obviously one of us was in New York and the other in Hollywood. My mother not only opened my mail, but if she didn't like what was in it, she would answer it. My lovely mother believed that the less you knew about unpleasant things, the better, and if something was worrisome, it was better to ignore it. So she saw to it that I worried as little as possible. In this letter, Tony said I was doing something criminal—his word, *criminal*—by telling my daughter that Vittorio Gassman was her father; I should tell her that he, Tony, was her father, and when she was eighteen tell her the truth, and let her choose. That letter is now in *my* safe-deposit box.

That Easter Sunday, we arrived home without the Easter basket. When we walked into the living room, my daughter was sitting on her nurse's lap and watching Ed Sullivan. Tony walked over to the television set and changed it to Steve Allen. He then walked into our bedroom. I saw my kid get off her nurse's lap and limp to the television set and change it back to Ed Sullivan. I smiled about this and went into the bathroom.

When I turned around I saw Tony take my child from her nurse's lap, carry her into her bedroom, and *toss* her onto the nurse's bed. Perhaps it was only two or three feet, but the next thing I remember is Tony standing in our bedroom, with blood pouring down his face and shoulder, whispering, "You killed me! My God, you've killed me!"

With that, I picked up the phone, dialed the Beverly Hills police, and announced, "This is Shelley Winters. I've just killed my husband," and hung up.

I was informed later that I had thrown a heavy perfume bottle at Tony's head, and it had connected. I have no memory of it. The nurse had closed my daughter's bedroom door, and she hadn't seen any of this. As we heard the sirens approaching the house, Tony picked up a towel to stanch the blood and pointed to some wooden shelves that were in the hallway, facing the door.

"We'll tell them that I hit my head on the shelf," he said. "They still have the death penalty in California."

With that, he smeared some blood on the shelf. He had plenty of blood to smear, as head wounds bleed profusely. I guess he was taken in an ambulance, and I was taken in a police car to the emergency room, I believe, of the Beverly Hills police station.

The police questioned me somewhere, but I could say nothing. I honestly remembered nothing. What I do remember is the policeman taking me into some sort of doctor's office. The doctor was sewing up Tony's head so I attacked the doctor and two policemen had to tear me away from him.

The next thing I remember is the police car taking me home, and I guess Kathy and my child were upstairs with my mother. The house was empty. I spent the next hour throwing all of Tony's things into the front garden—all thirty-two of his suits, all of his shoes, all of his sports equipment, and, especially, the Kahlua with which he had been mixing Black Russians morning, evening, and night.

When everything was in the street and garden, I called Stan Kamen and told him to come and get the stuff. I then took two sleeping pills and went to sleep, feeling that I might as well get some rest before the cops came to throw me in jail.

When I block, I *block*. Maybe I caught a glimpse of Tony during the next twenty years or so, but I blocked out his existence completely.

In 1982, at the Actors Studio, a couple of days after Lee Strasberg died, Elia Kazan was moderating Lee's class. He asked me to check the membership, as he wanted to find out exactly how many members were attending the Studio. He didn't want any observers at this first session after Lee's death. He asked me to check on the people coming up the stairs. I saw Brett Somers coming up the steps, and she was with a tall, sort of familiar, middle-aged, handsome man. I knew she was a member, but I didn't know who the gentleman was.

I asked him if he was an observer or a member of the Actors Studio. He was quite tall, and had gray sideburns, and sun-streaked brown hair. He was still slim, but he had a grown man's body, not a boy's. He looked familiar, but I couldn't place him. He had on a Hollywood sort of camel's-hair coat, boots, and a suntan.

"Yes, I'm a member," he said.

Puzzled, and assuming he was a California actor, I

asked him why he didn't attend the California Actors Studio—that I was sure he would find it very interesting.

"Shelley," said the gentleman, getting very red and staring at me, "don't you remember me—Tony, your friend, your ex-husband?"

I truly did not remember him. I wasn't pulling a number or anything like that. I'm sure I got as red as he did, so I said, "Please, Mr. Franciosa, take a seat. I'm a little confused."

Thank God, Al Pacino, who was coming up the steps in back of Tony, quickly jumped into the conversational gap, took Tony's arm, said, "Tony, we've never met, but I've admired your work for years," and showed him to a seat.

After the incident of the perfume bottle, I immediately saw a lawyer by the name of Harold Berkowitz. He tried to get me to sue Tony for a lot of money, since California was a community-property state and during our marriage Tony had acquired a great deal of money. But I knew that Tony had managed to get rid of a great deal. I didn't want any of it. I just wanted *out* as quickly as possible. Berkowitz prepared papers, and I signed them without reading them. I think Tony gave me $50,000 reimbursement for expenses incurred during our marriage, and I paid Berkowitz $10,000.

Then a strange problem developed. For months we could not find a summons server who could locate Tony to serve him with the divorce papers. I remember that during this time the newspapers were very kind to us. They never mentioned the perfume-bottle incident, and nobody came to arrest me. Oh yes, at one point Barney Balaban called me and offered me a half of a million dollars if I would not divorce Tony for a couple of years. He carefully explained to me that he did not want Tony raising his grandchildren. I carefully explained to him that I did not want Tony raising my child. I thanked him for the offer and hung up.

I was told by my agent that Barney Balaban blacklisted Tony for a number of years. Tony's barber was at Paramount Studios, and he could no longer even drive on the

Paramount lot to get a haircut. But Tony Franciosa's haircuts were no longer my problem. Just getting those divorce papers served was my problem. Some months later, in New York, I heard at the Actors Studio that Tony was staying at a hotel on Lexington Avenue, registered under a different name. So early one morning, I took the summons to that hotel and paid a bellhop $20 to take me to Tony's room. The boy knocked on the door, and, when Tony answered, we pushed it open, and I served him with the summons. He held it with one hand and put his other hand through a glass window. I didn't stay to find out which hand it was. I just kept going.

When the divorce became final, Tony married Judy Balaban, and they had a little girl. But then they were divorced, too, and Tony paid her alimony and child support till his daughter was eighteen years old, even though Barney Balaban had died and left Judy a great deal of money.

As I read the pages I've just written about Tony's and my relationship, I remember I've often wondered during the past three decades what Tony's version of our affair, marriage, and divorce was. Perhaps now I'll find out.

Through the years, I have seen Tony on television and in many films. He's had three successful television series. That takes a lot of disciplined work so perhaps all his agony was really related to me. Or Ava Gardner. Or Anna Magnani. Or Judy Balaban. But now that we're both "mature," I really would love to see Tony on Broadway again and *maybe* even act with him again. We got such great reviews together. Walter Kerr said, "Watching Shelley Winters and Tony Franciosa act is like watching two broken-hearted clowns."

Recently, I saw Tony in Italy in the flesh. He waved at me in a restaurant at Rome's Caribe-Hilton. I motioned for him to come over. He sat down and said, "Shelley, you really recognize me now?"

"Tony, if I didn't recognize you," I said, "it's because you've become so distinguished and handsome."

He returned the compliment, and then we both said,

"Cut out the bullshit!" and started to laugh and tease each other about the crazy days of the Fabulous Fifties and Sexy Sixties. In the course of our teasing conversation, Tony asked me why I'd never married again.

"To quote Tennessee Williams, I've had the best—not the second best, not the third best, but the best," I replied. "Marriage with anyone after you would be very dull."

He jokingly asked me what floor I was on, and I said, "Never mind, Romeo. I'll wave to you from the balcony."

19

I was now free, but really free. My obsession and pre-occupation with Tony's career and life were over. I began to realize that while I was so busy taking care of his emotional and acting problems, I'd given myself an excuse to ignore my own. I reconnected with the world, especially the aboveground testing of the hydrogen bomb, which was endangering all life on this planet; the terrible segregation and lack of opportunity of our black citizens; and the garbage-ridden tenements that lined the side streets of the Upper West Side, right in back of the luxury buildings of Central Park West.

I began to work with the new Reform Democratic Committee of New York. I rejoined the civil-rights movement, and I believe I was one of the first well-known people to take part in a sit-down demonstration.

Senator Hubert Humphrey and I and other civic leaders and Broadway stars sat down in the middle of Times Square TO BAN THE BOMB. Besides jamming all traffic around the Times Square area, we managed to make the front pages of the world press. This was part of a world-wide movement to stop the testing of atomic and hydrogen bombs. It took time, but by the end of the turbulent sixties, there was no testing above ground and I hope very little underground testing by either the U.S. or the Soviet Union.

I started to work for urban renewal of the West Side and of course for low-rent housing and middle-income housing. This was promised to the people of the Upper West Side by all the city and state bigwigs. But after they tore down a lot of landmark buildings, only a very small percentage of new buildings and renovated tenements accommodated those income groups.

I rededicated myself to working for all the civil-rights organizations that contacted me. I had forgotten that I could be an effective speaker, and the joy, satisfaction and self-esteem that I got from this reconnecting was most fulfilling.

I was hoping that my agent would find a wonderful new play for me, but none appeared. One lunchtime at Sardi's, my old friend Robert Ludlum, who now managed a theater in Paramus, New Jersey, approached me and said he was organizing various winter-stock packages and wouldn't I like to try out some wonderful recent Broadway play in various theaters that were opening on the Eastern seaboard?

We had a drink and thought about plays. I remembered that at the beginning of my relationship with Tony in 1955, I had been doing *The Women*. I had been so preoccupied with Tony and so terrified of playing the beautiful Crystal that I gave Mr. Fred Coe, the producer, a very bad time indeed. A couple of years later, when he was producing *Two for the Seesaw* on Broadway, his star, Henry Fonda, had begged him to read me for the part of Gittel Mosca. Mr. Coe refused and told Henry Fonda, ''I won't read her, because if I do, she'll be wonderful, and I'll have to hire her, and I'm too young to die of a heart attack.'' So Mr. Coe wouldn't audition me. He was a fine producer, and he died just a few years ago of heart failure, but I certainly had nothing to do with it.

So as Mr. Ludlum and I discussed possible plays to tour, I remembered how I'd longed to play Gittel Mosca, and I suggested *Two for the Seesaw*.

''That's it,'' Robert said. ''We'll get Frank Corsaro to direct, and I'll book you for a twelve-week tour, two weeks in each theater, in six of the best theaters in the East.''

I went home happy with the knowledge that I had a great part in a fantastic play and I would at last be on the stage again in front of live audiences. As I entered my apartment, the phone was ringing. As always in an actor's life, there is no work, or too much work.

Mr. Harold Hecht was on the phone. He was Burt Lancaster's partner and business manager. He told me that Burt was doing a film called *The Young Savages*. It was about a recent case that had appeared in the New York newspapers. Two teenage boys had assumed the personalities of cartoon characters to escape from their ghetto surroundings. Their imaginary games had become real, and they had done armed robbery and accidentally killed a policeman.

The film script accurately portrayed this real-life episode. Burt wanted me to play the mother of the boy who costumes himself in a cape and calls himself Batman. In the screenplay, Burt is the assistant district attorney who comes from the same environment as I do. When he was in law school, his character and my character had been sweethearts and later lovers. When he leaves the neighborhood, he leaves my character and marries an educated society girl, Dina Merrill. I don't think Burt ever enjoyed playing this unsympathetic role. I told Harold Hecht to send me the script, but in any case my salary would be $100,000 and I must have costar billing with Mr. Lancaster. Burt and I had known each other, in the biblical sense, when we had both started our careers at Universal. We had a lovely and sad backstreet romance for a couple of years, but I had not seen or heard from him since about 1950.

Now, one husband and several nominations and one Oscar later, he was contacting me and wanted to work with me in a film he was producing. But I decided not to be suspicious, and if the script was good, I would postpone my *Two for the Seesaw* tour. Harold Hecht called me back forty-five minutes later.

"Of course the salary is okay," he said, "but Burt gets billing alone above the title."

"Good for him," I told Mr. Hecht. "I pass."

Some days later I read in *The Hollywood Reporter* that

Lee Grant was to do this film with Burt Lancaster. It was to be shot with New York exteriors, and the interiors would be shot in Hollywood. Lee Grant is a good friend and a talented actress, and I was glad that she had gotten the role. I hoped that she would make a lot of money, which I knew she needed, as she had not worked in films for a number of years and her husband, Arnold Manoff, was critically ill.

I started to rehearse *Seesaw,* with Frank Corsaro directing and Al Morgenstern in the Henry Fonda role. *Seesaw* is a very difficult play, just two people holding the stage through the entire evening, and it takes them from the beginning of a romance, its ups and downs, to its bittersweet ending. Al was a joy to act with. He was a complete theater person, and as far as I know the only film he ever did was *No Exit* with Viveca Lindfors. To my knowledge he never had any film aspirations. He was completely at home on the stage, and that's where he wanted to be.

We were going into our second week of rehearsal of *Seesaw* when I was awakened one middle-of-the-night by a phone call from Lee Grant. She was so upset that it took me a while to understand what she was saying. It seemed they had been shooting on the Lower East Side, and she had been doing a scene with Burt Lancaster playing the prosecutor. In the scene, she denounces him for not understanding her son's plight, and she tells him he has sold out for money and is no longer connected to the lives of the ghetto children. When she had been shooting this scene earlier that night, Burt Lancaster had suddenly turned on her. They had begun fighting for real, and they had ended up calling each other terrible names, and she had walked off the film.

"I really think he wants you in the role," Lee said. "He is impossible to work with." He would not let the director, John Frankenheimer, direct, and she had only been able to do two scenes with him, when four had been scheduled.

"Would you please do this part?" she pleaded. "I'm afraid they will kick me out of the Screen Actors Guild, and I won't be able to work on the stage or anywhere.

My husband is ill, and I don't want to go out to California now, especially under such stressful conditions.''

I told her that I was in the middle of rehearsing a play that she had done on Broadway, *Seesaw,* and I was sure that Burt was not going to ask me to do her role in the film. All she said was, ''Please try. Please,'' and hung up.

Ten minutes later, Harold Hecht was again on the telephone. He gave me some long rigamarole about how I was the only one who completely understood this character in *The Young Savages* because I had come from a Brooklyn ghetto.

I listened carefully to him and said, ''Harold, it's still a hundred thousand dollars and costar billing, but now you have to buy out all the theaters I was to play in, or arrange your shooting schedule so I can perform in some of them that have advertised me.''

Silence on the other end. John Frankenheimer got on the phone and pleaded, ''Shelley, we're in the middle of the film. If we ever hope to finish it and not lose all the money we've invested, we will try to do what you ask. The script is on its way to you. We will not reshoot the scenes in New York. We will make your hair dark, the same color as Lee's, and we will just do your close-ups against a brick wall in Hollywood. In the long shots, we will dub your voice over the back of Lee Grant's head.'' (I wonder if Lee Grant ever got paid for the back of her head.)

I said, ''Whatever. Do your best,'' and hung up.

The money and how they shot the film weren't important. I just wanted to force Burt Lancaster to give me costar billing, which he did in the newspapers and on the screen. But quite recently a fan gave me a poster of *Young Savages,* and it says, BURT LANCASTER IN *YOUNG SAVAGES,* and under the title it says, COSTARRING SHELLEY WINTERS. Almost two decades later I'm still getting angry about it.

Frank Corsaro and John Frankenheimer had a powwow long-distance about how I could rehearse and perform *Seesaw* in Paramus, Westport, Mineola, and the Paper Mill Playhouse in New Jersey on alternate weeks, and film in Hollywood *The Young Savages* in between those weeks. Of all the insane things I've ever done in show business, this was the wackiest.

I arrived at Twentieth Century–Fox Studios in Hollywood and, lo and behold, the courtroom set was on Stage 27, and next door on 26 was the set of *Seesaw*, built exactly to the theater specifications. The game plan was that when I wasn't shooting *Savages* with Burt Lancaster with Frankenheimer directing, in between shooting I would go to the next stage and rehearse *Seesaw* with some Hollywood actor and with Sydney Pollack directing. Sydney was then Frankenheimer's dialogue director. Al Morgenstern would be rehearsing in New Jersey with some New York actress and with Frank Corsaro directing. Sydney and Frank would consult each other on the phone every hour or so to see if they were giving the actors the same blocking and direction.

I don't know if the reader is going to believe this, but it actually happened. A week into *Savages*, I had to fly to Newark and get a motorcycle escort from the airport to Paramus, Robert Ludlum's theater, and the first time I did *Seesaw* with Al Morgenstern was Paramus's opening night. It was perhaps my best performance on any stage. Al felt the same way. We had to never take our eyes off each other, because we did not know what the other one was going to say or do. How I managed to do this long, complicated two-character play in this way is a mystery. But the audience laughed in all the right places, the reviews were great, and we did SRO business for the whole run.

The following Sunday night I had to fly back to Hollywood to continue filming *Savages*. The weeks that I shot *Savages*, Al Morgenstern had to be paid in New York. Burt Lancaster's company had to reimburse the dark theaters where I was not able to play due to the shooting of the film.

It was so confusing to play two different characters of different ages that, at one point, I think I tried to leave Shirley Schrift in New York to do the play and send the movie star Shelley Winters to Hollywood to do the film. But not even I, with all my magical thinking, could pull that one off.

As the film progressed, I began to think I understood why Burt had wanted me in this role. I believe he did not know exactly what affective memory was, but I think he was living it out in the scenes we played. I almost never knew whether he was relating to me or the part I was playing or the Shelley of 1948. John Frankenheimer directed us very little, and the scenes were written brilliantly, eerie, and almost documentary in quality. I too found I was relating to the Burt Lancaster I had known in the late 1940s and not the famous, successful actor he had become. I think we both enjoyed the acting, but, off the set, we both were reserved and quiet with each other.

Burt had done many films since 1948, but this was the first time he had ever asked me to be in one. He did not talk about what had happened to him in the past decade, nor did I. When we were in front of the camera, it was as if no time had elapsed since we had seen each other. When we were just sitting around the soundstage, waiting for them to light scenes, we were almost like strangers, which in a way we now were.

Our strange relationship culminated in a dreadful real-life scene on the final day of shooting. We did the scene on the back lot, quite late in the afternoon. In it, my character denounces his for having deserted and betrayed the poor people he has said he became a lawyer to help and protect. He denounces me in legalistic language for having neglected my young son and allowing him to become a murderer and criminal. After a few low-key rumbles, Frankenheimer decided not to rehearse the scene. I just ran through my cues and lines with Sydney Pollack, and I assume Burt ran his lines with Sydney, too. They were not shooting Burt's close-up again, as of course he had done that in New York with Lee Grant. They had done all the exteriors in New York. They were just going to do a close two-shot, and then my close-up.

We got into the scene, and suddenly we weren't acting anymore. We both began to break from the dialogue and call each other terrible names. The language was appalling on both our parts. It got so bad that the crew, embarrassed, left their stations, and a security guard heard us a block away and came running with his gun drawn. Frankenheimer had turned off the camera and yelled, "Cut," two hundred feet ago, but we were almost ready to tear each other apart physically. When we ran out of breath, Sydney Pollack stood between us, and then we both left the set and climbed into our respective cars and drove away.

As I drove, tears were streaming down my face, and I didn't know quite why. When I became calmer, I realized this was probably the same scene in which Burt had had the fight with Lee Grant in New York that had caused her to leave the film. I didn't know what Burt and I had been screaming about—was it the scene in the picture, or were we blaming each other for what had gone wrong in our lives in the last decades? Me—two broken marriages. Him—it was rumored—an alcoholic wife.

I was very frightened and called my psychiatrist, who told me I was doing something called "acting out," which had nothing to do with the here and now. Then she advised that I should go back to work the next day and quietly finish the film like the professional actress I was. I did this. I apologized to Mr. Lancaster, and he apologized to me. When we shot the scene again, there were two cameras, one doing a close-up of me, and another camera doing a two-shot of both Burt and me, a very unusual expense and against the rules of the stagehands' union. They only allowed two cameras when there was a difficult physical stunt. Maybe the union realized that in some way, Burt and I *were* doing a difficult physical stunt. When the scene and the film were finally over, everybody at Twentieth breathed a sigh of relief, especially John Frankenheimer and the Hecht-Hill-Lancaster executives.

The next time I communicated with Burt Lancaster was through Western Union. He had just won the Oscar for *Elmer Gantry,* and my telegram said:

THANK GOD YOU WON ONE TOO. SHALL WE GO FOR TWO? CONGRATULATIONS SHELLEY

I got myself back to New York and to the here and now, and continued with my stock tour of *Seesaw*. Some nights I would wonder if on the stage I was reenacting my romance with Burt ten years ago as I performed Git-

tel's and her married boyfriend's story. Some or all of
the above are probably true.

Wherever I played in *Seesaw,* if it was close to New
York, I would go to rallies and make speeches in support
of Adlai Stevenson. He was such a wise, compassionate
man. I knew that if he became president of these United
States, the world and this country would return to the
ideals of brotherhood of Franklin Delano Roosevelt.
When I finished the tour of *Seesaw,* I ran myself ragged,
flying all over the country, appearing anywhere I could,
hoping to get the nomination for Adlai Stevenson.

The Reform Democratic Committee invited me to attend the convention as an unofficial observer. I could not
be an alternate because my state residency was question-
able. I believe I lived in New York at that time, but still
voted in California, despite the fact that I had been in
New York, on and off, since 1951. I had never attended
a convention before, and I was very excited at the prospect. I got together my most dignified clothes, business
suits, pearls, hats, white gloves, and sensible shoes.

Los Angeles was jammed. I've attended almost every
Democratic convention since that one, but none has had
the electricity and the sense of destiny that this spectacle
had. Presidential political conventions are peculiar to
America, and though they are a little wacky—the bands,
the straw hats, the frenzy of the delegates, and the
smoke-filled back rooms—still I believe they are one of
the best examples of our free society. I had my duplex
apartment house in Beverly Hills, which for the next
week or ten days I returned to only six or seven hours a
night to sleep. There was furious lobbying going on as
the Stevenson people were trying to hold onto their delegates, as more and more of them were swinging to Senator John F. Kennedy. I know during that period Mrs.
Eleanor Roosevelt never slept. She seemed always
everywhere.

The convention was in a large hotel, the Biltmore. It
was perhaps one of the hottest Julys I remember. Mrs.
Roosevelt was sitting in a box to the right of the auditorium. When Adlai Stevenson's name was placed in nom-

ination by Senator Eugene J. McCarthy, it set off the nearest thing to mass hysteria that I've ever seen. To quote *The New York Times*'s reporter William M. Blair:

> A wild, emotional demonstration for Adlai E. Stevenson shook the Democratic National Convention tonight.
>
> As the name of the man who led the Democrats in 1952 and 1956 was placed before the convention, the galleries erupted in a screaming roar that dwarfed all that went before. . . .
>
> It took the convention chairman, Gov. LeRoy Collins of Florida, twenty-five minutes to slow down the stamping, shouting show to get seconding speeches.
>
> Stevenson supporters from outside the convention stormed the floor. . . .

I sat on the convention floor in my Stevenson hat, praying that this wise man would somehow win the nomination and become president of our country. That night I attended a buffet supper, in some suite in the hotel, at which Adlai Stevenson and Mrs. Roosevelt spoke. They seemed happy and cheerful, but I sensed an undertone in their voices that depressed me.

The next morning, when I went down to the convention floor, my huge Stevenson button pinned to my shoulder and my Stevenson straw hat in place, I saw a group of Hollywood stars assembled to the left of the platform. As far as I was concerned, they had to be the younger, confused, flighty ones, because the only one I actually saw was Anthony Franciosa, wearing a huge John F. Kennedy button on his shoulder and a Kennedy straw hat on his head. I sat in my seat and wondered why I hadn't killed him when I'd had the chance.

When this group started up the right aisle to go to the platform to show their support of John F. Kennedy, I quickly rounded up some Stevenson movie-star supporters, and we dashed up the left side of the platform steps and marched to the center of the podium. We were about ten stars strong. They were over twenty, but we spread out and made ourselves look like more and we shined much more brightly.

When the polling of the delegates started later that day, I glanced up at Mrs. Roosevelt. She was quietly weeping. I could not believe it. The times I had seen her in person and on newsreels or on television, she had always been the most reserved, dignified, and composed woman I had ever seen. As the state roll was called, I became aware that Senator Kennedy was winning. I sat there most of the night, and I slowly realized that John F. Kennedy had managed to win the nomination. I will quote *The New York Times:*

> Senator John F. Kennedy smashed his way to a first-ballot Presidential nomination at the Democratic National Convention last night and won the right to oppose Vice President Nixon in November. The 43-year-old Massachusetts Senator overwhelmed his opposition, piling up 806 votes. . . .

I left the convention hall, drove back to my Beverly Hills duplex, and ate two tuna-fish sandwiches, drank three chocolate milk shakes, and took two sleeping pills, my standard tranquilizer. It didn't work.

I remembered when Stevenson had first run in 1952. I had been pregnant with my daughter, and I had been ill. In that very house, my husband Vittorio Gassman had somehow managed to carry the huge TV set into my bedroom. He had sat and held my hand while the election results came in. As it became obvious that the United States was going to elect General Eisenhower, and not Adlai Stevenson, to be president in this turbulent postwar world, Vittorio kept mumbling in Italian. When I asked him to translate, he said:

"If I say it in English, they will deport me. I am amazed that the American people are so stupid that they do not understand how valuable this man Stevenson would be to their own country and to the world."

So it was now 1960, and I had witnessed what I knew would be the final Stevenson defeat. I understood he was just not enough of a political animal. He could not go for his opponent's jugular.

The next morning, as I was trying to pack, the phone rang. It was a famous *Life* photographer named Paul Schutzer. He was an unconventionally handsome man I had met somewhere during Stevenson's campaign. Paul was Eisenstadt's protégé on *Life,* and he had done a story about Anne Frank with photographs of the attic in Amsterdam and the concentration camp where she had died. I remembered I had met Paul on a very cold night in Brooklyn, near a Stevenson-campaign platform on Flatbush Avenue. We had been waiting for Stevenson, sitting opposite the Lerner's store where I had worked on Saturdays when I'd been fourteen. Paul and I sat there in the dark for a couple of hours, reminiscing about our youths. His had been very similar to mine.

Paul had been assigned to follow various Presidential candidates and photograph them, but he'd already made up his mind that he was for Kennedy. We had had several spirited arguments about the candidates and he kept trying to convince me that, despite Adlai Stevenson's qualifications, Kennedy was the realist and the pragmatist.

Now, on the phone, he went into a long rigmarole about the necessity of the Democratic Party itself behind the candidate. I think I answered, "Bullshit." But he was really phoning to beg me not to leave for New York until the next evening. He wanted to pick me up at six o'clock to go to a victory party at Romanoff's. Bob Kennedy, who was John Kennedy's campaign manager, had asked to meet and talk with me. I hesitated and then felt it would be a good time to insult the candidate, so I agreed to go even though I was annoyed that when John Kennedy had made his victory speech he'd mentioned Lyndon Johnson and practically everybody else in the Democratic Party, but not Adlai Stevenson. And I felt he should have.

That afternoon, I didn't bother setting my hair or putting my eyelashes on or, for that matter, getting into my girdle. I just put on a black cocktail dress and pearls (not my real ones), combed my hair, and put on a little makeup, and when Paul Schutzer arrived I made him carry my suitcases out to his car so I could leave for New York on the red-eye at midnight.

We drove to Romanoff's and, though it was a warm California evening, I was cold. That usually meant that I was preparing to do something shocking, and I was frightened of myself. We walked into the bar at Romanoff's. Tony Franciosa, with Judy Balaban, was standing at the bar among other *nouveau* Kennedy celebrities. Tony took one look at my face, grabbed Judy, and scurried to the other side of the restaurant.

Paul Schutzer introduced me to Robert Kennedy, who graciously mentioned that his entire family admired my work in *A Place in the Sun*. I answered his graciousness by saying that I had a lot of friends in England and then asked if the rumor I had heard was true that when his father was Ambassador to the Court of Saint James he and his brother John had "taken a course at the Harold Laski School of Socialism."

Robert Kennedy laughed and said, "Miss Winters, I don't think I can deal with you. I'm going to pass you on to my brother," and took my arm firmly and walked me over to meet the presidential candidate. He introduced us, and the Democratic candidate said something complimentary to me. I studied John Kennedy's open, handsome, intelligent face, and blurted out:

"Senator, I hear your father is anti-Semitic."

Reporters were busily writing down what we said and taking pictures. Kennedy paused, then answered, "Miss Winters, truthfully, how do you get along with *your* father?"

"He's dead," I replied. "He wore himself out. He was a pattern maker and stood on his feet for forty years in a factory."

John Kennedy then said, "When he was alive, how did you get along with him?"

I had to answer truthfully. I remembered how I used to fight with my father over his antiblack bias.

"Well, I loved him, but we didn't agree about almost anything."

John Kennedy, the superb politician, responded, "Well, that goes for me, too. I can't do anything about my father. I can only try to make sure that the horror of the Holocaust never happens again, and the existence of the young state of Israel is guaranteed. That's one of the things I went to war about."

He gave me that wonderful smile, and I smiled back and thanked him.

Then Paul Schutzer escorted me to the back booth at Romanoff's. I was in a daze.

I decided not to mess with my political biases for a while and eat myself unconscious. Paul was photographing everything in sight, so I picked up the Romanoff's menu and asked for the prince. Mike Romanoff came and helped me order a huge dinner—shrimp cocktail, vichyssoise, Caesar salad, rare roast beef, creamed spinach, cheese and garlic toast, and a chocolate profiterole. Then he poured me some lovely French wine, and I had a wonderful dinner all by myself, eating away, while the fate of the country was being decided in the front of the restaurant.

Around 11:00 P.M., Paul found me, and he informed me that I'd better abandon my feasting and move if I wanted to make the red-eye. As we drove out to the airport, Paul asked me if I wanted a picture of myself talking with John Kennedy, but I told him:

"Not yet. I'm thinking about it."

He got me onto the plane just on time, and carried my suitcases to my seat. I guess they let him on board only because he was sporting a press pass. I gave Paul what started out to be a little chocolaty kiss, but he climbed into the empty seat next to me, and it turned into a sort of magazine cover kiss. Suddenly we weren't thinking about politics anymore.

"I'm flying back to Washington with Kennedy later tonight. I'll probably be up in New York next weekend." Then he disappeared.

I guess I'm a prototypical woman of the mid–twentieth century. So many of my life and romantic decisions have occurred on airplanes or in airports. I put everything on hold, took another sleeping pill and a martini, and became unconscious. My next memory is of being awakened by the steward and told I had to get off the plane, because everyone else had already left.

As I watched my favorite skyline approach through the limousine windows, I told myself that it was time I started to behave like a mature woman whose political loyalty was obviously valued by the Democratic Party. I also resolved to stop getting crushes on every Tom, Dick, and Paul who showed up to give me a lift. My divorce papers were barely filed, and the divorce would not be final for a year.

I was hugged and kissed by my family, and I gave them all the convention keepsakes. My daughter still has the Stevenson button I wore, and the famous silver pin of the sole of his shoe with a hole in it. After Molly and my mother admired all the presents, my daughter suddenly ran into my bedroom and brought me a play script.

"Mommy, it's a play, a play!" she said. "If it's a hit, you'll have to stay in New York."

Looking at her little face, I realized, maybe for the first time, that my child was getting show-business-wise in her attempts to keep her mother with her as much as possible. My kid was not yet in the first grade, and I knew that if I got her into the school I wanted for her, I would have to sign in blood that she would start the term at the same time as all the other children. I wouldn't ever be able to take her out of school to come with me on locations, and she would have to finish the term with all the other children. Those were the rules of the private school. So I hugged my kid and promised her that until she was in the first grade, wherever I went, she would go. If she couldn't leave New York, I wouldn't leave New York. She made me sit down then and there and read the play.

It was a rough draft of the play *Invitation to a March* by Arthur Laurents. It had a wonderful premise, but there were four women's parts, and I wasn't sure which one he had in mind for me. I called Arthur, whom I had known from my early Universal days, and asked him which role he wanted me to consider. He suggested I come out to his home in Quogue that weekend so we could discuss the whole project.

I told him I had to bring my child with me, to which he responded, "Great." So after twenty-four hours of rest, during which Paul Schutzer called me twice and I called him once in Washington, my daughter and I piled into the Jaguar, complete with suntan creams, heating pads, and ice bags, and journeyed out to Quogue. I had gotten directions from Arthur and an automobile club Trip-tic, so we only got lost twice, and in Quogue we managed to go to the wrong house. It turned out that the owners of "21," the Kriendlers, owned this house on the beach, but they greeted us warmly when we rang the doorbell. I was exhausted from driving my beautiful Jaguar, so Jack gave us some lemonade and lunch, and he drove us over to Arthur Laurents's house about a mile away. Then he walked back.

My kid immediately fell in love with Quogue, and Arthur, and we all had a lovely three days in which we discussed everything about the theater and a little bit about *Invitation to a March*. The play was not yet completed, and the part he wanted me to do was of a woman who was an independent thinker, earthy, and dedicated to the cause of women's independence. Arthur was ahead of his time.

The one problem in the play, as far as I was concerned, was that this character only had three scenes. Arthur promised me that the part would be expanded, and we were to go into rehearsal in four weeks.

My child had taught herself to read the winter before, and one afternoon while I was napping, she was going through some of Arthur's papers and, lo and behold, she discovered a file labeled "Tennessee Williams." When I awakened, she presented me with this file and said, "Look, Mom, Tennessee's little plays." I stared at her and realized that that was what she called one-act plays. (I don't know why Arthur Laurents had them.) One of them, about a strike in a shoe factory in St. Louis à la Clifford Odets, was not very good. It was obviously something Tennessee had written in his pre–*Glass Menagerie* days. But one of them was called *The Last of My*

Teardrop Diamonds, and it was glorious. Till this day, I regret that I didn't steal it. I have never seen it again, published or on the stage. And I don't know what happened to it. I made my kid put back all of Arthur's papers, carefully, because I didn't want him to think that his guests in the spare bedroom were rifling through his papers.

One of the plays I read later that night, and it was called *High Point Is Built on a Cavern*. Their house is sinking, but they don't notice. When I saw *A Period of Adjustment*, I realized that it was the expanded version of the one-act play I had read in Arthur Laurents's beach house. The one-act play was much better. It was a remarkable comment on the society of the fifties and sixties.

When Arthur reads this, perhaps he'll look through his files and find the folder of Tennessee's one-act plays I sneakily read in Quogue late one summer night in 1960.

All in all, it was a lovely weekend. I think Arthur must have total recall, too, because years later, when I read and saw *The Way We Were*, there were several stories that I told him that had happened to me and they ended up happening to Barbra Streisand. Oh, well, it looked good on Robert Redford and Barbra.

Besides, Arthur told me some stories about his college days that I've used when I want to impress people and they don't know that I never finished high school. I think we need another weekend in Quogue, Arthur, for the 1990s.

When my kid and I got back to New York, I conferred with my agent, and we both decided that it was time for me to do another play. Perhaps my decision was also colored by the fact that (1) Tony Franciosa now lived in Hollywood, and (2) I did not yet want to campaign for the Democrats, because I was not sure whom I wanted to campaign for.

Cheryl Crawford, who was producing *Invitation to a March*, sent a deal memo to my California agent, and when this little piece of paper finally got to me, I found out that I was starring alone above the title, and Eileen Heckart, Madeleine Sherwood, Jane Fonda (who was at the beginning of her career), and James MacArthur were costarring under the title. When I phoned him, my agent asked me if my role warranted being above the title over those other important theatrical names. I said I'd read the play again and call him back.

The play was still not yet completely developed, but I thought perhaps if those people were under the title, I should be under the title, too. But Arthur convinced me that since they were going on the road to New Haven, Cleveland, and Boston, I was the name that would sell the tickets, and I should stay alone above the title. Stupidly I agreed.

While I was waiting for the rehearsals to begin, I got daily phone calls from Paul. The first weekend he could, he came up to New York. Although I knew he was married, he never seemed to need to go to out-of-the-way restaurants, and, since I was still smarting from Tony's public unfaithfulness, I tried to get straight in my mind what living arrangement Paul had with his wife. It seemed she lived in Paris and they had an open marriage.

It was one of the happiest autumns I'd ever known in New York. I was suddenly meeting authors, scientists, and important political figures, who were treating me as an intellectual equal. When I was with Paul, maybe for the first time in my life, I felt no need to be "on." I didn't have to tell jokes to be accepted, and at last I could *listen*. I've often thought about and remembered this period in my life, and I hope at times I have recaptured it—or grown into it.

There was nothing I could do for Paul Schutzer. All my attempts to buy things or do things for him were gently thwarted. He paid the check, literally, emotionally, and figuratively.

Paul had a kind of fame that was much different from anything I had seen in Hollywood. He was a man who worked where the wars were fought, was at all the meetings of the important figures of the world, and the influence of his marvelous photographs was felt around the world. The photo essay he had done, "World Famine," was reprinted in magazines regardless of their political positions. We went to a lot of parties during this period and I got to know Tennessee Williams quite well, but we would stand over in the corner, and, because he had the same feelings of belonging only in St. Louis and not among the New York intellectuals, we both sometimes had one too many.

Paul was sending me funny postcards from the state of Washington all the way to Florida or wherever John Kennedy was speaking, and he would call me almost every day. A few years later, my need to talk to him got out of hand. I was in Hollywood doing some picture or other, and I hadn't heard from him for a while. Then I got a postcard from some hotel in Algiers. I immediately picked up the phone and asked the nice Beverly Hills operator to try to connect me person-to-person with Paul Schutzer at such-and-such a hotel in Algeria.

"I'll try, Miss Winters," she said, "but we're having some kind of problem with the Algerian telephone company."

A few minutes later, she called me back, and I was connected to Paul. He sounded a little strange and said, "Hi, darling! Where the hell are you?"

"Beverly Hills," I said.

"How the hell did you get through?"

"Oh," I said, "I just made a person-to-person call. What's going on there?"

Paul laughed, "Just a minute—I'll hold the phone out the window."

In a couple of seconds, I heard these strange explosions, weird boom sounds with an echo, very scary. When he came back on the line, I asked him what it was.

"Shelley, those were the plastic bombs," he said. "They're having the war right outside my window."

I knew they were having a war in Algeria, but I didn't know they were right next to his hotel. He laughed some more and then again asked me, "How the hell did you get through? My boss, Henry Luce, has been trying to reach me for days, and I can't get a call through to the States."

Until that second, I had not fully realized how dangerous Paul's work was, and then I remembered the only

39

40

41

*T*ony and I getting married in a rarefied atmosphere. The location for *Wild Is the Wind* with Tony and Magnani was high above Reno somewhere. I always suspected that Tony married me because he was more frightened of Magnani.

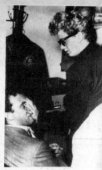

42–45

*H*ow not to buy a house at
auction if you're a movie star.

*A*t last, studying the way she had dreamed about. If only she could have gone up those steps a few years earlier.

*T*he happiest picture I've ever seen of Marilyn, taken at the Actors Studio sans makeup, with Arthur Miller, at the beginning of their relationship.

*S*ome Like It Hot, the picture she had the most fun with and proved she was a superb comedienne. I believe she would have had a long career with films like this. Billy Wilder told her to relate to both Jack Lemmon and Tony Curtis as if they were her best girlfriends. She pretended they were both me.

*M*y great director George Stevens, who convinced me at thirty that if I played Mrs. van Daan, who was fifty, I would act all my life. He was right. Even though I got the Oscar, it still incensed the president of Universal because I let myself be photographed this way.

*M*illie Perkins, myself, and Tony Franciosa the afternoon before the Oscars when he was nominated for best supporting actor for *A Hatful of Rain*. That night he didn't win.

53

54

*D*on't they look beautiful together? Wouldn't it have been nice if they had been making the same movie? Ava Gardner was doing *The Naked Maja* and Tony was doing *Goya*.

55

*M*arilyn, with her Golden Globe Award for *Some Like It Hot*, thanking me for sending her in the direction of the Actors Studio, while Tony watched, mesmerized.

*M*y daughter teaching me ballet . . . too late.

*T*he Rev. Martin Luther King teaching American mothers about caring for all children.

58

59

*H*ow husbands who are actors
cope when their wives win Oscars.
Yves Montand had Simone
Signoret and Tony had me.

60

*M*olly Epps, my beloved and longtime housekeeper, who
made me take that Oscar, as I had promised Otto Frank, to
the Anne Frank house in Amsterdam.

$\mathscr{P}$aul Schutzer, photographer extraordinaire, for *Life,* whose stories about world hunger, Anne Frank in the concentration camp, and many wars are famous classics. He was killed in a half-truck the first day of the Israeli-Egyptian War. As I look back, he was somehow the most important man in my life.

$\mathscr{M}$y Oscar at the Anne Frank house. They had to put it in a glass case because kids from all over the world would pick it up and whisper acceptance speeches.

*S*helley to Adlai: "Adlai, not everyone in your audiences went to Harvard!" Adlai to Shelley: "Shelley, not all these ladies went to the Actors Studio!" The little gold donkey was a gift from him for my good advice. I still think that if Stevenson had been elected president of the United States it really would have been a kinder and gentler society.

63

64

65

66

*O*nce a party unites behind a candidate, oh what a great and glorious party you have! As I worried about Kennedy's cavalcade being so late, and it seemed as if ten million people were crowding the Garment District, he said to me: "Now, Shelley, what would a method actress know about entrances?"

*W*hen I was Mistress of Ceremonies at the White House Press Photographers Ball roasting the president. This picture was on the cover of *The New York Daily News* with the headline: "Why is Shelley Winters crying as she looks at our young president?"

67

69

*J*ames MacArthur improvising my illegitimate son with me in *Invitation to a March,* while writer and director Arthur Laurents smiles with murder (no doubt) in his heart.

70

*S*ome 3 A.M.s when I see *Lolita* with James Mason and me on TV, I'm quite convinced that Charlotte is the best role I've ever played. And I again thank Kubrick with all my heart.

71

*A*ugust 18 is a birthday I share with Chris Jones, Robert De Niro and I believe Robert Redford. Chris Jones always shows up. Why William Merchant, the playwright, has a cake too, I don't know.

72

*M*aking up backstage for *Night of the Iguana*. If a Hollywood producer was out front, I would have an attack of Beauty and forget about ugly Maxine Faulk. The makeup changed dramatically.

73

*M*e being escorted by Alex Viespi (now known as Alex Cord) to an Oscar evening where I was a presenter.

74

*T*hree of the proudest moments of my life.

75

76

77

The Chapman Report: Frank sex—
discussed and acted with restraint
according to the Code. I don't believe
any of us achieved it. Claire Bloom,
Glynis Johns, Jane Fonda, and me.

Jack Warden backstage after the
opening of *Cages*. I think perhaps he
is the most brilliant and funniest
actor I ever worked with.

78

79

Geraldine Page, Rip Torn, Susan Strasberg, me, and Johnny
Strasberg in front of the Stanislavsky Theater in Moscow.

*M*y teacher Lee Strasberg at the Actors Studio. His students have won about three hundred Oscars, Emmys, Tonys, etc., in the thirty years he taught there.

*F*ull circle. Thirty years later, Vittorio Gassman attending a class with Eli Wallach that I am moderating at the Actors Studio. The next film he did after this session was *The Family* which won him prizes all over the world. I sometimes now call the Studio "The Young and the Rest of Us."

other combat photographer I'd known had been Bob Capa, after the Second World War, when I had been in rehearsal for *Oklahoma!* and staying at the Algonquin, and Capa had been running secret floating poker games all over New York.

Paul and I made jokes for five minutes in the middle of the Algerian War and then he said, "Darling, I'll stop in Beverly Hills on my way home. You do know how to write, don't you? Why don't you write, you rat?"

I hung the phone up, and a cold chill settled in my heart. I remembered Bob Capa had been killed stepping on a Thai mine.

It's hard for me to write about Paul. In retrospect, I realize he was the best friend I ever had. In the early sixties I really began to become knowledgeable about art, literature, museums, and music, and where the best food was in New York and not just where the celebrities ate. We always got the best service, not because of me, but because he was a *Life* photographer, and of course everybody wanted to be in *Life*. I never asked him questions about his life outside of his relationship with me, and he never asked me questions about my life outside of my relationship with him. At the time, I wished he would.

Some Sunday while I was rehearsing *Invitation to a March,* I was studying my lines when the doorbell rang and Paul walked in, carrying his little girl. She was about the same age as my kid and was gorgeous. I forgot about my play completely, and we had a wonderful Sunday in Central Park, the pony rides, the zoo, and the carousel. Watching my daughter, watching Paul play with his little girl, devastated me. He was a wonderful father and maybe it was my guilt that the nicer he was to my kid the more she missed Vittorio, perhaps.

When the play was rehearsed and ready to go on the road, Paul told me he had to "go photograph the Cold War," and he would write but certainly see me at the inaugural. I kissed him at Grand Central Station and said, "Don't be too sure that your candidate is going to win."

He kissed me back and said, "If you help him, he will."

As his train pulled out, I yelled, "I'll think seriously about it."

We had started rehearsals in New York and continued with rewrites in Columbus, Ohio, and we finally opened there. But that September day in New York was the worst start of any rehearsal that I've ever had. We started those rehearsals with Arthur reading the play to us, à la Charlie Chaplin, only Arthur Laurents was no Charlie Chaplin. It's an unproductive thing to do to actors. When a playwright does this to you, it blocks your creativity—he's giving you his results. An actor must create the thoughts that make the lines come out the right way. Arthur had written the play, and he was also directing it. What is usual and most creative is when a writer lets go of his play, hands it to a director who understands and agrees with the values he wants from the play, and the director guides his actors' interpretations until he gets those values. It is a creative process, and you go out of town because the audience is very much a part of this process. From the first moment, I felt diminished by this unusual rehearsal process. I felt that my part still was a minor role. I had a five-minute scene in the first act, a *tour de force* scene in the second act, and I came on stage at five minutes to 11:00 P.M. in the third act. This would have been all right if I had been below the title with the rest of the cast, but Cheryl Crawford and Arthur would not let me do this. So again I felt like a movie star who had been thrown into one of Arthur Laurents's plays for her ticket-selling ability and not her talent.

When we opened in Columbus, the play was three hours long. The first act was about an hour and a half. Madeleine Sherwood, Eileen Heckart, and Jane Fonda were indeed very good in the first act, so that by the time I showed up for my scene in the second act, the audience was surprised to see me on the stage. I think they had forgotten I was in the play, and when I disappeared during the long third act, and just came back for my five-minute scene at the end, they would applaud. I guess they figured it was my curtain call. I'm exaggerating a bit, but the curtain came down at midnight, and my fingers were all clumpy because, although I was starring above the title, I sat in my dressing room most of the evening, putting on layers of colorless nail polish.

Arthur and I had some really knock-down fights about the size of my role, since he didn't want to take out any of the things that worked in the first and third acts. The play was very long, so my role in the next couple of weeks didn't get any bigger. Columbus has a lovely square somewhere, and I remember, one 2:00 A.M., Arthur and me screaming at each other across this square. Luckily, everybody in Columbus went to sleep after Jack Paar, so we didn't make the front pages of the morning paper.

I began to stay away from the theater as much as possible and get there as late as possible. When you're trying out a play out of town, all you ever see is the lobby of the hotel, the lobby of the theater, backstage, and the stage. I've been in many cities all over America, especially the Eastern seaboard—Wilmington, Washington, D.C., Boston, Philadelphia, New Haven, Detroit, Chicago, and cities in North and South Carolina—and I have no idea what these cities look like, except for the lobbies of the hotels and the theaters.

One evening, after a matinee, I had dinner in my hotel room and decided to walk back to the theater as slowly as possible. When I got to that same square that Arthur and I had had the fight in, lo and behold, there was a huge Democratic rally going on. There was a platform built at one end of the square and banners and straw hats and lights and a band. It cheered me up considerably. There was a big clock on the front of an office building, and I checked it, and it seemed as if I had plenty of time to get to the performance.

Suddenly a motorcade arrived, and standing in back of a convertible car was John Kennedy. Accompanying him were Bob Kennedy, Pierre Salinger, and the mayor of Columbus. I had on regular eyeglasses, a babushka, a hat on over the babushka, and a long bulky coat. It was a very cold September.

As I listened to the Democratic music played by the Democratic band, my spirits began to soar. So what did this play really matter? My young country was going to take a new direction, and Adlai Stevenson would probably be Secretary of State. We would stop testing atomic bombs. We would sign an arms agreement with the Soviet Union, and the world and the U.S.A. would have a new era of prosperity and brotherhood, which we would send to the rest of the world, along with our money. I listened to the speeches, and, as the mayor introduced John Kennedy, I suddenly became aware of a very young man standing next to me, stuttering something. It was the very young Ted Kennedy. From my height of movie stardom, I looked down my nose at him. He managed to blurt out:

"Miss Winters, my brother would like very much for you to join him on the platform. He knows the contribution you made to the Democratic Party in New York State, and Ohio's Democratic Party needs you too."

I smiled at the kid, and said, "Are you all born with political savvy, or do you acquire it with your mother's milk?"

But I took his arm, and he escorted me up to the platform. I remembered I had cold-creamed my face at the hotel, so I had no makeup on, but I said the heck with it and sat in a chair on the back of the platform and to the left of John Kennedy, since I figured that's where I was politically. I cannot remember one word he said that night, but it was thrilling. The audience was hypnotized, as was I. When the speech was over, he introduced me and said:

"Miss Winters can only say a few words. She really should be in the theater right now."

I looked up at the clock on the bell tower of the office building, and it was 8:10 P.M. Curtain in those days was 8:30, and all actors were supposed to be in their dressing rooms when they called half-hour, which was 8:00. John Kennedy must once have gone out with a theater actress because he certainly knew that I was supposed to be in the theater at half-hour. I didn't care. There were many reporters and photographers standing below the platform, and they were writing down everything that he said. I made a very good speech, I believe—emotional, as usual. The important thing for me was that I finally endorsed John Kennedy and knew at that very moment he would represent and carry forward all the feelings of social responsibility and equality that had not been expressed in our country since Franklin Delano Roosevelt and Harry S. Truman.

The audience applauded, and John Kennedy shook my hand and thanked me, and all I said to him was, "No— thank *you*. I guess I have to learn how to look forward, and not back in anger."

There was a police escort waiting to take me to the theater. Arthur Laurents and Cheryl Crawford were standing at the stage door, white as sheets, as I rushed into the theater. That night my part seemed much bigger, and I remembered that famous theater adage, "There are no small parts; there are only small actors." I had learned that in films, and now I made it my own on the stage that night in Columbus. The second act of *Invitation to a March* was the best act in the play and one of the best acts I've ever done.

In spite of getting a severe reprimand from the Equity deputy, for the rest of the tour of *Invitation to a March* I flew all over the states of Ohio, Michigan, and Massachusetts to campaign for Democratic candidates and John Kennedy and Lyndon Johnson. I had to limit my campaigning to those states because the show played Columbus, Detroit, and Boston. Arthur tried to hold his temper, but, when I would show up at a rehearsal, he would grit his teeth and insultingly thank me for my presence. To be fair to myself, I was very angry that he'd conned me into this production and then presented me with a role that didn't warrant a star. To be fair to Arthur, he couldn't very well do otherwise; that was the structure of his play.

The first act is about some very sophisticated, rich, disillusioned people who come to a summer resort. Eileen Heckart's husband, a successful businessman, finds out that a woman whom he had a casual love affair with twenty years ago (me) has had his child and raised him by herself and has had a fulfilled and happy life. She lives on the beach, and she listens to a different drummer from the other women in the play. Jane Fonda played a symbolic sleeping princess who is regimented by her family. I think Madeleine Sherwood was her mother, and my son awakens her with a kiss, and they march together bravely into the future, making a better world for everyone. It was something like that.

The writing was very good, but the audience was not ready for this play. It was, after all, only 1960, and no one was yet recognizing the greed and disillusionment that were to characterize the unfulfilled lives of the newly rich Americans—symbolic or otherwise. No one yet had heard about happy unwed mothers.

20

When the play moved on to Boston, we rehearsed for a couple of days before we opened. There were rewrites for everyone, but not any major ones. My part remained pretty much the same. I think Arthur was having difficulties directing and writing at the same time. In the decades to follow, he did both those things very successfully, as with *La Cage aux folles*. Jane Fonda, Eileen Heckart, Madeleine Sherwood, and Shelley Winters would have been a handful for any director.

Before we opened in Boston, I called my agent in New York and asked him to make one more attempt to get my name below the title or get Eileen Heckart's, Madeleine Sherwood's, and Jane Fonda's names above the title with me. Eileen Heckart, whose name was first below the title, would not allow it. She refused to move. I felt that since she was very good and very funny in the play, when we got to New York, she was counting on all the critics saying things about this movie star who had dared to star alone in Arthur Laurents's play, and Eileen Heckart walked away with it. (Paranoia, thy name is actress.) Perhaps I was scared about opening on Broadway after the great reviews I'd gotten five years earlier in *A Hatful of Rain*.

Another problem was that the play was so long there had to be cuts everywhere, including my role, and I took it all personally. Opening night in Boston was a critical sweep for Eileen Heckart, except the review of Elliot Norton, who was one of the most distinguished of American critics. He gave me a rave review and said my talent and earthiness made the play work. Nevertheless, I notified the producer, Cheryl Crawford, that if Eileen Heckart continued to refuse to equalize the billing, either above or below the title, my two weeks' notice was effective as of then.

Farley Granger, my old buddy (who was also a friend of Arthur's), my mother, and my psychiatrist all came to Boston to try to reason with me. But by this time I was so paranoid that I felt Arthur and the rest of the cast were conservative Republicans, and I was the lonely liberal Democrat fighting through *Invitation to a March* eight times a week. I made possibly one of the worst decisions of my life and resolved to leave the play. I think it made other Broadway producers afraid of me, since my presence in the play accounted for much of the advance sale from the ladies' theater clubs.

Elliot Norton, the famous Boston theater critic, sounding like a fan, the following Sunday published practically an editorial about how I should not leave the play. But the die was cast, and the devil take the hindmost. I was not offered another play on Broadway for two years.

Farley stayed with me for a week in Boston and tried to give me the confidence to understand that, even though my role was not very big, the audience remembered me. But all I could feel was that I sat around for an hour, had one scene, and then sat in my dressing room till the end of the play. My fragile theater ego could not take it, at that point in my life. I was very lonely in Boston and spent many midnights walking around the Common, and many afternoons walking around the Harvard Yard, wondering what my life would have been like if I'd graduated high school and had enough belief in my intelligence to try to go to a university like Harvard. It was truly one of the low points of my life. Years later, when my daughter was accepted and attended Harvard, it was a dream come true, in a way, for me. It's very hard for someone who's not in the theater to imagine what it's like to get to a theater at 7:00 P.M., prepare for an hour, living in your character's experience, putting on your makeup, then have the curtain go up and wait for an hour to go on stage for a twenty-minute scene, and then go back to your dressing room until the end of the play.

Sometime in the second week, Celeste Holm reported for rehearsals, and, though I was very careful to get to the theater as late as possible, I did have an ache in my heart about someone else doing the role that I had created.

I phoned Kennedy headquarters in Washington, and began to do speaking engagements around Massachusetts within commuting distance of Boston. They also mailed an itinerary to me about joining a plane with a contingent of stars, who would crisscross the country for several weeks and appear in different cities with Kennedy, who would be in another plane. Since Paul Schutzer had rejoined the Kennedy campaign, he would be traveling with the candidate, but that had nothing to do with my decision to leave the play (Oh my God, wait until Arthur Laurents reads this).

I got back to New York on a Sunday, spent about three days with my daughter, and read the Boston paper. Elliot Norton had given Celeste Holm a so-so review, but still said the play needed Me. Celeste is a wonderful actress, and I think Elliot was just prejudiced and trying to teach me not to leave a tryout of a new play.

I kissed my daughter and then took off on the celebrity plane to work for a Democratic president, senate, and congress. I got to know the Kennedys quite well during this trip, especially Ethel, Joan, Eunice Shriver, and Pat. Peter Lawford was traveling with our plane, as was Ted Kennedy. We all had some wonderful times, but we were dedicated campaigners and worked very hard.

Over the years I've heard much gossip about John Kennedy. I got to know him quite well on these trips. He traveled with a doctor, wore some kind of back brace, and was often in obviously terrible pain. I would watch him make speeches after a day of traveling and stopping in two or three cities, and it was clear that standing on a cold platform late at night was a very difficult and perhaps dangerous chore for him. He was brilliant and a very political animal, and I have never been able to believe the sexual gossip I've heard about him. All I ever saw was a devoted husband and father, and he loved to try to tease Jackie out of the shyness she was prey to at this time. She didn't travel with his plane, but she would often join us at different cities.

Watching him walk stiffly to a waiting car after a long day would so remind me of Franklin Roosevelt. The whole man reminded me of Roosevelt, and I knew then, as I know now, that he, like FDR before him, would make great changes for the majority of the people in America, their aspirations, purposes, and living standards. Standing on a platform with my fellow actors, I developed almost a reverence for him. I memorized his features—his light-colored hair and the cowlick on the back of his head, the way his eyes slanted down as mine did (and those of my relatives in St. Louis), and his simple and direct contact with his audience. He never talked down to anybody. He assumed that everyone had gone to Harvard.

Sometimes, even then, I would get little waves of fear. It seemed to me that this man had never known evil. Though he had been in the war, I knew he was not perceiving the strength of the hate directed at him, mainly because of his position on civil rights, and could therefore not guard against it. Among my Republican acquaintances, I was hearing what they had said about Roosevelt —that he was betraying his class.

At a closing rally, when he was standing on Broadway and Ninety-sixth Street—this rally I had organized near my A&P store on election eve—I had a fleeting, strange wish, just for a second—a feeling that I wanted him not to be elected. In less than three years, I was to understand those feelings of foreboding. He was too open and honest to survive in the complicated Mafioso–greed-ridden society that developed in America. Someone else might call it intuition, but it was my perception of the hatred that existed against black Americans. For a time Lyndon Johnson was able to override it with civil-rights legislation that John Kennedy had planned. I hope, now in the eighties, with a new generation, it has not been diluted. Sometimes when I have a 3:00 A.M. case of the dooms, I wonder if it has.

In late October, I received a letter from Stanley Kubrick, who was in England, telling me that he was preparing a film script from the novel *Lolita* by Vladimir Nabokov, and he wanted me to meet Mr. Nabokov in New York to discuss the role of Charlotte, so would I read the book? Nabokov wanted my impressions of his novel. I was very busy with the election, but I managed to squeeze in time on planes and platforms to read *Lolita*. I was thunderstruck by Nabokov's genius and dazzling stylistic literary acrobatics.

Somewhere John Kennedy saw me reading *Lolita* and broke into laughter. He sent Pierre Salinger over to tell me I should get a brown paper cover for the book if I had to read it in such public places. In those days, *Lolita* was considered a literary scandal, although critics such as F. W. Dupee had acclaimed it a masterpiece. But I managed, as per Mr. Kubrick's request, to read the book and meet Vladimir Nabokov at Rumpelmayer's in between my campaigning.

I was greatly in awe of Nabokov, but he made me relax and had me discussing the pseudointellectual suburbanite Charlotte (my role) at great length. He had me meet his wife at dinner at the Sherry Netherland, and obviously she had to approve of me, which she must have, because the next time I returned to New York after campaigning, the film script of *Lolita* was waiting for me. I had many fights with my agent about signing this contract. I insisted that they had to wait to begin shooting until after the inauguration of John Kennedy so I could attend the inaugural ball.

"Shelley!" he shouted back. "Number one, what makes you so sure he'll be elected? Number two, they have Peter Sellers in this given time period to make the picture, and number three, after a worldwide search, they've got a kid named Sue Lyon under contract.

They're shooting it in England and making England look like America.''

Kubrick could not shoot the picture in the U.S. because of the censorship that existed in America before the sexual revolution of the late sixties and seventies.

"For God's sakes," my agent continued, "this is a chance to work with the great director Stanley Kubrick! Get off your damn campaign trail and get back to being an actress!"

After much screaming, we finally settled the contract as follows: I would leave immediately after the presidential election, and Kubrick signed in blood that I could come back to America from London and attend the inauguration and the inaugural ball. He would so arrange his shooting schedule that it would be possible.

I forget how much money I got for this film, but at Rumpelmayer's with Nabokov, during the final discussions, I had a tuna-fish sandwich and a chocolate milk shake, my standard tranquilizer, and at the Sherry Netherland with Mr. and Mrs. Nabokov, it was the only time I ever had oysters Rockefeller (they're awful—raw caviar on raw oysters).

Meanwhile, back at Broadway and Ninety-sixth Street on election eve, my English friends Peter and Mary Noble had joined the thousands of people waiting for Kennedy to show up, and, even though they were British citizens, the Nobles had red, white, and blue Kennedy straw hats on, and they stood in the rain in front of the A&P, shivering along with me, Mrs. Roosevelt, Governor Herbert Lehman of New York, and Governor Abe Ribicoff of Connecticut.

John Kennedy was very late, and I was getting angrier and angrier. Where the hell was his motorcade? I had organized this rally with my West Side Reform Democratic Committee, and, although I had traveled all over the U.S. for him, he was very late for my party. I dreaded to think what would happen if he did not show up. The least thing that would happen would be that I would never go to my A&P again. I'd have to shop for groceries on the East Side. Finally, in desperation, after having

kept the crowd quiet for two hours with my union songs,
I dashed into the A&P and called Pierre Salinger at the
Carlyle. Salinger told me that Carmine DeSapio had
taken Kennedy over to the silk-stocking district on the
East Side to make appearances for the rich people. They
only represented a few votes, as far as I was concerned.
Salinger promised to get in a car and find the candidate
and make DeSapio bring Kennedy over immediately to
my rally, because he had to be at the Coliseum by 9:00
P.M. for the huge television audience. I made Pierre
swear, by all that was holy, that he would do that immediately, and I went back to my rally, which by now was
pretty hostile. The mob had been standing in the cold rain
since 5:00 P.M., and the police had been trying to keep
order.

Just then, Mrs. Roosevelt got out of her limousine and
said a few well-chosen words to this immense, hostile
throng. Magically, they all became like fourth graders,
listening attentively to a loving but strict teacher. Bentley
Kassal, who was an assemblyman then, said a few words
in Spanish and was booed slightly. Either the crowd was
getting more restive, or his Spanish was lousy.

And then, at this most tense moment of the evening,
we began to hear the sirens of John Kennedy's motorcade. I rushed to his limousine door, threw it open, and
said:

"Senator Kennedy! I'll never be able to go to this A&P
again!"

He looked at me, a little confused, but I didn't bother
explaining. I just managed to utter:

"This interracial audience has been standing in the rain
since five o'clock."

Despite the cold, without an overcoat, Kennedy got up
to the platform, with help, and stood there in the rain. He
said something in Spanish, and maybe his Spanish was
better than Bentley's, because the crowd went wild. It
seemed to me that fireworks went off. How the police
kept the crowd back from the platform, I still don't know.
It looked as if people were jumping out the windows of
the tenements surrounding us. They quieted down after
twenty minutes, and Senator Kennedy said:

"Tomorrow we get a chance to vote for ourselves and our children—against the landlords, against the bigots, against the special interests. I'll see you at the ballot box."

I don't know exactly what happened next, but I was in a limousine with Peter and Mary Noble, Abraham Ribicoff, and John Kennedy. My two English friends were numb with excitement. When the limousine arrived at the Coliseum, they somehow got in the first row, and I was shoved onto the stage, where my fellow actors, who had journeyed across the country on the campaign plane, were seated. The crowd at the Coliseum went wild, of course, but all I noticed was that Mrs. Roosevelt was late getting to the platform, and Carmine DeSapio, who was sitting in the first row on the platform, refused to get up and give her his seat. He wanted to be near Kennedy so he would be in camera range. I stood up where he could see me, and I must have looked as if I was going to punch him out, which I was, so he finally got up and left his seat, which I held for Mrs. Roosevelt. Then I went back to the third row, where I belonged.

John Kennedy made a great speech that election eve, and I sat there with my fingers crossed, full of hope at the promise he offered to all of America, and especially to the postwar generations. I, like most Americans, was beginning to realize that we had won the long war but were losing the peace, and I knew in my soul that John Kennedy would reverse the trend toward cynicism, *greed,* and bigotry. I was sure of that, and that night I prayed for his election. I do not know exactly how they count the electoral votes, but, late that night, Bentley Kassal called me away from the television set, where I sat riveted with my family. Kassal told me that John Kennedy had carried our district. In a couple of hours, I knew that *that* district had carried New York City, which had carried the state, and I hoped the large number of electoral votes of New York would carry the election. Maybe again I was thinking omnipotently but that's what the now–Superior Court judge Kassal told me the next day.

The entire Democratic Committee was sitting in a large ballroom, watching the election returns. There were almost a thousand people in the ballroom, and there wasn't a sound. As each state was announced, and the number of electoral votes was added to the right, there would be cheers if it was for Kennedy and groans if it was for Nixon. In between the announcements, that ballroom was practically silent.

Paul Schutzer and I kept shuttling between the ballroom and the hotel suite, where the candidate and his large family were watching television. I would hold my breath when I was in the elevator, fearful of a large state swinging for Nixon. Paul was taking pictures in both places, but he was very sensitive to the reactions of the Kennedy family, and, even though there were a lot of reporters and photographers in that suite, they didn't bother the Kennedys too much. Paul kept taking close-up pictures of the various party workers, me included, watching the board with the election results. He was such a good photographer that you were almost unconscious of him photographing you.

It was almost 3:00 or 4:00 A.M. when we finally knew that Kennedy was elected. It was a joyful celebration, but there was a strange quality to it. It seemed there was almost a quality of relief in the victory. It was almost more important to defeat Nixon than elect Kennedy.

Later Nixon was to run, unsuccessfully, for governor of California. He was defeated. To this day, I cannot believe that California, after refusing to elect him governor, gave its electoral votes to make him president of the U.S. A few years ago, I read in the *Los Angeles Times* that there had been a fire in a warehouse in Van Nuys, California. The firemen found many ballot boxes with votes for Humphrey that had obviously not been counted in the Humphrey-Nixon presidential race. *The New York Times* also carried this story.

But in 1960, there was a mass feeling, especially in New York, of joy and relief that John Kennedy had been elected, if only by eighty-four electoral votes.

Election night, I could not go to the victory party, because I had to rush home and pack my things, my mother's things, my child's things, and Kathy and Molly's things. I had promised Kubrick and my agent that I would get to London as fast as I could after Kennedy's victory, and I was rushing to fulfill my promise. If Kennedy had been defeated, I doubt that I would have done *Lolita*. I think I would have been too sad and angry to pack.

21

Stanley Kubrick had been puzzled why I needed three adults and myself to take care of my six-year-old, but those had been my contractual demands—five round-trip tickets. We went on BOAC, so perhaps, since it was an American film being shot in London, they got the tickets free from the British airline.

In those days, the fancy hotels, like the Dorchester and the Savoy and Claridges, would isolate a wing or a section of a floor when they had actors staying in their hotels. So my entourage and myself were installed on the top floor in a wing that contained the Oliver Messel Suite, where Elizabeth Taylor and *her* entourage were staying, Jack Palance and his wife and children were in another suite, Kirk Douglas was there too, and the Shelley Winters Road Company.

Elizabeth was in London doing the first version of *Cleopatra*, with Peter Finch as Antony. I believe, in the early sixties, the studios had "blocked money," which they had to spend in the country where they earned it—this was true of Italy, France, and England—so some genius at Twentieth Century–Fox had this brilliant idea of shooting *Cleopatra* with all its gorgeous outdoor sets in London. The huge sets were crumbling in the British damp even as they were building them. Nevertheless, they managed to spend about £5 million (and a dollar was about four of what it is now) before they realized they had to do it in Rome.

At the first rehearsal of *Lolita*, I reminded Stanley Kubrick, Peter Sellers, and poor little Sue Lyon that they had promised I could go back to Washington for John F. Kennedy's inaugural. They promised again, and I phoned Paul Schutzer in D.C. to tell him I was having a dress made by the queen's couturier, Hartnell, and I expected him to spend some of the time, when he wasn't photographing the inaugural, dancing with me. He stuttered a little on the phone but promised that if he couldn't, Henry Luce would.

We had been installed in a beautiful three-bedroom suite at the Dorch, around the curve in the corridor from the elegant Oliver Messel Suite. The very night I arrived, Elizabeth called me and urged me to please come over for a drink and we'd reminisce about *A Place in the Sun*. I didn't know why it seemed so urgent right there and then.

I'd gotten my little family safely ensconced in our suite, and before you could say "Long live the queen!" I had "electric fires" placed in every room of this suite. Even though the Dorch was a hotel that catered to Americans, their idea of acceptable heating was about fifteen degrees below our American idea of central heating. I took an English shower (you sit in the tub and hold the spray over your soaped body), got into a housecoat, and traipsed over to Elizabeth's messy Messel Suite.

She had a secretary, a German couple, a chauffeur, and Eddie Fisher running around for her and her three kids. Various cats and dogs were underfoot as well. The kids were already in bed, and Elizabeth and I proceeded to drink gorgeous gin martinis and eat chili sent via TWA from Chasen's in Beverly Hills. During the next weeks, I realized that Elizabeth never ate anything from London for dinner. We had stone crab from Florida, smoked salmon from Barney Greengrass's in New York, steaks from Chicago, shrimp remoulade from New Orleans, barbecued spare ribs from St. Louis, white asparagus from France, linguini and clam sauce from Genoa, and, for all I know, chop suey from China. I think around noon every day she would call Howard Hughes and give him her order. I believe Elizabeth was originally British, and the food at the Dorch was pretty snazzy, though rich and boring after a while. But Howard Hughes must have had a crush on her, because every night there were different goodies from some faraway place.

It took about two days for me to realize that Elizabeth did not want to be alone with Eddie Fisher ever. She would leave for the studio quite early in the morning—early is about 10:00 for Elizabeth—and then start calling me about 8:00 P.M. insisting that I join her for dinner. Since my daughter would be fast asleep by 8:00 and my mother and nurse and Molly exhausted from shopping, I would usually trail down our private corridor and find out what was new on the menu.

Elizabeth and Eddie were beginning to be rather testy with each other, and I guess I was the damper that kept things from getting too volatile. London was damp enough already, and I didn't relish this role at all, but since I'd already seen Elizabeth through two engagements and followed her three marriages, I felt I should stand by and help her through whatever was going on in her young life at the time. Besides, it was fun.

I remember when we'd filmed *A Place in the Sun* together. She was seventeen, and she could not understand the fact that in a few months, when she was eighteen, she could move out and away from her parents and have her own apartment. So, consequently, she got engaged to not one but two different all-American football players during the shooting of *A Place in the Sun*, but, after all, the picture had a very long shooting schedule. As soon as the film was over, she up and married Nicky Hilton in a magnificently produced wedding that I believe cost over $1 million. All the events in Elizabeth's life have conspired to give her no idea of the value or reality of money. When we were just beginning to shoot *A Place in the Sun*, we both bought blond shirred beaver coats. I think they were $1,800 or $1,900. It took me four days of agonizing over my bank account to spend that much money on a coat. It took Elizabeth two minutes. When I asked the furrier if he could come down in price because we were buying two of them, Elizabeth went into gales of laughter. As a matter of fact, I saved us each $200. She was so delighted that she took me, her hairdresser, her makeup man, and her secretary out to a very expensive lunch and spent the $200.

During the time she was married to Nicky Hilton, she shopped most of the time, because she didn't want to stay home with him. The boy obviously had a very serious drinking problem. She constantly bought everyone presents, including her animals. Whatever Elizabeth's faults, lack of generosity is not one of them.

While she was married to Mike Wilding, he went broke. I don't think it ever sank in, because she proceeded to have not one but two very expensive children. (She couldn't work when she was pregnant and that cost them and MGM a fortune.) When nineteen-year-old Elizabeth looked at a merchant with those huge violet eyes, he gave her anything she wanted, even things she didn't want, and sent the bill to Michael two or three months later.

I remember once, during her second pregnancy, when I was married to Vittorio Gassman and also pregnant, we went up to Michael Todd's house to a barbecue. Todd had been living with Evelyn Keyes for a number of years. A very pregnant Debbie Reynolds and her husband Eddie Fisher were the other guests. As the evening progressed, we all decided to play poker. After a couple of hours, with the stakes getting higher and higher, the women dropped out. Michael Todd was a consummate poker player, and, in an hour or so, he had most of the chips in front of him. Vittorio was a little less than even, but Eddie Fisher and Michael Wilding were losing very heavily, and owed the bank a great deal of money. Suddenly, Michael Todd accidentally overturned the poker table, mixing up all the chips, 90 percent of which were his. Several thousand dollars were involved. He seemed to think it was very funny, and when I looked at Elizabeth, who was looking at Michael Todd, it flashed through my mind that sooner or later she was going to marry that man. It turned out to be sooner.

* * *

I remember well the great party that Michael Todd had for Elizabeth for the premiere of *Around the World in 80 Days*. Sixteen thousand people filled Madison Square Garden. Every single person seated in the Garden that night got a 22-karat-gold present. I got a Tiffany gold compact, which is still in the vault, and Marty Fried, a young director who was my escort, got a gold cigarette case. Elizabeth rode around the arena in a gold chariot, pulled by six white horses, wearing a dress made of nude-colored chiffon floating behind her, with that gorgeous body outlined and those violet eyes flashing fire. The sixteen thousand people cheered her beauty for fifteen minutes. I have never seen Elizabeth before or since look so glorious. Wearing a huge diamond tiara, she truly looked like a goddess who had decided to visit the earth. She and Mike Todd dwelled on Mount Olympus for the few short years they were together. Her grief at his death was so terrible that her family and friends despaired of her recovery. Thank God she had Liza and the other children. I think this was the reason she had to live.

Seeing her in London that winter, gazing at Eddie Fisher with despair, made me wonder how it had happened. What funny fate had brought her to this place? Had she married Eddie because he was Mike Todd's best friend, and so in that way she felt she had not lost Mike? It certainly seemed like that to me, that London winter.

Mornings, Elizabeth would want me to drive out to the studio with her. It was a long, foggy trip, and we would chat and laugh, or sleep, in the back of the big old Rolls-Royce they had assigned to her, but as our pictures progressed, we kept getting to work later and later. Whenever I went to her suite to pick her up after a hurried breakfast, Elizabeth would be with a salesperson from Harrods or somewhere, ordering some item that could be sent to her that evening. One morning at six o'clock, she was inspecting an exquisite handmade negligee, and she quickly ordered it in pink, blue, mauve, black, white, and nude. When we were finally in the car on the way to the studio, I asked her:

"Why do you have to buy these things before we go to work?"

"I'm getting two thousand pounds a day per diem," she replied, looking at me plaintively, "and I have to spend it by midnight, and I have no time to shop while we're shooting."

I looked at her in amazement and asked, "Who told you that?"

"When I looked at the contract, my agent had gotten me eight thousand dollars a day expenses to induce me to come to cold England to do *Cleopatra* in the winter."

"But, Elizabeth," I said, "why do you think you have to spend that eight thousand dollars every single day before midnight?"

She looked at me blankly and said, "Shelley, the contract says per diem, and you know how strange the English treasury is about taking pounds out of the country. Two thousand pounds amounts to about eight thousand dollars a day. It's paid to me in pounds, so I have to spend it here."

I took her hand and said, "Elizabeth, I guarantee you, you can spend it at the end of each week or on Saturday or Sunday. Why don't you buy Eddie a Rolls-Royce so he can get out of the hotel and not always be underfoot? He's pretty depressed with you working all the time, and he's alone with the kids and animals."

To my knowledge, Eddie never went to any of the tourist attractions that were all over London at that time, or even theater matinees. If I came home early, I would see him sitting in the bar, evidently since early morning, and not having tea. He was in a very depressed and despairing mood. He looked as if he was evaluating what he had done to his career and his life by divorcing the mother of his very young children, Debbie Reynolds.

Watching him getting quite drunk at the bar one night, I flashed on a time I had seen him on his own weekly TV show, when Debbie had been his wife, and his guest. She had been brilliant—a hilarious comedienne and great singer and dancer—but in the process she had made Eddie Fisher look like an amateur. I doubt whether she had realized that at the time. I guess she had thought she was helping him and his TV show.

In retrospect, I guess Debbie and Elizabeth rolled over poor Eddie like a couple of Sherman tanks. I had always thought he was a marvelous singer, and charming and funny. Hollywood just wasn't the place for him to have a fruitful life and career. Well, he wasn't the first, and he won't be the last.

In 1960, when I was holding Elizabeth's hand in the Rolls, she considered my suggestion about giving Eddie a car and said, "That's a good idea, Shelley. You're sure I can save the money up until the end of the week?"

"Order it on Saturday," I said, "and pay them three thousand pounds on Monday, Tuesday, Wednesday, Thursday, and Friday."

She believed me, and she bought two of them, one for Eddie and one for herself. Rolls-Royces were about $25,000 in those days.

Stanley Kubrick and James Mason were getting very annoyed with my lateness. When I explained to them about Elizabeth's £2,000 a day and how we had to spend it before we left for the studio each morning, Kubrick ordered me to have my own car bring me to work and notified Elizabeth's producer that I had to study lines by myself every morning. Spoilsport!

But I must say, working with him was an exhilarating experience. Kubrick understood one of the most valuable things a director can know. Young directors seldom know it. He would take the time in rehearsals to make you do exactly what he needed for a scene and make you think it was your idea and had come out of your own creativity and life experience. You never knew it until you saw the scene in the rushes. I don't know if a non-actor can understand this creative process, but it is the greatest gift a director can give an actor. I believe Stanley Kubrick, George Stevens, Robert Wise, George Cukor, and Roman Polanski are the only directors I ever worked with who understood the delicate mechanism of an actor's psyche. For instance, when a singer or a painter or a dancer shows a director his work and he changes or rejects it, he is addressing that artist's special technique. When an actor shows a director his work, he is exhibiting his looks, his voice, his mannerisms, his intellect, his total human experience, the whole complex mechanism that makes up a human being. When a director rejects or changes this, an actor feels rebuffed and rejected, and his creative talent is thus often blocked. A wise director makes an actor realize his performance, and does not impose it upon him.

I think the role of Charlotte in *Lolita* is one of the best performances I ever gave in any medium. She is dumb and cunning, silly, sad, sexy, and bizarre, and totally American and human. Until I saw the whole film cut together, I did not realize the gift that Kubrick had given me. I was enchanted with Charlotte and very proud of her. Kubrick had the insight to find the areas of me that were pseudointellectual and pretentious. We all have those things in us.

I found Peter Sellers and James Mason to be the strangest actors I've ever worked with. James Mason was handsome and sexy and very, very intelligent, but most aloof and technical. Perhaps it was Humbert Humbert, the character he was playing. He always seemed outside of his role watching himself—and me. I felt terribly frustrated when doing a scene with him, but, then again, when I saw the rushes, he was hilarious and marvelous. His asides were so quiet that, when we were acting, I never even heard them. He was constantly repeating the ends of my sentences, and while he seemed to be intently gazing into my eyes, his ears seemed to become another set of eyes, looking at my nubile fourteen-year-old daughter, Lolita. Well, they say about great acting, you must listen with your eyes and look with your ears. James Mason did this magnificently. I really had to work very hard to keep him from stealing every scene from me.

Peter Sellers seemed to be acting on a different planet. The audiences weren't very outer-space-conscious in 1961, but I never could connect with him. Whenever I complained to Kubrick about trying to connect with my two leading men, he would agree with me. But he didn't change their performances, and this very frustration that

I had in real life was what was so sad and funny about Charlotte. I never felt anyone was listening to me when I talked, except for the sound man. Again, I didn't understand the lonely quality it gave me until I saw the film.

Although I am fairly free sexually on paper or when I am alone with a husband or lover in the bedroom—in front of a camera or on the stage I freeze. There was a very simple scene of my wedding night with James Mason. I had on a silk robe, which I still have, and Kubrick wanted me to sit on the bed, drop the robe with my back to the camera, hold the cover up, get into bed with James Mason, and snuggle up against his back. Nothing showed. If I did the scene right, only my bare back would be exposed to the camera for a second. Then Humbert sort of starts making love to me, staring at a picture of Lolita over my shoulder.

I could not do it. I fell out of the bed, I pushed James Mason out of the other side of the bed, I tore the robe, I hit the mike with my head, I got the lines mixed up, I broke James's glasses. At one point he said, "I think there are a couple of other people in bed with us." Instead of being sexual, I was clutching the robe to my bosom. Imagine any awkward thing, and I did it during that day we were trying to shoot that scene. At lunchtime, they fed me gin, they cleared the set of the unnecessary crew (by now, the entire crew of *Cleopatra* had come over to watch "the klutz"), and Mason marveled:

"I can't believe you can't do such a simple thing! Drop the robe in the back, cover your bosom, get under the cover, and snuggle up against me."

I just couldn't, and, after spending a day trying to get this scene, at 4:30 P.M. Kubrick said, "Well, I know it's going to look silly, but keep the damn robe on and get in the bed and snuggle up against his back."

By now, we'd done a lot of takes. So the audience wouldn't know whether I'd taken off the robe or not, the camera panned in on a close-up of James Mason's face, which by now he could hardly keep straight.

So that's the way we did it, and it does look silly in the movie. If you rush out and get the cassette of *Lolita*, you'll see it's so. Thank God for dissolves.

That scene, though, broke the ice between James Mason and myself. At one point, when I was squirming with embarrassment under the covers with just panties on, Mason whispered to me:

"Would it make you feel more comfortable if I tell you that a long time ago my name was Moskowitz, and not Mason?"

"No," I whispered back. "The only thing that would make me feel more comfortable is if you lie absolutely still when I put my naked bosom up against your back."

"That would be very ungallant," James said.

I think that's the one and only nude scene I ever attempted in films.

I was seeing a lot of Peter and Mary Noble, who had two beautiful young daughters, Tina and Kara. Tina was a year older than my daughter, and Kara a year younger. Whenever I got back from the studio, my daughter would regale me with all the adventures she and the Noble children were having in and around London. After a few weeks, I swear she was developing a British accent and was absolutely addicted to high tea. If I got home early, she would put on her Mary Janes and little white gloves, and we would go down to the Dorchester lobby and have tea. Her nanny, Kathy, was overjoyed at how my boisterous New York kid was now behaving with proper British etiquette.

We would often go out to dinner, but my mother was suspicious of the food in the expensive restaurants. Molly found a section of Harrods that cooked delicious takeout food, and we somehow managed to have rare roast beef with horseradish dressing, brussels sprouts, and Yorkshire pudding, all heated up on a two-burner electric plate in the huge bathroom. I was getting what I thought was a lot of money for my per diem, but nothing compared to Elizabeth's. Since I could not take it back to the States, my mother, the nurse, and Molly were not trying to be thrifty. It was just that after a while you got tired of restaurant food. The living room of my suite had a large, low cocktail table, and we would all sit on the floor around it and have family dinners about three times a week. On Sundays we usually went to the Nobles', and if it wasn't snowing or raining we ate in their garden. England in November is cold, but they had a lovely gazebo in the garden with an electric fire.

Thanksgiving is an American holiday celebrating the pilgrims' escaping from Britain. Peter still felt Mary should cook a huge turkey for all the Americans who were filming in London away from their families. Peter got a huge turkey through his connections with the American embassy. Mary, Molly, Kathy, and Mother cooked a traditional Thanksgiving sit-down dinner for thirty-five people, including Albert Finney, Michael Caine, Sarah Miles, the Boulting twins, the Kubricks, Françoise Sagan, Sean Connery, Elizabeth and Eddie, and Peter Finch and his beautiful wife. Every time Peter and Elizabeth had a conversation in a corner, Eddie would have two martinis. In that version of *Cleopatra*, Peter was playing Antony to Elizabeth's Cleopatra, and they obviously had plenty to talk about. Very few people are aware that Richard Burton was Elizabeth's second Mark Antony, Peter Finch being the first. To this day I wonder what happened to all that film they shot that winter and why Fox hasn't released the Elizabeth Taylor–Peter Finch version in some form. I'm sure the American public would find it fascinating. That night, when we all trooped out onto Abbey Road to get in our cars, I had the feeling that Eddie Fisher was trying to run over Peter Finch with his new Rolls-Royce.

Stanley Kubrick kept watching Mary Noble, who had long red hair, and when she chose to, could be a bit of a vamp. That night he cast her as Clare Quilty's mysterious lady friend. Clare Quilty was of course played by Peter Sellers. I don't believe even Mary ever really understood her role. She was sort of Peter Sellers's alter ego, also his mistress, or his procurer. She was funny and eerie in the picture, but she would never question Kubrick about her motivations. British theater manners. I guess she didn't have to.

The work intensified on *Lolita*. I was working hard and didn't see Elizabeth for a number of weeks. In the middle of December, I heard that she had been very ill with pneumonia, and she had had a tracheotomy to save her life. When I called her suite around the twentieth of December, somebody very rude with a German accent grunted, "She's in Palm Springs!" I found out that Elizabeth was recuperating and would be back the night of Christmas day. I thought no more about it. I was glad she was getting well.

The next night I worked very late. It was rather unusual, because it was the custom on British stages for the shop foreman to call the quarter at 5:00 P.M., which meant the crew voted whether the scene in progress had to be finished that night or could go on to the next day. This was an artistic decision that the laborers made, which would drive the American directors working in London crazy. But that was the union rule. It sounds pretty weird, but if you were an actress over thirty trying to look beautiful all the time, you were pretty grateful not to have to do your close-ups at 6:00, 7:00, or 8:00 P.M., having been up since 5:00 A.M. Consequently, I always was very fond of the British labor unions.

James and I were doing the scene in which he finds out that I have sent Lolita away to camp, and from there she's going directly to a boarding school—and he makes up his mind to kill me. During this scene I find his diary and try to kill him. It was a tragic and hilarious scene, but it was very difficult to get the proper nuances Stanley Kubrick wanted. When I finally got it in rehearsal, the shop foreman and the crew seemed to understand that we had to work overtime to get this sensitive black-comedy scene which we were in the middle of, so we worked until 8:00 P.M. I fell asleep in the car going home, and the chauffeur woke me up when we got to the Dorch about 9:00 P.M.

When I opened the door to my suite, there was my daughter with three strange but familiar-looking children under the Christmas tree. The children were all bathed and pajamaed, and they were playing poker. There was a little girl about three and two boys about five and seven. My mother motioned me to be silent, and we listened to the little girl explain the most complicated rules of poker.

My daughter and the two boys were having trouble grasping the concept of an inside straight. So was I.

I motioned my mother into the bathroom and asked her where these children had come from. She said she'd found them in the stairwell, dirty and hungry. I asked her whose children they were.

"I don't know," she said, "but I wasn't going to put them out into the wet London street in front of the Dorchester."

I looked at my mother and the nurse Kathy and Molly as if they were nuts and immediately called downstairs and asked if anyone had reported three missing children. Puzzled and pompous, the hall porter said, "No! None of *our* guests *have* any children!" Obviously, he meant the transients, not us regulars.

Then I called the housekeeper and asked if any of the help had missed any children. They didn't quite know how to answer this strange question, and they said they would make inquiries, but they didn't think so. My mother was getting very angry and said:

"What do you want to do, call up the police and give them away? Can't it wait until after Christmas?"

The children finished their poker game and hot cocoa and toast, and I put the little girl on my lap and asked her her name.

"Liza Todd," she answered.

Then I found out the boys were Michael and Christopher, and I realized my mother had kidnapped Elizabeth Taylor's children. I had never actually met them, because I had only seen Elizabeth early in the morning, when we went to work, or late at night, after the children went to sleep. I asked my mother how long she had had the children, and she said, "Since ten o'clock this morning. I gave them breakfast."

Knowing that Elizabeth was in Palm Springs, I quickly called the manager and asked him to meet me in front of the Oliver Messel Suite and hung up.

I convinced him to use his key and open the door, since the phone wasn't answering. In his best British business manner, he informed me that Elizabeth, Eddie, and her secretary were in Palm Springs. But after much arguing, he opened the door. This suite had once been beautiful, full of rare antiques and paintings. Now, a remarkable mess met our eyes. The young German couple she had hired and four or five of their friends were dead drunk. There were trays of room-service food all over the place. The phones were off the hook, and the animals had obviously not been taken out for several days. They really had trashed the place.

The manager managed to wake up the male part of this high-priced couple. I realized this situation would be very unfavorable publicity for Elizabeth, even though she'd just been terribly ill. I read the riot act to this man and told him that if he wasn't out of the place in an hour with everything left clean and intact, he and his wife would be in prison and then deported back to Siberia. With that, the manager and I left.

I was shaking with anger. I called the Palm Springs operator, and she somehow located the house where Elizabeth was recuperating. In 1960, Palm Springs was a small town. She and Eddie were the guests of some Hollywood big shot, and she had indeed been very very ill. She was quite worried since she had not been able to get that German couple who were with her children on the phone. I assured her I had plenty of help with my nanny and housekeeper and mother, and we had her children in my suite.

She started to cry and asked me how her kids were. I reassured her that they were fine and did not tell her that my mother had found them in the stairwell dirty and hungry. I just told her that Liza was teaching them all poker. She kept weeping on the phone. She did not know where Michael Wilding or her mother and father were. Eddie got on the phone and told me that Elizabeth had been desperately ill and almost died in the few weeks I hadn't seen her. Elizabeth is not a great crier, but it took me a while to get her calm, and she promised me she would just worry about getting well. My mother would take care of them.

I know it is tough to raise one child by yourself, so I cannot imagine how a woman who is an actress and must travel all the time can raise three small children by her-

self, no matter how much paid help she has. Paid help is
not the same as love. Why Eddie couldn't have stayed in
London with the children is still a mystery to me, but
perhaps he wanted to see his own children at Christmas,
if Debbie let him. Elizabeth could have asked me to help.
I guess she knew how hard I was working and what a
tough director Kubrick was. I told her we would charge
presents at Harrods to her, and her kids would have two
Christmases—Christmas Eve and when she came home
to the Dorch on Christmas Day.

What followed was a glorious week for my daughter
and Elizabeth's children. I have always wanted to write
a children's book about the adventures of these kids the
week before Christmas. Perhaps someday I will.

Elizabeth had been carried to the plane on a stretcher,
and the children had not been out of the hotel since she
had left about two weeks ago. Every day, all day and
night, her chauffeur had sat out in front of the Dorch in
Eddie's Rolls-Royce. The children had never been taken
anywhere. My mother and Katherine proceeded to take
them to the pantomimes, they met Prince Charles and
Princess Anne at the circus, they went to the zoo, and
they met Father Christmas all over London. I think my
mother had as much fun as they did. Whenever I came
home from work, they told me about the great day they
had had. The huge staff at the Dorch brought them all
Christmas goodies. Mother too was stuffing them as if
they were Christmas geese with homemade food she'd
cooked at the Nobles'. They each gained about five
pounds. This was no chore for my mother, who loved
children. While I had been growing up, there always had
been an extra baby or very young child my mother was
taking care of for some neighbor. One we had so long I
began to think she was my sister.

I think the best night those children had was when I
was able to take them to the Old Vic to see a matinee of
Emil and the Detectives, a famous British pantomime.
When we came out of the theater, it was dark. Since it
was Christmas Eve, there were no cabs. I had given all
the chauffeurs the night off. It was cold and clear, and
the stars were shining above the Thames. Elizabeth's

children treated the walk home across the bridge as the greatest event of their young lives. When they were with Elizabeth or in the hotel, they always had to be guarded and supervised. Nobody knew who they were or cared, as they ran ahead and then back across the bridge and played on the deserted sidewalks, and, although my mother found it a bit of a hike, this freedom was the greatest gift we could have given those children.

It was very difficult getting the children to sleep that night, they were so excited, and I once again reminded them that their mother would be home the next night. They seemed to have the impression that since they had stayed in Shelley's "house" for a couple of weeks, my daughter would now stay in their "house" for the next couple of weeks. I began to realize that Elizabeth's children had lived in so many hotels that they thought of hotels as their house. I decided that I wouldn't discuss it until their mother arrived, and perhaps they would forget this plan.

Christmas Eve, I had all their little socks up on the mantelpiece, and Kathy and Molly had bought fanciful, funny little presents at Woolworth's and Marks and Spencer, which the kids called Marks and Sparks. We held back my daughter's presents because Elizabeth was bringing Father Christmas's presents to her kids. That Christmas dinner was a memorable one for the rest of the Dorchester's guests. I promise you, four excited kids can wreck any dining room, no matter how grand and pompous it is. We lasted through the roasted goose, but the *maître d'hôtel* gladly sent our Christmas pudding up to my suite.

Elizabeth and Eddie arrived around 4:00 P.M. Christmas Day, and I couldn't believe what she had brought my daughter: *two pink kittens*. I do not mean white or red —I mean Persian pink kittens. They are called creams. When they were curled up, they looked like huge pink powder puffs. I knew Elizabeth loved animals, but my housekeeper was allergic to cats, and I couldn't see dragging them back and forth from New York to California or wherever else in the world I had to take my family. But my child immediately fell in love with them. I found out later Elizabeth paid £300 apiece for those kittens—about $800 each. She'd ordered them in London from Palm Springs.

Elizabeth's children traipsed happily back to the Oliver Messel Suite. Elizabeth gave my mother a big hug and kiss, and a white mink stole, which of course I borrowed constantly. As I talked with Elizabeth, I realized she had somehow come to terms with Eddie, and she looked well and happy. Even Eddie looked happier, and, if possible, in some way sadder, too. I'm not sure, but I think Debbie had not allowed him to see his children.

My child was not able to take her eyes off those kittens for the next forty-eight hours. These cream puffs only ate shredded lobster and ground sirloin or Devonshire cream, which they would then throw up all over the bathroom. I would have to take them to the vet every twelve hours, and the vet that Elizabeth recommended charged the equivalent of $50 a visit. Either they had been taken away from their mother too early or they were just sickly or perhaps they were overbred or allergic to me.

These kittens were the cause of a great disruption between my daughter and myself. I made a great mistake. I let her have them and play with them until we were ready to go back to New York, and then I told her some nonsense like they were not allowed to fly or be taken out of England and gave them to Sue Lyon when *Lolita* was finished. When we got back to New York, my daughter immediately learned the truth from someone, and she has not forgiven me yet, almost twenty-five years later. They were gorgeous little animals with huge blue eyes, and they adored her. They slept with her, and she fed them from the palm of her hand, but they were so fragile and overbred, and Molly indeed had attacks of asthma when they got near her. I felt it was too dangerous to bring them home to New York.

To this day, Mary Noble is furious that she didn't take those kittens. She and Peter had about ten or eleven cats at that time, and they couldn't see their way to acquiring two more, but now they only have five, and they miss those two rare little pink creams. To make up for it, on a later visit, I gave them a blue angora kitten. Honest, they have blue and pink kittens in England.

Between Christmas and New Year's, there was a command performance, I have forgotten of which of my films, but it was a grand evening, and I was presented to the queen. I wore a beautiful white satin dress that I'd flown over to Paris one weekend to get, and Mother's white mink jacket. The Royal Cinema Board presented me with a gold medal embossed with Queen Elizabeth II's profile. Mother wore it in a gold casing on a charm bracelet for the rest of her life. She and Molly had been in the audience at that command performance. When I asked her why she was so fond of that medal, she told me when my father had been thirteen years old, he'd left Austria. His boat had stopped at Liverpool, and they hadn't let him off the ship. Something had been wrong with his papers. So England had not been very hospitable to my father, but the queen had honored his daughter.

I had been talking to Paul Schutzer on the phone in Washington, where he was still photographing Kennedy, and I had seen him briefly in Paris when I had gone to get my dress at Christian Dior's, but I was beginning to think he was a myth. I did not lose the self-esteem he had given me, so when I began to doubt his existence, I stopped. He was a dedicated artist, and of course his work came first. Also, his family lived in Paris, and that made him seem a little aloof. We sat in Fouquet's on a rainy night that November, and he told me he was catching a plane back to Washington. He handed me my invitation to John Kennedy's inauguration, all tied up with a pretty silver ribbon. He made me promise I would wear the Dior gown to the inaugural ball. I rode out to Orly with him, and he caught his plane for Washington, and I caught a plane back for London. I hate airports.

That New Year's Eve, I went to an elegant party with Peter and Mary Noble. It was given by Bryan Forbes at his Virginia Waters estate outside of London. Bryan Forbes was an actor and writer who later became a director and then head of a studio. It was a beautiful party, with the whole estate lit up, and I was thin and elegant, surrounded by the most desirable men in the world. I spent the evening dancing with Sean Connery and Albert Finney, and once I even danced with Ralph Richardson.

Suddenly, I decided I wanted to be home at the Dorchester with my family at the stroke of midnight. Riding back to London, I again began to wonder why I was so set on living in America—in New York or California. Many of the blacklisted artists from Hollywood were now living in London, and the best theater in the world was there. Whenever I was in England, I became involved in the intelligent, stimulating life that was there. My chums, fellow actors, and the British public treated me like an artist. Even the talk shows that I did then in London were witty and informed. The talk-show hosts never tried to make me feel or act like a blonde bombshell. I was an Oscar-winning actress who worked with great directors. The producers and agents in London were talking to me about working in the West End. Why, oh why, couldn't I make my life there? I couldn't. I was as American as apple pie, and, though I loved everything British, I had to live on my native soil, perhaps because I had been born in almost the exact center of America, St. Louis, Missouri. But I still don't understand why I couldn't have done a season on the West End then. Perhaps simply because I was too afraid.

We woke up my daughter at five minutes until midnight and had a little champagne and kissed each other. There were bells being rung in the corridor of our wing of the Dorch. Elizabeth Taylor's kids and Jack Palance's kids were running up and down the hall—I guess that's why the Dorch put the actors in a separate wing—and we all ended up in Elizabeth's suite, eating strawberries and Devonshire cream and telling ghost stories, and the adults drinking champagne.

Elizabeth looked radiant again, and Jack Palance's daughter and Elizabeth's son Michael, though very young, seemed to be flirting, if it's possible to flirt at six and seven. A couple of decades later, they got married, and I have always felt that their engagement started New Year's Eve 1961.

As I carried my daughter back to her bed, she whispered, "Mommy, is it 1961 for Blanche and Lolly in California, and is it 1961 for Daddy in Italy yet?"

I'm never sure whether it's earlier or later wherever I am in the world, but even then my daughter's mathematical mind had registered that it was eight hours earlier in California and an hour later in Italy. We watched the telly for a while, and I went to sleep. It was the first New Year's Eve since I had been a teenager that I hadn't had a hot date.

I was with my mother and child and friends who loved and respected me and working on an important film with a great director. I was willing to wait.

22

On New Year's Day, we were going to the Nobles' for dinner, which in England is served at 1:00 P.M. I have been trying for three decades to get the Nobles to have Sunday dinner at a civilized hour like 5:00.

My entire entourage taxied over to Abbey Road. Mary Noble was having one of her brilliant open houses for every writer and actor or actress in London. In retrospect I realize that Mary Noble was the Salka Viertel of London. Salka had run a famous salon in Santa Monica during the thirties and forties, frequented by all the talented young people in Hollywood at the time, the famous German refugees like Brecht, Thomas Mann, and Lion Feuchtwanger, and Dylan Thomas, Garbo, and Cukor. During the late fifties and early sixties Mary was doing the same thing on Abbey Road with very little money. Somehow there was always great food and wine and great conversation. Many a great romance and even greater marriages started in her basement dining room. Joan Collins, who I believe was eleven or eighteen at the time, was helping my mother and Kathy and me serve and clear the table. After we had stuffed ourselves, we all lay on cushions on the floor. My head was on Albert Finney's chest and I believe Sean Connery's head was on my chest. We were all dozing comfortably and watching Queen Elizabeth make her New Year's Day speech on the black-and-white telly. Everything seemed copacetic in the British Empire in the beginning of 1961. If the commonwealth was coming apart at the seams, the Queen didn't mention it that New Year's Day.

The filming of *Lolita* continued, and I enjoyed every second of it. Stanley Kubrick directed so quietly. When I would see the rushes at night, I was absolutely amazed. I had known a pseudointellectual suburbanite like Charlotte, the character I played, during my childhood days in Jamaica, Queens, and Stanley Kubrick knew what buttons to press in my acting computer to bring her back. Every time I watch the silly, sad woman come to life on TV I am impressed all over again. I am still hoping that I will work for him again sometime. When I saw *Clockwork Orange,* I sent Stanley Kubrick a letter saying how marvelous this film was and jokingly asked why I hadn't played the very British woman who gets raped in this film.

He did not get the joke. He sent me back a very stern reply and informed me that he would cast me in any role I was suited for in any one of his films. And that was final.

While we were shooting *Lolita,* I noticed that Kubrick always rode to the studio on his bicycle, and though the projection room where we saw the rushes at night was rather far away, Stanley would still ride his bicycle. I kept inviting him to get into my limousine, but he wouldn't. Finally one day, one of his aides whispered to me:

"Shelley, Stanley Kubrick two years ago decided he would not fly in a plane. Last year, he decided he would not ride in a car. He will only trust his bicycle."

I heard sometime later, after we finished the film, that he would only walk to the studio from his nearby estate. This is a strange quirk in the man who made the glorious *2001,* the definitive all-time space picture, and *Clockwork Orange,* which shows how it's not possible to be nonviolent in this violent world. I don't know how they got him to Ireland to shoot *Barry Lyndon.* Still he is one of the greatest directors I've ever been privileged to work with and is entitled to any eccentricity he needs.

We finally came to the scene of the dance in the high school gym, where Mary Noble, playing Peter Sellers's weird girlfriend, confronts me. This scene took several days to shoot, and I spent most of the time running around the gym trying to catch James Mason, who was looking hither and yon for Lolita. What none of us knows at that point in the story is that Lolita has already made contact with Peter Sellers's character, Clare Quilty, and she plans to run away with him. It took the art director many days to make a British gymnasium look like an American gymnasium, and even then he never got it right. It just looked like a weird gymnasium.

John Kennedy's inaugural was a few days away, and a blizzard over the ocean kept threatening London. I brought my packed suitcase to the studio the day before the inaugural, since I was going to fly to Washington, stay for two days, and then fly back. Toward the end of the shooting day, Peter Sellers and Stanley Kubrick and the MGM producer got me in a corner of this big gymnasium.

"Peter, you explain to her," Stanley said.

"Stanley, you're the director," Peter said. "You tell her."

All I could think of was that they were perhaps planning to replace me in the picture, although I'd already shot most of it, so all I said was, "What is it? For Chrissakes, somebody tell me."

Stanley Kubrick, rather white-faced and nervous, said, "I know we promised you that you could go to Kennedy's inaugural, but there is a blizzard over the Atlantic now, and it will invalidate our insurance. You cannot fly, understand!" I burst into hysterical tears.

"British television is photographing everything," Peter Sellers consoled. "They've promised to get President Kennedy to say something superpersonal to you on British television."

I knew I was stumped. The party I had dreamed about for the last year and that I had helped to make happen was going to go on without me. I took my suitcase and went back to the Dorchester. It was snowing, raining, and hailing. I did not want to go up to my suite of rooms and talk to my mother about it. I sat in front of the fireplace in the Dorchester lobby, tears streaking my makeup. I don't know how long I sat there. But finally a waiter came over with a tray with black coffee and a jelly doughnut and a cablegram and a double shot of brandy.

"Miss Winters," he said, "I'm sure everything's for the best."

I didn't know whether to tip him or slap him. Did the whole goddamn hotel know my travel plans? I wiped my tears and nose, took a slug of the brandy, and opened the cable. It was from Paul. It said:

FRAME THE INVITATION STOP IN MARCH YOU WILL BE THE MISTRESS OF CEREMONIES AT THE WHITE HOUSE PRESS PHOTOGRAPHERS' BALL STOP KENNEDY WILL GIVE THIS BALL FOR BOTH HOUSES OF CONGRESS THE CABINET THE SUPREME COURT AND ALL FOREIGN DIPLOMATS STOP YOU WILL BE THE ONLY WOMAN THERE STOP SO STOP CRYING DARLING AND HURRY UP AND FINISH LOLITA STOP PAUL

I did just that. *Lolita* was shooting in sequence, and my death scene was coming up. This time, I was going to be hit by a car accidentally. Up to that time in my film career, I had been strangled by Ronald Colman, drowned by Montgomery Clift, stabbed and drowned by Robert Mitchum, shot by Jack Palance and by Rod Steiger in two different films, and OH yes, overdosed with heroin by Ricardo Montalban. I knew how to be run over; I had done it a decade earlier in *The Great Gatsby,* but, thank goodness, British Equity was more humane. The director had to use a dummy of me for the car to run over. As a matter of fact, when they got through editing the picture, you didn't see me getting run over. You just saw James Mason's face when he got the news. His acting was so great I thought it was the most effective of any of *my* death scenes.

Toward the end of January, I was at last finished with *Lolita.* I knew that the role of Charlotte had been one of my best roles, and hoped that the members of the Academy of Motion Picture Arts and Sciences would feel that way, too. But when Oscar time came around, Ray Stark, who had something to do with the nominating and a big something to do with the releasing of the film, called me and asked if I would let myself be submitted in the Best Supporting Actress category. I refused. During a time in the early sixties the actor could choose which category he would be in. Like a dope, I said:

"Mr. Stark, I have already been nominated for Best Actress for *A Place in the Sun*. I have already won a supporting Oscar for *The Diary of Anne Frank*."

He tried to reason with me. "You get killed off in the middle of the picture," he said.

"I know," I replied, "but they talk about me all through the rest of the picture."

"Listen, kiddo," said Ray, who was an old friend and my former agent. "A year later, nobody remembers which Oscar you won. They just remember you won an Oscar. Be good to yourself and the picture. You're a shoo-in for the supporting Oscar."

I foolishly would not listen to him and repeated: "The Best Actress, or nothing." So, of course, I settled for nothing.

At the time I didn't realize that an Oscar means millions to a picture.

Lolita turned out to be a very prestigious film, and I should have listened to Ray's older and wiser mind.

But I probably would do it again.

When my part of the filming was over, for some reason Kubrick wanted me to stay an extra week, for postsynching or publicity or something. So my family went back to New York without me.

I was sitting in my suite, looking at the ever-present London drizzle and twiddling my thumbs, when my phone rang. It was Sean Connery.

"Now girl, how can you stay in London an extra week and not call me?" he asked.

"Sean," I replied. "You were in Liverpool playing soccer."

"That's true," he said. "But I'm here now, although I have to go back immediately. How'd you like to take the train to Liverpool? Have you ever been on a British train?''

I had to admit I hadn't, and that I usually motored around England.

"Okay," he said. "I'll pick you up at seven. We'll have dinner on the train, and we'll be in Liverpool in the morning. It's a lovely city and there is a new sensational band, the Beatles, playing there."

"What, no spiders?" I smart-alecked. "Okay, you're on," I said. "I just have to check with that Kubrick production department, and tell them where I'm going and when I'll be back."

I hung up, and I was happy and excited and exhilarated. I got permission from the production man and began to pack. I had forgotten to ask Sean what we were going to do in Liverpool and why we were going there. So I just took one evening gown, one cocktail dress, a pair of slacks, a couple of blouses, and underwear and tights. I knew it would be freezing in Liverpool, because I definitely knew that city to be *north* of London. When I added my jewelry and scarves and girdles and shoes and sweaters, I found out my overnight bag wouldn't make it, and I had to take a larger bag.

At seven o'clock I was waiting on the sidewalk with my large mink coat, fur-lined gloves, and a mink hat tied under my chin. Sean drove up in a snazzy two-seater. It looked very expensive and fast. He looked at me strangely and said, "Why are you taking this suitcase?"

"I don't know what plans you've made for Liverpool," I said, "so I came prepared."

He laughed gently as he put my huge suitcase in the trunk of his car. We drove to the station. He parked his car in a car park, and we started walking to the train with Sean carrying my enormous suitcase on his shoulder. I was holding my large purse and a thick book. It was a book that I had found out someone was making a film of, and I wanted to read it. I noticed Sean didn't have a suitcase for himself and commented on it. He just smiled.

We got on the train and Sean found our compartment and put my suitcase on the top berth. Then he took my hand and we went to the club car. After two pink gins I forgot to wonder why we were going to Liverpool—me with six high-fashion changes and Sean with just the suit he was wearing.

When the train pulled into Liverpool, Sean suddenly remembered he had to return to London, so we got off, had lunch, and took the return train back. British trains are gorgeous, romantic, and sexy, and the countryside is beautiful (I think).

When I arrived in New York, a notice was awaiting me from my daughter's school. I immediately went to see the principal as requested and she made me sign in blood again that I would always have my daughter back in school the opening day, which was usually a Thursday, and not take her out of school for any reason other than illness. I had kept her in England an extra two weeks. The students at this very good private school had orientation on Thursday and Friday, but the school term started on the following Monday. For the next twelve years or so, wherever I was working in the world I had to stop and get my kid back to Central Park West on some silly Thursday for orientation day of her school. For many years I wrote this into my film contracts. I was sad about losing this weekend with her but it was a great school and I guess they were right. Harry and Julie Belafonte's son went to the same school and there was a very dicey winter when they almost bounced this brilliant kid because the Belafontes were keeping him in their beautiful home in the Caribbean on orientation weekend. They finally had to sign in blood too.

Since Kubrick was such a prestigious director, and Nabokov was such an important author, and everyone in Hollywood knew I had played Charlotte, I was suddenly being bombarded with all kinds of scripts. My agent had raised my salary to some astronomical figure, but whatever the reason I could not even read them. If they had come from an important director I probably would have, but for quite a while the priority in my life was staying with my child.

Some weeks later I had an offer from Milton Katselas,

a new, young stage director who had just done a powerful off-Broadway play, *Call Me by My Rightful Name*. This was Joan Hackett's first major role and she was brilliant in this little off-Broadway production, which was superbly directed by Milton. He told me that the Paper Mill Playhouse was going to do three modern plays in repertory, and he offered me the female leads in *View from the Bridge* by Arthur Miller, *The Country Girl* by Clifford Odets, and *Two for the Seesaw* by William Gibson. This offer took my breath away. It was one of the most challenging theatrical assignments I'd ever attempted. I already had done *Two for the Seesaw* in stock but *Country Girl* was a demanding and difficult role. I had seen Uta Hagen do it on Broadway, and she had been marvelous, restrained and moving. It is one of Odets's most brilliant plays. The wife in *View from the Bridge* was not a large role, but I had long felt that she was the focus of the play, a woman who stands and has to watch her husband destroy himself. Many people feel that *Death of a Salesman* is Miller's greatest play, but I am not so sure that it isn't *View from the Bridge*. I remember standing in the wings performance after performance and listening to the lawyer's monologue at the end of the play: "The waves of this bay / Are the waves against Siracusa, / And I see a face that suddenly seems carved; / The eyes look like tunnels / Leading back toward some ancestral beach / Where all of us once lived. . . . / And I wonder at those times / . . . when we will truly have moved on, / On and away from that dark place . . . ?" It is Miller's epic tragedy—a man who has betrayed his comrades because of his own sexual needs. I felt that this was another of Miller's comments on the political life of America during that blacklisting period.

My agent was furious that at a time when I was so hot and my salary was so high I chose to spend six months at the Paper Mill Playhouse in a little town in New Jersey. There was no way to explain to him that I had decided that my family and my life were in New York. I wanted to be a theater actress, and playing these three demanding roles in these great plays would sharpen my acting instrument with a precision you cannot achieve in front of a camera. When you do a scene right in a movie it's a *print* and you never do it again. For the rest of your life you see that one performance and you cannot change or improve it. It's a superb experience but sometimes it's maddening. When you work in the theater in front of a live audience it's a constantly changing learning experience. Every performance is different and enthralling. And I repeat, an audience is the best teacher an actor can have.

Sometime during rehearsals of these plays Paul Schutzer phoned and reminded me I was committed to be the mistress of ceremonies at the White House press photographers' ball. As if I'd forget. At this massive banquet they roast the president during the after-dinner speeches. No press women were invited. Connie Francis, Lois Wilson, my publicist, and myself were the only women among about five hundred men.

Franklin Delano Roosevelt had initiated this custom during the thirties and sometime in the late thirties Eleanor Roosevelt gave a ball on the same night, for all the wives. Jacqueline Kennedy was so shy that she discontinued this tradition. Eleanor Roosevelt, when she heard this, commented, "There are many more important things for the president's wife to do than arrange wallpaper."

Jacqueline Kennedy had indeed restored the White House with Early American wallpaper, furniture, crystal, silver, and paintings. She had done a magnificent job, but obviously Mrs. Roosevelt felt that the First Lady should be doing things like going down in mines and checking the safety of miners, improving conditions in the South and Appalachia, exposing child labor practices, condemning greed, and alleviating poverty wherever she found it. I guess if I had my way it would be Saint Eleanor Roosevelt. Jacqueline Kennedy was too introverted and shy to use Mrs. Roosevelt as a role model.

I arrived in Washington for the press photographers' ball. Lois Wilson was carrying the beautiful dress I had bought in London. It was an off-the-shoulder black lace over nude silk. It had a waist-cinching black cummerbund and a huge taffeta skirt over a petticoat. Paul met us at the airport and he informed me that on the following day John Kennedy would give me a personal tour of the White House because I had missed his inauguration. As soon as I got to the hotel I called Molly and told her to put my kid on the shuttle plane to D.C. early the next morning. I wanted her to remember the experience of having our handsome, brilliant young president personally show us around the White House. So, she would miss a half a day of that damned school.

That night, I was so nervous it took me three hours to put on my makeup and curl my hair and get dressed. When President Kennedy approached me backstage I had a flash of intuition or insight and began to weep. I knew this man didn't believe that there were people who hated him. He did not understand hate. He only understood love, wanting the good things of life for all Americans. Whether it was his religion or determination to make the U.S. and the world a better place, he could not allow himself to understand that he was in mortal danger. Some photographer took a picture as he was questioning me and the next day the *Daily News* had a picture of that moment with the caption, "Why is Shelley Winters weeping as she talks to the President?" Of course this all happened in a second and I guess my conscious mind refused to register it. But I had grown up in a Brooklyn ghetto and I understood hate.

Nevertheless, when it was my turn to start introducing the various members of the press who had been roasting the president, I explained to this distinguished audience that I had missed the inauguration because I was filming *Lolita* in London. I still don't know why they laughed for three minutes. What was funny about that? Maybe they thought *I* was playing *Lolita,* but their laughter confused me so I kept changing the subject. I guess I was pretty funny in my introductions of the various speakers. They all told funny stories, kidding the president. At the end of the program when I introduced the president of the United States he congratulated me on my mistress of ceremonies techniques and he said to the audience, "All you gentlemen of the press have been ribbing me all night. But I bet none of you have ever done to a photographer what I have." Of course they all knew that when the president had met Jacqueline she'd been a photographer. He got the biggest and longest laugh of the evening.

It was a memorable event. There's nothing that boosts a girl's morale like five hundred important men in government complimenting her on how thin and beautiful she looks and how witty she is. When we were taking pictures at the end of the evening I told President Kennedy that I was bringing my daughter down from New York to see the White House with me. He said, "If Caroline is free I'll introduce them. She has as tough a schedule as I do but perhaps she can take a half hour off."

My child arrived early in the morning. I picked her up at the airport. The cabdriver gave us a short tour of all the glorious national monuments, then we drove up to the iron gate at the side entrance of the White House as instructed. They had our names at the gate and the cab was allowed to take us right up to the front door. I asked my child if she had studied American history in her school yet and she gave me a peculiar answer: "Not really, Mom. My teacher said he wants to make sure we're ready for it."

I didn't know what to make of that reply but I was quite sure my bright eight-year-old would understand the significance of what we were about to see. We walked into the White House and there was President John F. Kennedy waiting in the entrance hall with an aide to tour us around the public rooms of the White House. I guess he was giving me this personal tour because he wanted to thank me for helping him in his campaign and because I had been so disappointed at missing his inauguration.

I'm sure my daughter remembers more of this tour than I do. I was so dazed by Kennedy's presence that I can't quite remember what I saw. He took us into the Oval Office and he signed a copy of *Profiles in Courage* for me. "With thanks and affection," he wrote, "John Fitzgerald Kennedy." I realized that from this office decisions were made affecting the security and future of our planet. What an awesome responsibility.

I knew the dining-room wallpaper had been transferred

inch by inch from some historic house in Virginia. There was American antique furniture that had been donated to the White House by many of Jacqueline's friends and acquaintances. President Kennedy didn't say so but under the Roosevelt, Truman, and Eisenhower administrations the White House had gotten rather shabby. Kennedy did not have to tell me that fact, I saw it in the rooms that Mrs. Kennedy had not yet decorated. I seemed to prefer the shabby rooms. . . . They had a sense of history for me, but with my conscious mind I knew one must not live in the past, and certainly this young couple occupying this historic house were forward-looking people.

One of the most traumatic memories of my life is when the young president showed us the sign his Secret Service had above their booth at the side entrance to the White House. The sign said: IT TOOK ONE MINUTE TO KILL PRESIDENT ABRAHAM LINCOLN. My child and I stared silently at it, and the young president quickly took us to another room. I believe this personal tour lasted a full hour. We even went down in the elevator to the basement and there was a quite large swimming pool that had been built for Franklin Delano Roosevelt to exercise in since he had had polio. I believe President Kennedy used it daily for his back problem. He had been injured during the Second World War in his PT boat, 109. Much later, during the Nixon years, I learned that President Nixon had filled the swimming pool with earth and cemented it over. It is now the Washington press room.

As we were leaving and the president was saying goodbye Caroline came in from the Rose Garden with an aide. She had large men's shoes over her tiny ones and was flopping around in them. She and my child exchanged a solemn introduction and shook hands. Then Caroline walked toward the elevator. The aide was telling the president something, and Caroline had opened the elevator door and walked into the elevator and it shut behind her. The dignified young president forgot his position completely and he turned into a frantic father. In a controlled yell he said, "Darling, don't be frightened! Just press the white button over your head. Just press. Press it!" The door opened and Caroline clomped out. The aide grabbed her hand and the president looked as if he was going to kill him. But they quickly got into the elevator and I thanked the distracted president and I said, "I'll see you in three and a half years, Mr. President."

My daughter and I flew back to New York. I dropped her off at her tough school with a note that she had taken part of the day off to meet the president and see the White House and I hoped that they weren't going to expel her —and/or me. I got to the garage, picked up my Jaguar, and drove as quickly as possible to the Paper Mill Playhouse.

I resumed rehearsals with Joe Anthony, who was playing the actor in *The Country Girl*, with Milton Katselas directing us.

The role of the wife in *Country Girl* was most demanding. She is an intelligent, subdued, waspish lady who has been taking care of her alcoholic actor-husband for many years. In the first act of the play, the actor-husband gets a chance to star again on Broadway. Through the support of his wife he reclaims his self-esteem, talent, and health. It is one of Clifford Odets's most psychologically interesting works, but I think that the end of the play is false. In my opinion, Odets was influenced by commercial considerations and gave it a happy ending. The woman has been trying to give her husband the strength to get well so she can get out from under her terrible life of watching an alcoholic die—and so start her life anew. Odets calls him "a most cunning drunkard." At the end of the play she must pretend to believe that he is completely cured. She listens to her heart, she ignores her life experience, and she stays with this man who has made her life hell. I rehearsed this play for a month and played it in repertory for six months and did a great deal of research about alcoholism.

While I was doing the play, whenever I got to the third act all my instincts wanted to leave this husband I loved and go back and start a new life. But that's not the way Odets wrote it.

When I acted the subtext I would get a strange and sad

421

reaction from the audience. When I played it that way the audience seemed to know that it was a sad but lifesaving choice. When I played it that everything was going to be hunky-dory and he would be well forever they didn't believe it even though they applauded . . . they knew it was false.

Toward the end of this most fulfilling winter of great theater, George Cukor sent me the book *The Chapman Report*. This was a sixties novel about a scientific survey of case histories of the sexual lives of American women, loosely based on the Kinsey Report. How one of my most favorite directors in the world intended to make a film of this completely bewildered me. He asked me to study specifically one case history, an upper-middle-class woman who has a very happy marriage, two children, and a beautiful home and puts it all in jeopardy to have an affair with a handsome ne'er-do-well. Her husband finds out and she loses everything.

In some secret part of myself I quickly understood how the values of this woman had gotten so twisted by our society, which worships beauty and youth above all else. I decided that if the film was done in the summer I would play her and bring my entourage back to California. I would rent a modest little house on the beach and have a wonderful summer with my daughter when I wasn't filming. And that's what I did.

23

Before I left New York I called Rome and informed Vittorio that I was taking his daughter to California for the summer. Vittorio hates to talk on the phone but that day he spent an hour and a half arguing with me about how I must send our child to Italy. If necessary he would fly to New York and fly back with her to Rome. I could not hear him. I just screamed in anger.

I could not explain to him that a very dear friend of mine, Dawn Addams, had married Prince Vittorio Massimo in Italy about the same time Vittorio and I had gotten married. Since the laws in Italy declared at that time that the children belonged to the father, Dawn told me that when she had gotten a divorce the prince had taken their son and refused to let her even see him. Dawn told me that the Italian justice system supported this decision and although Dawn was a British citizen she did not see her son until he was ten. She said that then her father helped kidnap him off a beach. She had two bitter years of custody fights and ultimately she had to hand her child back to her ex-husband. I hear that the boy never had any consistent schooling and I believe he is now a Roman brat packer.

My ex-husband kept insisting that our child must get to know her grandmother and her Italian family but all I

423

would say was, "When she is ten I will bring her to Italy. Until then they can come to the U.S. and visit her."

I had taken her to England when I had done *Lolita* and *To Dorothy, a Son*. But because of Dawn's experience I would not allow her to get anywhere near Italy. That day after Vittorio called, I finally hung up and ran and got the airplane tickets to California.

When I showed up at Twentieth Century–Fox for wardrobe, George Cukor, the man who had discovered me and made me a star in *A Double Life,* kissed me and handed me the three-hundred-page film script of the book *The Chapman Report*. I kissed him and stared at the script in amazement. It weighed about two pounds. He explained later in his office that it would be edited and censored and he would send me the final version when it was ready.

The Chapman Report was a very explicit novel for its time. In the summer of '61, the sexual revolution had not yet fully arrived and the Hollywood censors were still very active. Even when I read the thick, marvelous script I did not understand how Cukor could film it. It was quite wonderful and he was able to cast it with Jane Fonda, Glynis Johns, Claire Bloom, and me because all of us thought it was an important film about the hypocritical double standard that existed in the U.S. then and now. Well, perhaps it's a little better now.

It had always amazed me that when a script is rewritten and/or edited, so much of the good dialogue is cut out along with the bad. In a later picture I finally found out why.

When a new writer is hired to rewrite a script he must rewrite 51 percent of the manuscript in order to get screen credit (union rules). So naturally that is his first priority. For many years I was dumbfounded as to why my scripts, when rewritten by very good writers, would often get worse. It was that old 51 percent requirement.

While I was waiting for the final script, and for a gorgeous wardrobe to be created by Orry–Kelly, I drove with my kid up and down the Pacific Coast Highway, looking at all the houses that had "For Rent" signs out. We finally found a darling green shack on a beach next to Malibu that, for want of a better name, the natives called Doggie Beach; all the middle-income families who lived there seemed to have a lot of dogs and children. My kid was in her glory. In New York during the winter she was of course cooped up, although I would take her ice-skating and sledding in Central Park as often as possible. She became a terrific skater and that summer she became a crackerjack swimmer too. Her first couple of weeks on the beach I could never get her or her little chums out of the water, except for when they traipsed through my house in their wet suits and sandy feet for sandwiches and milk. I never could keep enough baloney, peanut butter, or tuna fish in the house. There was no TV in that little shack, and when they got exhausted from playing outdoors they rested on exercise mats that I placed out on the foot-high balcony over the sand. My daughter introduced a new game to these L.A. kids—reading out loud. She had a large collection of the Bobbsey Twins, Nancy Drew, *Heidi,* and *Rebecca of Sunnybrook Farm.* There were an average of twenty children per afternoon and as I learned my lines in the family room I would hear them reading aloud to each other on the balcony. In the lovely twilights on the beach, I would listen to all their little voices reading. I would smile over my lemonade as I heard the little kids who couldn't read yet making up the ends of stories. It never seemed to bother the others.

One afternoon when I was drying off a kid who had come down the beach from Malibu, he said softly, "Mrs. Winters, your little girl's game is better than our big TV."

I asked him what he meant and he said, "Well, here on Doggie Beach we make up our own pictures."

I thought about that for a while. I called his nanny and suggested that she read to him and not just stick him in front of the TV. The lady said something very rude to me.

The lemonade I was drinking was strictly nonsugared because as per usual I was shaping up for a size 10 before I started the film. It wasn't difficult; I was so happy having my child to myself during this early summer. My mother stayed in Beverly Hills. I had given Kathy the summer off and Molly had stayed in New York. She had taken six months off and then was going to work for a physicist in England.

One day I was building elaborate sand castles with the children and the waves came in and flooded through the tunnels exactly as we'd planned. My hair was up in curlers covered with a babushka. I had on sunglasses which were crooked and cracked and an old, too-large bathing suit. Later, we were walking up the beach toward Malibu, collecting shells to add to our shell collection, when I suddenly heard a strange cracking sound. Since I had been in a lot of Westerns I immediately recognized that it was the crack of the kind of bullwhip that cowboys used in herding cattle or driving mule trains. My kid started to follow the sound. We looked over the fence of one of the houses of the Malibu Colony, and there was this well-built blond young man practicing cracking his whip over his head. I had seen stuntmen do this and I didn't think he was too good at it. His back was to us and, as we peeked, he put the whip down very quickly and started to practice drawing his guns. He had two six-shooters in holsters strapped to his hips. As he twirled the guns with both hands, he began to turn in our direction. We thought we were hidden behind the fence. Both my child and I were suppressing giggles at this young man who seemed to be acting out some secret fantasy straight from *Gunfight at the O.K. Corral.*

He was an attractive youth of about thirty and he had an ugly-handsome face with an interesting, broken nose. In a Texas accent so broad I could hardly understand, he began to spout Western lingo, saying, "You gunslingers better come out or I'll come in there and get you." We crouched, frozen. It was long before gang violence but I couldn't be sure this kid didn't have loaded guns. When he reached over for his whip again, which was a danger-ous-looking thing to be practicing with on a beach, I yelled, "Hey, kid! You could hurt somebody with that bullwhip!"

He immediately dropped it and said, "Miss Winters, I did not know you were there."

We straightened up. I've never been crazy about my voice but I guess it's recognizable all over the world as Shelley's special Midwestern/New York intonation. Despite all the speech therapy and Charles Laughton, I have yet to develop mid-Atlantic speech.

The young man came through a gate in the fence and hurriedly introduced himself. "Waal, ma'am, my name is Alex Vi-es-pi, and I shore know who you are. And this-here must be yore little girl."

I said, "How do you do," and my little girl observed, "It's very nice to meet you, Mr. Viespi. I never knew cowboys were Italian."

Alex looked stumped and with a shit-kicking elegant grace he said, "Why, ma'am, a lot of Eye-talians emigrated to Texas. My grandpappy's boat dropped anchor in Galveston." (I was to learn that Alex was a masterful liar but most of his lies were so enchanting I didn't mind.)

My kid said something to him in Italian but he just looked confused. I don't know that I believed him but, through that long summer when he would often visit our little green shack and practice his gunslinging and whip-cracking, he never dropped the deep Texas accent. He was an altogether charming and intelligent young man and turned out to be a very good actor now known as Alex Cord. But that summer he was going through his "Bonanza" phase, and it was very important to him that we believed he was a cowboy.

I did not start shooting *The Chapman Report* until just before my birthday. I had a wonderful two and a half months with my daughter. So when I started the film she went to a day camp somewhere in the Pacific Palisades and George Cukor saw to it that I had a Monday or Friday off almost every week. Alex was great at barbecuing and teaching kids how to fly kites on the beach. He set up a volleyball net and we had hilarious and exhausting games. The ages of the players ranged from five to seventy-five years, but each team had the same number of preteens, teens, more-or-less adults, and seniors, and usually three dogs played on each side. We became quite famous on the beach that summer. Even society people from Malibu and famous movie stars would walk down the beach to watch us play. Alex would captain one team and I would captain the other. That summer I spent $15,000 at the supermarket on picnic supplies. My business manager wanted to know what the hell happened to my plan for having a cheap summer at a shack on the beach. I tried to get him to deduct it for entertainment since all these producers and directors would join our game and then stay for hors d'oeuvres and cocktails. He couldn't. Sometimes at night Alex and the famous agent Freddie Fields would build huge bonfires (those were the days before you needed a permit). Since all the pretty girls from the Actors Studio would come weekends, my shack became the "in" place to be seen.

The next summer, my daughter was nine, and I took her to Italy to see her father. While she was visiting him I was comparing his awards in a glass case to mine and he presented me with something he had been given on a Western Italian picture he had done in Spain. He took out a gold sheriff's badge that said, "Sheriff Vittorio Gassman." It was 22-karat gold and about four inches in diameter. Until this minute I didn't know why he gave it to me. I just realized my daughter must have told him about my Italian cowboy on the beach the previous summer.

If I hadn't had that little shack I might have bought a house in Malibu which would be worth millions now. Instead, I have that wonderful summer in my memory. That was the summer that Charles Laughton came down to the beach and recited Shakespeare all night.

After my kid went back to New York on September 1, my mother hired a new housekeeper. Molly was staying in London with her physicist until the new year because he was ill, but she called New York every Sunday to make sure her kid was okay. She never bothered to call California to find out how I was.

The weekend after Labor Day, when I had to pack up all the things we had acquired at the beach, *nobody* showed up to help me. I guess Alex had to help his Malibu friend, whoever it was, get back to Beverly Hills too. Alex had left a jacket in a closet and as I packed it his wallet fell out of a pocket. Of course I looked through it and there was a membership card—the New York Bricklayers' union—saying "Alex Viespi, junior member of the union," with his picture. I somehow knew that the bricklayers' construction union was a father-son union, and since a great deal of construction was going on in New York, bricklayers made a great deal of money. I was so angry at Alex for not helping me pack that I considered telling him that he'd better go back to being a bricklayer from Floral Park, Long Island, and stop pretending to be a rodeo champ from Texas, but I never shot down his cover story till now.

Alex showed up at my Beverly Hills address during the shooting of *The Chapman Report* and explained he had been touring with the rodeo and his last stop had been Phoenix. His hands and face were rather bruised so either he was telling the truth or he'd been in a terrible fight. I gave him back his wallet. He looked at me strangely and said, "Ma'am, I do thank you for recovering my valuables." I never asked him, "Is your father a bricklayer from Floral Park, Long Island?" But I must have looked doubtful because he suddenly remembered he could speak some Neapolitan, but of course with a Texas accent.

I worked very hard on *The Chapman Report* and Jane Fonda told me all about what had happened to *Invitation to a March* after I had left it. Arthur Laurents was still furious at me and I don't even want to repeat the stories here because I hope someday Arthur will resume our friendship and maybe even write a wonderful play for me. After twenty-nine years I am still hoping.

One exhausted and exhausting weekend Alex was driving me around in my old convertible Cadillac because the Jag was in New York. For some reason we were going north on Rexford Drive. There was a white brick house at 711 Rexford with a sign, "For Immediate Sale." Alex said, "Let's go in and see it." I didn't want another house in California but I found it so charming I bought it that afternoon. When I got home I expected my mother to be angry. She said, "Shelley, for God's sakes, don't sell it now! Furnish it and rent it! Put in a pool! When you're not living in it, you'll make a fortune! Everybody's gonna want to live in Beverly Hills sooner or later!"

During the rest of the weeks of filming Alex and I attended estate auctions at nights and on weekends and I furnished the house completely for about $6,000. It had a huge living room and fireplace, a dining room, three bedrooms and baths, a den, and a huge old-fashioned kitchen with a restaurant stove, all on one floor, and it was on a half-acre of Beverly Hills property. I paid $72,000 for that house and never moved into it.

I leased it to Henry Weinstein and his wife. He called me about a year later in New York and said since the house had three bedrooms would I mind if Marilyn Monroe moved in with him and his wife. I believe that by then Marilyn had given up her apartment in New York and was looking for a small house like mine. Her marriage to Arthur Miller had broken up and she was sort of homeless. Henry was going to produce a film with her in six months or so at Fox called *Something's Got to Give*. I said gladly.

Although I never lived in that house and sold it a couple of years later, I still have a lot of the furniture cluttering up my Spanish duplex—especially a large, square dining room table that I instructed Marilyn to cut down to coffee-table height. It has always been shaky; no matter how I've tried I can't fix it and make it steady. I still use it, maybe because I'm still a symbolic thinker.

Sometime in October I got myself safely back to New York and away from Alex. I felt it was time because his cowboy accent was slipping fast. The next months I worked intensely at the Actors Studio. I decided to try to crack the classics and I did Juliet's famous tomb speech. I was an attractive young woman but certainly not near Juliet's age, which was fourteen. Laughton's beautiful rendition of Shakespeare's sonnets on my birthday made me want to fulfill his hopes for me. It was a very cold day in New York, and I was terrified of performing a classic in front of Lee Strasberg, Elia Kazan, and Cheryl Crawford. It must have been pretty good or pretty terrible because the other members of the Studio who usually were all too ready to inform the moderator of what they had received negative or positive from your performance were strangely silent. Lee asked me where I had studied Shakespeare and I told him, "With Charles Laughton."

Lee said I must continue working on Shakespeare because I had accidentally stumbled into a way of using Method work beneath the strictures of Shakespeare's poetry. As always, I was frightened by my accomplishments and I do not believe I ever did Shakespeare again.

I had a lunch date that day with Julie Belafonte, who looked the way Juliet should have looked, and we ate in a booth at Downey's. I was visibly shaken so Julie made me have an Irish coffee with an extra shot of whiskey in it. To distract me, she began to talk about the beautiful present Harry had just given her. She described what sounded like a very expensive diamond necklace, then she opened her sweater and showed me an exquisite diamond chain around her beautiful dancer's neck. It was scalloped with delicate, tiny diamonds. I gazed at it with longing. Since we were both having the $1.20 diet special for lunch, something seemed incongruous. I was in such a blue funk about having done all those pictures when I obviously should have been doing Shakespeare that I decided I knew how to cure my blues immediately.

"Julie," I asked excitedly, "where did Harry buy that?"

"Forty-seventh Street. The wholesale diamond district," she excitedly answered. "He knows somebody. I think the shop's called Mendelsohn's. I know the man. He had to adjust the necklace for me. You want to go over there and look at one like this? I'm sure he'll give you a great deal."

My plan to live frugally so I wouldn't have to do crappy pictures flew right out of my mind. Julie and I wolfed our lunch, had another double Irish coffee, left a fifty-cent tip, and dashed through the snow to the wholesale block on Forty-seventh Street between Fifth and Sixth Avenues. I was panting with desire as I entered the shop. I guess it's true that nothing turns a girl on like diamonds.

The owner was a big fan. He immediately informed me that he had a necklace similar to Julie's but with much bigger diamonds, and since I was an Oscar-winning actress I must have something commensurate with my position. He had us sit down on two leather stools and brought out a black leather box. I think I was sitting on my brains that afternoon. He opened the box and there was G*L*O*R*Y. It was a scalloped necklace composed of emerald-cut diamonds with baguettes in between, and only the diamonds on the back of the neck were half-karat round ones. Julie and I gazed hypnotized.

He quoted a rather reasonable price for what I imagined a diamond necklace would cost, but it was still an outlandish figure. Sanity returned for a second and I said, "But I have a diamond-and-sapphire pin and earrings and bracelet. This is only diamonds."

Julie, the soul of grace and balance, fell off her stool. The owner quickly left to get another box out of the vault, murmuring, "We have a beautiful investment here. Only fifty thousand dollars."

Julie and I both yelled, "Stop!"

I assured him I didn't want to see it. Then he said something strange as he showed it to us. "If you buy the first one, at any time you want to bring it back I'm sure that I can give you more than its value to trade it in for the diamond-and-sapphire one."

Julie said, "Shelley, it's not chic to wear everything matching."

After an afternoon of crazy negotiations in which I swapped the heavy 22-karat gold compact that Mike Todd had given me at the Madison Square Garden party for *Around the World in 80 Days* and a few other baubles, I left the shop with Julie with the first diamond necklace around my neck, not realizing that it would take me ten years to pay it off. At that point I think I was believing that he was practically giving it to me. What a salesman!

I had written him a check for $4,000 and given him the other gold stuff but I wasn't sure how much more I owed. As Julie and I walked through the snow we both became frightened, and she whispered, "I'm sure you can take it back anytime," and I answered, "No, Julie! I am entitled to a necklace! I did Juliet's speech so beautifully this morning."

In October I was invited by Ethel Kennedy to come to a house party at her and Bob's home in Georgetown. The invitation included a luncheon, a big party at the Kennedy house that night, and a cruise the next day on the Potomac on the *Honey Fitz*. I can never forget anything about this glorious weekend, though at times during the past twenty-five years I have tried to block it out. When I got to the hotel in Washington I carefully put my jewelry in the hotel safe, and when I showed up for the elegant lunch at Bob and Ethel's home the only jewelry I was wearing was Anthony Franciosa's Bulgari diamond-and-sapphire clip. We had an outdoor buffet and John Kennedy's sisters, Eunice, Patricia, and Jean, were sitting on the terrace. There seemed to be about a hundred children running all over the place, with goats, rabbits, geese, and other animals. Ethel and the Kennedy sisters just ignored the children. There were probably only about fifteen; they just seemed like a hundred. All through this lunch, not one of the ladies present reproved a child because of wild behavior. Ethel, seeing a shocked look on my face at one point, said, "Shelley, when you have a large family, they have to teach each other discipline and learn what is acceptable behavior to the group. If you don't do that, you go crazy. You'll see in a while. They'll all quiet down and behave like human beings."

And that's what happened during the course of the lunch. I discreetly examined the clothes and jewelry that the Kennedy ladies were wearing. "Understated elegance." None of them seemed to be wearing any kind of diamonds. Their engagement rings were small sapphires or emeralds and one was wearing a small ruby ring. Very unflashy were those ladies. I had almost worn my new diamond necklace and now I was glad I'd left it in the hotel safe. In the years to come I found out that most of their clothes were made by a Boston firm, Fiandaca. Years later I was doing a play in Boston and once I ordered a complete wardrobe from this couture house. The clothes are beautifully made of the best materials; they never seem to go out of style. They are so simply elegant and they seem to be designed in some kind of timeless way. When I wear their clothes I always look right whether I'm a size 16 or 10.

Recently when I was doing *84, Charing Cross Road* in Massachusetts at the Cape Playhouse, Albert Fiandaca came backstage and asked me plaintively, If he made me two evening gowns free, and the proper size, would I please stop wearing on the Johnny Carson show the one he made me in the sixties?

I answered, "But the Kennedy girls still wear the suits you made for them in the sixties."

Sadly he nodded, "Yes, I know."

The big party was held that night around the Bob Kennedys' swimming pool. Many celebrities were there from Hollywood and New York. Harry and Julie Belafonte escorted me from the hotel. It seemed to be a party for all the people who had helped JFK's campaign, and for some reason Ted Kennedy's entire Harvard football team was there. The food and champagne were great, as was the orchestra. All the college kids were doing the twist and at one point somebody put a large plank across the pool and then a conga line danced to cross it. Bob and Ethel were treating us all the way they treated their children.

I guess it was too undignified a party for the President and First Lady to attend, but it was a great party. At one point everyone had to suggest a new game, and I told Bob and Ethel about the new Hollywood game in which you choose up sides and you take one member of your team and wrap that person in pillows and sheets. Then everybody from the other team gets one feel and tries to guess who it is. Bob thought it was hilarious. Ethel knew I was making it up.

Around 2:00 A.M., I broke the heel of my sandal and sat down on a bench beside the garage. A young man tried to help me undo the strap and suddenly I was in his arms and he was kissing me. Although I was three champagne glasses into the party, I stopped the passionate kiss and stared at him. It was Edward Kennedy. I got terribly frightened. He quickly calmed me down and said, "For God's sakes, I was only trying to kiss you! What did you think I was trying to do?"

I hastily limped away, grumbling, "Only God knows."

I was rather disheveled in my strapless green chiffon dress but I hadn't lost any jewelry because I hadn't worn any. I was too intimidated by the Kennedy sisters at luncheon that afternoon. When Julie Belafonte noticed that I wasn't wearing the diamond necklace and asked why, I told her, "It's not only chic *not to match*. It's chic *not to wear diamonds,* in this administration at least."

Harry and Julie took me back to the hotel and they questioned me closely as to why I hadn't talked to one mature, interesting single man at the party. There had been plenty. I thought about it and said, "Well, kids, I guess I'm attracted to the kids." When we got back to the hotel there was a message at the desk inviting us to a barbecue lunch on the *Honey Fitz* and a cruise up and down the Potomac. Unfortunately Harry had to get back to New York for an engagement at Carnegie Hall and Julie preferred watching her husband perform to a trip on the presidential yacht.

Bright and early the next morning a Secret Service car picked me up. I was wearing an appropriate blue yachting outfit and a strand of my smallest pearls. I didn't know exactly who would be on the yacht but I hoped the president would be. As I walked up the gangplank there were about twelve sailors saluting and standing at attention. I felt like the honorary ambassador from Brooklyn and wished I had a red sash across my bosom. When I arrived at the bow I sat down in a deck chair next to Ethel Kennedy and she informed me that JFK had had to remain in the White House and Bob Kennedy was involved in some civil-rights crisis that was occurring in the South. But we were proceeding with the picnic.

Children were swarming all over the boat. The sailors were standing at attention but their eyes were glued to the children. I was sure one or more of them would fall overboard any minute. Ethel calmly ordered the cook to start grilling the hot dogs, corn on the cob, and hamburgers. She saw my terrified face and said, "I promise you, Shelley, they will take care of each other. If I allowed myself to worry about them, I would be in a constant state of anxiety. They are used to it." I wondered if the sailors had heard these words of reassurance and could relax while they were standing at attention. There were several other adult guests on the ship, but I can't recall who they were because suddenly the ship's radio became the focus of attention. It was tuned to some government shortwave channel and we all listened to Bob Kennedy talk to JFK. I'm not sure where they were but their conversation was fascinating. It seemed that there was a campus in the South, and a black youth was being refused admission, and the students and local police had barricaded the door, contrary to the law of the land. A White House representative was attempting to remonstrate with the segregationists and reach their humane feelings, if they still had any.

As we listened it sounded as if the Ku Klux Klan was surrounding this young person and the entire campus. After a couple of hours of bulletins we still had the barbecue, and Ethel turned up the volume on the radio. We then heard Bob Kennedy say, "Mr. President, don't you think it's long enough? Don't you think we'd better show those bastards we mean business?"

I heard JFK sigh and say, "Mr. Attorney General, call out the National Guard, we can no longer tolerate the philosophy of separate but so-called equal schools anywhere in this country."

I knew I was on the presidential yacht at a historic moment in my country's history. Ethel's vast brood settled down and sat around us quietly. Even the toddlers seemed to understand the historic importance of this moment. I got this shivery feeling as if I had just heard a continuation of Lincoln's Gettysburg Address; the freedom torch was at last being passed on after a hiatus of almost exactly one hundred years.

I quietly said goodbye to Ethel and all the children, and I got myself and my troublesome jewels back to New York and shoved them in a drawer in my bedroom. It had a lock but I had an attack of egalitarianism and felt it would be insulting to staff if I locked the damn drawer.

As Molly was still in England, I had hired a Southern black housekeeper. I had also hired a very refined young lady, a minister's daughter, to be sort of an unofficial nanny and see that my daughter got to school on time and did her homework, which nobody really had to do because she loved studying.

I must have been pretty impossible during this period. I was dressing as if I were related to the Kennedys and my voice was down an octave and calm and very precise and slightly Bostonian. I think for a while there I was thinking about going back to school—getting my high school diploma, going to college and possibly law school. But I got a dose of reality and just took a short-story course with Barbara Solomon, my upstairs neighbor, a marvelous writer who taught at Barnard College.

My California agent was sending me scripts but I had great hopes for *The Chapman Report*. I resolved that if this time anyone wanted to submit me for the supporting-actress Oscar I would graciously consent. None of the scripts I was being sent had good directors so I just would read the first page. I had finally caught on that if I was lucky enough to have a good director I could be very good. If not, I was average. I obviously needed a Stevens, Cukor, or Kubrick to do my best work. So I decided to wait for the release of *Lolita* and/or *The Chapman Report* before I accepted another film. Oh, if I could only have kept to that resolve for a couple of more decades.

It's a terrible quandary for an actor. You only get better when you work at your art, but you can only practice your art when there is a stage or camera. That's why I've loved the Actors Studio all my life. It's one of the few workshops available to professional actors so that they can work when they're out of work. Every other civilized nation in the world has state-subsidized theaters. The U.S.A., the richest country on earth, leaves its actors and playwrights to stagnate in inactivity.

I spent the next few months attending parent-teacher meetings, exploring New York with my daughter, and every Sunday going to see the film *Gigi*. I don't know why but that's what my kid wanted to do. I must have seen *Gigi* a dozen times that winter. One Sunday afternoon after seeing it we went to the Automat and, after filling our trays, we sat in a section reserved for mothers and children. My kid was explaining to me at great length why she liked the film so much when a fan interrupted her and said, "You are Shelley Winters, aren't you?" Whereupon my child turned on her with great anger and said, "No, she's not, it's Sunday, she's not Shelley Winters on Sunday." The fan slunk away. I looked at my child's angry face and knew there was no way I would ever be able to solve this problem. We walked back up Central Park West holding hands and saying nothing.

When a celebrity decides to live in New York there is some secret charity network that alerts all banquet rooms. I attended so many fund-raising luncheons at the Waldorf that winter, from the American Heart Association, the American Cancer Society, the National Multiple Sclerosis Society, Bonds for Israel, Red Cross, and Boys' Towns of Italy to the March of Dimes, that at one point the assistant manager offered me a suite there. I guess they were giving the impression to the women's clubs that if they held their function at the Waldorf Shelley Winters was included in the package. My luncheon activities came to a head one day when I was trying to get to a rehearsal. I got off the elevator at the Waldorf, rushed to a meeting room, made a splendid speech, and got a resounding ovation. When the applause subsided, the elegant lady in charge whispered, "Miss Winters, it was a stirring speech. But this is the fifth floor. This is Cerebral Palsy. I believe you're supposed to be on the third floor."

I didn't even break my stride. I rushed to the third floor, made the same speech for the National Tuberculosis Association, and rushed out in time for my rehearsal.

One afternoon the phone rang. It was Alex Viespi, who had not yet changed his name to Alex Cord. He had done some small films and/or television in California and he was staying at a hotel near my apartment. I agreed to meet him at Downey's and after I'd hung up I wondered why he'd sounded so strange. I soon realized what it was.

He'd lost his cowboy accent and was speaking your average American slightly New York English. But when I met him for cocktails at Downey's he was still wearing his Stetson and Western outfit. He had a five-minute speech prepared and memorized. He said, "Although I've worked as a bricklayer because my father was a bricklayer, and although my family lived on Long Island, I'd gone to acting school and run away from home and joined the rodeo when it was at Madison Square Garden." Where he'd learned to ride horses I didn't inquire. I assumed it was in Far Rockaway. I laughed and put him at his ease and asked what he was doing in New York.

Alex confided, "I think I'm ready for the stage. All movie stars have to work on the stage first, and I'm willing to pay my dues."

He was so naive, stupid, and endearing that I didn't know whether to slug him or kiss him. I told him I had become a movie star before I had seriously studied theater, although I had played little parts on Broadway. But I'd never thought I was pretty enough to be a movie star. It had all been sort of accidental. I told Alex to relax and I would ask Lee Strasberg if he could be an observer at the Studio for a couple of weeks.

If I'd given him a gold-plated saddle he couldn't have been happier. He laughed and jumped up and down in his high-heeled cowboy boots. Jim Downey walked over and said, "Hey, kid, don't bust the tiles." I noticed as they were talking that under Alex's fleece-lined cowboy jacket were holsters with *guns* on each hip.

I quickly told him to sit down and sent Jim for a couple of Irish coffees without the whiskey. I leaned across the table and whispered, "Alex, what the hell do you think you're doing, walking around New York with guns? Did you bring them on the plane?" There were no hijackers or security checkpoints then but it was not exactly good taste to carry guns around town as freely as he was. Alex whispered back, "They're not loaded, Shelley. I just practice fast drawing whenever I can. My agent has me up for a big Western—a feature, not a TV show." I then got really quite angry. I said, "Alex, we're going to walk back up Eighth Avenue to your hotel and you leave the holster and guns someplace in back of your closet. The rodeo is not in town now and you're liable to get mugged for the guns."

Alex was staying at a hotel a few blocks from my house. When he took the guns up to his room I looked around the lobby and realized that this was the same hotel, The Bolivar, where Anthony Franciosa had stayed when we were engaged.

I resolved to ship Alex back to California as quickly as possible.

Alex wanted to say hello to my kid so we walked up Central Park West that brisk, bright December day. The Manhattan sky was clear and sunny. Snow glistened in the trees. All the chic West Siders were thronging the streets with their bundled-up children, sleds, ice skates, and groceries. As we passed the Museum of Natural History Alex looked at the equestrian statue of Theodore Roosevelt. He stood there for a minute and said, "Shell, look at him. He was a cowboy and he got to be president."

"Forget it Alex," I replied. "Can't happen. You first try to get in Equity." (Ronald Reagan was still a cowboy actor then.)

We continued up to my house and Alex was suitably impressed by the marble lobby and the fact that when we got off the elevator there were only two apartments on the floor.

The kids weren't home from school yet, so the building was rather quiet. My new housekeeper opened the door and Alex walked into my huge living room. It was so big that in subsequent years I entertained the Bolshoi Ballet and the Moscow Art Theatre in it—but not at the same time. The dining room was half again as big. One of the stupidest moves of my life was selling this apartment. When my daughter went off to Harvard and Molly, my housekeeper, wanted her own apartment I got an attack of the dooms and sold it for $43,000. Recently Meryl Streep paid $2 million for it and I moved to a cold small apartment overlooking the Hudson River.

* * *

440

Oh, well, real estate investments have never been my strong suit and I have a suspicion that I don't like to own anything but paintings. Recently I heard a saying, "The first half of your life you spend acquiring things. The second half you spend getting rid of them." It's true for me. An example of this happened about a decade ago. I owned a beautiful house up on Coldwater Canyon in Hidden Valley. It was not too big, it had stone fireplaces and a beautiful view of the mountains, and it was modern and roomy. There was a suite of rooms above the garage that a housekeeper or guest could stay in. The house began, however, to be a headache. The mountain in back of it was covered in pink flowers but when the fire season approached the Beverly Hills police would make me strip the brush from the whole hillside and I would have to plant it again in the spring. Raccoons were living in the attic. I believe Marlon Brando, who lived on top of the hill, bred them.

Getting rid of raccoons is a very expensive process. The ASPCA has to come with a big crane, lure them into a cage, and then transport them by helicopter to some wilderness with a stream so they can gnaw on real trees instead of attics. There are all kinds of four-footed animals in the hills of Beverly Hills. I kept having problems with the roof, the pool, too much company, or feeling frightened when I stayed up there alone.

So after I'd had the house a couple of years I was shooting a picture in Rome and I read in the *Rome Daily American* that there were torrential rains and fires in the Beverly Hills, especially the canyons. I had rented the house to David Frost and Caroline Cushing, so I dialed their number immediately from Rome. A man answered and his voice sounded remarkably familiar. He said, "Hello, Shelley. How's the weather in Rome?"

"Yeah," I said. "Could I speak to Caroline or David?"

He informed me that they had gone to San Diego for a couple of days. It was raining cats and dogs and puppies around my house and he was taking care of it. He seemed to know me so well and his voice was so familiar that I didn't have the guts to say, "Who the hell are you?"

I said, "Listen could you do a few things for me about the house?"

"I can try," he replied. "Now don't tell me yet. Let me get a paper and pencil."

After a three-minute wait the voice came back. "Go ahead," he said. I listed: "First, see if the pool is turned off. The mechanism is behind a wooden fence near the hillside."

The voice said, "Just a minute, Shelley. I gotta write this down."

I waited another two minutes. He said, "Okay, go ahead." I said, "Ready? There's a six-foot rubber hose in back of that fence. Could you put one end in the pool, suck up the water from the other end, and put that end of the hose down the hill?" I explained that otherwise the pool would overflow from the rain and the house would be flooded. He sounded strange and said, "I'll do it or get somebody to do it."

"Thanks, and can you write all that down carefully please? Oh, and also, could you make sure the garbage cans are tightly covered and put them securely into the garage and close the door? When there's floods or fires, the coyotes circle the house and get into the garbage."

The voice weakly said, "I can do that."

There was another pause and he said, "Okay, enjoy Rome," and I said, "Thanks," still not knowing who the hell it was. I forgot about this overseas conversation for months. But when my sister and I were doing the inventory for the house for David Frost's secretary after the lease was up there was a book on the table in the guest suite. It was Richard Nixon's autobiography, which David Frost had obviously helped him with. Inside was written, "With appreciation for your hospitality, Richard Nixon."

When I complained to Caroline Cushing, she said, "There's nothing in the lease that says we can't have ex-presidents stay here." Angie Dickinson, who lived across the road, a staunch Democrat herself, wouldn't speak to me for a year. This was just after Watergate, so all the people in Hidden Valley had a party at my house and got a priest and a rabbi and a guru to exorcise the place. And I sold it soon afterwards.

But that December of 1961 in New York, Alex walked around my spacious apartment and he began to look a little puzzled. He said, "Tell me, Shell, why you live like a struggling actress in California and like a movie star in New York." I could not think of an answer. All I could reply was, "I'll take that up with my psychiatrist."

Then he asked me the $64 question. "Are you really ever going to move into that beautiful house you bought on Rexford Drive? Or did we just furnish it so you could have an investment?"

I thought a minute and said, "Alex, I'm working up to it. I hope some day I'll be able to have a pool, a tennis court, a gym, and a sauna, all the accouterments of wealth. But maybe I'm superstitious and think in some secret part of myself if I live like that my talent will disappear."

He was stunned. He said, "Listen, Shell, I want it all and more and as soon as possible."

I fixed some drinks for us at the bar and noticed a phone message from Frank Corsaro. It said, "Go to *Night of the Iguana* tonight and meet me at Sardi's afterwards. Urgent. Immediate."

I tried reaching Frank at his home, the Actors Studio, backstage at the Royale where *Iguana* was playing, and anywhere else I could think of, to no avail. I had been hearing the scuttlebutt all over town that Tennessee Williams's play, which had opened to glorious reviews, was in trouble, and I couldn't figure out why. I called the box office at the theater and there were indeed two fifth-row center tickets left for me. I informed Alex that he was taking me to see *Night of the Iguana* with Bette Davis, Margaret Leighton, and Patrick O'Neal that very evening if he could come up with an ordinary business suit and a pair of shoes that weren't boots. He looked abashed but said he would find some. I took him to the elevator and when the door opened my child got off; she was just coming in from school. She said, "Hi, Alex! What took you so long?" She had not seen him since Labor Day, but she obviously knew he was arriving. I hadn't known it, but I decided not to question her about it. I just said, "Leave your leggings on! We're going ice-skating!"

And so we did. She skated—I fell down.

That night as Alex and I sat in the fifth-row center we listened to the chatter of the audience. We'd arrived about ten minutes early. I tried to think why Frank wanted me to come this very night to see the play. I had seen it several times at the Actors Studio while Tennessee was rewriting it. Rosemary Harris and Madeleine Sherwood had played the two leads and Patrick O'Neal had created his role. Cheryl Crawford had produced it at the Studio. Now after several metamorphoses Bette Davis and Margaret Leighton and Patrick O'Neal had opened in it after rather a long tour. Chuck Bowden and Paula Laurence were producing it with Violla Rubber. I proceeded to watch the play and although the words were as lyrical as they had been at the Studio there was something very strange about the performances. Bette Davis seemed to be shooting her lines right at the audience, facing squarely front and not talking to Margaret or Patrick at all. She was getting uproarious laughs but I knew she wasn't that kind of actress. What the hell was going on? Only in the scenes when Bette was alone with Patrick was there any communication. Those scenes were powerful. It seemed to me that when Patrick had scenes with Maggie Leighton he became frozen—as if afraid to move. At the intermission I looked for Frank. I didn't dare go backstage because obviously Bette Davis was quitting or being fired. We sat through the last act of the play and I puzzled it all over in my mind.

Alex and I walked through Shubert Alley and entered Sardi's. There waiting for a table were my old friends William Marchant and Alex Fondas. I rescued them from being consigned to Siberia and asked them to join us at our front booth. I told Alex Viespi what a famous playwright William Marchant was and explained about Alex Fondas's birthday being on the same day as my child's and tried to find out what he was planning to dress up as the next Valentine's Day. I felt a little odd about having the men at my table because I knew Frank wanted to talk to me privately, so when I saw Frank come in I sent the two Alexes and the one Bill to the bar. They were old, dear friends, but when a star breaks contract, whoever's fault it is, it's a big theater scandal and secret.

As soon as Frank sat down he told me in whispers that even though the show had just opened and was a big hit, Bette Davis was leaving in ten days, hot or cold, suspended by Equity or whatever—nothing short of murder would make her stay in the show. It even turned out that she quit the next Saturday night. She just finished out the week. Did Bette Davis and Margaret Leighton hate each other so much that they couldn't act together? I tried to find out from Frank what was happening on the stage.

"Madeleine created the role of Maxine at the Studio," I said. "And now she's Bette's understudy. Why doesn't Madeleine go in?"

Frank told me it was very complicated. The producers, Chuck and Paula, who had taken the play away from Cheryl, had sided with Tennessee's agent, Audrey Wood, in demanding that the backers get no part of the movie sale. I looked at him in amazement.

"But the backers are always paid back first, aren't they, Frank?"

"Of course, but Tennessee always follows Audrey's advice—in this case, wrong advice. And he's such a hot playwright now that he can make these kinds of demands. We have sold a million dollars' worth of theater parties, but I think the ladies want to see a movie star. This is a long, poetic play and I'm not certain that even with the rave reviews it will run without Bette Davis or you."

"Or me?" I exclaimed.

"Yes. Please, Shelley. It's very important to me to have Tennessee Williams's play a hit."

If the play closed, I knew the Broadway producers would blame the director and forget the great reviews. I sat in that booth and examined my conscience. I didn't want to go into a role that had already been created by another actress. What I was looking for was a new play. But I owed so much to Frank and I admired Tennessee so much I couldn't refuse. If the play was a hit I would be able to stay in New York for many months with my child. Given all these positive considerations, the fact

445

that Bette Davis had been acting in a manner so foreign to her went completely out of my mind.

"Try it for a week with Madeleine," I suggested. "If business warrants it, and you have to have me, I will do the show. But I prefer that Madeleine play the role she created at the Studio."

Frank agreed and gave me a copy of the stage manager's script. He said to study the role and he would have the assistant stage manager mark my huge living room and teach me the blocking and the lines as soon as possible.

When I called my agent in California the next morning he almost came through the phone again.

"To go in as a replacement in a hit Broadway show is a very negative thing to do to your film career," he fumed. "It's bad enough to keep living in New York and acting in New Jersey. But this is really the pits."

I then repeated a now-familiar litany, and he joined in from California: "But I learn from the live audiences and I want to stay with my daughter in New York. And maybe Tennessee Williams will write me a great role in his next play." We finished speaking together.

He breathed a sigh of resignation and said, "Well, Ray Stark invested most of the money for the play and he'll probably make the movie. I'll make him guarantee that you do the role when it's made into a film."

Somehow this clause got scrambled in the hurry of getting me into the play and Ava Gardner did it in the film. As I think about it I wish I had let her have Tony Franciosa when we were in Rome. She might have turned down the movie then. Perhaps I would have gotten a Best Actress Oscar as I was very good and hilariously funny when I went into the play on Broadway. Modest, huh?

Alex Viespi and I walked up Eighth Avenue from Sardi's, me clutching the huge stage manager's script of *Iguana*. The Christmas lights were beginning to be turned on all over the city. I asked Alex if he didn't want to get back home to California in time for Christmas. He gave me his funny grin and said, "My home is in Floral Park, just over the bridge. My mother and father will be glad to have me home this Christmas.'' With a Texas accent, he added, ''This year is the first Christmas I'll have been home in three-four years.''

He was such a liar I couldn't tell whether he'd really been touring with the rodeo or not during his pre-Hollywood days. We walked into my living room and I gave the script to Alex.

''I'm going to put on my robe,'' I said. ''Go make us some tea and you'll read Maxine's scenes aloud with me.''

And then in a great Irish accent he lilted, ''So it's a cuppa tea you're after wanting, is it then, my fair colleen.''

I slugged him gently and went into my master bedroom suite to change into my customary flannel nightgown and faded chenille robe. As I reached for my furry bedroom slippers, I found a diamond-and-sapphire earring lying next to them on the floor. I picked it up and turned to put it in my unlocked jewelry drawer. When I opened the drawer, all my jewels were gone.

My new diamond necklace, Tony's sapphire-and-diamond earring (I was holding the other in my hand), William Holden's diamond wristwatch, Tony's Bulgari cabochon sapphire-and-diamond pin, Tony's diamond-and-sapphire bracelet, and Farley's diamond-pin question mark were all gone. What flashed into my mind first was how smart the Kennedy girls were, not to have diamonds and the responsibility thereof. Burt Lancaster's pearls were still in the drawer. My mind went blank. I awakened the housekeeper and the Southern girl babysitter but I was careful not to wake my daughter.

We all started to look. I was still clutching the earring. Alex wasn't quite sure what we were looking for. When I explained to him that my jewels were missing he immediately picked up the phone, dialed the operator, and asked for the police. When they connected him with the proper precinct he handed me the phone.

I told the police what had happened, giving them my name, address, and apartment number. I hung up. Alex said, ''Everyone sit down right where you are and do or say nothing until the police get here.''

I stared at Alex. It seemed to me he must be practicing for "Dragnet." It didn't dawn on me until the police actually arrived that the whole thing was quite serious. When it's over $100,000 it's grand larceny. I wasn't thinking about the money. I was just grateful that my daughter was sleeping quietly and safely in her youth bed and whoever had robbed me had been nice enough not to go near her. I made sure her door was firmly shut.

I didn't even feel anger. In fact, all I felt was gratitude. I guess I was in some kind of shock because Detective Enright took quite a while to question me and got very strange answers. He couldn't understand why I was so relieved and grateful to the robber. There were two policemen and two detectives in the house and some kind of lab man sprinkling my bedroom for fingerprints.

When I saw that happening I began to laugh hysterically and cry and the housekeeper went to the medicine cabinet to get me a Miltown. Detective Enright saw me take it and immediately said, "Do you have a prescription for these drugs?" I showed him the bottle and of course I did.

They wanted to question each person in the household in the kitchen so one by one Alex, the housekeeper, and the baby-sitter were grilled. As I walked down the hallway, I heard Alex giving the detective the Hotel Bolivar as his address in Manhattan. The police had taken the entire drawer that had contained the jewelry to the station house and there was white fingerprint dust all over the bedroom. I began to panic when I remembered that Alex Viespi had two guns and that cowboy holster in the back of his closet at his hotel and I was sure he had no permit. I looked up Alex Fondas's number in my phone book and called him immediately. If you ever have a robbery remember the phone is tapped immediately after a robbery.

When I got Alex Fondas on the phone I whispered, "Please go to the Bolivar Hotel. I will talk to the room clerk and he will give you the keys to Alex Viespi's room. Will you please do that? Take his holster and guns to some friend's apartment. Not to your apartment because they may search and question you and Bill because you were with me at Sardi's. Can you please do this for me, darling? I don't want him arrested for possession of prop guns because my damn jewels were stolen."

Alex Fondas, who was a big guy and had been a parachutist in the Army, was terrified, but he promised to do it. I quickly phoned the Bolivar. The room clerk recognized my voice and he promised to give Alex F. the key to Alex V.'s room. Of course the police were taping all of these conversations. It turned out that when Alex Fondas tiptoed into Alex Viespi's room he executed my instructions stealthily, carefully, and accurately, but when he saw a man in an overcoat in the mirror in the closet, he fainted dead away. Of course the man in the mirror was his own reflection. After I had given Alex Fondas his instructions, I put the phone down and hoped for the best or worst.

To make everything more confusing it turned out that the baby-sitter, a Southern minister's daughter, had a boyfriend by the name of Alex, whom I shall call Alex Dash. I found out later at the precinct that this case was known as Shelley Winters's Jewels and the Three Alexes: Alex Viespi, my beau, later known as Alex Cord; Alex Fondas, my friend; and the baby-sitter's boyfriend, Alex Dash. The very efficient Detective Enright, who was in charge of the case, was quite confused by this fact. I mean, when you have a burglary in a house in the movies or TV, the suspects don't all have the same name.

The following week was a nightmare. I believe it was the week before Christmas. Between learning the blocking for *Iguana*, buying Christmas presents, answering endless questions from Detective Enright, and trying to keep my daughter from knowing too much about the burglary, I became slightly crazed.

The morning of Christmas Eve, I discovered by overhearing two cops in front of my building that my phone had been tapped immediately after the robbery, so of course the detectives knew that Alex Fondas had picked up Alex Viespi's guns and of course knew where Alex F. had hidden them.

For some reason Detective Enright suddenly decided that Alex Viespi had to take a lie-detector test. The afternoon that Alex Viespi took the test I had to go to the matinee to see Madeleine Sherwood in *Iguana*. Frank Corsaro ordered me to cover my blonde hair and wear dark glasses and a coat with a stand-up collar, which hid most of my face. I got to the theater about five minutes early and sat in the back of the orchestra, making myself as inconspicuous as possible. Frank sat next to me and warned me not to open my mouth so no one in the theater would recognize my voice. Bette Davis had left the show after the previous Saturday night's performance, but there was no announcement in front of the theater or in the daily newspapers. As the lights were lowered, the stage manager announced over the loudspeaker, "At this performance the part of Maxine Faulk will be played by Miss Davis's understudy, the well-known stage actress Madeleine Sherwood."

After the announcement the curtain went up and the stage lights came up full but poor Madeleine never got a chance to open her mouth. Half of the audience stood up simultaneously and rushed to the box office to get their money back. This truly amazed me. I knew it probably was a theater-club matinee, but it was Tennessee Williams's play, and he was America's leading playwright. As the audience thronged up the aisle, Madeleine pulled a Shelley Winters. She came downstage and said, "Come on, ladies! Give me a chance! I'm really very good, and the play is terrific!"

Some of the ladies had the grace to go back to their seats and sit down, but obviously much of this matinee audience had come to see Bette Davis. Frank sat next to me, his body rigid with anger, and I can't say I blamed him. When the play started again he whispered to me, "There goes the Wednesday matinee. We played to an empty house last night. Almost the entire audience asked for their money back. If you don't go into *Iguana* soon the producers will have to close the show. I want you to rehearse on the set after tonight's performance."

It was, and is, against Actors' Equity rules to rehearse actors after they've performed a matinee and an evening performance, but none of the actors complained. They all understood that their jobs were in jeopardy. I left the theater at the first intermission to rush home and study my lines. Madeleine's Maxine Faulk was marvelous. It was hard to believe, given Margaret Leighton's delicate and lovely performance and Patrick O'Neal's powerful portrait of an alcoholic minister, that the audience would walk out on a great, poetic Tennessee Williams play. But they had, a great many at the intermission.

As I walked north on Eighth Avenue in the icy air, I could not imagine why Bette Davis had left the play in such an unprofessional manner. I knew Bette Davis was nothing if not professional, and I worried about what might have caused her to do this. She had obviously given her two weeks' notice before the play had even opened. Why? On my opening night a few days later I was to find out.

When I got back to the apartment Alex V. was having cocktails with Detective Enright. Alex F. was playing with my daughter, because the baby-sitter was out with Alex D.

Detective Enright stationed himself in my apartment almost twenty-four hours a day for the next few days. A uniformed policeman was in front of the building. I knew that Alex V. had taken his lie-detector test that afternoon but I didn't want to ask him how it had gone in front of the detective. When Detective Enright finally went into the kitchen to get some ice I whispered to Alex V., "Did the polygraph say you were guilty?"

He looked startled and whispered back, "Of course I'm not guilty. But I tried something interesting with the lie-detector test . . . I mean in case I ever have to take one in a movie."

I frantically whispered back, "For God's sake, Alex, what did you do?"

"Well, I took two of your Miltowns so I'd be calm and then I lied about every single question they asked me. Where I come from, who I am—all lies!" I sat down on the huge white marble cocktail table and could think of nothing to do but call the Chinese restaurant and order a lot of food for all the Alexes and the policemen and detectives.

* * *

That night, which was Christmas Eve, Harold Solomon, who lived upstairs, his wife Barbara, and Alex V. and I went down to the flower market to buy Christmas trees. It seems if you buy your Christmas tree late Christmas Eve you get ones that would normally cost $30 for $1 or $2. Harold Solomon, who was a millionaire, and a very astute and famous lawyer, could not see paying $30 for a Christmas tree. Barbara did not even try to argue with him. I got the feeling during the ride downtown that she was writing a story about my whole robbery, but the story never appeared anywhere that I know of. Then again she writes for very esoteric magazines like *The Nation*, *The New Republic*, and *The New Yorker*, and possibly *Playboy*.

Alex V. and I trimmed the Christmas tree, drinking eggnog, and then we went upstairs with Harold and Barbara and helped trim theirs. Their little daughters, Carla and Maria, seemed to know all about my jewel robbery. Although they were only six and eight they had wrangled all the information out of the elevator man. I tried to bribe them into not mentioning it to my daughter but over the years I have had a very strong feeling they did.

When I started to rehearse on the stage of the Royale at midnight Christmas Eve again I had that strange sense of *déjà vu*. What was going on in my life was so weird that Tennessee Williams's fantasy, *Iguana*, seemed like reality. I had often had the same feeling when I'd walked on the stage in *A Hatful of Rain*. The entire rehearsal period of *Iguana* is a blur. I just know that a week after Bette Davis had left the play I went on. There had been no announcement in the papers because they wanted to give me a few performances before the critics came. But that night when the stage manager announced, "Shelley Winters is playing the part of Maxine Faulk," the audience applauded and stayed in their seats. Nobody asked for their money back that night, thank goodness.

Since Detective Enright was showing up early Christmas morning, I got my kid upstairs to the Solomons' apartment, where she could show her little friends all her toys. I told Barbara not to bring her back down until I phoned. I wanted, on this Christmas Day, to have a lovely Christmas dinner with my daughter. I was going to get the police and all the Alexes out of my hair and to hell with my jewels. I was having bagels, lox, and cream cheese with Detective Enright when there was a knock at the door. It was my nosy elevator man and he handed me a present. It was a manila envelope tied with a pretty Christmas ribbon and my name and apartment number were typed on the front.

As I took it something jiggled inside. The elevator man closed the door and a few minutes later when I opened the envelope out slipped all my jewelry onto the coffee table, including Tony Franciosa's 6-karat diamond engagement ring, which I had thought was in the bank vault. I hadn't even reported that stolen. Detective Enright ran down the back steps. He obviously didn't want to wait for the stupid elevator man. The detective was in a hurry to catch whoever it was who'd delivered this envelope. But there on the table were my diamond necklace, Bulgari diamond-and-sapphire pin, diamond wristwatch, question-mark diamond pin, diamond-and-sapphire bracelet, and the other earring. I was quite grateful to have them all back.

I was carefully putting all the jewels back in a velvet jewelry box with a lock so I could take them to the bank vault when Enright came dashing in the front door. He obviously had a key. He grabbed the manila envelope, cursing curses I'd never heard before. He gingerly held the envelope while he called the station and garbled something violent.

Later I gathered that the policeman who was supposed to be on duty out front had gone down to the basement for a hot cup of coffee with the janitor. The elevator man could only describe the person who had handed him the envelope as someone male or female who was wearing a hat which covered the head, sunglasses which covered the eyes, and a coat with a stand-up collar which covered the face and neck. After this person had delivered the envelope he or she disappeared into thin air. The elevator man was getting very annoyed with Enright's questions. He turned to me and complained, ''Miss Winters, I've been delivering presents all over the building for several days. I can't remember every delivery boy for God's sakes. You got the jewelry back. What else do you want?"

Enright turned red, then green, in keeping with the holiday spirit. I answered, "Yes, I've got them back. Let's forget about the whole thing now. Okay?"

"Sure," Enright said, "and the next time this burglar steals he'll probably kill someone in self-defense. Okay?"

He grabbed the jewel box, gave me a receipt, and marched out of the apartment back to the station house, I hoped.

After several days of great detective work Enright found out who the robber was. It seems he had typed the envelope on a typewriter at the Sloane House YMCA on Thirty-fourth Street. He was the boyfriend of the baby-sitter—Alex Dash. It seemed that he and his girlfriend had been making love in my bed and she had said, "Look, there's her jewelry drawer. She doesn't want to insult the help by locking it."

For whatever reasons the kid couldn't resist. He had a previous record. He and some buddies in high school had swiped a car to go on a joyride, but he technically was a felon and guilty of grand larceny.

His family quickly shipped him to Puerto Rico and then called and asked me for leniency, so when Detective Enright brought extradition papers for me to sign I could not do it. I could not have some kid spending the next thirty years behind bars because I foolishly left my jewelry unguarded. Enright and the policeman were ready to kill me, but they agreed that they had only solved the case because the kid had returned the jewels. If he had thrown them into the Hudson River they would have never found him. So I bribed them with tickets for *Iguana* and a fancy dinner at Sardi's where they met all the theater and film stars, and I believe Enright was promoted. He became a lifelong friend and when he retired he became chief investigator for TWA. Because of his knowledge of movie-star jewels and their disappearances he was very successful at solving similar cases.

* * *

The whole run of *Iguana* is a blur. I stayed in *Iguana* until the backers were repaid, from Christmas until the beginning of September. After I served in *Iguana* I had an attack of hopelessness and decided to try California again.

The first time I walked into my dressing room backstage at the Royale, written on the mirror in very red lipstick were the following words: SHELLEY—AFTER YOUR FIRST OR POSSIBLY SECOND PERFORMANCE YOU WILL FIND OUT WHY I LEFT THIS SHOW. BETTE DAVIS.

Knowing how up-front Bette Davis was, I began to tremble with fear as I gazed at this message. What could she mean? Was some nut trying to shoot Maxine Faulk from the audience? Maxine walked barefoot on the stage. Was some deranged propman scattering broken glass on the stage? The two handsome Mexican cabana boys were played by Christopher Jones and Jimmy Farentino—not Mexicans, but certainly cabana boys. Did they plan devilish mischief against the character of Maxine? What could Bette Davis's cryptic message mean?

I soon found out. I went into the show a week after Bette Davis had left and Madeleine Sherwood had not washed Bette's message to me off the mirror. So whatever was going to happen to me must have happened to Madeleine, too, I reasoned. Madeleine (who was my standby too—even though I never missed a performance) either quit the show as a standby or never came near the Royale again, and just phoned in her whereabouts to the stage manager at seven-thirty. What was happening on stage was the following:

That matinee I had a wonderful first performance. The audience laughed and applauded my exits and entrances. The audience's response seemed much bigger and better than the ones that Bette Davis had gotten. Why had she just stood on the stage and shouted out her jokes? What a weird mystery.

My second performance was dismal . . . the evening audience laughed at nothing and I could see the first rows and they weren't even looking at me. I couldn't understand what had happened. I tried harder the third performance. Nothing worked. Finally, sometime between matinee and evening, Chris Jones, who was rather a mischievous young man, and later became a mischievous movie star, drifted into my dressing room and whispered, "Hey, Shell. I know you're big on all this Stanislavsky stuff, and this is my first show. But I think you ought to pay attention to what's happening on the other side of the stage while you're so deep in your Method stuff."

I didn't know what the hell he meant. But I decided to take his advice. That night, I just said the words and kept an eye on Margaret Leighton and Patrick O'Neal. Here's what was going on. Reader, concentrate.

A joke consists of two sentences: the setup and the answer. If the joke is properly set up—and everybody stands still on the stage—the audience will look and listen to the answer, and if it's delivered correctly, Method or not, they will laugh. *Iguana* is one of Tennessee Williams's most tragic plays—about a sensitive and intelligent alcoholic who is caught in the web of circumstance and goes to his almost certain death, like the iguana that is tied up under our stage veranda. Margaret Leighton and Patrick O'Neal had many long, poignant scenes. Tennessee wrote the part of Maxine Faulk for comic relief so their poetic scenes would work. If you do not give an audience a legitimate reason to laugh they will laugh in the wrong places because of tension. George Stevens made me understand that this was true in films as well as on the stage when he directed me in *Anne Frank*.

What was happening on the Royale stage was the following: Margaret Leighton or Patrick O'Neal would say the *setup* of my joke and then move slightly for a few seconds, keeping the eye of the audience so the audience was not looking at me or even listening. So when I gave the punch line they barely heard it.

It's hard to believe but that is what these two brilliant professional actors were doing. It took me about three performances to make sure. And then I understood why Miss Leighton had gotten such fabulous reviews and the great actress Miss Bette Davis had gotten some very good but many so-so ones. This is the device over which Bette Davis, the most professional of actresses, quit a hit show that had been largely sold out on the strength of her name.

Neither the producer, nor Tennessee, nor Frank, all of whom were supposedly such good friends of mine, had told me that this was what I would face. It's a wicked British stage trick and I have never seen it in an American production. Either Leighton, may she rest in peace, was so competitive with Davis—or she was so insecure that she wanted the audience to only remember her. She obviously had taught Patrick O'Neal to do it too—as soon as I started to get the attention of the audience she and Pat resorted to these stage tricks. The only way I could combat it was by delivering my lines straight and loud at the audience as soon as the setup of the joke was uttered. I stood this kind of acting for nine months. I would be damned if they would run me out of the show and close Tennessee's play. Frank Corsaro knew what was going on but he was powerless before that ego.

I finally understood why the audience became restless and why ticket sales of this great play were falling off. Audiences listen to only what they look at, unless the stage is completely dark. When Margaret Leighton was not on the stage Patrick O'Neal would become an Actors Studio actor again and I enjoyed those scenes. When I talked to the cabana boys or the iguana under the veranda I had fun, but the rest of the play was unbearable. I never envisaged having to act while defending myself or having to stand on a stage and watch two gifted actors destroy a play. That is exactly what they did and the play lasted about a month after I left. At some performances I felt as if I should make an announcement and give the audience their money back. But I had learned in the Westport School of Acting never to talk to the audience. I just gritted my teeth and prayed for Tennessee's sake the backers would get their money back quickly.

At one matinee performance the stepping on my jokes was so outrageous that I became enraged, and I pushed a cocktail cart which was part of the scene across the stage and knocked Patrick O'Neal over and he knocked Margaret Leighton over as he fell. The audience either liked this stage business or felt they deserved it. They applauded. I went on with my monologue, whatever it was, and felt very proud of myself. Frank rushed backstage during the intermission and told me I must be careful with the cocktail cart. I assured him it was an accident but it was so effective shouldn't we keep it in? He grinned and said, "No, Shelley. You might kill Margaret Leighton during one of her performances."

I rather thought that might be a good idea. This boring period of doing a play mechanically made me retreat into my adolescence again. I had never had a proper adolescence, certainly not the stressful one I had when I met Anthony Franciosa—I'd been working in the garment center when I was fifteen pretending to be eighteen. I'd been working in Woolworth's and organizing the retail garment workers when I was fourteen. I had never gone to proms or behaved in the normal carefree manner of a teenager. During my run of *Iguana* I made up for it.

Alex Viespi hung around New York and around the stage door. He became friends with Christopher and Jimmy Farentino. We carried that old Italian cinema proverb to new heights—"Only sleep on the boss's time." We partied every night and slept on the stage. Like the robot actors who had stayed in the show *Oklahoma!* for five years, I turned off my brain at 8:30 P.M. and woke up at 11:00 P.M. I could only perform in this automatic manner. Otherwise I would have gone crazy. It was self-defense. I eagerly awaited the end of my contract. But I'd be damned if I'd quit. Every night we would take the Jaguar out of Shubert Alley and Chris and Jimmy and Alex and I would find belly dancers in the Village, Mabel Mercer on the East Side, and jazz in Harlem. We once broke into Al Roon's Health Club at 3:00 A.M. for a swim. I was able to lock the door as we left, and thus escape arrest. We once ran out of gas on the West Side Highway. Nobody would walk to the nearest gas station. We just sat there, looking at the lights on the Jersey shore. There we sat—three handsome young men and a platinum blonde sitting on the hood of an enormous two-toned gray Jag with a British license plate. Christopher had thoughtfully provided several bottles of wine in the boot (trunk). Finally, à la Claudette Colbert in *It Hap-*

pened One Night, I showed a shapely leg and my three-inch heels in the headlights of the oncoming traffic. One car stopped and another one hit it—thankfully, not hard. While the drivers were yelling at each other, Christopher did something he'd learned in the Army. He siphoned off the gas from one car into a wine bottle, stealing enough gas for us to get off the elevated highway. Along with the British tools, the Jaguar company had thoughtfully provided a rubber hose.

I would try to stay out until my daughter got up at 6:00 A.M. to do her homework, and before she would go to school I would have breakfast with her, then I would sleep fast on matinee days or till 3:00 P.M. when she came home from school if there was no matinee. I didn't have to diet. I hadn't been so skinny since I'd been fourteen years old. I had no time to eat—just to drink. For some reason we never included any of the other cast members, especially the pretty girls in the show, in our nightly forays around Manhattan. In retrospect it reminds me of my film called *Bloody Mama* about Ma Barker, a lady gangster. She would never let any of her five sons have girlfriends. (But that's for the third book.)

I would often leave the theater in my blue jeans and sexy blouse costume and go to the Peppermint Lounge. We would often go to dinner at Sardi's on matinee days and although all male Sardi's customers had to have a shirt and tie to eat there, Vincent Sardi would seat us hooligans in a corner—Jimmy and Christopher and me in blue jeans and raggedy shirts and Alex in his cowboy gear. I guess Vincent figured everybody would see our orange makeup and my thick eyelashes and know we were in a play.

During the play, I was walking in the park with my child one afternoon, when a beautiful lady with platinum, purplish hair said to me in a very British accent, "Shelley, you are always dancing the twist wildly when I see you at Arthur's, and you never seem to have time to talk to me." I stood, stunned. Who was this beautiful, elegant lady with her couturier clothes, her platinum, slightly purplish hair, her elegant gloves and shoes? It took me a moment to register who she was.

The last time I had seen Sybil Burton she had looked like a dowdy little Welsh mouse, sitting among the sad Hollywood wives, while the celebrities were in another room and enjoying the party that was taking place at some big shot's house. The day I met her in the park the whole world was condemning Elizabeth and Richard and feeling sorry for Sybil. She laughed gaily and told me that she was making tons of money, that she and the very handsome young bandleader Jordan Christopher were getting married and were planning to have a large family. She was already expecting. They had bought a beautiful terraced apartment with many bedrooms overlooking the park, a block away from mine. They have had a very happy marriage. Jordan Christopher will never do a film unless his wife can come along wherever he works. (Did she or Elizabeth get the better deal?)

One of the producers of the play was a woman named Violla Rubber, an elegant theater-wise lady who knew what was going on onstage and knew how much it was costing me. Violla understood the reason for my rebellious behavior. One night she came into my dressing room during the hour wait I had while Margaret and Pat suffered on the stage. She wisely counseled me, "Shelley, the agony of performing in this play will pass in a few months. But you're an accomplished star of theater and films. You will want to work in England and to do other serious plays on Broadway. You have proved to producers that your drawing power can save a show. I was a great friend of Diana Barrymore's and I watched her destroy herself. Shelley, stop acting out your anger after the show. If you must do it, do it on the stage."

I listened carefully to her wise counsel, so I finally went to Lee Strasberg and discussed this professional dilemma. It was hard for him to believe that Patrick O'Neal and Margaret Leighton would do this to another actor onstage. So I bought him tickets in the fifth row and that night he and Paula came to the theater. After the show I met him in a quiet Chinese restaurant on Forty-sixth Street.

He quietly coached me, "Shelley, you cannot fight them in this manner. You cannot pretend that something that is happening on the stage is not happening. You must remember my first lesson, which is 'Use it.' Stop falling into their trap and stop trying to get laughs. That is the responsibility of the director. Use what Shannon and the spinster are doing and how they are insulting Maxine Faulk. Turn your back on the audience and act with all your talent. Ignore the audience and play the play."

I could not believe that I had not known to do this, after all the study and work I had done in the Method. That night I did not party. I went home and restudied the script, making my intentions and actions and affective memories clear. I called Violla Rubber and asked her to have the understudies on the stage at seven o'clock so I could rerehearse my role. By now it was the Ides of March but she got them to the theater as per my request. She and Frank watched from the audience. They came to my dressing room while I was making up. Frank had seen my rage when I had dealt in public with Tony Franciosa's shenanigans in Downey's. He looked at me quietly and said, "Tonight, Shelley, the play is going to be about Maxine Faulk. Never mind. I'll get Tennessee Williams to see it."

I said, "Do what you want, Frank. I can't stay in this play until September [when the backers would be paid off] and live, acting in this phony manner."

That night I turned my back on the audience and used my anger. Margaret Leighton was equal to the challenge, but Patrick O'Neal was shattered. I believe Miss Leighton had rehearsed him till he was also performing by rote, and I also believe they were having an affair—in other words, she was screwing him on- and offstage. But she knew how to use the new Maxine on the stage with her. She used her fear of my rage and horror and anger. At the end of our first scene the audience wildly applauded. At the intermission all the actors, who up till then had been divided into camps on stage left and right, crowded into my dressing room. I was weeping and trembling from the effort it had cost me, but they all congratulated me and said it was a different play. It was.

I have never made this stupid mistake again. To give Maggie her due, I believe she didn't say a word to Tennessee or Frank about the shift of emphasis in *Iguana*, but Patrick O'Neal was ready to kill me. He insisted that I was redirecting the play and it destroyed his role. We both were so stupid that we literally came to blows. He aimed for my chin but his blow accidentally landed on my bosom, and I hit him over the head with a beer bottle. Unfortunately it was a plastic prop beer bottle. The producers threatened to bring us both up on charges at Equity. I must say for Patrick he was between a rock and a hard place. He was trying to carry out the dictates of his inamorata and act with my Actors Studio–oriented Method. My will was very strong. And Patrick O'Neal finally rethought his role (I suspect with the help of Lee Strasberg). Shannon became more a victim of these two women than of alcoholism and he got bravos after the performances. At the matinee performance when he got his first bravos he again became my fellow actor and member of the Actors Studio and stopped the upstaging.

Business picked up and the play became a delight. We were finally speaking Tennessee Williams's beautiful words that expose the frail humanity in all of us. How a playwright depends on actors. If the performance we were now giving had been given opening night, Tennessee would have won the Pulitzer Prize for *Iguana* too, as he had for *Streetcar* and *Cat*. I wonder if when this book comes out I'll be able to dine at O'Neals' or The Ginger Man, the restaurants Patrick O'Neal now owns in New York.

When Tennessee saw the play he came backstage and waited for me in my dressing room. He gave me a big kiss and said, "I've been waiting six months and the whole rehearsal period to see my play. Why do actors need to be loved and liked on the stage?"

I was startled. I hadn't realized that I was playing for sympathy, but I guess I had been. Every human being on and off the stage wants to be understood and well liked. I hope I have never fallen into that trap again. If you act fully the audience will understand you; whether they like your character or not is unimportant. I have to keep remembering when I start a rehearsal of a play or movie that Richard Widmark achieved stardom and an Oscar nomination for throwing an old lady down the steps in a wheelchair. As a matter of fact, I put this knowledge to such good use that in 1965 I got another Oscar for *A Patch of Blue,* in which I beat up my blind daughter and try to turn her into a whore.

Tennessee began regularly taking me across the street to Harold's Show Spot on Forty-fifth during the hour-long scene in the third act that Maggie and Pat had. I'd gotten into a great deal of trouble in *Oklahoma!* when I'd done this, but Tennessee would tell the stage manager we were across the street having one drink and the poor stage manager would sweat for the hour we were there. But the assistant stage manager would come and get me in plenty of time. I would have one drink, but Tennessee would regale me with many wonderful stories while he had six. I recently found in my garage a play of his, unpublished and untitled, with notes in his own handwriting. I have another one in my New York apartment. I think it's called *The Last of My Teardrop Diamonds.* Either Tennessee or his companion Frank Merlo left them in my dressing room during *Night of the Iguana.* Or perhaps he gave them to me to hold while he was trying out *Iguana* at the Actors Studio. I must remember to give these scripts to the university that has his papers.

I especially remember Tennessee once telling me about his house in Key West. He invited me there many times. Alas, I never found time to go. He told me that when he got up early to write in Key West, he always went outside to look at the sky. If it was a certain shade of red, he would go back inside and get under the covers for the rest of the day. I tried to send Tenn to a psychiatrist to do something about his drinking. Even then, it was dangerous. I believe he briefly went to AA but he always seemed to know that he would die a strange and violent death. While Frank Merlo was alive he took care of Tennessee, so that he never suffered the consequences of his alcoholism. But after Frank's death Tennessee had one tragic accident after another.

During the run of *Iguana* I had dinner many times with Frank and Tennessee in a little apartment in an East Sixties brownstone which he complained about constantly.

He came to my apartment, which was huge and overlooked the park, and I tried to get him to buy one that was for sale above me. This great and famous American playwright pleaded poverty. I offered to lend him the down payment but he insisted he couldn't afford it. I finally called his agent, Audrey Wood, to say he seemed to want this big apartment so badly and all the agent said was, "Don't mix in. In reality he owns blocks of real estate, but he needs a little deprived place to write in. He doesn't feel he's entitled to a lovely apartment on Central Park West overlooking the park. He has his cronies and bars on the East Side. He's safer there."

I remembered Dylan Thomas had the same problem. Over the years I was to realize that home is where you function to the fullest. Never mind fashion or even comfort. Maybe that's why I cling to my Spanish duplex on the wrong side of the now-gone Beverly Hills trolley tracks.

One day Violla Rubber called me and asked me if I would please refuse to go with Tennessee to Harold's Show Spot during the performance. It was driving the producers crazy. Violla said, "Suppose something happens to you and you can't finish the third act."

Violla implored me not to put *Iguana* to this test, so I stopped going across the street with Tennessee. We would sit on the landing overlooking Forty-fifth Street— Tennessee, Chris, Jimmy Farentino and I. Tennessee would have little airplane bottles of brandy in his pocket and I was always terrified that the stage manager would think the actors were drinking. An actor can get kicked out of Equity for drinking backstage, although I don't recall anyone ever having been expelled from the union for this reason. I think it's just a threat. One night we were watching a show open across the street. It was sort of a play about Castro. Michael Ansara was playing Castro. We had seen an elegant opening-night audience go in at seven-thirty, and during our first intermission we watched that entire elegant audience walk out, every one of them. We couldn't believe it. Tennessee and I, Chris and Jimmy watched this mass of people run for cabs and limousines. This play closed before it opened. It was the playwright's first play, and I don't know if he ever wrote another. Tennessee sat there shivering, drinking brandy from those little bottles, empathizing with the playwright. Oh God.

Spring was springing up all over New York and the difficult winter was past. All the actors hung out together and Alex Viespi, who had gone back to California and done a segment of a very good TV Western, returned to New York. Jimmy Farentino was an official observer at the Actors Studio, but Chris Jones and Alex were sneaking in early and sitting up in the balcony and listening to Lee Strasberg. Both Jimmy and Chris suddenly had an attack of the Method. In May, after a performance, Frank Corsaro called the cast together for notes. He screamed, "Why the fuck have the cabana boys' parts gotten so important? They're only on the stage to move the props around. What the hell is happening around here?"

Tennessee hid under a seat. Chris and Jimmy and I had been hanging around with Tennessee, driving around Manhattan in my Jaguar after the show. Tennessee had been telling Christopher and Jimmy what to do in order to get the audience's attention. As a matter of fact, Chris was doing an interior monologue that Tennessee had written for him for an audition at the Actors Studio. No one but the audience had noticed that the cabana boys had developed their interior lives on the stage. We in the cast were so concentrated on our own roles that we hadn't realized it either. Frank screamed, "*Night of the Iguana* is no longer about Shannon and the death of the iguana. It's now about Maxine Faulk and her two Mexican studs."

I remained silent. The stage manager remained silent. Patrick looked like the cat that had swallowed the canary, and Maggie Leighton removed herself astrally. She was too British and professional to get involved in this Method brouhaha. Frank called a rehearsal for the next morning, sans Tennessee, and de-emphasized the cabana boys' roles, but he left Maxine Faulk alone.

Tennessee early had realized these boys were potential

movie stars, and Jimmy was dark and looked right to play a Mexican role. Chris Jones had almost blond hair, but Tennessee insisted he be in the show.

We were off Sundays and Mondays, so on Tuesday afternoon Chris would put black shoe polish in his hair, but by Thursday night it was almost out. So on the weekends *Night of the Iguana* had a blond Mexican cabana boy. I guess neither Frank nor the producers ever came to the show on weekends because it was sold out and they were in Connecticut.

New York was beautiful that spring. Alex acted as our chauffeur. In the early 1960s you could still go through Central Park at night. Our group now included Tennessee, Chris Jones, and Patricia Roe, who played the lesbian schoolteacher in *Iguana*. We'd circle the outer drive of the park, entering on the East Side, going up to 125th Street and around to the West Side. We would do this for a couple of hours, looking at the lights in the skyscrapers, smoking pot and hazily hallucinating. Most of the time we would end up at the Peppermint Lounge or Arthur's or one of Tennessee's secret haunts in the West Village. Tennessee would ramble for hours and if tape recorders had been as small as they are now, I would have taped everything he said. At a certain point about 2:00 A.M., he would speak pure and profound poetry. We then would deliver him to Frank Merlo around 3:00 or 4:00 A.M. He would never go home until he was just this side of unconsciousness. At his building we rang the bell, to the beat of "Shave and a Haircut, Six Bits." Frank would come running down the stairs and catch Tennessee as he fell.

Chris and Jimmy and Alex would deliver Patricia to her beautiful old apartment in a historic landmark building on Seventh Avenue, first stopping at the Stage Deli for huge sandwiches, which we would eat in her stately drawing room. After the boys delivered me home, God knows what they did, because they had a rule that they never went to sleep until the sun was fully up. Ah youth, where is thy fling?

In June, Alex showed up backstage looking as pale as the wall of my newly painted dressing room. He was clutching a script and announced to one and all that he had an audition for the greatest play of the century. The title was *To Play with a Tiger,* the theater adaptation of Doris Lessing's book. It was to be done in England on the West End with Siobhan McKenna. Alex rightly felt that it was the chance of a lifetime. When I read the play I agreed with him. It was about an intellectual British writer and her affair with a macho American writer fifteen years her junior. Doris Lessing had created the American character with extraordinary insight—he was a young Hemingway, the intellectual with muscles. It was a funny, sad, and beautifully written play. Why it never came to Broadway I don't know. If I could manage a believable British accent I would do it now. I've thought about it for the last twenty-five years.

For the next few days I worked with Alex on this role. He was a good actor, but did not have the life experience to make the choices that were necessary to make this pseudointellectual on the fringe of the literati come to life. We went over his long scene, idea by idea, thought by thought, and at the end of two or three days of rehearsing at the Actors Studio, when we could get the space, he was quite marvelous. During one rehearsal Lee Strasberg was sitting in the balcony. He had gone up there to examine the light panel, and he had sat down in a seat with the stage manager and listened to me coach Alex. I did not know Lee was there. At the end of a half hour he came down the steps and made his presence known to me. I was aghast. He gave me a little kiss and said, "Shelley, you really understand our Method work. It is habitual and finely tuned to your acting instrument. In the years to come you must study speech and make yourself play the great roles, not just the movie nonsense. This boy will get the role. He is very good. But when he does you're going to have to rehearse the whole play with him."

I thanked my wonderful teacher and watched him go down the steps to the office. I knew there was no way I could thank him for his many hours of teaching and hoped I could follow his advice.

I never did. I was caught up in the trap of movie stardom, my financial obligations to my family, and the trappings of success as defined by our society in the decade of the 1960s.

Alex had been speechless when I'd introduced him to Strasberg, but the great man had said that he was very good and with that confidence Alex went to his audition and got the role, his first legitimate role.

When I wasn't proud of him I was intensely jealous. Alex had to go to London and meet other producers and the director. Then they sent him back to New York while they had to read every British young actor who thought he had an American accent and every American actor married to a British actress with a permit to work in England. And only then would British Equity give the producers the right to have Alex return to London and star in this play. It took all summer long and I believe he went into rehearsal in the West End in September.

He starred in not one but two long runs on the British stage. He became the darling of the British critics. He also had his lovely Roman nose operated on before he left for London, and then he had another operation when he came back from his triumph in London. I think some important agent had told him to do this. When he came back to New York the next winter he was in a big television show, playing the part of a Russian spy. He was terrific in the show. His facility with accents was incredible. After all, two summers before he had almost convinced me he was a cowpoke from Texas when in reality he was a bricklayer from Long Island. But the sad thing that happened was that he was invited by Tyrone Guthrie to open the first season of the Guthrie Theatre in Minneapolis. He was to play Horatio and two other great classic roles and to stand by for Hamlet. My friend Rita Gam played the Guthrie that season. At a luncheon I had with Alex he informed me that he could not go work for $250 a week for a whole season. His agent wouldn't allow it. I warned, "Alex, fire that agent. You go pay Tyrone Guthrie $250 a week. You will learn things that you will use for the rest of your career. You will become a great theater and film star." Obviously the greedy agent won this argument. Not long ago, Alex played a role in a TV sitcom about a helicopter. He played a blond villain with a black patch over one eye, a limp, and a very nice nose. He's still a young man and if fate smiles he will have the career he deserves and will at last fulfill the early promise he showed in London and at the Actors Studio.

July arrived with all its heat, but I guess I'm one of the few people in the world who loves New York in the summer. Because of my name I'm always cold. In fact, I still hate air-conditioning. My friends have to find restaurants with gardens and no air-conditioning if they want to have dinner with me. We drove around the silent Wall Street area on Sundays, and up and down the West Side Highway and the East Side Drive. I had sent my child to a camp near the Grand Canyon that Julie Harris had recommended. It had classes in French and ballet and everything that I thought my kid loved. In the middle of that hot summer she sent me a telegram after being at this expensive camp only a couple of weeks: HELP HELP MOM THIS IS A CONCENTRATION CAMP AND I AM IN THE HOSPITAL. (She had a cold.)

I quickly had the counselors put her on a plane for California where my mother greeted her with sympathetic and open arms. *Iguana* ground on. I stayed in New York and everybody sweltered but me. My child went to day camp in California and we had a visit every night on the telephone. I longed to return to California. Nobody I knew was still in New York and some late Saturday nights we would drive out to East Hampton and visit various theatrical luminaries with homes in the Hamptons and Montauk. Even though East Hampton was sparsely settled in the early sixties I never wanted a home there. In a way it's like Malibu, a never-never land, and the culture shock when you return to the reality of New York in September is too great. Everyone leaves their problems in Manhattan and goes to Fire Island or the Hamptons in the summer, but the problems are waiting there and reach new proportions when everyone returns.

I don't know if it was my name that attracted the tourists or the strong air-conditioning at the Royale that I was allergic to, but the box office during that summer of *Iguana* stayed at SRO. Frank Corsaro had disappeared but Violla Rubber would call rehearsals when our performances got lazy. I had to sit outside the stage door on a chair placed on the sidewalk whenever I wasn't on stage because of the damned air-conditioning.

One night Tennessee and Frank Merlo took me to a literary party in a gorgeous apartment overlooking the East River. Alex was awaiting his work permit from England and was very nervous and jumpy and had not come along with me. As a matter of fact, I think Tennessee had included him out.

I don't remember whose party it was but many of the famous writers of the early sixties were in attendance—James Baldwin, Mary McCarthy, Norman Mailer, and Barbara Solomon. Tennessee, like me, got very shy in the presence of intellectual giants. I was afraid I would use the wrong word in the wrong place, but Tennessee just, somehow, was afraid. As was his wont, Frank Merlo would disappear when Tennessee entered a party. I guess he wanted Tennessee to shine on his own or for whatever reason. The party went along swimmingly. We listened while the wit flashed around us, and when I came back from the buffet with plates for Tennessee and myself, I found Norman Mailer quite drunk, towering over Tennessee. He was at his sexiest worst or best, depending on your point of view. He was funny and lethal, all at Tennessee's expense. I think history has already shown who was the greater writer, but at that time from my point of view Norman was verbally trying to prove he was. Tennessee seemed incapable of defending himself. I tried to protect him but I was no match for Norman who was on a roll. Suddenly it seemed that Norman was challenging Tennessee to come outside and settle the problem, whatever it was. I was not exactly sober but I was not drunk, and I could not believe what I was hearing. Norman back then was going through his prizefight period and was working out at the boxers' gym on Fourteenth Street and had recently stabbed his wife, Adele, who was a friend of mine. I did not want to get stabbed but I did not want him beating up Tennessee as entertainment in front of the entire New York intellectual community. Tennessee started to go outside and I followed, but when we all got to the street, Frank Merlo was somehow the person facing Norman, his fist at the ready. This quiet, peaceful East Side street had been electrified and people were hanging out of the brownstones and the entire party had moved to the street. Norman suddenly got less drunk when he realized his opponent was the brawny Frank Merlo instead of the frail Tennessee. I think Norman was going to out-insult Frank rather than fight. Tennessee had recovered his wicked wit by now and was shouting insults at Norman from behind me. Not one blow, however, was exchanged. Luckily or unluckily, the police arrived to stop the fight, to the disappointment and boos of the entire street.

The show ground on. Chris Jones, who had become the Peck's Bad Boy of the company and at all times looked so like my dead friend Jimmy Dean it was spooky, suddenly did something nice. He arranged a party for me at Daniel Blum's house. Daniel was a theater critic and writer, and he had an estate on the beach at Sag Harbor, Long Island. We left after the show Saturday night in my Jag and really tested its speed because we arrived by 1:00 A.M. There was a 90-MPH speed limit in those days, but I think the Jag didn't know it.

Sometime during the summer of '60, I had done a summer-stock tour in upstate New York, and I was driving the Jag to the airport to return to California and talking to my secretary, sitting beside me in the car. It was 6:00 A.M. Suddenly a car appeared alongside me, motioning me to the side of the road. When I stopped I realized it was an unmarked police car. The policeman looked at me white-faced and said, "Miss Winters, do you know how fast you were going?" I answered, "Just a few miles over the speed limit, I suppose." He looked at the elegant British speedometer on the burled-elm dash and informed me that I had been going 120 MPH. In that car it felt like 50. He took me to the judge in a small town off the New York Thruway, and the judge gave me a five-minute lecture and then leaned over and said, "Miss Winters, do you know where I can get product? I own two drive-in theaters in this neighborhood and I'm having some difficulty getting first-run movies." I flirted and gave him my agent's name and he let me off with a $100 fine and a warning that one more offense and I would lose my license. But for a few minutes there I thought I was headed for jail.

Meanwhile, on August 4, 1962, Daniel Blum showed me to a lovely guest house and he then showed Chris and Alex to a room in the main house. I was exhausted after a matinee and evening performance and the long fast drive, even at the Jaguar's rate. I creamed my face and got rid of my stage makeup, which I'd had on since 1:00 P.M., took a hot shower, and put on one of my glamorous flannel nightgowns. The ocean was lulling me to sleep when there was a slight knock on the door. Alex just had to talk to me about his script of *To Play with a Tiger*, which was under his arm. He was nervous because he was getting his return ticket for England any moment. Anyway, that's what he said. But he assured me that if I cued him in the role one more time, he would be able to relax and go to sleep in Daniel Blum's elegant main house. Believe it or not, for the next two hours I cued handsome Alex in the play he was to open in in London in October. Several hours later I was sleeping soundly and I assumed that Alex had gone back to his room and roommate. Suddenly there was a loud pounding on the door and before I could answer it Chris Jones had kicked the door open. He looked at Alex, who was sleeping on the floor with his head on the script, and yelled, "Hey, Shell, your girlfriend just committed suicide last night."

I stared at him, thinking, What a jealous little boy. I wasn't his mother. What right did he have to break in my bedroom door? He then repeated, "Your friend Marilyn. Marilyn Monroe. She committed suicide last night. We just saw it on the TV news."

The little bastard was smiling delightedly as he gave me this information. I had no reaction. I must have somehow gotten into my bathing suit because I went out to the patio where Daniel Blum and some other guests, including Mike Steen, a friend of Tennessee's, were having breakfast. They all were staring at me in a strange fashion. I asked Mr. Blum where the water-ski lessons were and he pointed a ways down the beach. Chris and Alex made motions to go with me. I think I hit them.

I walked down the beach feeling and thinking nothing. In some unconscious part of myself I decided that if I could stay up on the skis the very first time out *I* would not commit suicide. It was a selfish reaction, but that was what happened. I found the instructor and I must have looked strange, because he asked me if I wanted to postpone the lesson until the afternoon. I said, "No. Now."

He instructed, "Pretend the water skis are your feet, and you will balance on them. Let the motorboat pull you."

The motorboat and the rope pulled me off the beach and I stayed up on the skis the very first time. I swung around the motorboat some ways out and then I deliberately fell off the skis. I clung to one of them and began to cry hysterically. Or perhaps I was screaming.

The next thing I really remember is someone giving me artificial respiration on the beach. I had not drowned but I was still sobbing and my eyes seemed to be bleeding. My survival sense made me swim but it's very difficult to breathe *and* cry underwater, even though I had practiced it in a couple of pictures. All I could think of then was, If only . . . if only.

Marilyn had lived with Henry Weinstein and his wife in my rented house until a few months earlier, and then she had bought her own little house. I guess I was so busy with my own problems that I didn't take the trouble to stay in touch. All I could think was, Why didn't I have a service on my New York phone as I had on my California phone? But it had never seemed necessary to screen my calls when I was in New York.

I had been a role model for Marilyn, I guess. When I cut my hair short, she cut hers; when I got married, she got married; when I left Hollywood for New York, so did she; when I got into the Actors Studio, she became an observer. There's a Chinese proverb that says, When you save someone's life you are responsible for the rest of that person's life. I hope it isn't true. Anyway, so far I haven't committed suicide. But I had a mother and father and now a child and was able to reach out to my peers. I guess I was lucky. I never got as famous as Marilyn.

Although there was a pleasant weekend planned I could not stay in Sag Harbor anymore. We all piled into the front seat of the Jag and silently drove back to New York. No one spoke and I didn't cry. Perhaps I'm only allowed to cry underwater. We were going very fast and a yellow light began to flash on the dashboard. Neither I nor the young men paid any attention to it. Somewhere entering New York we got lost. We had been driving very fast for quite a while and I guess Alex was afraid to stop the car and ask directions. Around Nyack, New York, the yellow light turned to red but still we paid no attention . . . and then the Jag blew up.

As the steam and smoke rose from the hood I just sat there. Alex had to push me out of the Jag. Chris Jones somehow managed to carry me to the grass on the side of the thruway. I began at last to sob. I think the boys pushed the Jag to the side of the road. When I was finally able to stand up I said, "Leave it. Let's get a cab in Nyack." Only now as I write I wonder why I didn't remember I had a psychiatrist who in the summer lived in Nyack. Where had Marilyn's psychiatrist been? Where were Paula and Lee? All of her California so-called friends? She must have reached out for help. I think she had tried suicide a couple of times before that. Maybe she was drinking and forgot the number of pills she had taken. Since that day I have never had a drink after dinner because I often have to take a sleeping pill.

When we got in the cab I was still crying. When we finally arrived in Manhattan my apartment was empty. Molly had gone somewhere for the weekend. The boys called the doctor in my building and he gave me a shot. I wouldn't let anyone go back for the Jag. I didn't want it anymore.

A couple of months later a New York state trooper called me and told me that they had traced the ownership of that Jag through its English license plates to me. I said to the astonished officer, "You keep it. I don't want it." He hastily explained that the engine had "seized because of lack of oil," but that the Jaguar company was air-expressing a new engine to me through the Jag dealer in Nyack. I said, "Thank you, sir, but you keep it. I don't want it." And I hung up.

I never liked Chris Jones after that weekend, or trusted him. How strange fate is. He married Susan Strasberg, the daughter of Paula and Lee. Susan was a fine actress even then, but Marilyn had somehow usurped her position as daughter of the house. Lee and Paula were Marilyn's surrogate parents for a few years. Would Marilyn still be alive if I'd never moved to New York and joined the Actors Studio? Stupid question.

24

I guess I had a birthday that August, the eighteenth. If anyone attempted to say, "Happy birthday," I growled. I somehow continued in *Iguana* until the backers were paid off and I left the show September 1.

I had tried to get Tennessee to give some of his movie money to the producer to help pay off the backers (so I could leave sooner), but it seemed that Audrey Wood did not know how much they would be getting for the film of *Iguana*. It depended on how long the show ran.

At some point after I left, I believe Paula Laurence, the producer's wife, played Maxine. When I finished my last performance, I wanted to go onstage and say good-bye to the empty seats. One of Clifford Odets's lines in *The Country Girl* is, *"Nothing is quite so mysterious and silent as a dark theater . . . a night without a star . . ."* When I ran down the steps from my dressing room onto the stage I bumped into Margaret Leighton, who was still drilling Patrick O'Neal in his line readings. Poor Paula Laurence.

They probably kept the show running for a few more weeks to increase the movie money, but I didn't care to find out. All I knew was that although Ray Stark had promised me the role of Maxine in the film, he gave it to Ava Gardner. I would have loved to go to Mexico and *act,* or *whatever*, with Richard Burton. In those days he was famous for both. I imagined that Ava Gardner did the role for the same reasons, and not just to get revenge because I'd whisked Anthony Franciosa out of Italy.

I returned to my L.A. duplex in time to have two or three weeks with my daughter, who was now a very smart little girl of nine going on nineteen. Suddenly she said she was much too big to ride on the ponies anymore. Nowadays I keep looking at the huge Beverly Center Mall and wondering how those little pony rides on La Cienega were turned into this huge mall.

My agents were delighted and scurried around to find me a picture to do as soon as my daughter left for her school's orientation day. There still was a constant struggle between me and my agency; they were trying to force me to live and work in California and I was still determined to live and work in New York. Sure enough, an hour after I took my daughter and mother and Molly to the plane I walked into my agent's office and they were waiting for me. There sat the president and vice-president of the company, a woman agent, my agent, and the treasurer of this huge agency. There were several scripts on my agent's desk. For an hour and a half they regaled me with stories of how a star must strike while the iron is hot.

A star's "hot" life only lasts a few years, and I was hot. I believe my salary was somewhere around $150,000 per picture at that point. That's equal to about $600,000 now in purchasing power. The most expensive Cadillac then was about $5,000—that obviously is my measure of the value of a dollar.

I sat and listened patiently to all these bigwigs. I realized they were probably telling the truth, and this was the period that I could get secure and rich for the rest of my life. I didn't yet know that there is no such thing as security.

While they were haranguing me, I noticed a thin envelope on a side table addressed to me in care of my agency. They were talking at me so hard they didn't notice when I slipped it between the three movie scripts they had given me. I agreed with everything they said and promised I would read the scripts as soon as possible and let them know which film I wanted to do.

As I left I asked them to let me know in the morning which movie had the shortest schedule. They were rather puzzled by that request. One of them said, "Don't you want to know who the directors are?"

I wasn't interested in prestigious directors or producers or scenarists or studios. I just wanted to get back to my family and the New York stage. But I must say I was afraid to tell that to this important agency. They wouldn't have understood, and might not have wanted to represent me any longer. Even back then they were into packaging; that means if one of their stars agreed to do a film, then the agency would insist that the studio hire one of its high-priced, important directors and other stars they represented.

When I got home I sat in my garden under my two-hundred-year-old tall pine tree and read the script in the slim envelope addressed to me that I had recovered from my agent's office. It was an extraordinary play—in fact, two one-act plays. One was called "Snowangel" and the other "Epiphany." Together they were an evening in the theater called *Cages*. The title referred to "the cages of the human spirit," as the playwright later told me. They had been written by someone I'd never heard of, Lewis John Carlino. The producer, Judith Marechal, whom I also had never heard of, had sent me the plays in care of my agent and she was hoping to raise the money to do them off-Broadway at the York Playhouse, which was owned by Warner LeRoy. Warner was the son of the famous director Mervyn LeRoy, who had been my director on a little picture at MGM and had let me go test for *A Double Life*. I don't really think magically, but that day I did. I had stayed in *Iguana* many months and Bette Davis had gotten the opening-night reviews. *Cages* would be two roles that I would create.

The first play, "Snowangel," is about a sad, funny whore who tries to make a kinky impotent client understand that *love*, which he is trying to buy, is not buyable.

"Epiphany," the second one-act play, is about an ornithologist who is married to a powerhouse Madison Avenue lady. He is mystically trying to turn himself into a huge prehistoric bird in order to achieve dominance over his wife. At the end of the play when he was kneeling at my feet with his head in my lap, he tried to crow like a rooster, but only made hen. The audiences either were horrified or wept. Carlino was way ahead of his time. I think he was posing a question, Do men get weak if women get strong? In the sixties, this play was called theater of the absurd. Now it would be called a social document.

The afternoon I read these new plays I ran, not walked, into my house and called Miss Judith Marechal, whoever she might be.

She was overjoyed to hear from me and informed me that if I did the plays Jack Warden would do them too. Jack was a great comedic film and stage actor. I was happy and I was stunned. She took my silence for doubt.

"Miss Winters," she said, "I have put a deposit on the York Playhouse and as soon as their current bill closes we'll have the theater."

I was shivering with joy. Whoever the hell Lewis John Carlino was he was a great playwright. I quickly read the movie scripts and when they told me the shooting schedules I immediately accepted Paramount's *Wives and Lovers*. I sent Judith Marechal a telegram of intent, accepting *Cages*.

The only problem was, Hal Wallis, producer of *Wives and Lovers*, thought I had accepted the leading role in his film, but I wanted to do the funny secondary role opposite Ray Walston. That role was wonderful; the leading role was blah, a suburban wife and mother. Besides, the shooting schedule for the character I wanted to play was only four weeks.

My agent remonstrated with me. I've forgotten what the other two pictures were but they were leads in important pictures with long schedules. I didn't care. I wanted to do a film quickly and get back to New York.

"Shelley," he argued, "it's a second lead in *Wives and Lovers*. If you won't do it, Janet Leigh will play the lead opposite Van Johnson. You're a big marquee name and the part you want to do is very funny but it's opposite Ray Walston, who is not a leading man."

"That's great," I answered. "Ray's an original comic talent. I long to work with him. I saw him four times when he played the devil in *Damn Yankees* opposite Gwen Verdon on Broadway. They were fantastic."

I hung up on my agent and pondered about playing a second lead. What the hell was he talking about? I'd gotten an Oscar for a supporting role in *Diary of Anne Frank*, and I remembered what George Stevens had said. He'd told me that if I switched to character roles while I was still young, I would act for the rest of my life. Besides, when you do a secondary or supporting role you often get all the glory if the movie's a hit and none of the blame if it's a flop.

Wives and Lovers was an important film. The script was charming and funny and Edith Head would design my clothes. I spent the next week at the Beverly Hills Health Club, mostly in the sauna, studying the plays "Snowangel" and "Epiphany." When I was size 10 again I reported to the Paramount wardrobe department.

I couldn't go to any of the parties or charity benefits that I was being invited to. I was still on the A list in Hollywood's social scheme but Alex Viespi (who now was beginning to be known as Alex Cord) was in England becoming a star and I did not have an escort.

In New York I will go to any affair with another woman or alone, but in Hollywood if you don't have an attractive escort the other women present are afraid of you (as perhaps they should be). The nice photographers are ashamed for you and don't take your picture.

Even now, with women's lib, they hardly ever do. The paparazzi and fans in front of Spago look the other way if you're with another woman or alone, they're so humiliated for you. If you're with a man, even if he is unknown, they ask his name or the *Enquirer* makes up a profession for him, usually calling him a producer. God forbid you go to dinner with someone not famous or not in the business. I still go to Spago often—it's the best food in Hollywood—with other ladies.

As soon as they saw the rushes and okayed my departure I left for New York on the red-eye. My agents could do anything they wanted to. The only offer I had around the East Coast was to lecture at, of all places, Harvard on the subject of the *theater of the absurd,* which was just beginning to explode around New York. Nudity, radical politics, new concepts of the male-female relationship, black humor—the sixties were under way, and the theater was in the vanguard.

Judith Marechal called me and told me that we could not have the York Playhouse or the money for *Cages* until after the first of the year. I told her I would wait and began to get to know the playwright, Lewis Carlino, whom I invited to my house every other day because I suspected he was starving. He had had one play done off-Broadway and he was living with his wife and small child in some cold-water apartment way, way over on the West Side. In my opinion he was indeed a genius and I kept remarking that I didn't know what to do with my child's old crib and mattress and baby clothes, which were cluttering up my closets. Molly would manage to send him home with these articles and packages of food and I would pretend I didn't know. I was so glad this brilliant playwright had written two such great roles for me, and besides, he was such a lovely human being. He was slim and shortish and dark with dark, twinkling eyes, but there was something very Tennessee Williams–ish about him. He had a shy, pretty wife whom I met only once and they both were ecstatic that Jack Warden and I were going to do his play. In the years to come he would become a famous screenwriter, director, and producer, but then he was living in appalling poverty. During that winter Judith Marechal was able to raise enough money to advance him small amounts to live on. Alex Cord had left some overcoats and jackets in my apartment when he left for England, and I swiped one and gave it to Carlino. It was too big for him in the shoulders and he said, "Do you have these in all sizes?" He twinkled at me and I twinkled back, saying, "Maybe. Want to put in an order?"

Carlino wrote every day, often in a warm corner of my

living room. He helped me with my Harvard lecture—thank goodness, because when I got to Kirkland House in Cambridge, I soon realized that the undergraduates had set up the blonde bombshell for verbal slaughter. They were planning to roast me, but I stunned them with my erudition, not only about the sixties theater of the absurd but more particularly the labor movement in America and how it was expressed on Broadway in the late thirties and forties and fifties. I didn't tell them that I had been briefed by a scholarly playwright from Yale.

At the end of the lecture, instead of inviting questions I sang them my union songs, à la *Meet the People* and *Pins and Needles*. Many of these Harvard boys were then the sons of millionaires, but they joined in and yelled "Strike!" on cue. I looked at all those kids closely. I knew that Harvard was the mecca and birthplace of Kennedy's Camelot. That evening I had dinner with the entire student body of Kirkland House.

I can't remember the name of the restaurant but I remember I had succulent lobsters with garlic butter. We took over the whole place. These ardent Ivy Leaguers were all so young, beautiful, eager, and optimistic and the world was unfolding for *them*. The pessimism of the late sixties had not settled in yet. I had to keep reminding myself that nineteen-year-old college boys were too young. They all took me in a jolly caravan to the airport. At the shuttle I waved to them and prayed there wouldn't be another Korea.

I made lifelong friends and many of those young men, who are now bank presidents, stockbrokers, lawyers, and writers, visit me on both coasts. Of course, after that experience my daughter had to go to Harvard, which she did and graduated *cum laude*.

Judith Marechal still did not have all the money for the production of *Cages*. *Suddenly Last Summer* was still playing at the York. Being a workaholic, I did not know what to do with myself. I concentrated on becoming a crackerjack ice skater; I never made it, but my kid got pretty expert. Frank Corsaro would go with us sometimes to the Wollman Rink in Central Park and he was an expert speed ice skater. He could outskate anyone on the rink.

One cold winter afternoon, we all traipsed back to my apartment for hot chocolate and cookies, and I found a film script that someone had left with the elevator man. It was called *The Balcony*. I immediately sat down to read it and was furious. It was weird and disconnected writing, and besides, it was another hooker madam part; in fact, the whole picture took place in a whorehouse. With my daughter going to fine schools, I did not want to play a film hooker part since I was going to do one off Broadway that winter. So I threw the script on the floor in disgust. To this day I've never really learned how to read a film script. I guess I'm a theater actress and mostly look at the dialogue. I thank my lucky stars that Frank was in my apartment that day. Sometime later Frank picked up this discarded script and in a reverent voice said, "My God, Shelley, they're going to make a film of Genet's *The Balcony*." I said, "What, Frank?" He told me, "It's still playing off Broadway—two years now. It's the quintessential theater of the absurd. Jean Genet wants you to do it? Who the hell's gonna direct it?"

I looked at Frank's amazed face, then took the script from him and read the attached letter. I pretended I'd dropped the script on the floor accidentally. I rushed into my dressing room, first locking the door, and then I carefully read the attached letter and the script. The letter was from a Mr. Joseph Strick. He seemed to be a new director-businessman, and he was doing this film independently. He had bought the property from Genet in Paris.

I hadn't known who Dylan Thomas was but I certainly now knew who Jean Genet was. Though France's most celebrated writer of the time, Genet was in prison. I had seen scenes adapted from his novel *Our Lady of the Flowers* at the Actors Studio and I had heard Lee Strasberg and Harold Clurman discuss him in the writers' and directors' unit at the Actors Studio. At the time I was a little vague as to whether he was a living or dead playwright and I was ashamed to ask anyone, but when the film was completed and Genet saw a rough cut in Paris, he sent me a letter, which Barbara Solomon translated for me, and I knew he was alive.

"I have seen many productions of my *Balcony* in many languages," Genet wrote, "but your madam is absolutely the definitive madam. *Merci.*"

Joe Strick told me that Genet felt that I very much understood the mother in the madam. The play and the screenplay were indeed before their time. *The Balcony* is about men who need to act out their political kinkiness. The madam arranges the "scenes" with costumes and props and girls. All these episodes are performed against a background of revolution or civil war. It sounds like 1990, but it was over twenty-five years ago that we made this film. There was nothing salacious or explicit in the film, and the *New York Times* critic wrote that our film was "relentlessly funny, shaggy, shocking." But some holy-roller magazine they quoted in the ads said, "Unfit for exhibition to man, woman or child!" Compared with today's films, like *Fatal Attraction* and *The Unbearable Lightness of Being*, *The Balcony* was *Rebecca of Sunnybrook Farm*.

I was afraid my agent wouldn't allow me to do this offbeat film which was truly theater of the absurd, but it had a message which I only really understand in the context of today.

The Balcony is not available in cassettes and I've never seen it on TV. I wish Joe Strick would rerelease it. Back in the winter of '62, when I called him at the phone number on his letterhead, we made the following deal. He had directed an experimental film produced by his company, City Film Corporation, and he invited me to see it at the Paramount screening room. City Film would produce *The Balcony* too and if I played the madam I would get 20 percent of the company, including its past films and its future films. For the actual work on *The Balcony* I would get scale, which then was about $500 a week. In the flush of joy at being offered a film of Jean Genet's I immediately accepted. Joe Strick also convinced Peter Falk, Leonard Nimoy, Peter Brocco, Ruby Dee, Kent Smith, and Jeff Corey to take stock in City Film and work for scale. The only one who refused and wasn't interested was Lee Grant (smart girl). She insisted on being paid her regular salary. After Joe Strick finished *The Balcony,* I don't know what happened to the money but we actors got paid very little more money. The next I heard of Strick he was in Ireland filming *Ulysses*.

I believe *The Balcony* was shot in New York. I remember exactly everything else about it. I wanted so badly to stay with my daughter that probably one of the incentives for doing it was that it was shot in New York, but I'm not positive. We shot the film on one stage in a television studio. The famous MGM cameraman George Folsey photographed it in pristine black and white (I hope they never colorize it).

There were lots of sexy girls in skimpy costumes running around. Peter Falk knocked on the studio door a lot but whenever I opened it Joe Strick would cut to newsreels and stock footage of various civil wars and revolutions. I even think there's a long shot of Lenin in that film. Strick really was an excellent editor—though 90 percent of the film was shot in this huge TV studio the audience never felt claustrophobic. But perhaps at times you do have a sense of watching a filmed play.

I got Frank to phone the Circle in the Square where *The Balcony* was still playing and we got house seats that very night. It was a marvelous production and I wished they'd been able to use those actors but the name of the game is selling tickets, and stars attract the public, then and now.

The film was to start in a couple of weeks and since it was a very low-budget film Mr. Strick asked me to wear my own clothes—anything I thought was appropriate. I studied the role. Since the woman is a lesbian I, of course, wore a sexy tailored suit, padded shoulders, a cinched peplum, and short tight skirt. What goes around, comes around.

I had to pull Marilyn Monroe's trick, which meant I brought my size 12 suit into wardrobe and they altered it to a size 10 so that it was skin tight. I remembered, when we used to go shopping, my late, sweet friend would try on dresses that were size 12, and if she liked them she would buy them in size 10. I got hoarse trying to convince her that she should buy them in the size that she wanted to wear them. But she would always say, "I'm swollen today," "I've had a lot of Coca-Colas," "It's my period," or "I'm losing five pounds."

Lauren Bacall is the only other actress I knew who did something like this. She tried on dresses size 12 and bought them size 16. Her theory then, and maybe now, was that the looser clothes were on you, the thinner you looked. I just aim for size 12 and buy them that size whether they fit me or not. I now have a closet full of beautiful size 12's that I'm praying will fit me by the time this book is published.

This suit for *The Balcony* ended up a light cocoa brown and had a very low V neck. The skirt had a slit up the side and I wore black nylons and my F.M. satin sandals.

Kim Stanley recommended a lesbian bar and I went there one night with Violla Rubber and her friend to study the ladies. I didn't notice anything unusual about the behavior of the patrons. I had a wonderful dinner there, a very good steak and salad with fresh Roquefort dressing. I went to the ladies' room several times, but noticed nothing special or different. It was a couple of years later that I realized that Violla and her friend were lovers. I just knew that Violla was a very compassionate woman and her friend was a crackerjack aggressive agent.

I talked to Kim Stanley about the role. She was rehearsing *The Three Sisters* at the time. It was very gracious of her to take time one morning, before a session at the Studio, to help me with this difficult role. She is a brilliant teacher and as an actress she is a national treasure. I hope I repaid her for this help a couple of years later. Bryan Forbes sent me the film script for *Seance on a Wet Afternoon*. I loved the script but I was committed to do a TV show with Marty Balsam called *Two Is the Number*. So I sent the film script to Kim and convinced Bryan Forbes that she was such a great actress that if she got the part it wouldn't matter that she wasn't a film star.

I won an Emmy for *Two Is the Number* and I am the only American actress who has ever won the European

TV award, which they give out at the spring television festival in Monaco. The award is solid gold and is a six-inch-tall statuette of Thisbe on a real jade rock.

I doubt whether I would have been as memorable as Kim Stanley in *Seance*. But when I have 3:00 A.M. middle-of-the-night dooms, I think about not doing *Seance*—could I have been as good as Kim Stanley? Well, I would have been different—and I wouldn't have had that Emmy on my mantelpiece. But would I have had a Best Actress Oscar for *Seance?* Kim was nominated that year—she should have won. What silly wonderings!

I don't know if Joe Strick noticed my lack of lesbianism in the rushes or whatever, but one morning I was doing a scene with Lee Grant, who was playing my lover. She is working a switchboard in this surrealist brothel and I had a page of dialogue. I give her my diamond earrings, which she has coveted, and Peter Falk, who was playing a despotic surrealistic military dictator, is loudly knocking at the door of the stage brothel. Since we went in and out of the script while we were shooting I was never sure of how to play a scene. Sometimes we were the characters in the film and sometimes we were real-life actors à la theater of the absurd. After we had done the scene twice and Mr. Strick had printed a take he drew me aside and whispered, ''This time, I want you to give Lee one of the earrings. Say some of the dialogue, give her a big passionate kiss, give her the other earring, smile and then go answer the door.''

I looked at him askance. I couldn't believe he was serious. But he was. I asked him, ''Shouldn't you tell Lee what I'm going to do?''

He whispered back, ''No, no. I want her surprised reaction on film. After all, there are many clients and fascist policemen sitting around this brothel waiting room.'' Never one to balk at a Method challenge I thought about this scene and decided where in my dialogue I would kiss Lee.

''Action!'' the director yelled. I handed Lee Grant one of my diamond earrings in a sexy way, then, petting her throat, I spoke some of the dialogue and then I gave her a big wet kiss, holding the back of her head.

She was seated and I was leaning over some kind of rail. I finished the dialogue and threw her the other earring and exited the scene. The director yelled, "Cut." Lee Grant exploded in anger.

"She ruined my hair," she shouted. "Just ruined it."

She said not a word about the kiss, she just insisted we do it again, and I must kiss her without messing her hair. I refused to do it again. So, on film, Joe Strick had her take a little mirror out of her purse and repair and fix her hair for the next scene. I wasn't embarrassed while kissing her, but I was sort of embarrassed afterward. Lee Grant wasn't embarrassed at all and was furious at me because I wouldn't do it again. She had very gooey lipstick on and it got all over my mouth and upper lip. I informed her I was sorry, but no matter how much she begged, I wouldn't kiss her again.

Over the years we have had lots of laughs about this. As I write I'm amazed to realize how my life has been intertwined with Lee Grant's. Some years later we had a terrible fight on a film called *Buona Sera, Mrs. Campbell* with Gina Lollobrigida. I've forgotten what the fight was about now but we didn't speak to each other for a number of years. Now we're very good friends again and we spell each other when we moderate at the Actors Studio. She is an accomplished director now, besides being a teacher and an actress, and her daughter has a hit show on television.

Toward the end of filming *The Balcony* Judith Marechal notified me that *Cages* would go into rehearsal the Saturday morning I completed the Friday all-night shooting of *The Balcony*. Howard Da Silva directed and we would have three weeks of rehearsal and three weeks of previews. I was a little aghast at this information as most plays have four weeks and I was playing two distinct characters in "Snowangel" and "Epiphany." I had planned on having a few days' rest between the two jobs. But I worried needlessly. Howard Da Silva was an inspired director whom I had worked with when he had played my husband in the film version of *The Great Gatsby*. He had been in the Group Theatre, and had often been directed by Harold Clurman.

The creation and the playing of the two roles in *Cages* was a fantastic experience. The role of Connie was far from the whore with a heart of gold that I had often played in films. She's a very funny, feisty, angry, compassionate character who is proud of her profession and abilities. Her struggle to make a trick understand love was often hilarious and sad.

The character in "Epiphany" is a driven career woman who, no matter how she tries, cannot put her job on the back burner and recognize her husband's mental illness. Every performance with Jack Warden was different and most marvelous fun. Some nights I felt as if I had waited all my life to act with him. The suspense the audience felt was shared by the actors on the stage. Nobody knew what was going to happen the next minute. I could not wait to get to the theater each night, and even the weekends, when we did a backbreaking five performances (7:00 P.M. and 10:00 P.M. on Friday and Saturday and then one on Sunday). That meant doing ten one-act plays in three days. For each act, which was an hour long, I had to create a completely new persona. But I never resented the work, I always loved it. I acquired a degree of technical control of the audience that I have not experienced before or since. The only other actor I have seen do this was Marlene Dietrich when she performed at the Café de Paris in London. She could make the audience laugh or not laugh with a gesture. It's not something you learn along with the Method. You only acquire it with a great role and a great director and costar and many, many audiences. We could make them cry when we wanted to and laugh when we wanted to, depending on the needs of the play.

I loved the plays so much that when I would accidentally skip a page or two because I had such long monologues—I couldn't just keep going the way you're supposed to—I would pause, then remember what I had left out and go back and put the pages in.

Jack Warden would turn his back to the audience and

roll his eyes like a Las Vegas slot machine as I filled the audience in on the information I had left out. We would somehow return to the proper place in the script and keep going while the stage manager, holding the book in the wings, was pulling his hair out. So what if it loused the light cues up a little? The audiences roared.

Howard Da Silva managed to get very restrained, funny, and deep performances out of both of us. I still hope that someday we can do these plays on film; my hooker Connie could easily be in her middle sixties. And Jack Warden's john could be in a wheelchair.

Creating a role from a printed page is a special experience—you cannot possibly know what the writer based the language and the character on, and it is the actor's special experience to supply the physical characteristics, the thoughts, and even the soul of the human being.

My agents were very annoyed that the show was such a hit and for many months I refused to leave it. I was working for a paltry $500 a week. We stayed at the York Playhouse and played to SRO audiences until the next Labor Day.

One night toward the end of the run my ex-husband Vittorio Gassman came backstage with my little girl and watched the performance from the wings. After the performance they came to my dressing room. It had been a good show. He began to talk to me quite rapidly in Italian. I said, *"Lentamente, per favore,"* which means "Slower, please." He was about to play *Kean* in Milan. He said, "What a marvelous, remarkable actress you are. It is too bad I could not teach you my voice and physical techniques and you could have given me your training and willingness to act so deeply and profoundly." "And if my grandmother had balls, she would have been my grandfather," I answered.

While I was doing *Cages,* Albert Finney was doing *Luther* by John Osborne, and was beginning to show up at my stage door. He would get very annoyed on Fridays and Saturdays when I had to work until midnight but he would console himself at a popular East Side pub, P.J. Clarke's, until I finished. The drinking capacity of English actors has always amazed me. Later, when I tried to keep up with Michael Caine when we did *Alfie* together, I found out it was impossible.

There's something in the British water or air that gives actors that proverbial hollow leg. Of course their gin is not as high-proof as ours but I still don't know how they drink for three or four hours and are still lucid and in complete control of all their faculties. I would meet Albert at P.J.'s or various restaurants and bars on the East Side. His living arrangements were complicated at this point and for some reason we could not go to his place. I certainly never brought any of my beaux back to my house. I think in twenty years, if I remember correctly, only once did Sean Connery spend the night on my couch —well, most of the night.

Albert and I ate lunches and suppers together and necked in the park, in alleyways, in cabs, in hallways, and on rooftops. We did everything but. . . . It finally became a very sore issue. He insisted we either go to a hotel or call it quits, that we were too old to have this kind of relationship. I could not see myself or Albert, who was a big star with great reviews in *Luther*, checking into some seedy hotel, so I bought a new Cadillac. It seems ridiculous now, but this was, remember, the pre-sexual revolution early sixties, and then as now Finney was a very private person. But it was getting dangerous to park by the lake in Central Park and I was amassing parking tickets. There's no place to park on the East Side when you're in an off-Broadway show.

Albert Finney was the funniest, sweetest, and sexiest of men. But since I could never figure out a way to resolve this problem he drifted away, probably finding a blonde with her own private apartment.

I had gotten extraordinary reviews in *Cages*, as had Jack Warden, and so I began to do every newspaper interview and television show that originated in New York. One early morning I posed for the Sunday cover of the *Daily News*, whose circulation was in the millions. It was a long, grueling sitting. I had a performance that night. In those days color photography took a lot of lights and you had to sit very still. Anyway, that's how I remember the

Daily News color-photo cover, because later that day I was so angry over this sitting that I was trying to make a right turn off West End Avenue and I accidentally hit a *Daily News* truck with my relatively new Cadillac. It was my fault but the driver apologized profusely and somebody took a picture of us and I gave him an autograph. But then again, his truck was hardly dented, and my beautiful convertible brown Cadillac with the pigskin seats was quite damaged. In fact, the Cadillac company had to send to Detroit for some new part for the engine and get an entire new fender. They were rather slow about delivery until I discussed this problem on "The Tonight Show." I remember the discussion but I can't remember if it was Jack Paar or Johnny Carson.

One night before the show the stage manager informed me that Ambassador Adlai Stevenson was in the audience. I wish he hadn't. In fact, that night I was so angry with the stage manager that he never again informed me of special people in the audience. But I was so honored and nervous at Stevenson's presence that I think I was acting à la Paula Placard ("Audience! Pay attention and get my message!" I should have called Western Union if I wanted to send a message. I think I was just awful); but he came backstage to my dingy little dressing room afterwards and was most complimentary. I was so in awe of him I stuttered. He was so gentle and kind and he invited me to have lunch with him at the United Nations. I was most flattered by his compliments. But that October when I left the show to go to Italy and do a film, *Time of Indifference,* I found out through the grapevine that Adlai saw the play again with Mercedes McCambridge, who replaced me. My goodness, even great statesmen are fickle.

But that spring and summer, whenever I did not have a matinee, I would find myself at the United Nations, listening to their debates. I was not yet disillusioned with the dream of a world peace organization and in the years to come I would keep breaking my heart over the way they voted.

* * *

One morning I received a call from the State Department inviting me to attend the first film festival in Moscow. I was elated but fearful that I would not be able to attend due to my many performances a week. I felt that Adlai Stevenson had something to do with this invitation. It was also the hundredth anniversary of Stanislavsky's birth, and of course many of the stars of the Actors Studio were invited, being devotees of his Method. It turned out that Geraldine Page, Rip Torn, Lee and Paula Strasberg, Susan Strasberg and her brother Johnny, Stanley Kramer, and many other American celebrities were going to attend this first open film festival in Moscow.

This was the height of the Cold War and the Berlin crisis and, I must say, I did have some trepidation about an artistic safari to the Soviet Union. But, I reassured myself and my fellow Actors Studio members that we were going with representatives of the Association of Motion Picture Producers and nothing could be safer literally and politically. The McCarthy era was still around.

Someone from Stanley Kramer's office called me and told me *Anne Frank* would be shown at the festival out of competition and I was to prepare an easily translatable nonpolitical speech to deliver at the showing. I asked whoever I was talking to what pictures were being entered in the festival competition. I was amazed to hear that we were showing *West Side Story* and *The Defiant Ones*. I could not understand why Stanley Kramer was showing American films with self-critical messages to the Moscow actors, directors, and judges.

For the next week or two I argued with Judith Marechal, Actors' Equity, the theatrical producers' association, and my agent, and it finally came down to me threatening to give my two weeks' notice unless Judith let my understudy go on Tuesday night. I felt I could fly to Moscow Sunday night, since it was later in Russia than it was in New York, arrive almost before I left timewise, and be back in time for the Wednesday performance.

This trip reconfirmed my time disorientation for the next decade or so. Judith finally agreed with me but unfortunately the New York press announced I was leaving the play to "go work in Russia." So Judith closed the play for three nights. We were dark Monday anyway, so I would just miss Tuesday and Wednesday—two performances. My agent got some strange queries from the American Legion at that point. Judith put a big announcement in the press the Thursday I came back, and the TV and radio news carried this nonsense event, that I had come back to the play from Russia, as if it were an international incident. I had never left the play. The people who had gotten their money back now scrambled to get their tickets again. So Miss Marechal upped the ticket prices. If Miss Marechal had let my understudy go on Tuesday and Wednesday nobody would have thought that I had left the play. I just should have said I had a bad cold and gone to Russia.

When the limo came to pick me up after those exhausting ten acts since Friday evening, I hurriedly took all the orders from the cast and crew for things Russian, and went to sleep in the back of the limo on the way to the airport. It had been raining in Manhattan but when I got out of the limo at Idlewild there was a full-blown hurricane whirling about the airport. I'd been planning to take TWA all the way to Moscow because it was the only American carrier that flew around the world in those days. But TWA was not taking off. No airline was taking off in that weather except Air India. So I told the TWA clerk I was going Air India to Paris and to book me on Aeroflot from Paris to Moscow.

Two porters rushed with me through the airport to the little Air India counter. I think Air India had been flying only a short while. Air France had been their carrier. So now in effect I was taking "Air Chance" to Paris.

I had a thrilling and delicious flight to Paris. I barely made the Aeroflot plane but they had waited for me, three minutes. They searched me and all my luggage in Moscow and there were two Russian Orthodox priests standing waiting at the airport. Only when I left Moscow and saw them again did I realize they were employed to stand at the international terminal all the time to prove to the travelers from the West that there was freedom of religion in the Soviet Union.

25

George Stevens, Jr., who was representing his father's films, met me at the Moscow airport with the equivalent of a Russian limousine. On the long drive to the Mokva Hotel he read off a list of instructions. He lectured me closely about exactly what I was to do and not to do while in Moscow. I didn't pay much attention.

All I could think about was the time in 1939 when my sister and I had walked from Brooklyn to the World's Fair in Flushing Meadow and only had enough money for the entrance fee. We saw practically nothing but the Russian Pavilion because she had to get back to her hospital in Coney Island where she was a student nurse. I remember we had been most impressed because we had seen a Russian tank and a pretty Russian girl had explained in robotlike English the current Stalin five-year plan. When I had asked her if they had beauty contests she hadn't answered and just looked dazed. Lo and behold, last night I saw a Russian TV program that included a beauty contest. My, how the mighty have fallen! Now I have to go to another festival in Moscow and teach them about women's lib.

That morning in Moscow my nose was glued to the window of the limo. There were brand-new factories and blocks of flats. It looked a great deal like the outskirts of

London. The chauffeur spoke some English. I remember seeing a little peasant's house with a thatched roof between two very tall buildings. We had come to a stop and I asked the driver why that little peasant's shack was there. He turned around and proudly informed me that the man who lived there was very old but he was a hero of the Bolshevik Revolution and they would not move that shack until he died. I don't know if that was true but it was great propaganda.

The hotel seemed inelegant but very clean, warm, and cozy. The only odd thing was a concierge on my floor at a desk where I was to pick up and leave my key. Later when I talked to other members of the American delegation I found out there was a concierge on every floor who watched every room. When I was unpacking I did have the strange sense that it was perhaps the only hotel in the world where the television watched you. Although I turned the set on and turned the knobs all during my whole stay at the Mokva Hotel I never saw a television program. Perhaps in 1962 the television sets in the Mokva Hotel were awaiting the installation of a television station in Russia.

When I went down to dinner, Ambassador Averell Harriman was sitting at the table I was assigned to. Wouldn't you know, the first course was vodka and caviar. It was served sort of boardinghouse fashion. A waitress served the fresh gray caviar and the pumpernickel bread from a tray but the vodka was right on the table. After the first course I realized I was going to have to be very careful about how much vodka I drank while in the Soviet Union.

People were constantly getting up, making toasts and speeches. I was quite hungry and when the waitress finally arrived with the main course there on the big plate was *oluptchez* with gravy—just like my Aunt Zizel used to make. *Oluptchez* is three different kinds of meat with rice rolled in cabbage, spiced and cooked. It looked and was delicious. I was very hungry and I took three *oluptchez*. I remember I had tried to make *oluptchez* during the Second World War but had failed miserably. I had tried to roll the meat in fresh cabbage and tie it with a thread. I didn't find out until this trip that you're supposed to steam the cabbage first so it's soft and you can roll the meat in it.

All twelve people around the big round table, I assumed, were from the American or English delegation. I finished two *oluptchez,* my hunger gone, and I pushed my plate away. I began to engage a very attractive blond man named Michael in a conversation about the purposes of the British and American delegations at this festival. Suddenly the waitress was screaming at me in Russian. After a long tirade Michael translated and explained to me what I had done. He had a British accent but he spoke Russian rather well and I thought he was the interpreter for the British delegation. I had left one very large piece of *oluptchez* on the plate. The waitress was explaining to me that I was welcome to take as much as I could eat, but the peasants in Georgia had grown and fed the cattle, the Manchurians had harvested the rice, the Ukrainians had grown the cabbages, and I was wasting all their effort by throwing it away. I quickly grabbed the plate and gulped down the rest of the *oluptchez,* washing it down with plenty of vodka as Averell Harriman and the American consul watched me.

That waitress was right. I realized that Russia had barely recovered from the terrible afflictions of the Second World War, and it was drilled into every Russian child's head never to waste food, or anything for that matter. I, having been in the affluent U.S. during the Second World War, had only known that occasionally I couldn't get a steak. I was properly mortified when I realized this. When we had arrived the Russian government had issued us ration books with food stamps. When I gave the waitress my ration stamps at the end of the meal I gave her an extra one. I guess it was the right thing to do because she gave me a big smile and a kiss on the cheek.

The next morning we gathered in front of the hotel, and Stanley Kramer counted noses. Everyone had slept his or her hangovers off and we were all neatly dressed and ready for the Kremlin.

Can you imagine holding a film festival in the U.S.

Senate? Maybe it's not a bad idea. At the time it seemed rather odd as we marched over the cobblestones to enter the huge fortress of the Kremlin. I felt as if I should be on a sled with a fur hat and a long scarf, sliding over the cobblestones to the tune of Tchaikovsky's "Marche Slave." I communicated my fantasy to some of my fellow actors and we all had this eerie sense of Russian history from viewing all the MGM spectacles we'd grown up on. Somebody said he felt "like *Rasputin*," and we all broke into nervous laughter. It was obviously not the right thing to do. Khrushchev was just a few feet in front of our group and he and his entourage turned around and glared at us. We stood riveted. He scolded us as if we were naughty children, but nobody translated, and so we all continued solemnly marching into the Kremlin—the Kremlin, where Stalin and his Comintern had met.

We all quickly sat in our assigned seats and put on our multilingual earphones. There was a little desk that folded in front of me and seemed to pin me to my seat. The huge hall was decked with flowers and the flags of all nations, of course including the American flag.

For the next hour and a half I listened to Khrushchev lecture us about the responsibility that *"an artist must have to the people."*

My emotions went from shock to fear to interest, then I began looking around at the flower-decked stage and auditorium trying to recognize stars from other countries, biting my nails, nodding, and dozing off.

Rip Torn and Geraldine Page were sitting on my right. I must have been gently snoring because Geraldine poked me under the seat. I couldn't believe I had dozed off. Here I was at one of the key moments in modern history, when the East was first opening its doors to the West, and I was sleeping through it. But I had flown ten thousand miles, had a lot of vodka, and barely slept. As I tried to concentrate on what the English interpreter was saying on my headset, I had the definite feeling that my translator spoke English well but I didn't understand a word, as when you listen to certain Shakespearean actors who *recite*. You don't understand a thing they say because they don't understand what they're saying, à la Maurice Evans, who recites beautifully.

Then the commissar of film spoke for an hour while I made a valiant effort to stay awake. I kept reminding myself of the politically important place I was in. Finally Stanley Kramer spoke and I could take off the damn headset at last. He spoke about people understanding each other under and over and around the problems of their governments. Humanity, he said, had a common aim—the protection of their lives and the security and welfare of their children and the continuation of the species and the planet. I was no longer bored and was thankful that I had been able to make this important trip and help represent the U.S. film community at this First Moscow Film Festival. I remember thinking, Wouldn't it be great if we took from Russia such things as socialized medicine, government support of theaters, and perhaps publicly supported TV that didn't sell you anything. Even back then I felt a lot of my life was stolen by the TV commercials. Perhaps we could give to Russia the incentive of capitalism, our high standard of living, and the concept of personal freedom, that government exists for the people, not the people for the government.

On a huge screen clips were shown from the various films that were entered in the festival. That lasted another hour and a half, and after "The Internationale" was sung we staggered out of the Kremlin. As I hobbled on my high heels, I remembered that the last line of "The Internationale" was, in English, "The international soviet shall be the human race," and I also remembered the bumper stickers in America that said, "Better Dead Than Red." I prayed that in the future these slogans would change so the planet would survive.

We were all herded to a cocktail party in some huge restaurant honoring the directors of the films that were entered in the festival. I tried to find out why *Anne Frank* was entered OUT of competition. After many vodka toasts the only thing I understood was that the plight of Anne Frank and her family was not politically correct according to the Soviet party line.

Susan Strasberg's room was next to mine and we went

back together to the Moscow Hotel to change into evening clothes. We walked through Red Square rather thoughtfully. She had played Anne Frank on Broadway for two years. As we got our keys from the prison matron–type concierge I asked her what she thought "not politically correct according to the Soviet party line" meant. Calmer and wiser than I, Susan said, "Remember, Shelley, Russia is the land of the pogroms."

I went into my room, kicked the television set, and took a Miltown. In those days I traveled with a small pharmacy. I put on a slinky white jersey evening gown with diamond earrings, a bracelet, and a diamond clip on my shoulder. I had a white mink cape and after Susie's reminder of that chapter of Russian history I hoped I reminded them of White Russia and the elegance they had missed. For some reason I also put on my gold charm bracelet, which matched nothing. Charm bracelets were very much the vogue in the sixties. It had charms from all the important films I had done, usually given to me by the director. I suddenly was finding myself rather anti-Red, but as I dabbed myself with Collage perfume I reminded myself of the reasons I had become part of the American delegation. My hair was quite long then and platinum, for the hooker part I was playing in *Cages*. I usually wore it up, but that night I let it hang to my shoulders.

As I entered the ballroom some man with a beard looked startled and asked, "Marilyn Monroe?"

I quickly shook my head no and as I passed a full-length mirror I looked at my reflection. If you squinted real hard, and you were nearsighted, I vaguely resembled Marilyn. Why had I worn a glamorous, revealing white evening gown to this dignified reception? Was I unconsciously representing her or wishing that she had been able to live and come to the Soviet Union with me?

I quickly had some more vodka and caviar and although I smiled and parroted the few Russian words I knew, my depression deepened. I guess I attended the dinner and I sat next to Michael again. We went to the one restaurant they had in Moscow then with dancing.

It was quite late at night and Michael asked me if I

would like to go to a Russian party. I vaguely remembered George Stevens, Jr., saying something about staying with the delegation, but I wanted to see unofficial Russian people and question them about their human feelings. So I got in Michael's car and we drove for quite a while. I asked him if we were going to the Bronx section of Moscow and he laughed and said, "No, my apartment. It's just another ten minutes."

I gazed at him bleary-eyed and said, "You're an Englishman. Why do you have an apartment in the suburbs of Moscow?" I had been assuming he was the British group's Russian translator.

Michael laughed and answered, "Because I'm a Russian."

I couldn't quite digest this. "But you speak English with a British accent! Aren't you in the British delegation?"

He said, "Of course not! I'm the English translator for the British delegation. When I was a child I was educated in London."

I stared at him. I couldn't believe I had made such a silly mistake. I quickly sobered up and wondered if there were taxicabs in Moscow so that I could safely get back to the Mokva Hotel. We stopped at what looked like a housing project with new buildings, acres and acres of them.

We went up in a little elevator, while I wondered if I should make a dash down the steps. We entered an apartment and there really was a party going on. There were about ten men and women at the party. A man was playing a guitar and a woman was playing an accordion. They were all very cordial to me and I had a blurred impression they thought I was Marilyn Monroe's stand-in or sister. Michael was not enlightening them. He began to drink rapidly and he was funny and I think he answered my questions truthfully. It seemed his parents had been imprisoned by Stalin for many years. His father had died in prison and his mother had somehow gotten him to London when he was an adolescent. I never asked him why he had returned to Moscow but recently I saw a picture of him in *The New York Times* identifying him as part of a Russian delegation to the U.N. His hair was now white but it was Michael, all right.

At the party that night I sang my union songs for this group of Russian citizens, but I had a feeling they didn't really know what a union was. During the course of the night or morning I wanted to answer the call of nature and asked Michael where the bathroom was. He pointed to a door. I opened it and there was a tub and a sink but no toilet anywhere. I came out and had to ask, "Where is the toilet?" He said, "Oh," and pointed to the door of the apartment. There was a toilet out in the hall. There were four apartments on his floor and one toilet out in the hall in a brand-new building. When I returned and questioned him about this he got very angry and defensive and said, "Russians don't spend much time in that room!"

After a while I reminded him that I had to get back to the Mokva Hotel. It did cross my mind to wonder whether men raised under communism made love differently from the men raised under capitalism, but I never found out.

It got later. Some lady who was serving tea and cakes disappeared, I assume to go to work. Michael was passed out, unconscious. Really unconscious. Finally after the last person left I gathered my courage and decided I would get back to the Mokva Hotel alone. Somehow.

I walked down the six flights of stairs because I wasn't sure I knew how to work the elevator, and walked out into the sunny street. It must have been about 7:00 A.M. by then and many people were rushing to buses and sort of trackless trolley cars. There seemed to be a lot of automobiles in the street for Moscow. I spoke to a few passersby but no one spoke back or acknowledged my presence. As I trudged along I began to think I was invisible and had died and gone to heaven and my soul was still wandering around the suburbs of Moscow. But I was getting very cold in my little white mink jacket and thin white jersey evening gown. No one, but no one, was looking at me. The passersby wouldn't acknowledge my existence, but the more I sobered up, the more I knew I was real. I was hungry and cold and scared. I didn't have any Russian money and didn't know what bus to take. Here I was, this blonde, obviously American lady, in a white slinky evening gown and a white mink jacket and diamonds, wandering around the Bronx section of Moscow, and no one would acknowledge my existence. Finally I stood at what I thought was a bus stop—sort of across the street from a little green park. The first bus that came along was so crowded I couldn't get on. I think someone pushed me off. I stood there weeping with frustration and a car with a man and a woman in the front seat stopped. They opened the back door and motioned me in without looking at me. I got in the back seat and collapsed.

I whispered, "Mokva Hotel, *pozhaluista*, Mokva Hotel!"

The lady driver said, "Okay, okay. Down. Down. You stay down."

I lay on the back seat of that Russian car and wondered if this was the KGB or where the hell I was and what the hell I was doing there. Why hadn't I stayed in Warner LeRoy's theater on York Avenue? What was a drunken idiot like me doing in a strange car on a highway on the outskirts of Moscow? After all, my great-grandparents had escaped from these same streets. Why hadn't I memorized their lesson and stayed safe at home on Central Park West?

After what seemed like hours we arrived at what I hoped was the back door of the Mokva Hotel. The lady said, "Up!"

I sat up with my hands braced on the front seat, ready to strike if the Russian police came out to get me.

The man and woman smiled at me and the man said, "Very good, Anne Frank."

I smiled through my fears back at him and then, like a dope, took off my diamond clip to give to them. The woman shook her head no and pointed to a gold mezuzah charm which was on my charm bracelet. I twisted it from the bracelet and handed it to her. She kissed it and smiled, putting it in her pocket. The man said, "Out!"

I got out of the car and they very quickly drove away. There was no one around. I trudged through the alley to the front of the Mokva Hotel, wondering how those young people had had any religious education. Her eyes had lit up when I'd given her the mezuzah—mezuzahs obviously weren't purchasable in the Soviet Union. I walked into the lobby with my head held high, as if it were the most normal thing in the world to stroll through the lobby in a slinky white evening gown, at 9:00 A.M. When I got to my room I said a prayer for the safety of that couple and for the safety of the state of Israel and hoped that young couple got there someday. And I went to sleep.

The next day was your standard tourist day. The Russians were into thrift so this time we had a bus, a comfortable bus, but certainly no limo. The Actors Studio contingent piled in with our cameras and I noticed for some odd reason that Rip Torn had a fishing rod with him. I knew he was from Texas and an outdoorsy type but I hoped he hadn't come to the Soviet Union with a hunting gun. Our first stop was the new GUM department store. It was a beautiful new store and there were lovely things from all over the world on mannequins and the shelves, but the natives were strolling around the place as if it were a museum. No one was buying anything. I thought it was perhaps because they didn't have the rubles. But although the translator didn't say so we finally figured out that there wasn't *anything* for sale. It was all for display only. We were finally steered toward the tourist shop where I bought some beautiful Russian amber beads, graduated and twenty inches long. I bought beads for every female friend I felt I had to bring a present to. In each department we visited, we were given little tie tacks and we finally figured out they represented every organization in the Soviet Union, including the Communist Party, the Young Communist Party, and the Preteen Communist Party.

I had acquired a very attractive, intelligent interpreter, and, as the day progressed, I realized she had been assigned to me personally. Somehow I felt Michael had had something to do with this. But when I would ask a Russian salesclerk a question and the clerk would answer me with a lengthy Russian speech, she would say, "No, I don't think so" . . . "Yes—tomorrow" . . . or "It's coming in."

The only department that had things for sale was the liquor department. We all loaded up with Stolichnaya vodka as presents to our male friends and relatives. It was not yet being exported to the U.S. What we also found was fresh caviar. I have never before or since had such marvelous caviar. It was gray in color and very fresh, packed in ice, shipped direct from the Black Sea. I tried to smuggle some back into the U.S. (you're not allowed to bring food through customs), but the customs officer confiscated all my communist caviar. I'm sure they enjoyed it in Queens or wherever.

After the exhausting tour of GUM we toured some other buildings and then did the required visit to the tombs of Stalin and Lenin. They were under glass, but I decided I wouldn't look. I preferred to see Lenin live on late-night television newsreels. After we asked all day, the guide finally took us to the Moscow Art Theater. It had been built before the Russian Revolution and the tour guide made sure we saw all the things built in Moscow after the Revolution before he would take us there.

It was midsummer and the Stanislavsky Theater Company was touring the vast Russian provinces. They had left the set of *The Cherry Orchard* standing on the stage.

Like pilgrims journeying to Mecca, we Method actors silently tiptoed into this historic theater and were seated in the front row. We all, including Lee and Paula Strasberg, sat silently for a long time and listened to the ghosts.

A very old actor who was now the curator of this theater/museum didn't say a word for the longest time. So Lee began to lecture us quietly on how Stanislavsky had evolved his Method (which he called System) and how his company had functioned and worked before, during, and after the Revolution. My interpreter was obviously fascinated and quickly translated into Russian for the old actor.

A couple of years earlier I had entertained the entire Moscow Art Theater in my apartment when they had played New York. Two of the actors, a man and a woman, had given me their names, which I had written in my appointment book. I gave these names to the old actor. His face lit up and he brought us all immediately backstage and then opened a door. We saw what we knew was Stanislavsky's dressing room. I don't know if this was on the guided tour or not. But his makeup and his robe, his costumes and his eyeglasses, were there as if he had just left them. Obviously the Soviet government valued and preserved what Konstantin Stanislavsky had given to the world of acting.

I saw a pile of papers on the chair—all odd pieces, some brown, some white, some torn pieces of newspapers—and a pencil was laid carefully on top of them. I asked the fragile old man what they were. He smiled and then explained to us that during the revolution sometimes the actors in the company did not have access to blank pieces of paper and/or pencils, so Chekhov would slowly dictate his plays to the assembled actors and they would slowly write down their roles onto whatever blank pieces of paper they could find in their homes. We stared at him in amazement. He reassured us it was so. It took Chekhov sometimes weeks to do this. But then Stanislavsky discovered that by the time the play was dictated his actors had not only memorized their roles but somehow had absorbed them into their own personalities. The very act of writing them in their own handwriting not only seemed to help them memorize the roles but made their talents create the characterizations and made them free of the words.

If I got nothing else out of my trip to Russia I learned a technique that I have used and will use for the rest of my life and that I teach to my students. After you have studied a play you must write out the role, every single word. Just print the words of your cues.

I once agreed to do *Virginia Woolf* with a week of rehearsals at some small summer-stock theater. I memorized and absorbed that enormous role and character in three days, writing it out in my own script, which is only legible, even to me, when it's fresh. I did that play in that week of rehearsal and learned how to play it from the audience reactions.

At the Moscow Art Theater, Susan and Johnny Strasberg, Lee and Paula, Rip Torn and Geraldine Page, and I wandered around the stage, the dressing rooms, the space underneath the stage, the orchestra, the boxes, the balcony, and the lobby for hours. The guards and our interpreter got very annoyed with us, but the old actor sat on a comfortable chair on the porch of the set and dozed off. He obviously wanted us there and he was an old Bolshevik and there was nothing the young Communist officials could do about it. When we were ready to leave we kissed him goodbye and when Lee Strasberg shook his hand, he said something to Lee in German, which I understood.

"The revolution did not only take place in the government buildings and in the streets, it also happened with the playwrights and the actors and the directors here. They helped change this society."

We all waved goodbye and we Actors Studio actors walked slowly out of the Moscow Art Theater.

The next year the Actors Studio did *The Three Sisters* on Broadway. Kim Stanley, Geraldine Page, Barbara Baxley, and Shirley Knight performed what I think was the most hauntingly beautiful and moving production of Chekhov I have ever seen. The play opened with a wonderfully orchestrated party scene with the balalaika being played on stage and drinking and talking. Kim Stanley sat stage right and looked at her lover across the stage and one watched her blush from her bosom up to the roots of her hair. I have never seen the like on *any* stage. Old people who were alive to see Eleonora Duse told me that she also could do that. When Geraldine Page said at the end of the play with all the longing in the human soul, "To Moscow, to Moscow, to Moscow," the silence in the audience was like thunder.

When *The Three Sisters* was taped for TV Lee Strasberg asked me to play Natasha and Sandy Dennis replaced Shirley Knight. I believe Barbara Baxley and Shirley Knight were in Hollywood doing films. They had moved the set from the theater to the TV studio and we did it live like a play with three cameras. Lee was taken ill with the flu the day we got on camera and Kim Stanley directed us. Paul Bogart was in the control booth and just called the technical shots of the camera. It is the best classic work I have ever done and Kim has ungently joshed me whenever I have met her since that show because I don't stretch more and try to do the classics.

Geraldine Page had her first baby at forty and what I remember so vividly about that production was discussing a scene with her in her dressing room while her toddler stood between her legs, nursing and hanging on her knees, as she put on eyelashes. Not long ago I went to Geraldine's memorial. The entire film and theater world seemed to be in the theater that afternoon. It was held in the Broadway theater she had been playing in when she died. We all celebrated her life and her art and the legacy she inspired and gave to the theater. I have seen her last picture, *The Trip to Bountiful,* many, many times, and I still marvel at her deep Stanislavsky performance. When you watch her in that film you have the sense of watching a documentary; that's how deep and real she was. I'm so happy she got the Best Actress Oscar before she died, and not after.

When we all sat in that bus in Moscow going back to the Mokva Hotel from the Mokva Art Theater we thought about the knowledge that had been handed on to us and Lee walked up the bus aisle and just looked at our faces. We knew that we had connected with the intention of our teachers and he was communicating to us that, in our lifetime, we had an obligation to hand on to the next generation what we had learned from him and the Group Theatre and what they had learned from Konstantin Stanislavsky and his Russian company, the Moscow Art Theater. Everyone on that bus that day was destined to become a teacher in addition to carrying on a career as a professional actor. Somehow that day in that Russian bus Lee made us aware of our life responsibility to the next generation of artists. Acting is a special art. Only if experienced actors pass their knowledge on to the next generations does it live. You cannot learn acting from a book. Some actors are born with an extraordinary acting talent but most hone and learn their skills from directors, teachers, and audiences. The mores and style of each generation change, even what they laugh at. When you see an old sitcom you thought was hilarious twenty years ago, you soon realize it now isn't even amusing. But Jimmy Dean, who studied the Method with many teachers and directors, created portraits of cool anguish that have electrified young people for thirty years, although he only did three films.

When we see silent films, only Eleonora Duse and possibly Lillian Gish seem relevant today. The rest of the actors seem stylized and phony. Like language, the interpretive art of acting is a living thing that must change, and it does.

One morning in Russia, I attended a huge press conference with *Pravda* and *Izvestia*. Somehow, I found myself alone, fielding questions from members of the Eastern-bloc press. Geraldine Page for some reason had not shown up and had stayed in her hotel room, and I guess the rest of the Hollywood contingent was doing tourism. I found myself answering the strangest questions from the Russian reporters. The American films which they had been seeing at the Kremlin as part of the film festival included Sidney Poitier and Tony Curtis in *The Defiant Ones*, shackled together, the victims of a racist Southern sheriff played by Theodore Bikel. In *West Side Story* they saw the anger and hatred of the Puerto Rican and Italian population in New York, pitted against each other in Hell's Kitchen. The Moscow reporters were insisting that these films which were so self-critical were financed secretly and were underground films. At first I didn't understand their questions. I just kept saying they were big capitalist pictures financed by American banks and done by American artists at big studios. They got quite angry with me and then I realized that behind their anger was longing and their real frustration was that they could not possibly hope to make such self-critical pictures in Russia. Then I understood why Stanley Kramer had showed these films in Russia. Only now, over twenty-five years later, with the beginning of *glasnost,* are their artists allowed to do anything even faintly critical.

At great length at that Soviet press party I explained that one of the great advantages of democracy was that artists could criticize and expose the existing evils, whatever they were, and in this way help to change them. I told them I had often been attracted to roles with directors like George Stevens because all of Stevens's films addressed "man's inhumanity to man." The Eastern-bloc reporters just stared at me. There was a long silence after my explanation. Some of them understood English, but later a British translator told me that the artistic commissar who had translated my reply had explained that I was a foolish American actress with a lively imagination. The Russian reporters did not smile and I do not believe they accepted this explanation of his.

But later during the festival they each individually made a point of drinking a vodka with me and discussing Chekhov, Dostoevsky, and Theodore Dreiser. I didn't understand a word they were saying. I think they were telling me how those writers had criticized monarchist Russia, but I can't be sure since I only caught the names of the authors. They also said "Konstantin Stanislavsky" a lot. They knew that I knew that they knew that Stanislavsky had started his theater when the czar was on the throne and had his secret police controlling Russia.

Later that night I attended the cocktail party given by the French film delegation. I hadn't seen the films they had entered because I had been too busy being a tourist and giving press conferences. I also accidentally skipped breakfast and lunch and was glad because the hors d'oeuvres at the French party were scrumptious. Since fresh caviar was so plentiful in Moscow the French chef had figured out a thousand ways to serve it. I tried every single one of them, drinking countless toasts with the various French film directors and actors. I never made the dinner which everyone else marched into sometime around 10:00 P.M. I marched into the elevator at the Mokva Hotel. I believe that night it went sideways, and I had to hold onto the rail because it was circling up and down. When it got to my floor I think I was sitting on the floor of the elevator, but I managed to get my foot squeezed into the door so that when it opened it wouldn't close again. The concierge, who was shaped somewhat like a tank, soon pushed the elevator door open and began to yell at me in some language I didn't recognize.

The next thing I remember is being in my bed in my nightgown and throwing my brains up into the wastepaper basket. I was so ill I felt as if I were dying. I managed to stagger to the bathroom and drink a lot of cold water and bring a glass of water back to my bed. I tried to see which of the assorted pills and vitamins on the tray next to my bed were for stomach upset but I couldn't read the labels so I took one of each, washing them down with Mylanta. Five minutes later I again began to throw up nonstop. In between throw-ups I staggered into the hallway, threw up there too, and then fell down, and the Sherman tank concierge, I assume, carried me back to bed.

Pretty soon there were two young men in white coats standing around my bed. The concierge kept saying, *"Doktor, doktor."* I screamed at them, "You're not doctors! All Russian doctors are women!" I had read that somewhere. One of the young men leaned over to feel my stomach and I noticed he had steel teeth. I began to think I was in a spy movie and they were going to take me away to torture me. In those days the Russians didn't care about looks and porcelain teeth; the dentists just made sure they were functional, and steel teeth probably are better than porcelain.

They were trying to get me onto a stretcher that was lying on the floor. I just held onto the headboard, screamed, threw up, and kicked them. They were pulling at me but I managed to yell, "Interpreter, interpreter!" Suddenly they let go of me and began looking at all of the pill bottles in the tray. Their expression changed from anger to terror. All three of them began to yell at me in Russian, and all I could make out was, "Marilyn Monroe! Marilyn Monroe!" At that, I began to cry with wrenching sobs.

Until that very moment I had not really allowed myself to feel my grief over Marilyn's death. I remembered how she had talked Russian to Khrushchev and how she would have loved to have come on this trip.

The tank concierge suddenly turned into Mother Russia and got a bowl of cold water and began yelling at the so-called doctors and washing my face and cleaning up the mess on my bed, the floor, and I presume the hall. The young doctors just stared at me. After I had put on a clean nightgown I phoned the American embassy and asked them to wake up Averell Harriman. When I got him on the phone, I explained that I had eaten too much caviar and had had too much vodka and I had thrown up for a few hours but it wasn't serious and they were trying to drag me to a hospital. Harriman reassured me by telling me they had wonderful hospitals in the Soviet Union.

"It sounds to me as if you're having a gallbladder attack, perhaps," he said, "and Soviet medicine is very advanced."

I burst into another spasm of sobs and informed him that if I needed a gallbladder operation I would have it in English, and hung up. My pretty young interpreter arrived and Mother Russia began giving me some kind of Russian liqueur or medicine. It tasted awful but seemed to stop my throwing up and crying spasms. She was holding me in her arms as if I were a baby. She and then the doctors and my interpreter had a long Russian argument. I went to sleep. My interpreter gently woke me some time later and informed me that they were all afraid I had tried to kill myself the way Marilyn had, when they'd seen all the strange pills all over the floor. She managed to make me understand that the Soviet Union was having enough trouble with the Cold War and they certainly didn't need a blonde movie star committing suicide during their first film festival. The Western press would say they had killed me secretly or some damn thing.

I began to throw up again. The young doctors wanted to pump my stomach—if I refused to go to the hospital they could do it in the bathroom.

That is exactly what we compromised on. Perhaps the United States and the Soviet Union could do the same thing about nuclear bombs. Just get rid of it—all of it! These young doctors certainly got everything I'd eaten in the last three days out of my stomach and the interpreter and the concierge gave me a gentle enema. I indeed had swallowed too many pills, but to this day I think it was Tums and vitamins I took and not the sleeping pills.

They gave me strong tea and walked me around the hallways of the Moscow Hotel until the sun was streaming through the windows, and only then did they let me fall into an exhausted sleep. But first we all agreed with many oaths that we would tell no one of this incident— but no one. Mother Russia crossed herself and the young interpreter and the two young doctors put their hands over their hearts. I don't know who they were swearing to. I did the same, making a Jewish star since they obviously expected some sign from me. If the story had come out, they would have gotten into trouble for not having taken me to a hospital. Only because of *glasnost* am I telling it now. When I got to New York I found out I had an inflamed gallbladder, so Harriman's diagnosis was right. Despite several gallbladder attacks since I have still not had a gallbladder operation in any language.

Late that afternoon I was informed by Stanley Kramer that the Russians, who were usually very thrifty about travel, would give me, Geraldine Page, and Rip Torn an entire Aeroflot plane if we left the Soviet Union immediately. They knew I had to get back to my play and were making an unusual exception. That's what they said, but the rest of the American delegation stayed the full ten days. I had planned to stay five but I guess I only stayed three. I never found out what Rip and Geraldine had done other than bring a rod and reel to the U.S.S.R.

On the way to the airport my interpreter told me all about herself. She was in her early twenties and spoke English with almost no accent. She was a linguist and spoke several languages fluently. She lived in one room in a huge flat and her husband and she planned to have a baby soon. She would have to quit her job and get pregnant because the state taxed you very heavily if you didn't have children. She was planning to have two children close together because she would have to stay home with them until they were six, but she would get her seniority when she returned to her job after seven years.

She asked me why I had divorced Anthony Franciosa. I puzzled over the question but I finally said, "I was older than he was, and he was very immature." In rather a superior manner she replied, "No Soviet woman would ever say that about her husband." I wanted to slap her but instead gave her a bottle of Collage perfume and another to give to Mother Russia, the concierge. She was delirious. In those days imported things like Collage perfume were never available to the general public.

Rip and Geraldine and I sat in this huge plane with all the empty seats and wondered who had arranged this and why. I thought I knew why I was being sent home but I didn't tell them. As I looked out the window of the plane at the vast reaches of the Soviet Union I resolved that someday I would come back, be careful what I ate and said, go to Leningrad, and see the Hermitage Museum, Siberia, and the Black Sea, where a cousin of mine had fished for caviar toward the end of the Second World War after he had walked from Warsaw to Minsk at fourteen years of age. Well, at least on this trip I had walked around Red Square and the Bronx section of Moscow.

26

Our special Aeroflot flight landed in New York and the reporters were waiting. Aeroflot had as yet no regular scheduled flights to the U.S.A. When interviewed we only had nice things to say about the Soviet Union and I hope the Soviet Union had only nice things to say about us.

I now began to perform again *Cages* eight performances a week. I must have lost ten pounds during my purging in Moscow; the wardrobe lady had to take in all of my costumes.

Shortly after I got back I got an urgent call from Albert Finney's dresser. Finney had played *Luther* for a year in England and had opened it for the producer David Merrick on Broadway. Even though he had gotten rave reviews he still felt stale in the role. Like most English actors, he had negotiated a contract so he could leave the play in New York after one hundred performances, and those one hundred were almost done. I had seen the play before I'd gone to Moscow and he did indeed seem a little monotonous in the role—well, as monotonous as brilliant Albert Finney could be. We had a drink after that performance and discussed how one keeps a long-running role fresh.

He attended the Actors Studio for a couple of sessions

and listened to Strasberg carefully, but he was truly going crazy having to repeat the same role for a year and a half. I asked him if Martin Luther had ever had any doubts about the validity of his purpose, when it was costing so many thousands of human lives. In one strategic scene in *Luther* a man wheels a dead young boy in a wheelbarrow in front of Martin Luther. He pauses and Luther looks at this youngster's bloody face and crushed skull. When I had seen the play I wondered about Finney's choice to have Martin Luther stand absolutely firm in his faith. Martin Luther above all was compassionate and human and it must have cost him dearly to see the chaos that followed when he nailed his declaration of freedom to the church door. I felt it was important for an actor to try to explore the opposite of his character's thrust. Perhaps ambivalence is the cornerstone of good acting, as it so often is of real life.

At that point Finney would try anything, he was so bored repeating the same lines eight times a week. I was again in the theater the Monday night that Albert changed his performance. When the young boy's corpse was wheeled in, Luther's faith was shaken. Finney took an enormous pause, and in the silence it seemed as if he was asking God to reaffirm his mission. This moment on the stage changed the whole second half of the play. It became uncertain, alive, and interesting.

One of my beaux from when I was very young was an actor by the name of Ted Thurston, who was playing one of the monks who chant in *Luther*. I met him in Downey's a few days after Finney had altered his performance, and he told me the whole shape of the play had changed. Everyone in the show was responding to the difference in Finney's performance.

When I got Albert's phone call that day I was hoping that he was going to invite me to see the play again. Instead he asked me to picket it. It seemed that David Merrick was trying to pull a shenanigan with the Actors' Fund benefit. This benefit is a Broadway tradition, always done on the hundredth performance of a play, on a Sunday night. The actors forgo their salaries, the proceeds of the house going to actors who are in need. Merrick had moved this benefit by thirty-two performances, trying to force Finney to stay in the play another four weeks. Albert was furious at this blackmail. He said he would leave the play as per contract, hang around New York, go bowling with me after the show, and go back into the show for the Actors' Fund benefit. But he refused to stay in it these extra weeks. American Actors' Equity and British Actors' Equity that season were having a lot of brouhaha. Many English actors and shows were on Broadway and British Equity was still making it very difficult for American actors to work in England.

Finney felt that *Luther* was a hit and that an American star could easily replace him without harm to the show's box office. Merrick had had plenty of time to sign such an actor. He had been either unwilling or unable to do so. Finney was leaving the play that Saturday night and since Merrick had not put a notice in the papers or, so far, a notice up in the lobby that Albert's understudy was going to go on as of Monday, Finney was rallying his fellow actors to picket David Merrick in front of the theater.

That Monday night I showed up in the lobby and there was Albert with three or four picket signs saying ALBERT FINNEY IS NOT ON THE STAGE! ALBERT FINNEY HAS LEFT THIS SHOW! So, starting at 7:00 P.M., before the 8:30 curtain, Shelley Winters, Albert Finney, and another off-Broadway friend of Albert's walked up and down in front of the theater. The public who had lined up to buy tickets began returning them to get their money back, en masse. I believe David Merrick called the police but we were within our civil rights and there was nothing they could do. I never wonder why David Merrick never, never hired me for any of his countless shows. But fair is fair and contracts must be honored and actors must not be blackmailed. Or so it says in the Actors' Equity constitution.

Ambassador Stevenson got me an admissions pass to the gallery at the U.N. and I would sometimes have lunch with him at that elegant restaurant in the U.N. Building. We had been friends since he had run for president in

1952 and I had often campaigned with and for him. Even though he had been defeated in that election and John Kennedy later had won the Democratic nomination in 1960 I had watched his importance as a world figure increase and indeed John Kennedy had been wise in appointing him as U.S. ambassador to the U.N. He had a subtle sense of humor and he would often gently josh me into using my perfectly good intelligence when I was still under pressure to retreat into my blonde-bombshell image, which by now was getting into middle-aged blonde-bombshellishness.

When I made a charity luncheon speech, if it was at the Waldorf, he would sometimes stand in back of the ballroom in the shadows of the hall and listen to me. The ambassador's quarters were in the Waldorf Towers. He would later critique my speech and try to advise me how to think in an orderly way and how to marshal my facts more insightfully. I in turn was trying to teach him to be more emotional so as to appeal to the unintellectual, emotional masses. He wouldn't or couldn't do it and would just smile wisely and try to make me understand that you mustn't condescend to the public. You must appeal to their most discerning instincts of brotherhood and fair play.

One evening after my performance we were sitting in his study overlooking the beautiful nighttime spectacle of midtown Manhattan, listening to the late news. Some important event that concerned the U.S. and his position at the U.N. was announced on the program. He was very angry and turned off the TV and in a surprisingly bitter voice said, "Your hero has feet of clay, as do most popular heroes." Something had happened that he should have been informed of and the cabinet and president had bypassed him. I can't remember the event but I remember that it seriously impaired his effectiveness at the U.N.

I got both of us another drink of Scotch and just listened. There was nothing to say or as a matter of fact to understand. It was too involved for me to grasp. This was sometime around my birthday, August 18, and since it was one of those traumatic decade birthdays Stevenson had bought me a little present. I believe I've mentioned in this book how the Kennedy ladies never wore diamonds because they were too flashy. Adlai Stevenson knew this and he also knew my fondness for gems. He opened a little box and handed me a blue sapphire ring. The stone was beautiful. It had two subtle baguettes on the sides. I didn't know what to make of this. I should have been flattered and honored, but instead I panicked.

"Is this birthday present a friendship ring?" I whispered. "Which hand and/or finger should I put it on?"

Adlai looked at me very quietly and seriously. "It can be whatever you want it to be," he said.

After a long pause, in which he said nothing, I put it on the middle finger of my right hand and like the retarded idiot I sometimes am I said, "It fits and it looks nice on that finger, doesn't it?" I never was invited to the embassy of the United States at the United Nations again. Ambassador Stevenson was too vague or I was too frightened.

I still have that beautiful sapphire ring and depending on my self-esteem at any given moment I wear that ring on the second finger of my left hand or whatever finger on my right hand.

I had left *Cages* to do a film called *Time of Indifference* in Italy. Adapted from a book by Alberto Moravia, it was a penetrating study of the rise of Fascism. A new hot young Italian director by the name of Francesco Maselli was to direct. It was being produced by a famous Italian producer, Franco Cristaldi. I, Rod Steiger, Claudia Cardinale, Paulette Goddard, and Tomas Milian were to star in it.

When you're in an off-Broadway play you are working for minimum or a little more than minimum. My agent had taken this aspect of *Cages* personally and had made me feel as if I were taking money out of his pocket, so when I accepted *Time of Indifference* he pouched a TV script called "The Way from Darkness" to me. This would be done in California and if I hurried I could squeeze this show in before I left for Italy. This television drama was for the prestigious "Alcoa Premiere" series and I was to be paid $25,000 for ten days' work, a week of rehearsing, and three days of filming. It was to be photographed with three film cameras, the way television sitcoms are now photographed, which was very innovative then. Lucille Ball had pioneered this technique of photographing with "I Love Lucy." I can't remember what "The Way from Darkness" was about but it was very serious and very dramatic, and since I had worked for six or seven months for practically nothing I needed that $25,000 . . . so I found myself alone again, back in my apartment in Beverly Hills.

While I was rehearsing the Alcoa show I got a call from Sean Connery. He was at the Beverly Hills Hotel and he wanted me to go that very evening to a press showing of a film he had done with Ursula Andress called *Dr. No.* He was very nervous about the film; in fact, he hated it. But the producers, Cubby Broccoli and Harry Saltzman, were offering him a lucrative contract to do another film about this same James Bond character.

The public had not yet seen this film. There was a preview theater under the Lytton Bank across Crescent Heights from Schwab's drugstore. He would pick me up at seven. We would have drinks and hors d'oeuvres in the lobby of the theater and then see the film and have dinner afterward. I believe, though I am not sure, that Sean was engaged to Diane Cilento at that time. Anyway, she was in London and she also hated the picture, Sean told me, and she felt that Sean would be selling out his talent if he did another Bond picture. Until recently I had thought Diane Cilento nuts about this matter, but Sean Connery has just won an Oscar for *The Untouchables,* and who knows, maybe she was right. He might have had a different kind of career.

That night I went with him to the preview theater and we met Ursula Andress and John Derek at the cocktail party. Joe Wiseman, who was a friend of mine with whom I had acted in *Saturday Night Kid,* was sitting in a corner with a double martini, paralyzed with fear. He whispered that he played a corny villain in *Dr. No* and he felt it might ruin his career, which was composed mostly of playing villains in important films. He had been one of the original members of the Group Theatre, and most of his villains were very Method.

After a couple of martinis and stupid responses to the questions the press were asking Sean and me, we went in to see the first press showing of the film version of Ian Fleming's *Dr. No*. After fifteen minutes I had to move away from John Derek, Ursula, and Sean. I was enjoying myself hugely and they were describing in whispers whatever had taken place on the set when Terence Young was directing them. The special effects were great and Joe Wiseman was marvelous, the ultimate villain. When we walked up the aisle and came out of the theater that night, Sean was a superstar.

Ursula had been very good but mostly they had photographed her gorgeous body. Sean was handsome, graceful, elegant, debonair, and sexy sexy sexy. How this young drayman who had thrown around barrels of beer so recently in Scotland had achieved this sophisticated performance was almost a mystery. As I stared at him I remembered that much of acting is keen observing and automatic personalizing. Sean had it down pat.

The press was overwhelming him but we managed to get out of the theater in fifteen minutes and thrifty Sean took me to the back booth of Schwab's for dinner. His excuse was, nobody would think of looking for us there at night. In those days Schwab's was not only open and functioning, it served dinners. I was so excited about his performance in this film I had to order my standard tranquilizer: tuna-fish salad and tomato on rye toast and a chocolate milk shake. Sean had no idea what a sexual turn-on he was on the screen. He still felt the whole thing was glitzy, mannered, and dangerous. He went on in this fashion for ten minutes. As he voiced these sentiments I continued staring at him and finally interrupted him with, "Sean, if you truly don't want to do any more Bond pictures, just ask for some outrageous sum like a million dollars a picture for three pictures." He started to laugh almost hysterically and I joined in. I'm not sure we were both laughing at the same thing. He had been so poor and now I knew he was going to be a billionaire. But at the time he felt this was a great way to turn down two important American producers who worked out of England.

As the world knows, they accepted his terms. God only knows what he got after those three Bond pictures, but I have seen every Bond picture and most of them are quite wonderful entertainment. Though there have been two or three other James Bonds since he relinquished the role, none of them, but none of them, have had the élan of Sean Connery. It is a part he has made uniquely his own. Though he now has an Oscar, I'm sure he remembers what fun it was those days when women fainted at his feet. Or maybe he doesn't. Maybe, like me, he has gladly made the transition to character roles. Next time I see him I must ask him.

After an exhausting performance in the unmemorable "The Way from Darkness," I jetted to Europe with Sean. Sean got off in London and I arrived in Rome enthused and happy that I was to do such an important film by a famous novelist and with such an important cast and important director.

I registered at the apartment hotel, the Residence Palace, where the production had reserved a two-room apartment for me. When I had been in Rome before I had always stayed at the Hotel de la Ville, and of course I had stayed in our apartment when I was married to Vittorio. The last time I had stayed in Rome, when I was married to Anthony Franciosa, I had stayed at the Excelsior.

The Residence was in a new section of Rome that I didn't know, and I felt lonely and strange. My daughter was arriving from New York as soon as she finished her school year. She had never been to Italy before. She was ten years old and I felt it was an appropriate time for her to at last meet her Italian family. Her father had been to New York and California many times, but I had never let her come to Italy before because of my friend Dawn Addams's plight. This was another reason I had accepted this film, so I could be in Rome with her.

I had fittings with a famous Italian couturier, and the six costumes he made for me were gorgeous. Since I was playing a remittance woman, sort of Paulette Goddard's personal saleslady and cosmetologist, I couldn't understand why I was wearing these gorgeous clothes. *Time of Indifference* was set in Italy in the middle thirties when the aristocracy and the rich were very rich and the poor were very, very poor. But these clothes were so classy and art decoish that I stifled my artistic truth and let the seamstresses work. They gave me these clothes after the filming and I have worn them in *A Patch of Blue, Wild in the Streets, Bloody Mama,* and a picture I recently completed called *Touch of a Stranger.* They have finally fallen apart, but the last was a black chiffon dress, bias cut à la Jean Harlow, with a white chiffon collar. It barely held together until the end of the filming. I wonder if Signore Cristaldi, the producer, or Signore Schubert knows that their wardrobe from *Time of Indifference* was worn in several other American films. In fact, I wore one of these dresses, a black-and-white floral print, for the next decade, in *A House Is Not a Home, Harper,* and *Diamonds.* In fact, the black-and-white print photographed in color kind of navy blue–and–white, so I insisted that Joe Levine, who produced *House,* rent me a real sapphire-and-diamond necklace, which I subsequently wore in all those films. After the many weeks of rental, Marvin Hime, jeweler to the stars, let me trade in my old diamond necklace and buy this one for a very few thousand dollars. Joe Levine, Paul Newman, and Menahem Golan don't know it but they bought me a diamond necklace which I have worn to one Oscar-cast and a dinner for General Omar Bradley. Now it rests in the bank vault.

Meanwhile, back in Rome, while postproductioning *Gli Indifferenti* (as *Time of Indifference* was called in Italian), I awaited my child's arrival and had long discussions over the phone with Vittorio's sister Maria about what an American child was used to in New York. Maria was a lovely lady and reassured me. She had two daughters of her own and lived next door to Vittorio, and the game plan was that my kid would spend the week from Monday until Friday, while I was working, with Vittorio and his family, and the weekends with me. I had never shared custody of her before and I had dragged her on every location I could and every tour of summer or winter stock.

Even before she arrived, I was jealous and angry. Both Vittorio and I went to the airport to meet her. I was barely polite to Vittorio. Logically, I knew that he was happy and excited to have his daughter at last in Rome to meet her Italian family, but logic had no place in my feelings. Our ten-year-old got off the plane wearing a chic hat, dark glasses, and white gloves. She gave us a friendly wave and in a most adult manner went through customs. She hugged her Daddy and gave me a lot of kisses, and we got in his car, which was some expensive, fast Italian model.

He drove me back to the Residence Palace. I got out of the car and they sped away, my child and her father. I stood on the pavement in front of the hotel for a long time. I had had to leave her so many times for film locations, and now it almost seemed as if she was getting even and leaving me. I knew it was only my imagination but I felt desolate.

There was a cinema on the ground floor of the Residence that only showed Elvis Presley films. There were a lot of American and English residents in that part of Rome and I guess they parked their children at this theater when they didn't know what to do with them.

It was quite early Sunday afternoon but I went into that theater and sat down in the darkness and wept. I didn't know why I was crying so bitterly but I had never felt so lonely in my life. Elvis was up on the screen being funny and sexy and I sat there sobbing, rather loudly. A little boy came over to me and said in Italian, "Lady, did you get hurt?" I gave him a rather wet kiss and got tears all over his face. Then I pulled myself together, walked out to the lobby, and took the elevator up to my apartment. I ordered something from room service—anything but spaghetti. The *maître d'* sent a bottle of wine compliments of the Residence, but I didn't drink any of it because I knew I was going to take two sleeping pills.

* * *

In those days, filming in Rome was much more civilized than it was in Hollywood, or for that matter the way it is in Italy now. The studio car picked you up at nine. You drove to the set, you had a leisurely cappuccino while they made you up and then you reported for work about eleven or twelve o'clock. You acted till 1:00 P.M., had lunch until 4:00, slept or rested or whatever, and reported back to work until 8:00 P.M. Maybe the working hours are a little less than Hollywood, but I'm convinced they get more work done. When you get up at 5:00 A.M. and report for work at 6:00, you begin to fade after lunch and the afternoon seems endless. I hope that with the new independent spirit in Hollywood they will revert to Italian hours.

Some years later I did a film in Paris with Roman Polanski, *The Tenant*. Although the film was technically very difficult, the shooting schedule was only six weeks. I am convinced that it was because of the French hours of working: noon to a civilized 8:00 P.M., then everyone has a delicious French dinner.

Gli Indifferenti started in chaos and ended up in shambles. It seemed that the producer, Cristaldi, was making a film about a romance between Claudia Cardinale and Tomas Milian—and the director, Maselli, was making a political picture about the rise of Fascism. But this was sort of par for the Italian film scene in those days. Everyone in the film spoke a different language. Rod Steiger, Paulette Goddard, and I sort of spoke English. Tomas Milian, who was Cuban, spoke Spanish, and Claudia Cardinale just made sounds. She had been born and raised in Tunisia, had spent a few years in Spain, and had arrived in Italy at eighteen. Of course, she was Cristaldi's girlfriend. That was the reason for the whole operation.

She was a lovely, sad girl, beautiful and quiet, rather stunned to find herself a "movie star." I once asked her why she always looked so unhappy. She smiled her Mona Lisa smile and said in some language, "That must be the mystique of female Italian movie stars. We must always appear to be suffering silently."

The film director, Francesco Maselli, barely spoke En-

525

glish and he had a British lady who was rather graying and spinsterish as his assistant and translator. The problem was, she had left England thirty years earlier, and during the thirties, forties, and fifties the English language had changed. She spoke Italian like a native but her English was rather rusty. We were working from an Italian script but speaking our own languages since the film would be dubbed into the appropriate language of each country it was released in. There was such an ideological difference between the producer and the director that the words the actors spoke were being constantly changed and argued about.

A couple of years later when this picture was to be released in America, Rod Steiger and I had to dub it into English. That meant speaking into a microphone while you watched your lips move on the screen and trying to sync the sound with your lips. When we got ready to do it, we found that Maselli had stolen the sound track and we had no guide track to copy. We finally had to get someone from the deaf-and-dumb institute to read our lips and tell us what we had said on the film. It is always rather difficult for me to dub because I hesitate when I speak naturally and I have irregular breathing and speaking patterns. Dubbing *Indifferenti* was a nightmare. In fact, shooting the whole film was a nightmare.

The only relief was Tomas Milian, and we became fast friends, and I do mean friends. He had lived in New York for a while and he was a member of the Actors Studio before he emigrated to Rome. He was doing lots of artistic pictures in those days but since has become a big Italian TV star. He has made a lot of money doing a series about an undercover cop and I don't think he longs for the stress of acting deeply anymore. I know I certainly don't. Well, I think I don't.

I would long for weekends when my daughter would be delivered back to me. We would go out to the beach at Fregene from Friday night till Monday morning. The production understood and would give me late calls on Monday morning while I returned my daughter to her father's household.

During the week, to distract me, Tomas Milian showed me a part of Rome that I had never known existed—the struggling young actors' and workingmen's cafés and restaurants. We visited Visconti's beautiful house on the Appian Way. He was filming at the same studio, Cinecittà, and I got to know him quite well.

The first film that Vittorio had ever taken me to in Rome had been over a decade ago, and it had been Visconti's *La Terra Trema*. I remember that this film had started with a message across the screen in Italian. I asked Vittorio what it said and he told me, "This picture is in Sicilian because Sicilians do not have the opportunity to learn Italian." It was a great film about a hopeless strike by fishermen in Sicily against the monopolies that buy their catch, and about the church helping the monopolies to break their union.

The early sixties was the era of great directors in Italy. Rossellini had peaked after his revolutionary innovation of neorealism. During this period I got to know Vittorio De Sica, Fellini, Antonioni, and Zeffirelli. They all seemed very like George Stevens. When I have my 3:00 A.M. case of the dooms I wonder, if I had learned Italian and stayed in Italy, whether I would have worked with these great directors. They certainly seemed to respect my work and to like me.

Sometime in the middle of the shooting of *Indifferenti*, I finally realized that Maselli was trying to make an important anti-Fascist statement.

The film took place during the period when Mussolini used the indifference and greediness of the Italian people to grab power and became the dictator who eventually destroyed Italy. All the nouveau riche characters in the film were politically apathetic and only cared about material possessions and didn't pay attention to or give a damn about what was happening around them—rather like the American society of the eighties.

I wondered why I, who usually research films so closely and often try to make a sociological or political statement with the role I am playing, had warded off the knowledge of what this film was really about. Perhaps it was because of the subtle blacklisting that was still going on in Hollywood.

I was attracted to the film and on some unconscious level afraid of it. When I faced this I began to help Maselli as much as I could. I stayed on the set and watched scenes that I wasn't involved in and translated for him into English as best I could what he had written in Italian.

Why this film has never been shown on American TV to my knowledge puzzles me. Rod Steiger gave a powerful performance in it, and I think my scenes with Paulette Goddard were very funny. I remember one in which I was giving her a facial. I had worked with her in *The Women* and she had worn different sets of jewelry every day and she did the same in this film. It was rather difficult to get around her diamond necklaces while I was giving her neck and face a facial, but we had very amusing scenes together. She was indeed fun to work with in this film, rather zany, and she would tell me long, rambling stories about how stingy Charlie Chaplin was, ignoring the fact that she was the only woman in his history who got a lot of money and jewels from him. I told her about the open house on Sundays at Charlie and Oona's that I had gone to. She was amazed.

"I can't believe he spent money on food for strangers, talented or not," she said.

I think my daughter became allergic to filming at this point. Her father began shooting a film and when she wasn't sitting on his set she was sitting on mine. Shooting a film is the most boring thing in the world unless you're personally involved in it. You spend a whole day getting three or four minutes of actual footage. She must have paid attention, though, because sometime during her adolescence she heard someone ask me how many frames go through a camera per minute. She remembered the number, though I no longer did.

She was loving her Italian family and having fun with her cousins and half-sister who was about five years older and was taking her all over Rome, to the zoo, the Villa Borghese, puppet shows, and special plays for children. A few years later her father did something called Teatro Tentro in which the government built him a movable tent and he performed, twelve hours a day, all the Italian classics for the schoolchildren of Rome. At that time I think he practiced reciting on his kids, because they all learned Dante. I knew it was silly but I began to be afraid on Monday mornings when I brought her back to his house that she wouldn't want to come back to New York with me, or that Vittorio wouldn't let her come back.

One Friday night when I picked her up Vittorio insisted I stay for dinner. I can't remember who his wife or mistress was at that point—I think it was Annette Stroyberg —but it was a large family gathering, with aunts, uncles, sisters, and children. The chatter was going around the table in three languages and Vittorio and I began to have a heated discussion about world film and the American and British theater.

Suddenly we became aware that we had been arguing for about an hour, and no one else had said a word. All the relatives had remained silent and just were looking and listening to us. We both laughed at this incident in a rather embarrassed way. The silence that followed was louder than our discussion and almost as long.

In the years to come, when Vittorio came to New York to visit, my daughter would tell him to meet her at my apartment at six o'clock, and she would show up after seven. It took us quite a while to catch on that she was trying to get us to talk ourselves out before her father took her to dinner. She obviously wanted her father's attention completely on her. After that famous evening in Rome I would find excuses not to visit my ex–Italian family anymore, although I loved them dearly, especially Vittorio's mother and sister.

Weekends my kid and I would stay at a little *pensione* at the beach, La Firenze. It was sort of stupid to stay there because Vittorio and I had had romantic weekends there when we were courting. But my friends Paul Bogart and his wife, Jane, were staying there with their children, who were then about the same age as my daughter, and they would have lots of fun on the beach.

One Sunday lunch we went to a restaurant down the coast that was vaguely familiar, and then I remembered I had been there with Vittorio. During that lunch my daughter corrected me on an Italian word that I unknowingly had long mispronounced. Vittorio had loved to tease me by teaching me inappropriate Italian words. This restaurant's specialty was little black mussels steamed in garlic and butter, and you opened them like peanuts and could eat a bushelful. I think this fish is indigenous to Spain and Italy and nowhere else in the world. When I ordered a large dish of steamed *cazzo*, my very young daughter looked at me strangely and said, "Mother, the word is *cozze*. You have to be very careful of your vowels in Italian, Mom." I looked confused and asked her what the word I had said meant, and she whispered in my ear, "Mom, *cazzo* means a man's penis. *Cozze* means the mussels."

I blushed several shades of red and realized I had been confusing that word for over a decade. Anthony Franciosa had never noticed the difference. But his ancestry was Neapolitan.

That evening, when we drove back to Rome, Tomas Milian was giving an end-of-the-picture party for the cast. He had many beautiful antiques and statues in his apartment off the Piazza di Spange. There was a torso of a beautiful young man that he told me Visconti had given him. He told me that he wanted to present it to my daughter because I had helped the director, Maselli, and him with the film *Time of Indifference*. The bust was very old and it was almost illegal to send it out of Italy because there was a new "preservation of antiquity" law that had been passed in Italy in 1960, but legally he could send it to my daughter because she was half-Italian.

The statue was two feet high and so lovely it looked as if Michelangelo or one of his students could have done it. It was hardly chipped and very, very valuable. He told me he would take it to Naples and put it on a boat and the forwarder in New York would notify me when to pick it up. I thanked him and kissed all the actors goodbye and told Tomas I would see him at the Actors Studio in a couple of months, when he was planning to come to New York.

My role in the film ended the next Monday and Vittorio

took us to the plane. My daughter kissed her daddy good-bye and promised that from then on she would spend all of her summers with him. As the plane took off I looked at the earth of Italy and wondered why so much of my happiness and angst was related to it. My daughter had a fluent Italian conversation with the Italian stewardesses all the way to New York, although they chatted too quickly for me to understand anything. But after eight hours we landed on American soil.

I got home the Thursday after Labor Day and thank goodness I got my kid in school in time for orientation day. New York was beautiful, crisp and sunny, and for once I was not being an obsessive workaholic. I enjoyed New York, attending the theater almost every night.

Tennessee Williams was hanging around Downey's and the Studio again, and we would sometimes walk up to Fifty-ninth Street and take a hansom cab through Central Park. It was quite expensive even then and most of the time I would pay. Tennessee always lived as if he were on the edge of poverty, but I understood this, being a Depression baby myself.

Tennessee wouldn't start his serious drinking till nightfall, but although I saw him many times in Hollywood and New York, I never remember once having a meal with him or seeing him eat a bite of food. And I would know if we had eaten together, since I remember almost every meal I've eaten. I remember going to the Four Seasons with Tennessee and having an elegant dinner. Tennessee just drank. I don't remember him getting drunk, he just waxed poetic and then suddenly became comatose.

One cocktail hour we found ourselves in Paula and Lee Strasberg's huge apartment on Central Park West. Lee, as was his wont, questioned me about my role in *Time of Indifference* and I told him about my experience with Francesco Maselli and how I hadn't realized the sociological and political implications of the film until the middle of the shooting. I had then turned my artistic brains around to help the director. Lee listened to this Italian work experience and then informed me that he had been carefully listening to my critiques of scenes at the Studio in the past year.

"From among all the actors of your generation at the Studio you can articulate the use of my Method the most accurately," he said. "Both Cheryl Crawford and Elia Kazan know this. As a new member of the board of directors of the Actors Studio you must take time out from your acting career and start teaching and moderating at the Actors Studio."

He then turned to Tennessee and said, "You attend the actors' and directors' session, Tennessee, and you are one of the greatest playwrights of this century. We understand that you're very shy, but we think you must do the same, and try to give your poetic knowledge to the next generation." Lee Strasberg always spoke in the royal "we."

After that gentle urging Tennessee never came to the Actors Studio again. But I started teaching and moderating. I did not know how much I had absorbed about acting until I began to teach it. As the widow lady in *The King and I* sings, by our students we are taught.

That night, when I rushed home to have dinner with my kid, she handed me a telegram. It was an invitation to a dinner honoring General Omar Bradley. President and Mrs. Kennedy, Eleanor Roosevelt, Adlai Stevenson, and many stars of theater and film who had worked in Kennedy's campaign would be on the Waldorf dais. I spent the next week dieting and exercising, very nervous about the fact that I did not have an appropriate escort to take me to that dinner—certainly none of my Downey's chums.

Nevertheless, I went to Bergdorf's and let myself feel rich. All the salesladies helped me try on every single evening gown in the store. I finally settled on a cobalt blue satin off-the-shoulder gown, which had a huge puffed skirt gathered up underneath to the knees. It had a very tiny waist, which I managed with a very tight waist cincher. With it I planned to wear my traded sapphire-and-diamond necklace, earrings, and bracelet and a sapphire ring.

Women's lib had not quite arrived but I bravely went to the dinner alone, in a rented limousine.

When I arrived at the Waldorf I was ushered into a gold and brown velvet room with two long rows of gold chairs down the middle. I was given a cocktail and seated in a gold chair that had my name on it. I'd been so nervous about being late that I was the first to arrive. A waiter offered a tray with lovely hors d'oeuvres but I was afraid of spoiling my beautiful gown, and the waist cincher was really too tight for me to eat anything. The room began to fill up with celebrated people from politics, the theater, and films. Lo and behold, Henry Fonda was my dinner partner and I did not have to march in alone. When everyone was finally seated on the little gold chairs, music played and we marched onto the huge dais in two orderly rows: the politicians on the high dais and the theatrical personalities on the lower dais. Paul Newman and Joanne Woodward were seated to my right, and on Henry Fonda's left were Marlene Dietrich, Art Carney, and Henry Morgan. I think every well-known actor who believed in the New Frontier was on that dais that night.

On the dais above us was a gallery of Democratic notables such as Mrs. Roosevelt, Mike Mansfield, Sam Rayburn, Lyndon Johnson, Ted Sorensen, Arthur Schlesinger, Jr., Robert McNamara, Stewart Udall, Bobby Kennedy, Pierre Salinger and all the rest of the New Frontiersmen, and of course President Kennedy and General Omar Bradley. Alas, Adlai's chair was empty, as was Jacqueline Kennedy's.

I went up to the dais to say hello to the president and chat with Mrs. Roosevelt, who was seated on his left. I looked for Mrs. Kennedy, whom I somehow had not really met yet, but didn't see her anywhere. When I asked when Mrs. Kennedy would be arriving, the president immediately spoke to someone across the empty chair. Mrs. Roosevelt looked at me without expression and said in a very even tone, "She's still at the airport on Air Force One. Her hairdresser can't get her hair right."

I couldn't think of a reply to that one. I said, "Oh," and went back to my seat. Mrs. Kennedy never showed up that night. I think she was too shy and intimidated by the presence of the strong former First Lady. It surprised all of us, because Jackie had made such an impression in France and Berlin. But I believe she was still terrified of Democratic public appearances.

Adlai Stevenson arrived during the first course and took his seat. He smiled and nodded to me and I sat on my hand with the sapphire ring. We had a glorious dinner and for once I can't remember what I ate. Somehow the empty chair on the upper dais was filled—everyone moved one seat closer to the president.

Then began an evening of extraordinary, hope-filled, inspiring speeches. America was loved and very prosperous in the early sixties, but Kennedy's speech was focused on what can happen to a country when it is completely materialistic and ignores its responsibilities to the citizens of the world who live at poverty level.

After the glorious evening Henry Fonda dropped me off at my apartment and on the way we talked about the rocketing career of his daughter, Jane. She was still attending the Actors Studio sporadically, and I had done *Invitation to a March* and *The Chapman Report* with her. She was under the spell of an Actors Studio Svengali named Andreas Voutsinas, who now has a theater and school in Paris. Although he was a fine teacher he was the most egotistical Greek I've ever met, but whatever it was he did for Jane Fonda and Tanya Lopert and Madeleine Sherwood must have been positive.

He fancied himself the inheritor of the Strasberg Method, and when he took an actress under his wing he literally lived with her day and night, worked on her plays and pictures with her, coached her, and God knows what else. I remember Jane complaining in her earliest Actors Studio days about her "piano legs." She did have rather thick ankles. While she was under the spell of Andreas, for hours she would do special ankle exercises, and he would wrap her legs and ankles in athletic bandages soaked in brine. As they dried they would shrink. Jane would cry with pain, but she now has lovely ankles. I believe her mania for exercise started under Andreas's tutelage. I remember once looking in their refrigerator and seeing nothing but health food. I thought, Eck! How awful. But I'm allergic to health food. Then and now, it makes me sick.

The early sixties was the beginning of the youth cult in the U.S. and sometime around then Jane decided she would never get old. So far, she hasn't, and she is indeed an accomplished actress.

The previous fall and winter, Broadway had a British invasion—Georgia Brown in *Oliver!;* Anthony Newley in *Stop the World—I Want to Get Off;* Alan Bennett, Peter Cook, Jonathan Miller, and Dudley Moore in *Beyond the Fringe;* Hermione Baddeley in Tennessee's *The Milk Train Doesn't Stop Here Anymore;* Margaret Leighton and Anthony Quinn in *Tchin-Tchin;* and Vivien Leigh in *Tovarich.* It seemed that no matter where you looked, English actors were playing in British or American plays on Broadway. In 1963, if an American musical or play was done in London, unless it was a big star whose name sold tickets the British would not give an American actor a work permit.

There was a great deal of brouhaha among the American actors about this. British Equity and American Equity were in great conflict. There were several fistfights in Downey's, Harold's Show Spot, and P.J. Clarke's. It seems there were also fights in pubs in London's West End—so Shelley, the great peacemaker, decided that since she had such a big apartment and had entertained the Bolshoi Ballet, she'd invite all the British and American actors working on Broadway to a Thanksgiving buffet dinner to discuss what would be fair for all English-speaking actors.

I proceeded to call all the actors I knew on the phone and invite them. I decided to go backstage and hand-deliver invitations to the British and American actors I did not know. I got busy on the phone inviting alphabetically the ones I did know. When I got to Henry Fonda, who was in New York performing in a play, I told him my idea and he thought it was a good one. But he suggested that I invite Adlai Stevenson or Ralph Bunche, who were famous diplomats and knew how to arrange such peace negotiations. If not, he thought, I should notify the Central Park West precinct in my neighborhood. It was a very sore subject, he warned.

I thanked him for the advice and proceeded to call the next person on my alphabetical list, who was Jane Fonda. Andreas screened the call and then finally connected me with Jane. She thought it was a great idea, but suddenly in the middle of our conversation she stopped talking and said, "Do you consider yourself a good friend of mine, Shelley?"

"Of course."

"Did you invite my father?" she queried.

"Of course. He's in a play on Broadway. I'm inviting all the casts of all the plays on Broadway."

"If you are a good friend of mine you'll uninvite him," she demanded. "I really mean that, Shelley."

I knew she did. I replied, "I'll think about it," and hung up.

During the sixties and seventies, Jane would love her father intensely for some months, then hate him for other months. I gathered that her parents had been divorced when she was quite young, and I later read that her mother had committed suicide. While we were in *Invitation to a March* a childhood friend of Jane's committed suicide. Jane had not been able to perform the play without the assistance of a doctor. That morning, as I sat holding the phone, I remembered all this, and I decided to do as Jane wished and uninvite her father.

When I got Henry on the phone, all I got out of my mouth was, "Hank, do you mind if—"

And he interrupted me, saying, "I understand, Shelley. Jane doesn't want to be in the same room with me."

I couldn't answer. He said, "It's okay. I understand. I'll tell Olivia about it." His voice sounded as though he was weeping.

I believe he was.

In later years, when Jane was able to be friends with her father, she did a wonderful Mark Rydell film, *On Golden Pond*, with him just before he died. I was so happy she was able to do that. She was able to forgive him and herself, and I hope he wasn't too ill to understand that Jane had helped him win the Oscar for Best Actor he had long deserved.

I spent that entire morning phoning all the members of the Studio playing on Broadway. Then I had my brunch and put on the television and began to write the invitations to my Thanksgiving party for all the British and American actors I did not know. A special news show was on TV, and there was a crowd cheering in Dallas. I looked up and saw Jacqueline Kennedy and the president waving at the crowds. I was happy at how victorious and radiant they looked. As I watched, I heard some gunshot noise, like pops, and I saw John Kennedy's head go forward and then another man jumped onto the back of the limousine and then I saw Jacqueline, in her lovely suit, now covered with blood, trying to crawl out of the car.

Molly came running in from the kitchen. I was sitting on the floor, writing on my marble cocktail table. Molly sat on the cocktail table next to me. I kept writing the invitations. Molly took my hand and held it, stopping my writing. It had to be some kind of strange made-up news story. But as we watched, people were screaming and running for cover and an announcer said, "The president has been shot." I don't remember the rest.

Molly turned off the television. We sat staring at each other. Molly and I had been active in civil rights, and we both loved John Kennedy. We couldn't move or cry. We couldn't imagine that it was real or in any way deal with it. We just sat there. In a little while my daughter walked in the door. They had dismissed the entire school. She was crying. She looked at Molly and me and said, "Mom, they shot the president. I think he's dead." I held her in my arms. After a while, I asked Molly to turn on the TV again. All I remember of that terrible day is the picture of poor Jacqueline, standing in the plane with the blood on her clothes, looking at Lyndon Johnson as he was sworn in. Then I remember seeing news clips of Johnson getting off that plane and Humphrey looking at him with accusing eyes—or perhaps I imagined it. But I am an actress and I have developed the art of reading people's thoughts and that's what I saw.

After a while, Barbara Probst Solomon took my child up to her apartment. Molly went to her church in Harlem. Then it was dark, and I was sitting with Barbara and Tennessee Williams in Downey's. I could not cry. I don't think I felt anything. It was too traumatizing to think of. I heard myself saying that I wanted the record of "The Lonesome Train." It was a recording about Lincoln's funeral train. I remembered it from Roosevelt's death.

We walked up Broadway to the Colony record shop. It seems to me the whole city was completely still. Even the sign on the *Times* building was shut off. No one spoke. Tennessee was carrying his little dog. We got the record and somehow got a child's phonograph with a winding handle. I don't think either of us said a word.

We walked over to P.J. Clarke's on Third Avenue—I guess we wanted to be with other people. Tennessee guided us. We sat down in a corner and listened to the recording of "The Lonesome Train," about carrying Lincoln's body home again. In this very Irish bar no one was drinking. Everyone was looking at each other in disbelief and despair. I think every single person who was alive in the world that day remembers where he was that afternoon and night. It was a trauma for all who had love and hope for the future. Only the haters celebrated.

Henry Madden, a very tall Irish friend from the Actors Studio, came to the back of Clarke's with Dorothy Kilgallen and her husband, Dick. They all sat down and listened to my endless playing of "The Lonesome Train," Lincoln's funeral dirge. I couldn't feel grief. I don't think I felt anything. Henry, who was a religious Catholic, at last suggested that we find a church and say a prayer for John Kennedy's soul. It seemed like the only thing to do.

The Kilgallens had their car. Tennessee sat in front of the limo with his dog and the chauffeur. It was the middle of the night and we couldn't find any church that was open. It seems to me we tried all the famous ones, and they were all closed.

Henry finally suggested a little church that was way west on Forty-third Street. It was for the bums and homeless who even then populated the Times Square area. We pulled up in the Kilgallens' limo and entered this very crowded church for the poor of Times Square and Ninth and Tenth Avenues. We each lit a candle for JFK. When we got back in the limo Tennessee turned the radio on. The news seemed to be just about the assassination and Lyndon Johnson's swearing-in. There was no news from Texas. Strangely, the Texas news was blacked out. They had taken Kennedy's body on Air Force One back to Washington, D.C. There was something almost refugeelike about the way the people on board that plane had fled Texas.

Barbara Probst Solomon told us about the article she had written for the November 1963 issue of *Harper's* about the hatred in Texas. Texans were carrying guns and she just about warned that no government official who stood for civil rights should go to Texas at that time.

As we rode up Eighth Avenue Barbara kept asking, "Where's *Oswald?*" They had said he'd been apprehended, but there seemed to have been a clampdown on any information about his whereabouts or whether he was the sole assassin. I was too numb to think about it. Dorothy Kilgallen, who was an investigative columnist, looked out the car window and said, "I am going to find out the truth, who wanted this, who did it, and how and why our wonderful young president was murdered."

In the year to come, she would be the only reporter to interview Jack Ruby, the man who would shoot Oswald, ostensibly the sole assassin. This shooting happened the following day in Dallas on camera. Dorothy herself would die soon thereafter under rather mysterious circumstances. It seems that everyone who had any direct connection with that assassination died mysteriously.

It was dawn. The limousine dropped off Tennessee and then Dorothy and Dick and proceeded up Central Park West. Henry Madden asked the driver to wait and Barbara kissed me and went up in the elevator. Henry, who was then and now a liberal Democrat, I knew would now go and get drunk. I kissed him goodnight and rang for the elevator. Henry left the lobby. When the elevator came I told the operator, "Never mind." I waited awhile to make sure Henry had driven off, and then I decided to take a walk in the park.

I was in despair. Since childhood I had believed that good must triumph and now it seemed the opposite had happened to the whole world and me and my family. I walked for a long time through Central Park and found myself at the Bethesda Fountain. This is a majestic, very old fountain in Central Park where I and my fellow Studio members had bicycled on Sundays. I had often brought my child there in her stroller when she was very little. There was no one else around. I sat on a bench and looked at the big winged angel in the middle of the fountain. I thought about another time in my life when I had been in despair, in the Piazza San Marco in Venice, when I had faced the reality of divorcing Vittorio.

As usual, when I am in the depths of despair some survival mechanism deep within me activates and I summon up that tough survivor, Shirley Schrift.

That night I saw her walking toward me around the Bethesda Fountain and once again noticed her kinky dirty-blonde hair, the falling-down ankle socks on her skinny legs, the thrust of her shoulders, and her indestructible grin.

At fourteen, in the depths of the Depression, this kid had organized Woolworth's.

At fifteen she had fought the mounted police in front of Ohrbach's during a vicious strike.

At sixteen, because she couldn't get into the WACS, she had married a navigator flying the London-Africa bombing route, and with her daily letters had encouraged him to fly eighty missions when he could have come home after fifty. He had helped destroy the terrible Nazi war machine.

Shirley took my hand and whispered, "Didn't Mrs. Roosevelt say it was better to light a candle than to curse the darkness?" I wiped my tears. We held hands and she helped me home through Central Park that cold dawn. And in the decades to come she helped me light a lot more candles.

TO BE CONTINUED, I HOPE!

INDEX

PICTURE CREDITS

Private Lives of Very Public People